MARY, MOTHER AND WARRIOR

For Elizabeth Ahlenar —
With all best
wishes. Looking
forward to seeing your
work in print, soon,
as well —

Linda Hall

✠ ✠ ✠

Mary, Mother and Warrior

THE VIRGIN IN SPAIN AND THE AMERICAS

✠ ✠ ✠

Linda B. Hall

TERESA ECKMANN, ILLUSTRATIONS EDITOR

UNIVERSITY OF TEXAS PRESS
Austin

Requests for permission to reproduce material from this work
should be sent to Permissions, University of Texas Press,
P.O. Box 7819, Austin, TX 78713-7819.

(∞) The paper used in this book meets the minimum requirements
of ANSI/NISO Z 39.48-1992 (R1997) (Permanence of Paper).

LIBRARY OF CONGRESS CATALOGING-IN-PUBLICATION DATA

Hall, Linda B. (Linda Biesele), 1939–
Mary, mother and warrior : the Virgin in Spain and the Americas / Linda B. Hall ;
Teresa Eckmann, illustrations editor.
p.   cm.
Includes bibliographical references and index.
ISBN 0-292-70602-2 (cloth : alk. paper) —ISBN 0-292-70595-6 (pbk. : alk. paper)
1. Mary, Blessed Virgin, Saint—Devotion to—Latin America—History
2. Latin America—Religious life and customs.   3. Mary, Blessed Virgin,
Saint—Devotion to—Spain—History.   4. Spain—Religious life and customs.
I. Eckmann, Teresa.   II. Title.
BT652.L29H35   2004
232.91′ 098—dc22   2004012817

✠ ✠ ✠

For my students and their mothers,

and

to the memory of Jayne Spencer (1948–2004),

good friend and warrior

Contents

✢ ✢ ✢

A Note on
Translation and Orthography

✠ ✠ ✠

THE SCOPE OF THIS TOPIC has involved many languages, including indigenous languages from Latin America in which I lack facility. When the translations are from Spanish or French and the original language is provided in the notes, they are my own. If translations from any languages are given only in English, they are the translations of the authors cited in the notes. As for Spanish orthography, which varies enormously across time and region, I have done my best to record any quotations accurately in the way they appear in the source that I used, and that is acknowledged in the notes. I have avoided the use of *sic* except where most necessary so as not to impede the reader.

Acknowledgments

✠ ✠ ✠

IN THE COURSE of researching and writing this book, I have incurred many debts. The wide-ranging and synthetic nature of the topic has led me into contacts with many scholars in regions and disciplines far removed from my original area of expertise. Further, given the importance of the visual images in this work, I have been enormously helped by the artists and photographers who have created many of them and the individuals at museums around the United States and the Hispanic world who have made other works of art available to me. I am grateful to all of them, more than this simple acknowledgment can convey, and hope that I have used their help wisely. I know that this help—and interest—on the part of many individuals has made this work far better than it otherwise could have been.

I was fortunate during the early months of my research to receive a Fulbright Association grant for a six-week seminar in Peru, Argentina, and Brazil. Although I have not included Brazil as a prominent part of my work—finding this very complicated country too different from Spanish America to fit cohesively into the volume—the experiences in Argentina and Peru have led to my selection of these countries as major foci of the book. Norma González and Marcia Koth de Paredes, Fulbright directors in Argentina and Peru respectively, and Ralph Blessing and Cynthia Wolloch from Washington helped me in every possible way. Traveling through three countries in the company of eleven fellow scholars from various disciplines was an enormous privilege and helped me see many things I would not otherwise have seen. I want particularly to acknowledge among my companions in that extraordinary trip Lucía Garavito, Andrew Boeger, and Rachel May for their ideas and interest in the project. The Fulbright Association made it possible for me to return for several weeks in 1998 to Cuzco, where I was able to do follow-up research and to observe the Corpus Christi celebrations there from start to finish.

Amy Remensnyder and William Christian have furnished encouragement as well as enormous help from the field of Spanish history, and I have constantly kept their work in mind as I have observed, researched, and written. The works of Louise Burkhart and Carolyn Dean have fascinated and inspired me, though I have only been in contact with them by telephone and e-mail. In Argentina, Eloisa Martín, Patricia Fogelman, Alejandro Frigerio, and Ricardo Salvatore have provided encouragement and guidance in regard to the Virgin of Luján, to the enigma of Eva Perón, and to the larger project as well. A conversation in Paris with Serge Gruzinski gave me new perspectives and ideas, as has his voluminous work as single author or in collaboration with others on matters cultural in colonial Spanish America. Readers of the manuscript for the University of Texas Press have provided helpful suggestions that, I believe, have notably enhanced the text.

During the course of the writing, I benefited from the group of scholar friends who form the Santa Fe Seminar: Sandra Lauderdale, Richard Graham, Richard Flint, Shirley Flint, Peter Linder, Curt Schaafsma, Polly Schaafsma, Shirley Barnes, Barbara Sommer, Jim Dunlap, Suzanne Stamatov, Cal Riley, and the late and much-missed Benjamin Keen. The seminar read with care; critiqued my ideas, facts, and perspectives; stimulated my thinking; and consistently renewed my enthusiasm. No scholar could have a better set of colleagues than these. Any shortcomings that remain, of course, are entirely my own.

It will be obvious to the reader of this volume that the illustrations are crucial to an understanding of what I have to say. I am grateful to Blair Woodard for working with me on ideas about these illustrations at an early stage of the project. I worked with museum officials who have gone out of their way to make available many of the images that appear in these pages. Donna Pierce and Julie Wilson of the Denver Art Museum helped early in the project and then straight through to its conclusion, not only with the wonderful images in that repository but also with ideas and contacts for other illustrations. Hector Rivero Borrell, Eduardo Ancira, and Ricardo Pérez of the Museo Franz Mayer in Mexico City and Mark Roglan and Kay Johnson of the Meadows Museum at Southern Methodist University in Dallas also made available images from those extraordinary collections and went out of their way to make sure that we got them in time. Fred and Jann Kline of Fred R. Kline and Company in Santa Fe, New Mexico, first showed me the fascinating statue of the Virgin of the New World and made information and photographs available. Stella de Sá Rego, curator of images at the Center for Southwest Research at the University of New Mexico, helped me once again locate precisely the historical photographs I felt I needed.

Most important of all, I want to thank the artists and photographers who have made their own work available. Ester Hernández, Alma López, and Carlos Callejo have let me use their images, which not only illustrate points I wanted to make but have led me on to new ideas. Susan Gandert, Andrea Heckmann, Baird Pogue, María Elena García, Gabriel Cardona, Aaron Anaya, and Jacqueline Orsini Dunnington have provided wonderful photographs, full of the color and the liveliness of the Hispanic devotion for the Virgin. Teresa Eckmann has not only provided some of the photography itself, but she also has served as picture editor, consulting, copying, captioning, and helping place the illustrations. Her help in the last stages of the manuscript has been crucial in its completion.

I want to express my appreciation to my students at the University of New Mexico and at the University of California at Los Angeles. I have discussed this work with students on so many occasions that I can no longer discern a line between their ideas and my own. And finally, I owe much to the authors whose scholarship appears in my citations. This book would not have been possible without the exceptional body of work that exists to draw on. I have done my best to acknowledge the contributions of others carefully. In these ways, the book that follows must be viewed as the result of a long collaborative process.

MARY, MOTHER AND WARRIOR

CHAPTER ONE

Introduction

＋ ＋ ＋

I HAVE WANTED to write this book for years. During the seven years that I spent in Colombia, 1961–1968, I was fascinated with the enormous reverence for the Virgin Mary that pervaded that country. I was particularly intrigued that this reverence crossed gender lines, with men as fervent as women if not more so. In a country troubled terribly by violence, this feminine vision of unconditional love, peace, and forgiveness held a power like no other. In the years since my return, I have observed the same fervor in many other parts of Latin America and among Latino populations in the United States. My years of residence in San Antonio, Albuquerque, and Los Angeles have confirmed that reverence for María is strong on this side of the border as well. Sometimes this fervor is visible; sometimes it is interior, known to me only through conversations with the reverent and from the ubiquitous home altars to her throughout the southwestern United States, Central America, the Caribbean, and South America. What has become clear to me is that what I thought of as an image or symbol is, for many Latin Americans and Latinos, a palpable presence, an understanding and giving being to whom access is proximate and immediate. Where did that reverence come from, and why is it so powerful?

My interest has been further and most importantly stimulated by my students. In the past eighteen years of teaching about women in Latin America, I have used the Virgin as a theme of study and have received dozens of thoughtful and often emotional communications about her from my students at Trinity University, the University of New Mexico, and University of California at Los Angeles. I want to share several of those stories here.

The first was told to me by a Peruvian woman, about her grandmother. Her *abuela*, she said, in her eighties and after bearing six children, had begun to insist that she herself was virgin. At first the family worried that she was becoming senile and somehow simply didn't remember. After our discussions in class, the young woman said she believed that what her grandmother was saying was that as she approached death, she was both whole and clean. She also indicated that perhaps her *abuela* was dealing with the impossible task of living up to the example of Mary as both Virgin and Mother.

Another student, a native New Mexican, told me that her mother, fleeing an abusive marriage, took with her only her two daughters and her image of the Virgin. This story resonates with a woodcut from El Salvador in the 1980s of villagers fleeing in terror from the army carrying with them a statue of Mary. In disastrous circumstances, the precious images of Mary are saved. My New Mexican student went on to tell me on a later occasion that her weeping mother had told her not long before that she had decided to leave the statue not to her but to her sister. This decision had been made, she said, because it would mean more to the sister, a practicing Catholic. My student agreed that this choice was reasonable, but the mother was not consoled, still suffering from her judgment between her two children. Clearly, she believed that the Virgin's power inherent in the image would accrue to one child, relatively imperiling the other.

On two other occasions, after an introductory lecture on the subject of Mary, I have had students come to my office visibly shaken. On both occasions the students said their mothers had told them that they were products of virgin births. One woman was Hispanic Catholic; the other was Irish Catholic. Both of their mothers had been very young when they conceived— and both were unmarried. Quick marriages to boyfriends followed, and in neither case had the marriage worked well.

The stories are suggestive. First of all, they make clear that the Virgin Mary presents an impossible ideal for living women, a mother without sexuality, and that this ideal in turn fosters in some a sense of inadequacy and insecurity, sometimes even denial. At the same time, Mary presents a picture of wholeness and integrity, of nurturing and healing and power, which is comforting and validating. In fact, it is to this impossible model that women turn for comfort in their failings and sorrows and for help in their necessities. And this figure is always with them, a constant and familiar presence.

Given this constant sense of presence, it is less surprising that individuals, and sometimes groups, have believed that the Virgin has actually physically appeared to them. Most of these appearances, these face-to-face encounters with the sacred, I believe, never become public knowledge. They are kept, secret and personal, in the internal world of the beholder. Others come to public attention, sometimes provoking highly emotional devotion. When these sorts of experiences occur, I believe as William Christian writes, that these are "eminently social visions" and that "what people hear the saints say, or the way they see the saints, reveals their deepest preoccupations. The changing faces of divine figures over the last six hundred years lead us to changes in the societies that meet them."[1] In the context of this study, it is not important to discern whether these visions were "real." What is important is that people believed that they were real and that they reacted to them as such. For our purposes it is how and why they did so that is important, and what happened as a result. Further, the legends that grow out of these appearances have real effects; these effects may be even more important, and frequently are, than they were in the original incident.

Apparitions are only one sort of appearance, of course. Far more often, the public manifestations involve the miraculous appearance of an image, on a window or mirror, inside a cloak, hidden down a mine shaft, buried under a mosque. The appearances of the images of the Virgin in Miami near and in the home of Elián González's Florida relatives were seen by those opposed to Castro's government as divine signs that the child should remain safely, as they saw it, in the United States.

Other stories of Mary's appearances and miracles, again with real effects, grow up as justifications for or illustrations of a devotion already in place.[2] Still others are promoted actively by those with particular interests in channeling the fervor such belief and devotion engender. Kings and queens and religious orders and politicians and soldiers, as we shall see, have engaged in such promotion, either out of devotion or cynically. What we are looking at here is the development of a spiritual complex, the history of a set of beliefs, focused around a female figure. This set of beliefs interacted with and helped shape cultural attitudes and behavioral patterns. These attitudes and patterns, in turn, crystallized into institutional forms, which then interacted with new cultural and historical settings in new ways. Out of these changes, the attitudes and patterns themselves are transformed. Still, there is continuity here. Over the centuries millions of human beings have believed that the Blessed Virgin Mary is the Mother of God, and millions continue to hold this conviction. Yet they have acted on these beliefs in ways that fit their own times and historical circumstances; these beliefs have had enormous human consequences. This book is about some of those actions and interactions in Spain, in Latin America, and among Latinos in the United States.

The sense of Mary's presence helps explain the intense reverence for her of those engaged in migration and resettlement, and many of the stories here involve just such situations. As they travel and sense that she is with them, the dangers, fears, and loneliness of new territory are assuaged. This reverence may even be intensified in those engaged in violent conquest. Confronted by violence and the need to commit it, they are comforted by the sense that they are doing it for her, with her approval, legitimized in her name. Throughout the Reconquest of Spain and the Conquest of the Spanish New World, the men engaged in those enterprises felt that she was with them, carried her banners, were animated by the thought of her, saw her appear above the fray, dedicated their actions to her, and believed that she aided their victories.

Throughout these endeavors, images of Mary, both painted and sculpted, were extremely important. The Spanish prayed to them before leaving the motherland, brought them on their campaigns and journeys, put them in conquered mosques and in native sacred spaces that they converted to Christian churches—often dedicated to the Virgin. Art historians have noted that among the many images with which humans interact, those of Mary have been particularly powerful.[3] These sorts of phenomena will be a focus in the pages that follow.

These images of the Virgin were (and many still are) powerful. They significantly enhanced the sense of the Virgin's presence. People who believed in the Virgin's power felt her presence in the representation, not apart from it. Although theologically the idea that she is within the image is murky, nevertheless that is exactly what many believers felt and feel. One source tells us, "The theological view of such images is that they are windows into the eternal world of revelation and that they capture, albeit imperfectly, the realities of which the gospel speaks."[4] The significance of images has been much contested in the Christian world, particularly in the period of iconoclasm in the eighth century and the Protestant Reformation in the sixteenth. The Council of Trent (1545–1563), in reaction to the forces of the Reformation, reaffirmed the significance of such images, provided that superstitious usage be avoided, and at the same time approved the honoring of relics and the veneration of saints, the most important of whom has been Saint Mary.[5] In discussing the iconoclastic heresy, Peter Brown notes the interactive process when he states, "The icon was a hole in the dyke separating the visible world from the divine." However, in the case of the Virgin, such an image, it seems to me, was more of a welcoming helper in attaining access to the divine than she was an absence, as the terms "hole" or "window" might imply.[6] Marina Warner is closer to the sense of what I mean when she says, "A sacred image was not an illusion but the possessor of reality itself, and the beneficent forces that flow through icons and relics of a holy personage like the Virgin bring them to life."[7] The Virgin, as a human and accessible person *re-presented* in an image, becomes a conduit between the human being and the divine. This same sense of liveliness and efficacy, it seems to me, persists today in interactions with the images of the Virgin.

4

These images need not be located exclusively in holy places. Small tokens that the devoted can keep in their pockets or wear around their necks convey a sense of her presence with the carrier. This feeling may also appear in regard to larger images of significance to a given community, some of which indeed may be the models for the smaller, personal ones. Recently, art historians have begun to study such phenomena. What I am describing is what Hans Belting has noted as the likeness considered as a person. He says:

> The image, understood in this manner, not only represented a person but also was treated like a person, being worshipped, despised, or carried from place to place in ritual processions: in short, it served in the symbolic exchange of power and, finally, embodied the public claims of the community.[8]

Mamacha Carmen is transported to the main temple the day before the Feast of the Virgin of Carmen on July 15, 1998, in Paucartambo, Peru. Photograph by María Elena García.

We shall return to this point frequently as we see the Spanish bringing the Virgin Mary as religious idea, psychological construct, and physical image to their New World. Europeans of the fifteenth century and forward believed that the efficacy of these images could "affect even (or perhaps especially) the youngest of viewers, and affect them not just emotionally but in ways that have long-term behavioral consequences."[9] The idea and image of the Virgin appealed to indigenous populations as well, especially as a nurturer and healer. So in addition to being a comfort and a justification for those engaged in discovery and conquest, Mary became powerful in bringing indigenous peoples, at least in appearance, into the Roman Catholic faith. At the same time they were to some degree brought under Spanish control.

David Freedberg has emphasized the power of images, studying "the active, outwardly markable responses of beholders, as well as the beliefs (insofar as they are capable of being recorded) that motivate them to specific actions and behavior." But he goes on to say:

An image of the Virgin of Remedios is arranged for a Corpus Christi procession in Cuzco, 1998. Photograph by Susan Gandert.

6

We must consider not only beholders' symptoms and behavior, but also the effectiveness, efficacy, and vitality of images themselves; not only what beholders do, but also what images appear to do; not only what people do as a result of their relationship with imaged form, but also what they expect imaged form to achieve, and why they have such expectations at all.[10]

The relationship between human and image is interactive, and clearly so. The ways humans act toward images and the responses they believe that they get influence the way they and other observers respond in the future to these representations. Freedberg also discusses "the ways in which the god is in the image; in other words, how it becomes charged with presence."[11] In Latin America, the evident belief of the Spanish in the power of the Virgin and the benefits springing from her favor were conveyed to indigenous peoples not only by preaching and catechizing but also by example. Further, Freedberg points out that images not only can mediate in the process of acquiring and giving thanks for supernatural help but also "can elevate beholders to the heights of empathy and participation."[12] The Spanish used the figure of the Virgin in just this way, for indigenous peoples and for themselves.

It is important to understand and remember that according to Roman Catholic theology, Mary is not God but the Mother of God. She is fully human, the vehicle through which Christ became flesh, but not herself a deity. As the Constitution of 1964 emerging from Vatican II reminds us, "We have but one Mediator [Jesus Christ] . . . The maternal duty of Mary towards men in no way obscures or diminishes this unique mediation of Christ . . . For all the saving influences of the Blessed Virgin originate, not from some inner necessity, but from the divine pleasure. They flow forth from the superabundance of the merits of Christ, rest on his mediation, depend entirely on it, and derive all their power from it."[13] Still, Mary assumes a place above all other humans. While she may not be adored as a deity, she may be revered. This reverence is not as exalted as the adoration (*latria*) due to God, Father and Son, but it is nevertheless more intense and more reverent (*hyperdulia*) than that due the saints (*dulia*). Further, there are four dogmas that distinguish her from other humans: her divine motherhood; her virginity; her immaculate conception, which means that from the moment of conception she herself was freed from the stain of original sin; and her bodily assumption into heaven at her death. The first two dogmas had been recognized by the early Church and were well in place by the time of the Spanish arrival in the Americas. The Immaculate Conception, though its proclamation as dogma would not take place until 1854, was a doc-

The Virgin Mary is framed by symbols taken from the Song of Solomon *that are usually associated with the Immaculate Conception. The sun and the moon here are personified in an indigenous manner. Note especially the devil figure enclosed within the moon at her feet.* Immaculate Conception, *artist unknown, eighteenth century, huamanga stone, Ayacucho, Peru, 28 by 20.4 cm. Denver Art Museum Collection, anonymous donor, No. 1983.397.*

trine strongly pushed by Spanish theologians and powerful political figures from the late thirteenth century forward. Many of the artistic representations of Mary in Spain and in the Americas reflected the iconography of the Immaculist vision of Mary. Associated with the Woman of the Apocalypse and conflated with the Virgin of the Assumption, she was pictured standing on the moon, either full or crescent, clothed with the sun, sometimes crushing the serpent of evil beneath her feet, usually pictured alone without the Christ Child. She is shown floating visibly above the ground, an indication of the association with the Assumption. This fourth dogma was not declared until 1950 but was also important to the Spanish of the fifteenth and sixteenth centuries, though not in such a defining way as the Immaculate Conception.[14]

Reverence for the Virgin and entreaties to her, of course, are addressed to her properly as a mediator and intercessor with her Son. Her power flows from and with Christ. Though it is an efficacy that is dependent on her motherhood, it is deeply significant nonetheless.[15] However, it is quite clear that many of those who petition her see Mary herself as powerful, numinous, and supernatural. Still, it seems to me that her resonance and power and particularly her accessibility are enhanced in the human psyche by precisely her own humanity. In 1979 the prominent Brazilian theologian Leonardo Boff called for a reconsideration of the theological position on Mary in his work *O rostro materno de Deus* (*The Maternal Face of God*), but he moved both boldly and cautiously. He asserted on the one hand that

> Mary incarnates the new creation that God is forging from the old. She likewise embodies what the Church ought to be as a community of the redeemed. Only in Mary does the Church actualize its archetype and its utopia . . . As the most eminent member of the Church, then, she occupies a corresponding place among the links of the salvific mediation binding all men and women: she is venerated as Mediatrix of All Graces, for in union with the Holy Spirit and her Son she is full of grace. Thus, Mary is associated with her Son, the Holy Spirit, and God himself in such wise that she is raised to the level of Co-Redemptrix.[16]

But Boff was cautious, prefacing his discussion by subordinating himself and his ideas to the Church.

> The task we set before ourselves is risky, and the theoretical and practical pitfalls numerous . . . We make no attempt to impose our position. We submit it to the better judgment of our critics and of the Church itself. The new knowledge that we use, and the change that society is undergoing where women are concerned, constitute an invitation to revitalize and recast traditional perspectives of faith on Mary. If theologians will not assume this task, who will?[17]

And the issue is by no means settled. As we begin the twenty-first century, there are widespread petition drives to have her named co-redemptrix with Christ, yet it is extremely unlikely that Pope John Paul II will take any such step, despite his own strong reverence for Mary. The petitions have asked him to proclaim a new dogma, that Saint Mary is "Co-Redemptrix, Mediatrix of All Graces, and Advocate for the People of God," in large part echoing Boff's language. Such a change would elevate her theological status signifi-

9

cantly and approach a recognition of the feminine face of God. This change of status has long been rejected by the male hierarchy of the Church, including a group of Mariologists commissioned in 1997 by the Holy See to study the issue.[18]

Yet the debate on Mary's significance continues inside and outside the Church. Popular reverence for Mary has often made Church leaders nervous. However, the very refusal over the centuries to elevate her status closer to that of a deity seems to have added to her power and appeal; as a real woman, however exceptional, believers see her as someone who shares their difficulties and can sympathize with their problems. She remains both accessible and understanding.

It is therefore not surprising that the Spanish would have taken her with them, in their minds and hearts as well as in physical images, during their struggle to expel the Muslims from the peninsula and later to conquer the indigenous peoples they encountered in the Americas. It is self-evident that she was seen as Mother, not only of God but of themselves, but perhaps not so self-evident that she was also seen as Warrior. Yet she appeared in their prayers before battle and on the banners that they carried into the fray. Her intervention was credited with Christian victories in Spain, Mexico, and the Andes. Although Saint James, Santiago, the apostle who is credited with evangelizing Spain, was the figure who most often appeared above the battle on a white horse with his sword raised, the Virgin frequently appeared as well and sometimes took an active part in defeating the enemy. It is important to recognize that she was and is recognized as a powerful aid in troubles of all kinds and that her role in conquest and colonization was often perceived as active and direct. She has led human beings to do violence on many occasions, among them the Reconquest and Conquest, the Latin American independence movements, and the repression of individuals and of social movements. She also has protected them, they believe, in their chosen endeavors.

Yet in her role as protector and nurturer, the version of Santa María emphasized by the evangelizing Christians in the wake of the Conquest, it is not too surprising that she would be an appealing figure for devastated native peoples. Probably some of them feigned reverence for her in order to protect or ingratiate themselves vis-à-vis the Iberians; others, according to reports, continued to revere their own gods, male and female, but to call on Mary as well. Nonetheless, it does not strain the imagination to consider that some of them may have found her initially appealing. Paintings and statues of her, especially those representations as a nurturer holding her Son, were beautiful and tranquil. Being assured that she was the Mother of All by Catholic priests, perhaps they believed. Perhaps such belief helped them maintain sanity in what Rolena

*This painting depicts an event in 1370 in which the Virgin Mary intervened to save the Christians
from a night ambush by revealing the presence of hidden Moorish troops with her radiant light.*
The Battle between Christians and Moors at El Sotillo *(part of an altarpiece)*, Francisco de Zurbarán *(1598–1664), ca. 1637–1639, oil on canvas, 335 by 191.1 cm. All Rights
Reserved, the Metropolitan Museum of Art, New York, Kretschmar Fund, No. 20.104.*

Adorno has called "the swirling madness of the open contests between the old gods and the new."[19] There must, at least initially, have been a strange edge to revering a figure so important to those who had wreaked so much havoc in their world. In any case, as the decades and the centuries passed, belief in her power and efficacy surely grew into more than a sham and a substitute. These various adaptations were different at different times and places, as community, family, and individual needs and beliefs determined. What was and remains widespread is a belief in her presence, power, and significance.

Another point should be made here. In Iberia and in Latin America, the Virgin took many forms. She was called by many names—Pilar, Monserrat, Guadalupe, Copacabana. Some of these advocations were extremely general and not associated with a particular place; they usually were tied to specific doctrines or devotions or particular attributes of Mary, such as the Immaculate Conception, Our Lady of the Rosary, the Virgin of Remedies (Remedios), the Virgin of Sorrows (Dolores). These images were distinguished by special iconographies, which usually were recognizable but often became conflated. Other advocations, which may be representations of the wider designations above, are tied by legends of appearances or miracles to particular locations. These may significantly affect both the secular and sacred landscapes. In late medieval Spain, for example, Monserrat and Guadalupe "were the two poles of Iberian devotion."[20] Networks of pilgrimage connected villages within the region, stimulating devotion and political and societal cohesion, not to mention economic activity. This pattern has continued in Latin America, with Guadalupe in Mexico as the pre-eminent pilgrimage destination now drawing more visitors yearly than any other Roman Catholic site except the Vatican. But there are many other Marian locations in Latin America—among them Copacabana in Bolivia, Chinquinquirá in Colombia, and Luján in Argentina—all with their Marys and all with significant national as well as religious content.

Other advocations are strictly local, often being the objects of particular devotion within a smaller community, even a neighborhood or a particular social or ethnic or economic group. The devotion to these advocations is often carried on through brotherhoods, sometimes including women or even dominated by them. The histories of many brotherhoods go back hundreds of years, and although the social and historical contexts have changed radically, habits and practices of devotion may significantly resemble those of earlier centuries. Throughout the layers of advocations, in which the Virgin may be dressed differently, may be perceived as performing different kinds of aids and services for her devout, may have changed her attributes and her actions over time, and may even have distinctive personality traits and favored followers, she is nevertheless only one person, the Virgin Mary, Mother of God. Yet she is not exactly one person, although theologically it is clear that she is one and unique. Here we are back to the issue of her inherence in the image. She is at once universal, regional, local, and even personal, at least in the minds of her believers. Again, she is present, and the use of advocations makes it possible for human beings to tailor their relationships with her and their beliefs about her to current needs and cultural contexts.[21]

The ways in which Mary became important and revered in Latin America varied enormously across the geographies and cultures of the Spanish and Portuguese empires. Although the Iberian vision of the Virgin predominated, it should be emphasized that this vision was by no means uniform, varying from region to region and even from person to person. The indigenous cultures and visions of the sacred were even more varied. And yet another element must be considered. Among the migrants to this new region were African slaves, bringing along their own notions of the sacred and the sacred feminine. These ideas became part of the mix. While the Iberian view of Mary tended to reassure them and justify a position of dominance, the indigenous and African versions frequently denoted resistance. The interweaving that resulted has given rise to a huge number of cults of and personal devotions to Our Lady, far more than could be studied by one person or covered in one book. My purpose is only to open the discussion.

This book, therefore, is a series of essays, discrete but connected, which look at several stages in the development of Marian reverence in Latin America. These essays address both the cultural and political dimensions of that devotion and the ways in which that devotion carries over to the present. I intend Chapters II through VI as a synthesis of the developing cult of the Virgin in colonial Spanish America. I begin in Chapter II with Spain in its Mediterranean context up through 1492, that crucial year in which Christian forces finally conquered the Moors of Granada and Columbus encountered the Americas, to establish a baseline understanding of Marian reverence. In the next four chapters I explore the Conquest and colonial period in Spanish Latin America, especially in the areas that now are Mexico and the Andean highlands of Peru and Bolivia. Here I look at the devotion of the group of men involved in the Spanish discovery and Conquest and the ways in which Marian devotion became entangled and combined with the indigenous sacred in Mexico and the Andes.

Although a great deal of selection is involved in the preceding section, that process necessarily becomes even more stringent moving forward in time. The next essays are more specific but add other regions of Latin America to the two discussed above. In Chapter VII I examine the development of three national advocations of the Virgin in Latin America—the devotions to the Virgin of Guadalupe in Mexico, to the Virgin of Copacabana in Bolivia, and to the Virgin of Luján in Argentina. In the nineteenth century these phenomena became linked with the independence movements and then with the new nation-states. The themes of the perceptions of the Virgin's power and strength, combined with her political potential, continue here. All have roots in the colonial period, and those of Guadalupe and Copacabana are particularly strong and linked to the areas of focus in the previous four chapters. A consideration of the Virgin of Luján introduces an important region not considered in earlier chapters and a significantly different case, one less strongly rooted in the colonial past but powerful nonetheless.

In the last three chapters I look successively at the case of a powerful individual and at the significance of Marian devotion and the Marian model in her life and in her political success; at a group of late-twentieth-century Marian celebrations in the Hispanic world, including Spain, to search for continuing similarities and for significant differences; and at the reverence for the Virgin among Latino groups in the United States. The first of these, Chapter VIII, moves to twentieth-century Argentina, considering the ways in which Eva Perón, the Mothers of the Plaza de Mayo, and the Argentine military of the 1970s and 1980s used Marian imagery and symbols to establish political resonance and their own political and personal legitimacy. Evita, a highly public figure, offers us an opportunity to see in the life of one woman the operation of Marian models in interactions between herself and the people of Argentina. This chapter argues that Marian symbols and behaviors, woven into the political activities of Evita, were important implicit and sometimes explicit factors in her political appeal. In fact, surprisingly, her strong identification with the Virgin and with ideals of motherhood so revered in Argentine society, and her framing of her activities in these terms, helped her break away from societal norms to achieve significant public power and even devotion despite her childlessness and her sexual past. I believe that Evita had completely internalized the Marian model, which she then carried out in her role as the wife of the president. Because she believed in this identification so thoroughly, it was effective during her lifetime, and she established a strong political resonance with the masses of Argentina. Yet when the Peronist movement tried to use this symbolic (and spiritual) connection cynically after her death, it failed. Later, the Mothers of the Plaza de Mayo and the Argentine military, in their confrontations during the Dirty War in the 1970s and 1980s, both used Marian symbols to support their political positions. Again, the Virgin as model and symbol was lived out and ideologically positioned in ambivalent, conflicted ways.

In Chapter IX I consider recent reverence for the Virgin in Spain and Latin America by looking at several contemporary festivals with significant Marian content that I have been able to observe: Corpus Christi in Cuzco, Peru, in 1995 and 1998; Semana Santa in Seville, Spain, in 1999; and the pilgrimage to the shrine of Guadalupe in Mexico in December 1999. These celebrations show fascinating continuities and illuminating differences in relation to earlier rituals and with each other. They reflect present concerns including local and national issues along with strong links and associations to the past. The last main chapter of the work looks at Marian devotion among Latinos in the United States, again focusing on recent years but also noting continuities and changes.

A connection that has emerged throughout my research and teaching on the Virgin is the one between individuals and their own mothers. Repeatedly during the years that I have been working on this book, Latino/a and other friends and colleagues and students have asked me if the book was finally in print because they wanted to give it to their mothers. While this reaction reflects to some degree a generational falling-off of religious beliefs—even popular ones—among individuals further removed from the experience of migration and dislocation, I believe it also reflects the way in which the figure of Mary connects mothers and children on a powerful affective level. Another story illustrates the point, I think. The wealthy father of a Mexican friend is a follower of Gurumayi Chivilasananda, the female guru of the Siddha Yoga movement, and has pictures of her all over his San Diego apartment. He also has a striking and valuable collection of paintings of Guadalupe. His daughter believes that the basis for this extraordinary Guadalupan collection, exhibited side-by-side with images of a contemporary female spiritual leader, is his connection to the memory of his own mother, who was devoted to the Mexican Virgin.[22]

Recent feminist theologians have been extremely critical of the theology of the Virgin Mary within the Roman Catholic Church, contending that it has reinforced women's institutional and personal inferiority. Elizabeth Schussler Fiorenza, for example, has argued that "The Mary myth" is rooted "in a male, clerical, and ascetic culture and theology . . . The myth is a theology of woman, preached by men to women, and one that serves to deter women from becoming fully independent and whole human persons." She questions whether "the myth can give to women a new vision of equality and wholeness, since the myth has almost never functioned as symbol or justification of women's equality and leadership in church and society, even though the myth contains elements which could have done so."[23]

Though this view has merit as a theological argument and may well describe the effect on some women that is indicated, it does not ring entirely true for me as regards human experience of Latin Americans devoted to the Virgin. As I have worked on this volume, themes that have emerged to me most vividly are that of the Virgin's perceived power and that of the empowerment that reverence for the Virgin provides to her devotees, both male and female. Far from being the meek and mild figure depicted to me in my Protestant youth, she is often seen by them as active, effective, legitimizing. Her actions can invert or reinforce relations of dominance; the vision of her is ambiguous and ambivalent among members of the same cultural milieu and even within an individual; she can be challenging and transforming. Although she may be used in an attempt to reinforce gender ideologies of passivity and obedience for women and other subordinate peoples, she may certainly be used to empower them as well. I consider, in fact, that in Spain and Latin America and among Latino populations in the United States, belief in the Virgin has been empowering and that this empowerment has been more important than any sort of gender-related restrictions based on the model of Mary as Virgin. Of course, the effects have varied greatly depending on time and place. As Els Maeckelberghe has recognized, "It is a complete illusion to think that you have a clearly defined figure if you just pronounce the name 'Mary' . . . It is a very flexible name that can be adapted to the needs of the time when and the place where it is invoked."[24] Indeed, for men and women, the belief in her presence and ubiquity make and have made her useful as model and helper in overcoming adversity and refashioning their own behavior within or in opposition to cultural norms. This story is a complicated one. What you find between these covers is, I hope, a beginning to discussions and understandings.

CHAPTER TWO

The Spanish Reverence

✠　✠　✠

IN ORDER TO UNDERSTAND the impact of the Virgin Mary in Latin America, it is essential to understand the way in which her cult and image fit into the sacred landscape of Spain, metaphorically and literally. Muslim invasions had pushed well into the north of the peninsula during the late seventh and early eighth centuries, and Christian resistance grew in the following centuries. The Virgin would be increasingly linked with the efforts to force the Moors south again, an effort which would be completed largely by the end of the thirteenth century. The final elimination of Muslim control, however, would not be concluded until the watershed year of 1492, when Isabel and Fernando, the Catholic Kings (known more popularly in English as Ferdinand and Isabella), would take Granada. Isabel and her consort were highly devoted to the Virgin, as were most of the Spanish of their time. Their entrance into the city of Granada in that year met ragged and hungry Christian captives released from its prisons, walking in file behind a cross and an image of Mary.[1]

The year was significant. Only a few months later, Christopher Columbus would make his famous voyage to the New World, encountering there not only the possibilities of riches (though not enough, initially, for his tastes) but also souls for conversion.[2] Columbus, like so many of his time, was devoted to the Virgin, long regarded as the protector of mariners and identified with Stella Maris, the North Star, by far the most important of all stars to sailors and essential for navigation in the fifteenth century.[3] Indeed, Mary as Stella Maris is still revered in Mediterranean communities.

The Virgin was connected with other crucial matters during the period known as the Reconquest, during which Christian forces, when not fighting each other, were driving Muslims slowly south. Many of these same themes would recur in Latin America from the moment of encounter through the sixteenth century and indeed into the present. Mary was particularly connected to conversion in the Spain of Muslims and Jews and in the New World of indigenous peoples; to fertility, of humans, fields, and animals; and to health and especially protection from epidemics, reflecting the European plagues of the late Middle Ages and the terrible devastation from European diseases in Latin America during and after the Conquest. It is likely that parents bereft of stricken children, and children left orphans, would respond to the powerful images of Mary as a devoted and helping mother. She occupied the position of the most powerful intercessor between humans and God on land and sea. She also was identified with war and conquest, particularly of peoples perceived as non-Christian. Some scholars believe that Marian devotion in Spain was related to earlier mother goddesses, often those associated with fertility and closely tied to the Spanish landscape.[4] In fact, it would be an error to imagine that the Iberian Peninsula before 711, the date usually used to signify the farthest Moorish advance, was securely Christian. Only in 589, if we are to believe the standard accounts, did the Visigothic King Recarred declare himself and Spain to be Catholic rather than Arian, settling the issue of Christian disunity at least in ideological terms. A Christian Spain, in which the Church was securely bound to politics and developing Spanish nationalism, continued to be a work in progress during the years leading up to 1492. Still, it is perhaps useful to see the Reconquest as a sort of civil war in which religion played a major role.[5] However, Christian forces often fought each other on the peninsula before 1492. Isabel's own succession to the crown of Castile in 1474 was heavily contested by other Christian hopefuls.

It would also be a mistake to see the peninsula at the beginning of the Reconquest as entirely Muslim to the south, with Christians only in the far north. Christians, known as Mozarabs, lived in all parts of the Muslim-held territory; Muslim slaves were brought north, and Muslims continued to reside in reconquered regions. And all regions contained Jews. Relationships between the three groups were often strained and sometimes violent, and in ordering Jews expelled, Isabel brought to culmination a process long under way. Muslim expulsion shortly thereafter was also the result of a long process. The differences between these populations were framed in religious terms often associated with the Virgin. What would be Spain was being defined through religion, both institutional and popular, along with territorial and political struggles. We shall see the continual intersection of these three arenas of contention.

Moreover, the process of Reconquest created a frontier. Never very firm, always dangerous, the territories newly regained were not easy to repopulate with Christian settlers. Historian Peter Linehan has commented of the Castilian kings during the twelfth century, when much territory fell to them, that they "governed not a kingdom but a space," a great deal of it empty. In order to inhabit it, *fueros* (privileges of various kinds) were granted to those moving into this liminal area. This settlement was accompanied by anxiety, as kidnapping, attack, and enslavement by opposing forces or simply bandits were always possibilities. The sense of uncertainty, and perhaps loneliness, was accentuated by the breaking up of extended families. Linehan suggests that in compensation for these lost relationships, spiritual kinship mediated through the Church became increasingly important. The presence of Catholicism was more and more manifest across the Spanish landscape as churches large and small were built or installed in religious spaces, often previously Muslim.[6] The larger urban churches were frequently converted immediately and named for the Virgin, a sign at one and the same time of Christian dominance and motherly love and reassurance. In the countryside, some sacred spaces also became linked with stories—sometimes describing apparitions—about the discovery of her images. It seems likely, however, that in many cases this ideological connection was made later, after perceived miracles made these spaces and images seem powerful and they had already attracted popular devotion. The usual legend indicated that these representations of the Virgin had been buried, hidden in a cave, or otherwise protected to save them from the Moors and on discovery manifested in various ways that they wished to remain and be revered in the locations in which they had been found.[7] The images and many of these sites would become enormously important as centers of Christian devotion. The eleventh, twelfth, and thirteenth centuries, coinciding with the major push of the Reconquest, seem to be the years in which the Virgin became a major object of peninsular devotion, as shown by the more frequent use of her name in documents and of church dedications. In this regard she was replacing earlier devotion to the saints, often of local origin, who were not readily available in the conquered territories. The possibility of using saints was also affected after the thirteenth century by the increasing unwillingness of the hierarchical Church to approve new canonizations.[8] These factors made the Virgin, favored by the endless possibilities for the development of new advocations that could be related to the local situation, particularly important in the establishment of Catholicism in the conquered territories.

The reverence for Mary around the Mediterranean had grown gradually between the sixth and twelfth centuries. During the period of Christian persecutions in the earliest centuries after Christ, it does not seem that a cult of the Virgin developed immediately. The Council of Ephesus in 431 had given tremendous impetus to her status when she was proclaimed Theotokos, the Mother of God. Ephesus, where she is said to have resided in the care of Saint John after the crucifixion, was apparently already the site of devotion, and her new title led to torchlit celebrations there on her behalf. Other important developments in the growth of her cult were the establishment of feasts in her honor, notably two commemorating the Annunciation and her virginity. The latter was celebrated all over the Roman Empire, including Spain, though on widely varying dates ranging around Christmas. The date in Spain was December 18, and many celebrations for the Virgin in Spain and Latin America still fall in that month. Her status was further elevated when in 451 she was declared ever-virgin, at the time of conception, during her pregnancy, and after the birth of Christ. Pope Martin I proclaimed her virginity a dogma of the Church almost two hundred years later, in 655.[9]

Her cult was quickly associated with victory over enemies. In Constantinople in 626, it was images of the Virgin paraded around the city's walls that were believed to have saved it from the attacks of the Avars. An account of the siege from that era tells us that the patriarch of Constantinople, Sergios, placed an image of Mary above the Golden Gate, one of the main entrances to the city, and warned the foe that the Mother of God would defeat them. Mary further became a center of community, "a symbol of urban integration."[10] Reverence for Mary was dealt a terrible blow in the Byzantine Empire by the rise of Iconoclasm in the eighth century and beginning of the ninth century. Yet the repression associated with this movement led in part to the rise of Marian worship in the West, as religious fugitives wanting to continue their reverence for images were forced out and came to Rome and Sicily. The popes of the eighth century honored her with new paintings and statues, especially as Maria Regina, the Queen, in part because her worship might emphasize their secular power; the Virgin later became the patroness of the Norman kings in Sicily. Mary was becoming political.[11] Recarred himself founded a cathedral in Toledo dedicated to Santa María in 586 or 587. It is significant that in Toledo only two or three years later he would proclaim for Spain the rejection of Arianism in favor of Roman Catholicism. There were also a few claims of Marian relics dating from about this time, probably touch relics of some kind connected with her from the East, or perhaps images, since her bodily Assumption into Heaven had long been claimed.[12] The fall of Jerusalem to the Muslims in 638, yet another reorientation of sacred space, caused great shock throughout Christendom, leading to the rapid development of legends in which pious acts and miracles were linked with the holy places.[13]

It may be that the earlier Mediterranean reverence for mother goddesses made the development of Marian devotions rather easy both in the cities and in the countryside. Alfonso X, the Castilian monarch of the thirteenth century and great devotee of María, acknowledged this connection in Law 43 of his *Setenario*, which was titled "About how those who worshipped the earth, really meant to worship Saint Mary, if they understood it well." It explained that in adoring the earth they were actually praying to the Virgin. Among the seven ways in which Mary was linked to the earth, the document went on, was her complete freedom from the stain of sin, as the man-god Jesus Christ grew in her as plants grow in the fertile soil. The supporting discussion made the connections between Mary and the earth in startlingly graphic ways. The Virgin was like the earth in that the Holy Spirit had cultivated and opened her body so that Jesus Christ could descend into it and become Man and God. The watering of the fruit of her womb was related to her virginity, before, during, and after birth. Finally, she produced the most beautiful fruit of all beauties possible. The argument continued that Mary, the Mother, made possible all the good things brought to the world by her Son.[14] It seems fair to ask, however, given the strong metaphorical connection between María and the earth that Alfonso was proposing, what or whom he himself was really worshipping.

The city of Toledo became particularly identified with the Church and the Marian cult in a number of ways. During the seventh century, several Church councils were held there. Attempts—only consolidated just before the Muslim takeover in the early eighth century—were made by Church leaders to make it the center of Visigothic political control as well. It was also a center of anti-Jewish sentiment, with Church documents comparing Jews to ulcers and leprosy within the Spanish body politic—or perhaps body religious. The Spanish bishops even promoted a decree of enslavement for the Jewish population, which was proclaimed by Ervig, the last Visigothic king to control the city. Significantly, this document also mentioned Mary's December 18 feast. The decree soon became a moot point as the Muslim conquest swept over the area. Already, however, as one historian has phrased it, "the conviction that *patria* and *genus christianum* were consubstantial had been an article of episcopal faith."[15] Later centuries would produce versions of the Muslim takeover that would blame the Jews for letting in the Saracens while the inhabitants of Toledo were out of the city performing Palm Sunday devotions.[16] This story is certainly apocryphal, but it reflects the early hatreds and tensions. The Muslims, moreover, were disinclined to move strongly against Christians or Jews; such people, collectively called *dhimmis*, were at this time guaranteed freedom of religion in Muslim territories. Only in the twelfth century with the arrival of the fundamentalist Almohads in al-Andalus, the Muslim-controlled area of Spain, would persecutions be more of a problem.[17] Moreover, the Muslims were in hostile territory, far to the north and away from their base, and their numbers were limited. The terms of surrender were therefore not odious. Taxes, not significantly greater than those paid to the Visigothic king, went to the new masters. In return, religious freedom was guaranteed and local autonomy respected. Still, for Christians the change rankled, with profound shifts in status and a heavy sense of loss. Among the relics thought to have been taken from the city at the time of the Muslim conquest—varying from Saint Peter's right sandal to some of Mary Magdalene's famous locks—were quantities of the Virgin's milk, a bodily relic satisfactory because it could have been collected before her ascent into Heaven or miraculously thereafter.[18]

Mary, according to later texts, had already dignified her cathedral in Toledo through an appearance there in 662 to Ildefonso, the reigning bishop. This specific apparition would be repeated again and again in various European compendia of miracles in the next few centuries, including Alfonso el Sabio's remarkable thirteenth-century work, *Las Cantigas* in praise of Mary.[19] The story, as told in the ninth century, was that Ildefonso, later to be sainted, had entered the church to celebrate a new *missa* that he had composed. He was preceded by a number of clergy, but when the portal of the church opened and heavenly light shown around them, his companions dropped their torches and fled. Ildefonso, left alone, then beheld the Queen of Heaven sitting on the ivory throne from which he was accustomed to addressing his congregation. She called him to her with the following words: "Hasten, loyal servant of God, to receive from my hand a gift I have brought you from the treasure of my Son; you may wear this vestment only on my feast days, and because you have remained in this life with the vesture of glory, in the life to come you shall enjoy with other servants of my Son the realm of glory."[20] Ildefonso's strong association with the Virgin was enhanced by his own writing in her praise, especially *De virginitate perpetua Sancta Maria*. He was said to have had a role in establishing her December 18 feast day just a few years before his vision. The liturgical texts that accompanied this celebration, containing prayers on the themes of the Annunciation, the birth of Jesus, and the perpetual virginity of Mary, were also believed to be his work.[21]

The appearance of the Virgin also conveyed great honor on the cathedral as well as on Toledo and enhanced the city's claim in later centuries to religious preeminence. When the Visigothic King Wamba was anointed in Toledo in 672, early sources indicated that it was in his own praetorian church. In the ninth century, however, sources contradicted earlier versions by claim-

Plate I. The pious Saint Ildefonso, a seventh-century bishop of Toledo devoted to the Virgin Mary, is depicted receiving a golden chasuble from the Virgin Mary. The Investiture of Saint Ildefonsus, *Juan de Borgoña (1470–ca. 1534), 1508–1514, tempera and oil on wood panel. Courtesy of the Meadows Museum, Southern Methodist University, Dallas, Algur H. Meadows Collection, No. 69.03.*

ing that the inauguration had taken place in Santa María's cathedral.[22] Thus, two centuries later, history was being rewritten, more securely binding together Church and State in a place belonging to God's Mother.

Another devotion was developing in Spain during the ninth century in the northwest, beyond Moorish control. This was the cult of Santiago, Saint James, and later stories connected him both to military conquest and to the Virgin. We cannot be sure precisely when he began to be a focus of reverence. The idea that this apostle proselytized Spain had reached western Europe by the late seventh century but was initially rejected; after the Moors swept north in 711, a different sensibility seems to have formed around the issue. Probably around the beginning of the ninth century, after savage attacks by the Moors had been repelled, the belief developed that the apostle was buried at Saint Mary's church near Iria Flavia in Galicia. Remains believed to be his were discovered at what would become Santiago de Compostela at some time in the first half of the ninth century, and Alfonso II had a small church built there. His successor, Alfonso III, was much more generous, providing lavish gifts and endowments. By the eleventh century, it was a well-established pilgrimage site. Meanwhile, the significance of Saint James, who would become known as Santiago Matamoros (Saint James the Moorslayer), was becoming attached to military and political protection and victory. Alfonso III regarded him as protector, military and otherwise, but it was probably not until the twelfth century that he became closely associated with aggressive Christian kings in victories against the Moors.[23]

The legend of Santiago became closely associated with the Virgin, although it is difficult to determine precisely when the various versions connecting the two developed. It is likely that they are readings backward from later centuries. Nevertheless, they tied the Virgin closely to Saint James, Christian unity, and victory over the Moors. One version of the legend ran that after the Crucifixion the Apostles scattered to proselytize. James had gone to Spain, where, after much discouragement, he succeeded in converting nine Iberians to the new religion. He was then visited as a special honor by Christ's Mother herself.[24] Another version of the story was that Saint James, while preaching in Mugia near the Cape of Finisterre, was shown a stone that had been used in the embarkation of Our Lady in Jerusalem as she was departing for Spain—an indication that she had actually preceded him there. Still, failing pitifully at conversion, he was ready to return to the Holy Land when Mary appeared to him on the outskirts of Zaragoza by the banks of the River Ebro. Surrounded by a dazzling light, she was standing on a pillar of stone brought from Palestine. After she had encouraged the apostle to be of good heart and to continue his work, she vanished, leaving the pillar on the ground.[25] Yet another modern version claimed that as Saint James prayed with a group of followers on the banks of the Ebro, the Sainted Virgin appeared and asked that they construct a chapel for her at that site. They immediately built a small oratory in her honor. As time passed, it was replaced with a more splendid building, which still conserves the name Pilar. The devotion continues to this day, having been recognized by Pope Clement XII with its own feast day, October 12. This Marian image was still linked with military power at the time of the French invasion in the nineteenth century:

> The Virgin of Pilar says
> that she doesn't want to be French,
> that she wants to be captain
> of the Aragonese troops.[26]

I think it is fair to believe that it was so associated during the Reconquest as well.

Yet another later version of the Santiago legend indicated that the body of James, who was beheaded at Caesaria, was miraculously made whole again and then disinterred and rescued by knights manning a ship of stone. His corpse was taken to Galicia in northwestern Spain, where the pagan queen initially refused burial. However, she was convinced by various miracles to permit interment in the old Roman cemetery. In 812 (other sources say 814), a hermit saw a bright light above an unused field. He persuaded the religious authorities to excavate, and Santiago's body was discovered intact. Saint James then assumed leadership of the Christian forces fighting the Muslims, appearing in the sky above the battle of Clavijo in 844. He was riding a white horse and killing Moors by the thousands. From that point on, he was known as "Santiago Matamoros," Saint James the Moorslayer, and Christian troops going into battle would shout his name along with that of the Blessed Virgin. Santiago de Compostela, his resting place, became a major European pilgrimage point by the next century. The name Compostela itself may have been associated with the Virgin as star, perhaps taken from the Spanish "campo de la estrella" or the Latin "Campus Stellae," that is, "the ground where the star shone."[27] This association would not prevent Santiago and the Blessed Mary from becoming competitors for reverence in the future. Unsurprisingly, the Santiago legend was not the only reinterpretation that was taking place. Later historians reconsidering Visigothic Spain were more formally developing a discussion of Covadonga, the battle at which, according to tradition, the Reconquest commenced in 722. According to the new versions, a small band of Christians led by Pelayo (possibly a man of royal lineage) routed an enemy force of 187,000 and began the push South.[28] Again unsurprisingly, Saint Mary was linked strongly with Pelayo and his struggle. According to the legend, when the Moorish tide swept north, Pelayo and his men took refuge in the mountains of Asturias. There the leader, pursuing an outlaw, encountered a cave in which an image of the Sainted Virgin was guarded by a hermit. The outlaw, having taken refuge in the same cave, prayed for the protection of the hermit and the Virgin. Pelayo sank to his knees in front of Mary's image, begging her pardon for the abrupt entrance he had made into her sanctuary. He then agreed to pardon, in turn, the man he had been pursuing. The hermit prophesied that Saint Mary would reward this noble action, providing Pelayo great triumphs in his lifetime. After his victory against the Moors, Pelayo, now king of Asturias, is said to have returned to the cave, where he thanked the Virgin with fervor for his victories and dedicated his life to the defense of the Cross against the Moors. Saint Mary is now the patron of Asturias.[29]

At the same time that the Santiago cult was developing in the North, the reverence for Mary in Mozarabic communities to the south was growing as well. An example may be found in the radical Christian movement in the city of Córdoba that produced forty-eight martyrs for the cause between 850 and 859. Muslim rule had not been harsh; the initial conquest had not been primarily for conversion, and monotheists—"people of the book"—including Jews and Christians, had been permitted to keep their religions and to be governed by their own laws. In al-Andalus (Muslim Spain), these laws were Visigothic. However, no public religious displays other than Muslim were permitted. From the middle of the eighth century and accelerating in the ninth century, there was an increasing drift in the direction of Muslim Arab culture—more conversions to Islam, more Arab dress, more interaction between communities. Between 822 and 852, the first period of rule by the Umayyad Arab rulers that united al-Andalus, wealth and culture increased, raising the level toward that of Abbasids in Baghdad. Many Córdoban Christians were dazzled by the wealth of the Umayyad court and the financial opportunities it afforded. Between 20 and 30 percent of the population were Muslim by 850; 50 percent had converted by 961; 90 percent were no longer Christian by the time Córdoba was retaken by Christian forces in the first part of the thirteenth century. The Córdoban movement of the ninth century may well have been a reaction against these rapid changes.[30]

Because the Muslim rulers were more concerned with protecting their own people from dangerous ideas than with converting Christians, martyrdom had to be sought out. The two major charges against the forty-eight beheaded in these years were, first, denigrating the prophet Mohammed and, second, apostasy to Christianity—usually on the part of Christians who had one Muslim parent and were automatically considered to be Muslim. These people went about deriding Mohammed as a "magician, an adulterer, and a liar" and warned that Hell awaited his followers.[31] As many of the martyrs were from mixed-marriage families, a high degree of tension, particularly in terms of gender expectations, can be imagined. Such issues as notions of modesty for women and the availability of divorce for Muslim men could cause a great deal of trouble. The largest subgroup among those condemned, however, were monks and nuns, marking the significance of monastic communities in keeping Christianity alive and viable. About half were clergy or lived under monastic vows. Other Christians saw them as simply causing trouble, but the martyrs' supporters believed the movement to be justified as a protest against the horrors of Muslim rule.[32]

The great chronicler of these events was the monk Eulogio, or Eulogius, as he is usually designated. This observer, who was eventually martyred himself, often referred to the Virgin Mary in his *Memoriale Sanctorum*, calling her the Blessed Virgin Queen of the World. He invoked her help against Satan, associated for him with the Moors. He also emphasized her virginity and purity, perhaps at some level a protest against the marrying of Christian women with Muslim men.[33] It is not surprising that Mary would be invoked in such circumstances; the mystery of the incarnation, in which Christ took his human form from Mary, was the Christian theological principle to which Muslims most objected.[34] Still, Mary was certainly not rejected by the Koran, which acknowledged that Christ had been conceived by virginal Mary. Nevertheless, Christians seem to have seen their own strong reverence for perpetually Virgin Mary as a major point that differentiated them from Muslims.[35]

The Reconquest of Spain accelerated during the eleventh and twelfth centuries, and the growth of the cult of the Virgin in both the peninsula and the rest of Europe coincided with it. Mary occupied a position at the center of popular devotion during these years.[36] Toledo was taken by Christian forces in 1085, and from that point forward its archbishops strove to make it the strongest diocese in Spain. As magnates on the Spanish frontier, they exerted this power and wealth in the effort to reconquer territory and to reestablish Christian religious and civil development in the area. As early as 1088, just three years after Toledo was returned to Christian political control, the pope gave the Toledan archbishop authority over those sees still under Muslim rule, including the not-yet-reconquered Seville.[37]

The Reconquest of Toledo and points south was linked with the Virgin in important ways. The eleventh and twelfth centuries were a period of heightened Marian devotion throughout Europe, but this devotion was manifested particularly strongly on the Castilian-Moorish frontier. As one historian has pointed out, "The late medieval frontier was a Mariological one."[38] Typically, the major church in a reconquered town would be named for Mary, a direct and vivid assertion of Christian power. It was usually located on the site of the chief mosque. The pattern was for the Christian ruler, after a triumphant entry into the conquered Muslim city, to hear mass in the newly converted mosque, now dedicated to the Virgin.[39] A significant example was the Great Mosque at Córdoba, but the pattern was repeated over and over throughout the peninsula. Along the frontier, the major churches on the Castilian side were dedicated to Mary, and her statues and other images were said to have played major roles in Christian victories.[40] Once installed, churches and images of the Virgin became viewed as highly resistant to recapture, as they would later in Mexico. As a poem in the *Cantigas de Santa María* in the thirteenth century pointed out, the Muslims had attempted unsuccessfully to destroy a church of the Virgin at Murcia. The text explained, "Muhammad

will never have power there because she conquered it [the church] and fur-
thermore she will conquer Spain and Morocco and Ceuta and Asila."[41]

Below the River Tagus—that is, south of the city of Toledo—the association of the Virgin with Christian power and Christian devotion was vivid.
William Christian has pointed out that in the sixteenth century the ratio of
major shrines dedicated to Mary and her mother, Saint Anne, was 26 to 20 in
relation to those of other saints in the region north of the Tagus; south of it,
the ratio was an astonishing 27 to 3. He traces this difference to the period
of the Reconquest. Yet in New Castile in the sixteenth century, local chapels
to the saints remained significant, with 32 percent devoted to Mary and 62
percent to the saints.[42]

The association of the Virgin with the success of the Reconquest was
emphasized by stories of the Marian devotion of past leaders. Sancho Garcés
of Pamplona, a tenth-century leader, was reported to have prostrated himself before Santa María de Irache, asking her intercession and promising her
the fort of Monjardín should he win it. In 1003 the Conde de Besalú, before
the battle of Torá (now Lérida), reminded his companions that the Virgin
and Saint Michael had protected them in the past and urged them on to
victory. When Cuenca was reconquered in 1177 by the King of Castile with
the help of the King of Aragón and the military orders of Calatrava and
Santiago, they were accompanied by the bishop of Burgos, who hung Mary's
banner on a wall during the final assault.[43]

The most spectacular victory was that at Las Navas de Tolosa in 1212,
only a few years after the appearance of the *Poema de mio Cid*, an epic celebrating a warrior leader of the eleventh century who in fact had fought for both
Christian and Muslim rulers. The poem shows him as a complex character
fighting enemies of both faiths. Still, the figure of El Cid, Rodrigo Díaz de
Vivar, became a tool for Christian recruitment for the upcoming campaign.
By this time, the fight had become identified with Castile, with the Castilian
court firmly established at Toledo. The poem vividly describes the hero, turned
away from his home at Burgos after difficulties with King Alfonso VI, paus-
ing by the Church of Santa María before leaving the city. There he knelt
down and "prayed from his heart," promising the Virgin reward should he
survive and prevail. On leaving the city, with his horse turned toward Mary's
church, he asked, "May your grace support me, Mother in Glory . . . and
help me and aid me through night and day." He struck a bargain with her,
saying, "If you do so, and I enjoy good fortune, I shall offer at your altar fine
and rich gifts; it shall be my duty to have a thousand masses sung."[44] Later,
the poem avers, he paid his debt, sending "gold and fine silver contained in a
gourd, full to overflowing," to pay for a thousand masses in Mary's church in

Burgos, with the balance left to his wife and daughters.[45] Apparently, his actual daughters were named Cristina and María, although they are named differently in the poem.[46] Perhaps his identification, or at least his wife's, as devoutly Christian was not so fanciful. Moreover, during the years that the historical El Cid ruled in Valencia, he converted the principal mosque into a cathedral dedicated to Our Lady.[47]

The battle at Las Navas de Tolosa was without question the key to the retaking of the South by Christian forces. This conflict was led initially by Castilian King Alfonso VIII, as the kings of León and Portugal were busy fighting each other. However, many of their vassals did take part. The military orders of Calatrava, Temple, Hospital, and Santiago all participated. Initially, the French provided a force of perhaps sixty thousand men, by

The Cathedral of Santa María at Burgos, Spain, houses the tomb of El Cid (1026–1099), a national hero revered for his victories. Photograph by Baird Pogue.

29

*Arco de Santa María, the main gate to the city of Burgos, Spain, constructed out
of the eleventh-century walls. At the top of the arch is a sixteenth-century sculpture
of the Madonna and child Jesus. Photograph by Linda B. Hall.*

Alfonso's estimate. Castilian troops were drawn away from their fortified
cities, a gamble that left these population centers essentially unprotected
should the drive against the Muslims fail.

Meanwhile, the caliph was preparing for the decisive battle in Seville,
where African troops had been encamped for months and where reinforce-
ments from Morocco and southern Spain gathered in the spring. The battle
was joined on Monday, July 16, 1212. The Christians had risen at midnight on
Sunday, first hearing mass, confessing their sins, taking communion, and
going forth vowing to conquer or die. Just before the battle, the main French
force had deserted, leaving only a handful of French knights. A small force
from previously hostile Navarre arrived at the last minute. The military orders formed the core of the main body of troops, and Spanish Archbishop
Rodrigo, a major figure in this crusade, commanded the rearguard with

Alfonso. Early on, a counterattack by the caliph's troops caused some Christians to flee, but the Moors were routed quickly by a charge led by Alfonso and Rodrigo. This movement reportedly was led by a bearer carrying the cross and another the royal banner adorned with images of the castles of Castile and of Our Lady, the patron saint of Toledo. The arrival of the cross and the banner was noted as the key to turning the tide. The king of Castile, seeing the image of María attacked by stones and arrows, redoubled his efforts, forcing the caliph to flee. The bearer of the banner, it was noted, was miraculously uninjured. Although years of desperate struggle remained, the way to the South was opened. Córdoba itself was retaken under Fernando III, later San Fernando, in 1236, and its great mosque was quickly dedicated to the Virgin by Archbishop Rodrigo's deputy, Bishop Juan. According to tradition, Fernando carried with him an image of Mary, which he installed in a watchtower on a mountain near the city. The location became a pilgrimage center.[48]

The struggle for the South was now closely connected with the Crusades to recover the Holy Land. Indeed, Pope Innocent III had ordered Rodrigo, then the new archbishop of Toledo, to urge Alfonso VIII to attack the Almohads, granting crusading privileges to those who would fight. Given the well-known problem of the Spanish Christian princes fighting one another, the pope enjoined all of them to help in the effort and ordered the bishops to excommunicate any king who attacked Castile while Alfonso's effort was in progress. During the hiatus between the reigns of Alfonso VIII and his successor, Fernando III, the military orders continued the struggle. They were aided in the most significant Christian victory, the recovery for the Order of Santiago of Alcácer do Sal, by Dutch and Rhenish warriors on their way to the Crusade against Egypt proclaimed by the Fourth Lateran Council in 1215. This castle, guarding the southern approach to Lisbon, had been granted to the order in 1186 but taken by the Muslims again in 1191.[49]

During Fernando III's reign, which lasted through 1252, the greatest movement against the Moors was completed, leaving a Muslim ruler only in Granada at the southern tip of Spain, that region now in vassalage to Castile. By 1247 this Christian king had established siege lines around Seville, which resisted until November 1248. The Virgin was once again associated closely with this victory. Fernando's great devotion to the Virgin was manifest when he entered the city bringing with him (according to legend) the image of the Virgen de los Reyes, the Virgin of the Kings, on a special open float constructed especially for this moment of triumph. He is said to have installed the image in the royal chapel of Seville's great mosque, which was converted into the Catholic cathedral devoted to the Virgin of the Sede. The Virgin of

Battles, an ivory image he had carried on his saddle, was also placed in the cathedral. There is another similar tale. By the end of the fifteenth century, about the time of the European discovery of America, another image of Mary in the Sevillian cathedral was closely associated with Fernando. This image, according to the story, had been kept in the city's mosque during the years of Muslim control. The account given to visitors was that during his siege of the city, Fernando had a vision indicating that if he would revere this image, the city would soon fall to him. Indeed, the city fell, Christianity was victorious, and the image of the Virgin was released from captivity. Fernando, it was said, thereafter took the image with him in future battles against the Muslims.[50] Stories of the Virgin's favors to Fernando would be recounted at length by his son Alfonso X in his *Cantigas de Santa Maria*. Mary was becoming more and more identified with the process of conquest and with the differentiation of Christian peoples from others. At the same time, these stories link the Spanish crown closely with tangible images of Mary.

Meanwhile, Jaume I of Aragón was moving down the eastern side of the peninsula establishing the basis for a great maritime empire. In Valencia, the major area conquered, the Christian settlers were confined to the cities surrounded by a "sea of subject Muslims." Jaume's own devotions were intense and directed toward the Virgin, despite his vindictiveness toward his enemies and his well-known eye for the ladies. As one prominent scholar has noted, "It is nothing new in the psychology of pleasures that the Blessed Virgin should exercise so immediate an attraction." Jaume himself wrote about one occasion when he had been faced with dangerous conditions at sea. Turning to Our Lord and his Mother, he addressed her specifically as the "bridge and path of sinners," invoking the "seven joys and seven sorrows you had from your dear Son." He was saved. Forty years later, he again faced a storm at sea. Arriving safely, he "went to the Church of Holy Mary of Vallvert to thank her for the favor and the good." He ordered that her image be carried for triumphal entries, and he dedicated to her the main churches in cities like Majorca, Murcia, Valencia, and Alcira. While waiting for Murcia to surrender, he prayed to the Virgin and, upon victory, set up her altar there. Later, under attack, he refused counsel of retreat, as the Lord had granted Murcia to the crusaders because of Santa María's intercession with her Son. The turning point in the advance across Valencia came after a council of war in her church. The key fortification for this drive he named the "Hill of Holy Mary." He viewed his crusades as Marian "deeds" within a knightly code of honor.[51]

But it was under Jaume's son-in-law and Fernando III's son, King Alfonso X of Castile (1252–1284), that the reverence for Mary became most entrenched, both spatially and ideologically. This effort coincided with the attempts to fuse the newly conquered territories of Andalusia into his empire and to establish something like a unified culture. Although Alfonso was unable to advance the Reconquest greatly in terms of physical space, he consolidated Christian control significantly. In particular, he was able to extend Castilian power to the Atlantic coast, providing an opening—though not one that would be used effectively—to Africa. While seeking to impose direct rule on Muslim vassalkingdoms in the South, he was met by resistance led by Muhammed I of Granada, the remaining non-Christian stronghold. In a plot that included plans to capture Alfonso, the Muslims rose, killing Christians and capturing fortresses south of Seville such as Arcos and Rota. Alfonso escaped, however, and reacted vigorously to reassert Christian power. When Arcos was retaken, according to the legend now scribbled on the wall of the church, an image of the Virgen de los Nieves was discovered in an old mineshaft—where presumably she had been hidden during the Muslim sweep north.

Given Alfonso's determination to expel the Muslim population and resettle the area with Christians, the appearance of the Virgin's image would give comfort to new settlers and legitimacy to Christian claims on the region. With Jaume of Aragón's Reconquest of Murcia and its deliverance to Alfonso, the Castilian monarch was able to extend his policies throughout the portions of southern Spain under his control. Most Muslims were expelled and the region resettled, principally with Cataláns, so that there were few of the former in his realms after 1284. Castile now enjoyed hegemony over much of southern Spain, which became a land of Christians determined to stay despite the proximity of Muslim Granada. Granada itself remained in an ambivalent relationship to Castile, moving back and forth between degrees of vassalage and independence, until Fernando and Isabel completed the Reconquest of the peninsula in 1492.[52] The region at the edges of Granada and Andalusia now became a frontier, sometimes disputed and always liminal, between Christian and Muslim cultures.

However, Alfonso's most significant contribution to the cult of Mary was literary and ideological. Deeply devoted to the Virgin, he led a team of artists, writers, and composers in the production of a collection of stories and poems in praise of Mary, some popular throughout Europe and others directly related to the peninsula during the Reconquest. Still others were personal statements (and personal histories) by Alfonso himself. The collection, known most widely as the *Cantigas de Santa María*, is interesting to analyze within an understanding of his commitment to the creation of the state, defined by one author as "the integration of king and community into one corporate unit."[53] Although the *Cantigas* follow in a line of European collections of Marian miracle stories, they are remarkable in terms of the extraordinary number of miracles recounted, 356, while others range in the neighborhood of 25 to 60. They also vary widely in origin and setting, with a large number repeating stories known throughout the Christian West, others relating directly to sanctuaries or locations in the peninsula, and still others recounting miracles that affected the king himself. It is striking that while the earlier stories in the volume are internationally known, the later ones are heavily focused either on Iberia or on personal stories involving Alfonso.[54] It is clear that this enterprise went well beyond other previous compilations, and it is especially striking that the project was undertaken by a monarch in the process of consolidating his holdings. As Maricel Presilla puts it, "one has to bear in mind that Alfonso X was a culture-hero engaged in an almost messianic process of state-building. His efforts required, above all, a consensus both at the secular and religious levels. The cult of Mary, which was the most deeply rooted form of religious expression in the popular mind, provided Alfonso with all the means he needed to achieve symbolic consensus."[55]

Moreover, the *Cantigas* fit well with his other intellectual endeavors, including the writings on law, history, and astronomy compiled during his reign. As Presilla indicates, the *Cantigas* form one component "of a highly structured ideological model aimed at the reorganization of thirteenth-century Spanish society. Such an attempt indicates that Alfonso was consciously reacting to the immediate challenges presented by the halt of the Reconquest in the middle of the thirteenth century and to the long-term consequences of the process of territorial expansion such as: inflation, intragroup violence, population shifts, religious diversity, a frontier mentality, and acute cultural dissonance."[56] But while the *Cantigas* were a potent ideological set of documents, it should not be forgotten that they were also a potent and poignant statement by Alfonso of his own personal faith.

While some of these illustrated songs addressed various of the Virgin's nurturing and healing qualities, others were devoted to the increasingly clear distinctions being made between Christians and the other inhabitants of the peninsula, notably Jews and Muslims. Some were related to the triumph of Spanish arms, the miraculous releases of Christian prisoners, and the establishment of Christian hegemony over southern Spain. The theme of hegemony was pursued most importantly in a cycle of song-poems related to the Puerto de Santa María, a new city that Alfonso established on the Gulf of Cádiz as a port he hoped to use for further conquests in Africa.

Alfonso's personal devotion to the Virgin and its relationship to his empire are emphasized in the first of two introductory poems. It names Alfonso and his realms, reaching from León and Aragón in the north to the recently conquered (and rather tenuously held) Jerez and Murcia to the south. These songs of "honor and praise" are dedicated to the Virgin Santa María, Mother of God, to document her wonders. This sense of Alfonso's deep devotion continues throughout, although the songs themselves were no doubt written by a team of writers. This enormous compendium, though with many authors, is a personal document of the Spanish monarch.[57] In the second poem, also introductory, he describes himself as singing her songs: "And what I wish is to tell the praise of the Virgin, the Mother of Our Lord, Holy Mary, the best thing that He made; and so I want to be her troubadour, and I ask her to desire me as her troubadour and to want to receive my song wherein I wish to reveal the miracles that she worked."[58] The relationship between Mary and her patronage of a historical Spain is immediately made clear by the second of the songs actually in praise of Mary, which recounts her miraculous appearance to San Ildefonso—Alfonso's namesake—in her cathedral at Toledo in 662.[59] The themes of nationalism and expansion and of Mary as the protector of the kings of Castile in these endeavors is reinforced in Alfonso's *Primera Crónica General*, in which it is recalled that the three kings who participated in the battle of Las Navas de Tolosa on the Christian side all carried banners of Santa María la Antigua. This advocation, it goes on to say, was known to all as the patroness and conqueror of all Spain.[60]

The accounts are full of the miracles of Mary as she cured and revived the faithful from the horrors of leprosy, rabies, blindness and deafness, ailments of the throat, and even death itself. But these cures were often linked to Alfonso's imperial project—integration in social, religious, territorial, and political terms. The location of cure miracles shifted to the Virgin Mary in the center and South, away from Saint James of Compostela in the North. In addition to venerating the Virgin, Alfonso perhaps wanted to diminish the influence of Compostela, which could compete for power with the crown. As Peter Linehan has put it, "In the Cantigas Santiago is regularly upstaged by the Virgin."[61] A particularly interesting story (Cantiga 321) involved a young girl healed at Córdoba, to the south on the road to Seville. Córdoba was a center of Muslim power for centuries and was only returned to Christian control by Alfonso's father in 1236. Even after that date, it remained no more than a military outpost. The story recounted that the child, suffering from a tumor in her throat, had been taken by her mother to Alfonso, believing erroneously that the king's "healing touch" could cure her. The king replied that such a royal healing touch was "nonsense" and advised the distressed mother to take the child to the image of the Virgin. She was instructed to wash the image with pure water, which should then be saved and drunk by the afflicted youngster from an altar chalice for five days in a row. The five days corresponded to a day for each letter in María's name. According to the story, the child recovered completely. This account illustrates both the authority of the king in this recently conquered location as well as the healing power of Mary, now directly operative within a former Muslim stronghold.[62]

The most graphic cure stories refer to Alfonso himself. These stories are so specific as to the ailing king's symptoms that a tentative diagnosis can be made about some of his conditions. In Cantiga 209, the king fell desperately ill in the town of Vitoria with fever and intense pain and was saved by the miraculous intervention of the Virgin when a copy of the *Cantigas* was laid on his body. This story is very close in time and proximity within the book to another, which recounts that Mary had saved him from a conspiracy led by his brother.[63] These accounts have been dated to approximately 1272–1279, close to the end of Alfonso's life. It seems that he was suffering from a serious malady that waxed and waned in intensity, possibly renal failure or heart disease, along with a cancerous facial tumor that affected his eye socket. The Marian miracles recounted would presumably be periods of relief or remission. Although his actual condition remains speculative, it is clear that Alfonso was seriously ill and in severe pain during the last years of his reign. This suffering led to an ever greater devotion to María.[64]

The *Cantigas* also relate directly to the challenges that Alfonso faced in integrating a large non-Christian population into a Christian political empire. Alfonso employed Muslims and Jews at court, and he realized that his social and political project would benefit from assimilating and acculturating these peoples. It should not be forgotten that the *Cantigas* were meant to be performed at the king's court and elsewhere. Not surprisingly, then, a number of them were addressed to condemnations of the religious minorities and a lauding of conversion to Christianity. This theme occurred early, in Cantiga 4, when Mary saved a young Jewish boy, Abel, whose father had thrown him into the fire for associating with Christians. The boy's mother, Rachel, prayed to the Virgin to rescue him, which the Virgin of course did. Mother and son were converted happily to Christianity, while the cruel father died.[65] Cantiga 107 relates that Santa María saved a young Jewish woman caught in sin who was thrown off a cliff by her people. The young woman cried out to Mary the Queen to save her, pleading, "If you are as they say, and you help those anguished who commend themselves to you, save me among sinners, as I am in need. And if I remain alive and well, I will become Christian, before the next day dawns." Mary intervened and helped her fall safely near a fig tree. The woman arose and continued on her way, saying, "The Glorious Mother of God shall always be blessed, she who was merciful to me. Who would not serve her?"[66] Courtiers of other faiths listening to these songs and skits would certainly have gotten the message.

Jews helpful to Christians appear in the *Cantigas* as well, leaving open the hope of integration and conversion. Cantiga 25 describes the case of a Jewish moneylender who helped a Christian who had failed to obtain aid from his own friends. Although the case may be read as an instance of Jewish avarice, it can also be seen as an example of Jewish tolerance, as the moneylender accepted as pledge only Christ and his Holy Mother. Although the Jew later tried to pretend that the loan had been left unpaid and thus take advantage of the borrower, he ultimately relented when the true story was revealed by the Virgin, and he accepted conversion.[67] Jews who did convert often chose names associated with Mary, perhaps to prove their sincerity and/or zealousness. A notable example from the next century was Pablo, bishop of Burgos, the former rabbi and leader of his community, Solomon ha-Levi. He and his children, several of whom became important in church offices, took the surname Santa María.[68]

Moors within the new boundaries were also targets for conversion, while those outside remained dangerous enemies. The Moor as a threat or a treacherous enemy appeared in these Marian stories, but he or she was also a possible convert.[69] Muslims might save themselves or their loved ones from the perils of death and damnation through the intervention of the Blessed Virgin if they were willing to become Christian. Alfonso, though amenable to having his court populated by Jewish and Muslim scholars, was looking to the homogenization of his kingdom. Through the Cantigas, which were to be publicly performed, he was putting pressure on these groups to assimilate and showing them the advantages to be gained thereby.

It is in the cycle of song-poems concerning Santa María del Puerto that Alfonso's reverence for Mary becomes most entwined with his social, ideological, and imperial purposes. This advocation is directly connected with Alfonso's attempts to consolidate the holdings gained through his father's victories by firmly establishing a Christian naval base on the Gulf of Cádiz. Such a Castilian presence would make it possible not only to guard the straits against invasion from Africa but also to launch further crusades in that direction. Moreover, an established Christian community on the Guadalete River might make it easier to control Muslim populations still entrenched up the river valley at sites such as Jerez and Arcos. These were the populations that had begun to test Alfonso's mettle almost immediately after he took the throne in 1252.[70]

Alfonso therefore moved in approximately 1260 to fortify and develop the town for naval operations, although it is unlikely that there was much of a settlement there until much later in his reign. His naming of the town, previously called Alcanate or al-Qanatir, was by no means capricious. Santa

María, close to the southern extreme of Castilian holdings and almost on the frontier of Christian and Muslim territories in land still disputed, would distinguish the Christian realm from that of the infidel. She would protect Christian forces and at the same time be ready to lead these forces to further conquest. The Moors of Jerez, although they had submitted to Christian rule, protested the name change and the reinforcement of the Castilian presence in southern Andalusia. Nevertheless they eventually acquiesced. Alfonso's only expedition to Africa, the sack of Salé on the Atlantic coast of Morocco, was launched from that point.[71] Settlement of the port was delayed by the revolt of the Muslim populations of Jerez, Arcos, and other populations further inland along the Guadalete in 1264, but the port's development remained a priority for Alfonso throughout his reign.

One legend that developed around the discovery of the image of María indicates the way in which she could be used later to legitimize Christian control of the area. According to the story, in 1264 Alfonso was contemplating the ruins of the ancient city of Alcanate when, led by an apparition of Mary, he encountered an image of the Virgin beneath the ruins of a Christian chapel. Along with the statue was a parchment that recounted the following story. In 1062 Hamer Hairán had occupied the port and moved into the fort that contained the chapel. His beautiful daughter Leila was convinced of the truth of the Christian faith and especially the infinite goodness and mercy of the Mother of God, although she did not renounce her Muslim faith publicly. She fell in love with a Muslim nobleman, whom she converted as well, and they began to search for a way to flee to Christian territory to seek baptism. Her father discovered their plan and, furious, tried to force the couple to renounce Jesus Christ. They preferred martyrdom. Hamer Hairán had them slaughtered in the corner of the chapel, right over the image of Mary hidden there years before. Alfonso reportedly read this account with great emotion and immediately had a church dedicated to Mary to house the image and to serve as the center of the newly Christian city.[72]

The cycle of song-poems that treat Santa María del Puerto exists within the larger work as a kind of mini-narrative that, scholars emphasize, had personal significance for Alfonso. The works are notable for their directness and the realism of their presentation, naming various associates—including Alfonso's scribe, one of his favorite artists, and his brother Manuel—as the beneficiaries of the mercies and miracles of this particular advocation. Alfonso fostered this devotion to the point that he founded a military order devoted to it, the Order of Santa María, to guard the Spanish coast. It was also known as the Order of the Star to emphasize the significance of Mary as the Star of the Sea, protector and guide of mariners.[73]

Many of the stories involve the ways in which María nurtured, protected, and aided the new inhabitants of the port. In particular, a number of Cantigas discuss the curing or protection of children, a theme sure to be reassuring to potential settlers. In one case, she even resuscitated a child who had died of the fever.[74] Although these cases did not take place in the port but rather in Jerez and Seville, they served to emphasize the goodness and the safety to be had in the service of María and presumably under her protection in residence in the new settlement.

In other stories, she protected settlers in southern Andalusia from various vicissitudes ranging from the loss of sheep, which were found unharmed despite being surrounded by wolves, to attack by pirates, on whom she took vengeance.[75] In another she clearly protected her own interests when she saved from harm thirty men who were excavating land for her church when a tower collapsed almost on top of them. The spared men then worked with such zeal in her behalf that the resulting church was said to be well built and very beautiful.[76]

The remaining years of the thirteenth century and most of the fourteenth were spent in consolidating lands already held and continuing to bring them under the territorial and cultural control of the monarch. Successor kings followed Alfonso X's devotion to Mary and his practice of establishing sacred Marian sites. This effort was not only conducted on the front lines of opposition to the Moors but also in areas to the north and west of the newly conquered territories. The most famous of these was the new devotion to the Virgin of Guadalupe in Extremadura, an area extremely lightly held and subject to bandit raids.

As the legend goes, priests fleeing from Seville at the time of the Moorish invasion encountered the River Guadalupe and there dug a cave where they placed the image of Saint Mary that they had brought with them. Centuries later, a cowherd missing one of his animals went searching into the mountains and found it lying dead. On butchering the creature he opened its breast in the form of a cross. He was amazed to see the carcass revive and rise to its feet. Immediately the Virgin Mary appeared to him, ordering him to return to the town and explain to the local priests that they would find the statue of her on that site. On returning home, the cowherd discovered his wife in tears, as their son had died during his absence. He immediately promised the child to Saint Mary of Guadalupe, and the young boy arose well. Then the cowherd went to the priests and urged them to join him in returning to the place of her appearance with him; they hastened to the spot and discovered the image. The discovers carried away stones in the area as relics, and the statue immediately began to heal those who came to her with afflictions.[77]

The story may be apocryphal, but the fame of the image spread throughout Spain in the fourteenth century. King Alfonso XI was the first monarch to promote the Guadalupe cult enthusiastically. Establishing a shrine of Santa María de Guadalupe, he helped introduce some measure of royal control to the Extremaduran badlands. Not only would this cult bring pilgrims into the dangerous area, reassured by the presence of a healing Mother, but it also would lead to settlement as economic opportunities grew around the shrine.[78] At the same time, Alfonso XI was rethinking the route of the *mesta* through which transhumant flocks moved seasonally from one part of Spain to another. In 1339 his officials redirected that route to run through Extremadura and western Andalusia. In this way he not only ensured the traffic of Christian pilgrims but also the constant movement of flocks.[79]

The shrine thrived during the fourteenth century, but corruption in its administration led in 1389 to its delivery to the Hieronymites. The monastery continued to enjoy royal favor through the administrations of the succeeding monarchs down to and including the reign of Isabel and Fernando, who quite reasonably were known as the Most Catholic Monarchs. During their reign the cult of Mary would become even more important than before. Isabel was strongly associated with the Virgin, particularly with the advocation of Guadalupe and the doctrine of the Immaculate Conception. The latter idea, while rather vague in meaning in the fifteenth century, had to do with Mary's freedom from original sin from the moment she was conceived. Though the theology of this idea was not clarified until it became dogma in the nineteenth century, it was clear in Isabel's mind and in the popular religion of the time that it emphasized the purity of the Mother of God. The devotion to the Immaculate Conception, as measured by the number of vows to observe that day, December 8, was rising rapidly in Castile during the last decades of the fifteenth century, coinciding in time with Isabel's rule.[80] She endowed three chaplaincies to the Virgin of the Immaculate Conception—significantly, at Toledo, at Seville, and at Guadalupe.[81] It is likely that the association with the Virgin was particularly appealing to Isabel, a woman raised strongly Catholic whose own marriage to Fernando had been consummated, apparently very enthusiastically, before the dispensation permitting it had been obtained from the pope. Although she was unaware that approval had not yet been secured, she must nevertheless have felt that her reputation was sullied despite her ignorance. She probably also had concerns about her immortal soul.

Isabel and Fernando reinvigorated the Reconquest, which had largely bogged down after the time of Alfonso X. Isabel was by all reports intensely religious and determined to unify her realms within the Christian religion.

The Immaculate Conception, *Bartolomé Esteban Murillo (1617/18–1682)*,
ca. 1655–1660, oil on canvas. Courtesy of the Meadows Museum, Southern Methodist
University, Dallas, Algur H. Meadows Collection, No. 68.24.

Her identification with Mary seems to have been strong. She became very
fond of the monastery of Guadalupe, traveling there often for spiritual renewal and to consult the monks, who were known for their medical expertise, about health and especially fertility matters. For example, she visited
there in 1477 at a time when she was especially eager to give birth to a male
heir. The following year, Prince Juan was born. Isabel loved the time that she
spent at Guadalupe, calling it *mi paraiso*, "my paradise." She also constructed
a residence in Guadalupe using funds confiscated from *conversos* (Jews converted to Christianity) attacked by the Inquisition and later an oratory above
the altar, where she prayed with her *Book of Hours*. A beautiful copy of this
book that she seems to have possessed may have belonged first to Juana
Enríquez, the mother of Fernando, and then Isabel's own daughter Juana.
Two of the pictures show a very fair, red-haired queen in her devotions. In
one image the queen kneels at the foot of the Virgin Mary and her Child.
The pictured queen is in a robe of ermine and red fabric. The Virgin is also

Plate II. Queen praying before the Virgin and Child. Libro de horas de Isabel la Católica,
edited by Matilde López Serrano (Madrid: Editorial Patrimonio Nacional, 1969).

regal, sitting on a throne and crowned as the Queen of Heaven. Interestingly,
the two figures are of the same size. In another plate the queen in ermine and
red again prays to Mary, but this time the figure of Mary is double in size.
Mary holds the Christ Child while towering above the courtiers, but the red-
clad queen, clearly the same individual as in the earlier illustration, is in front
and well separated from the rest. That figure holds a book opened in prayer,
perhaps supposed to represent the very *Book of Hours* in which the picture
appears. Matilde López Serrano suggests that the images of the queen may
be of Juana Enríquez, though Isabel's mother-in-law, who died of cancer the
year before her marriage to Fernando, was known to be rather dark. The
name Johanna appears on the text of folios 356 through 359 and could have
referred to either Isabel's mother-in-law or to Isabel's daughter Juana, who is
thought to have had the book after Isabel herself. In any case, the name
seems to have replaced another, which has been effaced. It seems at least
possible that the book was produced for Isabel at the behest of her

bridegroom's family, identified with the coat of arms of Aragón and Enríquez on folios 37 and 343, and that it was Isabel, fair and redheaded, who provided the physical attributes of the queen, though it strikes me as unlikely that she herself would have been accessible to model from life. If it were meant to be Isabel, these images might have been of her own reverence.[82] Whether or not the portrait of the queen was a representation of either Isabel or her mother-in-law, these depictions would certainly have presented Isabel in an image that reflected her devotion—humble, despite her rank, before the Holy Mother but identified with her.

The birth of Prince Juan reinforced the identification of Isabel with Mary. It was reported that when she gave birth she exclaimed, "Oh, Sweet Mary." This report may have been an invention designed to link Isabel with the Woman of the Apocalypse of the Book of Revelation (in turn linked iconographically with the Immaculate Conception) who, with a cry, gives birth to a son. Yet it is significant that writers in her service sought to connect Juan's birth with that of Jesus and the contribution of his mother with that of the Virgin. Isabel's chronicler, Pulgar, made the connection clear: "And with the great supplications and offerings and pious works that she made, it pleased God that in that city she conceived and gave birth to a son who was named the Prince Don Juan." He continued, "In those days that the King and Queen were in Seville, the King of Granada sent his ambassadors." The biblical resonance to the story of the Three Kings was obvious.[83]

The association between Santa María, Isabel, and the Reconquest was strong. Another of her chroniclers, Diego de Valera, wrote to her "that just as our Lord wished that our glorious Lady might be born in this world because from her would proceed the Universal Redeemer of the human lineage, so he determined that you, My Lady, would be born to reform and restore these kingdoms and lead them out from the tyrannical government under which they have been for so long."[84] Here was combined not only Isabel's achievement as the mother of the new heir but also a reiteration of her responsibility to restore Christian government to the entire peninsula. Just as Mary could be seen both as the Virgin of Battles and as the deliverer from evil, so could Isabel.

Fernando was also devoted to the Virgin. His sword carried a message invoking her aid and protection, and even before he became king he founded a chivalric order dedicated to the purity of the Virgin and to the final conquest of the Moors with the Virgin's help. It should be remembered that the Christian-Moorish frontier at this time was eschatological; that is, it was widely prophesied that the devil or anti-Christ would appear in Seville; that the forces of the Spanish king would embark from the port of Cádiz; that a terrible battle would follow; and that then the messianic forces of the Christians would drive out the Moors and conquer Granada. The Spanish king who would accomplish this feat was known as "the hidden one," widely thought to be Fernando.[85] If Fernando was the hidden one, then Isabel could certainly be associated with the Virgin as the conquest of Granada came to fruition in 1492. As Isabel's project to push Christianity to new lands proceeded, Saint Mary would accompany those she sent to do her mission.

And the Virgin Mary who would arrive in the New World would be very much like the one who had accompanied Christian forces in defeating the Moors. Loving and nurturing on the one hand and strengthening and fortifying her troops in battle on the other, she would place her name throughout the new landscape of the Americas.

CHAPTER THREE

Discoverers, Conquerors, and Mary

✠ ✠ ✠

IT WAS ISABEL'S AND FERNANDO'S MISSION of Christianity and conquest that led to the voyage of Christopher Columbus to America, and Columbus carried this intense devotion for Mary across the ocean. In a real sense, his mission was a continuation, both spiritually and spatially, of the Spanish Reconquest of the peninsula. But the discoverer was by no means the only European to bring the Mother of God with him as he encountered what was for him a New World. Virtually all of the leaders who initially came to explore and conquer shared the reverence for Santa María that characterized the Spanish monarchs and Columbus and his men. Their invoking of María in new locations and contexts repeated the patterns being used in Europe, as they wrote to the crown, composed their wills, and wrote their remembrances. Though these patterns could be dismissed as formulas, in my opinion the formulas and their ritualistic nature are significant and meaningful, and Saint Mary's position at the center of them is significant and meaningful as well.[1] Not only did she continue to nurture and comfort those far from home, now in even more unfamiliar and dangerous circumstances and territory, she also animated them as a warrior leading them against hostile forces.

For Columbus, his voyage into the unknown was closely connected to his religious beliefs. In his own spirituality, the devotion to and reliance on the Virgin was intense. His voyage was wrapped round with Marian imagery; his progress was marked with geographic locations dedicated to Mary. This reverence, within the context of expanding Spain, was entirely natural. The Reconquest had been placed securely in a context of Marian devotion and protection against hostile, non-Christian foes, and Santa María had long

*Plate III. In this early-sixteenth-century painting the Virgin is depicted spreading her mantle
over the Spanish. King Fernando is depicted to the left of the painting, while Columbus,
Vespucci, and one of the Pinzón brothers are shown kneeling on the right. Note that they soar
with her on clouds above the sea. Many contemporary vessels are shown in the water beneath
her feet. This image was produced during the lifetimes of Cortés and Pizarro.* Virgin
of the Navigators, *Alejo Fernandez, ca. 1535, Real Alcazar, Seville, Spain.*

been viewed as particularly concerned with mariners and protection from
the dangers of the deep. A number of the *Cantigas* of Alfonso X involved
rescues of imperiled sailors; Alfonso's father-in-law, Jaume, credited a maritime escape of his own to the Virgin, as Columbus would later. Mariners of
the time were accustomed to singing the *Ave Maria* at sundown to guard against
the perils of the night and perhaps to welcome her star—Polaris, the North
Star—so essential at that time to navigation. We know that Columbus himself prayed regularly to the Virgin Mary, and he is believed to have carried a
Book of Hours with him on his voyages. A beautiful *Book of Hours* belonging to
the admiral after the Discovery still exists in the Biblioteca Corsiniana of
Rome. Of course, it contains, most importantly, the Office of the Virgin, a
guide to daily prayer. According to one authority, Columbus balanced per-

sonal, guided prayer with the more general devotions fixed by the Church; it is touching to imagine him using this volume.[2] He often included invocations to Mary and Jesus in his letters, asking for them to accompany him as he went about his life.[3] Though these might be read as formulaic, his naming of his discoveries in the European New World further attested to his piety for the Virgin.[4] There have been persistent rumors that Columbus was Jewish or of Jewish descent.[5] If so, it would not have been unusual for him to practice his Christian beliefs with a special emphasis on Marian devotion, as was the case of the converted rabbi Paul of Santa María, who became bishop of Burgos (see Chapter II).

Columbus's own "Mystical Signature," a much-analyzed and debated formal signature that is more a signifier of his identity than a rendition of his name, includes important references to Mary. Although it varied from time to time, typically it looked roughly like this:

```
          .S.
.S.       A        .S.
X         M         Y
El Almirante [The Admiral]
```

Alternatively, the last line sometimes read "Xpo FERENS," which all agree means "Christ-bearer," a point to which we will return. Crucial here, however, is that many signatures and marks of the time reflected those things important to an individual's self-identification. For example, a contractual statement signed by a number of late fifteenth-century fishermen in Puerto de Santa María included anchors, boats, oars, fish, and the like. John Fleming suggests that Columbus's formal signature is in fact a kind of mariner's chart, focused not on map reading but on star reading and reflecting his own spirituality. According to Fleming, the stars on which Columbus based the signature were those of the constellation Ursa Minor, in which Stella Maris, the North Star, appears, and the central axis of the signature, reading top to bottom .S. A M, was built on the incipit of that most famous of all Marian and mariners' hymns, the *Ave Stella Maris*. The crossbar may have been taken from the phrase "StellA mariS."[6]

The Marian imagery surrounding the voyage itself is pervasive. Columbus left from the port of Palos, close by Cádiz, the point of departure of the many Jews being forced out of Spain by Fernando and Isabel after the defeat of Granada. It was also close to the Puerto de Santa María, where the Virgin's presence had been so consciously located by Alfonso X two centuries earlier. Some of Columbus's sailors actually came from that town. Columbus's flagship, reflecting the regard of mariners for the Virgin, was named the *Santa María* and was also contracted in the Puerto de Santa María. Before departure, in the monastery of La Rábida, where he had been housed and encouraged during his entreaties to Isabel and later while he prepared for the voyage, he prayed to the image of the Virgin of the Angels to whom the monastery was dedicated. In fact, his departure date—August 3, 1492—was determined in relation to her feast day, August 2. By choosing this date, Columbus and his sailors could attend the festivities, so important to the Franciscans at La Rábida and to those in the communities from which the sailors came. Further, and probably more important, they could depart secure in the knowledge that they had invoked the protection of the Virgin.[7]

Given the circumstances of his departure, then, Columbus's voyage was covered by the protective mantle of Mary. The ships left from an area protected by the Virgin, after invoking her help on her day, with her ship carrying Columbus and leading the way, following her star. As an added reassurance during the voyage, the mariners, following the custom of the time, prepared themselves against the dark by saying the Hail Mary at nightfall.[8]

The impression of Mary's name on the New World was almost immediate upon the arrival of the mariners at landfall. Although the first island was named San Salvador, for her Son, the second was named Santa María de la Concepción. It honored the Virgin in the advocation that had become so popular in Spain in the preceding decades, was favored by the queen, and so clearly indicated her purity. The devotion to the Immaculate Conception was no doubt strong in Columbus's consciousness, as this idea was being pushed heavily by his patrons at La Rábida, the Franciscans. In its precise theological meaning, this doctrine is a bit abstruse, referring to the Virgin's freedom from original sin from the moment of conception. Devoted laypersons nevertheless supported it as a generalized way of honoring her purity, her state of being "without stain." This naming of the island took place only about six weeks after the departure from Spain. A month later, on December 6, two days before the feast day of Concepción, Columbus named a harbor on the island of Española Puerto de la Concepción.

Traveling home with just two ships after the Santa María was lost in the islands, Columbus and his men had cause to call on Mary.[9] The Niña and the Pinta, hit by bad weather, lost contact. The Pinta went on ahead, but the Niña was hit full on by the storm. The admiral decided to call on the Virgin, rather than the Lord, for aid in this crisis. In his mind, presumably, Saint Mary would be more sympathetic than her Son. She was promised that one of their number would undertake a pilgrimage to the shrine of Santa María de Guadalupe, carrying a five-pound wax candle, if they were spared and returned safely to Spain. Chickpeas, one marked with the cross, were put in a hat and mixed well. The admiral himself, perhaps not so accidentally, drew the first lot, which was indeed the cross-marked garbanzo. The storm continuing, they drew lots again to send a pilgrim to the sanctuary of Santa María de Loreto, a place where, according to Columbus's log, "Our Lady has performed and performs many and great miracles." This time a seaman of Puerto de Santa María was chosen, and Columbus promised to pay the sailor's expenses. Still the storm did not abate, and a third lottery to choose a pilgrim to spend the night at Santa Clara de Moguer near their home port of Palos and to arrange for mass to be said also failed to calm the storm, despite the fact that once again Columbus himself was the chosen person. The situation was becoming critical, as the ship was sailing with little ballast, provisions having been largely expended. Now all the sailors and the admiral made a vow that as soon as they hit first land, they would all go in procession in their shirtsleeves to pray in the nearest church dedicated to the Virgin. This last vow nearly led to disaster.

Although the wind began to abate and the sea to subside after sunset on February 14, the danger had not completely passed. One of the sailors spotted land dead ahead on the morning of February 15, although it took them three more days of struggle with the winds before they could make landfall there. It turned out, appropriately, to be Santa María, the southernmost and one of the smallest of the Azores. However, these islands were Portuguese-controlled, and only extremity led Columbus to harbor there. Still, the initial reception was promising. The mariners were welcomed by the people of the island, who marveled at their amazing escape from such terrible weather and at the news that they brought of the discovery of the "Indies." Nearby, in what must have seemed marvelous rather than coincidental, was a village called Nossa Senhora dos Anjos, Our Lady of the Angels, the same advocation of the Virgin to whom Columbus had prayed at La Rábida before departure. The name of the village and a chapel dedicated to her commemorated an appearance of the Virgin surrounded by angels to a stranded fisherman several years earlier. However, threatened again by winds and weather, Columbus and the crew were forced to move the Niña to a more sheltered harbor out of sight of the village. Three men were left on shore to obtain fresh provisions and water for the crew. That evening three villagers hailed the ship, and Columbus sent for them to come aboard. The visitors brought provisions and a welcome, insincere, as it happened, from the captain of the island. They also brought information about the small chapel, and Columbus decided that the time had come to fulfill the last vow.

At dawn on Tuesday, February 19, Columbus sent half the crew ashore with the messengers, asking the latter to find the priest and arrange for him to say mass. The priest was indeed found, and the sailors, clad in their shirts—which were the proper garb for penitence—crowded into the chapel. While saying their prayers before an old Flemish triptych, which, according to Samuel Eliot Morison, still adorned the altar in the 1940s, they were attacked by the men of the town and taken prisoner by the local official. The Portuguese had been angered by Castilians poaching along the Guinea coast, and it seems likely that the official suspected that Columbus and his men had been engaged in just such an enterprise. Columbus, sailing closer to the village, saw men and horses on the shore. The horsemen dismounted, climbed into a boat, and came out to the Niña with the intention of arresting the admiral. After a shouting match, Columbus sailed away, but two days later he returned to the island to try to recover his crew. By this time the priests had intervened, and the seamen were released.

It is interesting that in the sequence of events Columbus called on the Virgin rather than the Lord for aid when in peril and noted in his journal that he feared "that Our Lord might wish him to perish." A long passage followed in which Columbus tried to restore his faith in God's favor as had been shown in permitting him to discover the Indies and in giving him "all he had asked for." Yet his distress continued, caused, he said, by his "weakness and faint heart." It was Mary's mercy that he trusted. On arrival at the island, however, thanks were initially given to Our Lord, not to his Mother. It seems that Columbus never doubted her goodwill but felt that the Lord would be difficult to deal with without His Mother's intervention.

Further bad weather continued to delay his return to Spain. The Niña was forced into the River of Lisbon in early March, renewing the danger that Columbus and his men would be arrested by the Portuguese. He therefore made the best of the situation by writing to the Portuguese king requesting permission to proceed upstream to the Portuguese capital city. João received him graciously, congratulated him, and sent him on his way. Finally, on March 15, 1493, the Niña reentered the harbor at Palos that it had left seven and a half months before. The sovereigns were eight hundred miles away at Barcelona, so Columbus hastened there and lingered for several weeks. The delighted monarchs quickly approved a second voyage. However, diplomatic negotiations with the Portuguese and with the Holy See to clarify the rights of peninsular powers in the Indies delayed his departure.

His return trip to Seville to prepare the second journey was made even longer by his need to fulfill his vow to Our Lady of Guadalupe at her shrine in Extremadura. Along the way he passed through Trujillo, where it is certainly likely that a thirteen-year-old named Francisco Pizarro came out to see his entourage pass. Three days later, constantly ascending through the defiles in the sierra, Columbus arrived at the monastery of Guadalupe, so significant to Isabel herself. The ancient image housed there, said apocryphally to have been carved by Saint Luke, had a widespread reputation for aiding sailors as well as sovereigns. The monks were particularly interested in the Indians whom Columbus had brought along, seeing in them the first converts of that race to Christianity. They requested that Columbus name an island after their monastery on his next voyage, and so he did. On descending from Guadalupe on his way back to Seville, Columbus passed through the town of Medellín, where he was probably seen by a young boy named Hernán Cortés.[10] These encounters in his travels to Saint Mary at Guadalupe perhaps piqued the imagination and ambition of the future conquerors of Peru and Mexico. Both of these men would take a devotion to the Virgin Mary with them to the Americas.

Columbus's devotion to Mary seems to have intensified by the second voyage. The expedition left in October, only seven months after arrival back in Spain and well under a year since the Virgin Mary had, he believed, saved the Niña. By this accident of timing, they avoided the hurricane season, and the passage across the ocean lasted less than a month. Arriving in the islands on November 3, Columbus named the first island they spotted Dominica, for the Sunday landfall, and the second Santa María la Galante, "for love of the ship in which he sailed," and, no doubt, for the ship's namesake, lost on the first voyage.[11]

The admiral continued naming islands for the Virgin for several days. By November 4 Columbus had spotted a mountainous island that he named Santa María de Guadalupe, fulfilling his promise to the monks back in Spain months earlier. On November 11 he named no less than three islands for Mary: Santa María de Monserrate, Santa María Redonda, and Santa María la Antigua, all important advocations of the Virgin in Spain, and the latter two in Italy as well.[12] In fact, in his first eight days in the islands, he had named five of six discoveries for Mary, an outpouring of devotion onto the landscape unmatched in his other voyages. On the evening of November 11, they made anchor off a much larger island, which Columbus named for San Martín, it being the vigil of his feast day. Interestingly, that name did not stick; it became known as Nuestra Señora de las Nieves, Our Lady of the Snows. When the island became English in 1630, it retained its name and is still known as Nevis.[13] That completed the string of islands named for Mary for the time being; many of the remaining islands discovered on this trip were named for various other saints, but some were named for features of the landscape and even for animals.[14]

This outpouring of devotion for María is not too surprising, given Columbus's belief that it was the Virgin who had saved the Niña less than a year before. Further, the mariners, grateful for her aid, had just experienced a relatively quick and easy trip from the Iberian peninsula. His selection of advocations was very much in keeping with both his own reverence and his keen political sense. The first, Mariagalante, was a tribute to the ship in which he traveled and to her namesake. The second, Guadalupe, was the advocation to whom he had first appealed in the midst of bad weather ten months earlier and to whose shrine he had made an arduous pilgrimage only weeks before. The reasons for Santa María de Monserrate are not far to seek. Columbus had just visited Fernando and Isabel in Barcelona, in Cataluña, while they saw to Fernando's Aragonese realms. The Virgin of Monserrate was the patroness of Cataluña and one of a handful of very influential regional advocations in the peninsula. Known in Catalán as Montserrat, her legend echoed that of other advocations, particularly that of Guadalupe. As the later story went, her image had been venerated as early as the seventh century. In the year 717, fearing the Arabs, a group of Christians hid her in the most forbidding nearby mountain, Monte Serrado (serrated mountain), so known because its summits resembled the teeth of a saw. More than a century and a half later, the legend tells us, three shepherds observed that on a Saturday night a rain of stars lit up the mountain like torches. The following Saturday, the shower of stars was repeated, leading the shepherds to communicate this information to the nearby town of Olesa. The phenomenon continued for two more Saturdays, at which time the parish priest contacted the bishop. Led by the two clerics, the town processed toward the extraordinary lights, all the while breathing delicious aromas and hearing celestial music. On arrival at a cave they found an image of the Virgin Mary. Filled with joy, they fell to the ground, adoring, blessing, and claiming her as their protector.

The crowd tried to remove the image from the mountain, but it became extraordinarily heavy, too heavy for them to move, a pattern that would become familiar in the Spanish New World as well. The bishop, in order to honor the will of the Mother of God, then ordered that a chapel be built to house the image at that site.[15] Although historians place the founding of the resulting shrine and monastery at a later date, there is no doubt that by Columbus's time it was an important regional pilgrimage center. It is even possible that Columbus, previous to his visit to Guadalupe, went in pilgrimage to Montserrat at the time of his visit to the sovereigns in Barcelona. In any case, the honoring of this advocation would have pleased Fernando, who was reported to be less enthusiastic about Columbus's endeavors than was the queen. Montserrat was a most significant advocation of Mary in his own realms in the eastern part of the peninsula. Columbus's son Fernando, in his version, reported that the selection of the name had to do with the island's height and configuration, but the story does not lessen the likelihood that Columbus wished to please his king.[16]

Santa María Redonda is an interesting case. Perhaps Fernando Columbus was right, and it acquired that name because it was "so round and smooth it seemed impossible to climb without a ladder."[17] The physical appearance did not negate the Marian devotion, though it may well have reflected the shape of the Pantheon in Rome, dedicated to Saint Mary and the Martyrs but better known as Santa María Rotunda. This remarkable edifice was built by the Emperor Hadrian in the second century and dedicated to "every known God." It was the first pagan temple in Rome to be Christianized, a process that occurred under Pope Boniface IV, and it reflects the Virgin's appeal and importance that this sacred space was rededicated to her. If the circumference of the dome, a perfect hemisphere, continued down to floor level, it would form a perfect sphere because the height and the diameter of the interior of the building are identical—133 feet. Huge and daunting, the church was indeed "round and smooth." When the building was dedicated to Saint Mary in 609, a small altar was placed opposite the door, and an icon of the Virgin and Child was displayed upon it. The recently restored icon, now exhibiting the seventh-century image, is still on display for the visitor, dwarfed and tiny and luminous within the huge structure. It is one of the few remaining surviving icons of the period.[18] The contrast between the size of the building and the image of Mary and her Son is memorable. Perhaps, if Columbus was aware of this sacred site, it influenced his naming of the strikingly configured island, though there was at least one church dedicated to Santa María la Redonda in Iberia at this time.

Santa María la Antigua, perhaps, may also have found its roots in Italy, though it was clearly connected with the Iberian peninsula as well. The church of Santa Maria Antiqua in Rome was also a converted classical building, but it was up and functioning in the seventh century. However, the building itself had been sealed by a landslide and was not excavated until 1900. Still, the advocation was popular in the Mediterranean area in Columbus's time. The reader will remember from Chapter I that Santa María la Antigua was a favored devotion of Fernando III, the Castilian monarch who extended the Reconquest far into the South of the Iberian peninsula in the thirteenth century. Later canonized as San Fernando, his carrying forward of the Reconquest may have held special significance for Columbus. After all, Columbus named one of his two sons Fernando, a name in no way traditional in the Columbus family but rather representative of an Iberian and above all an Andalusian devotion; probably not coincidentally, it was the name of his sovereign as well. It does not seem too far-fetched to imagine that Columbus identified strongly with San Fernando, a fellow carrier of Christianity into dangerous realms. Certainly Columbus had a messianic sense of mission similar to that of the Castilian monarch two and a half centuries earlier. The priest Bartolomé de Las Casas, who knew Columbus, reported that when the admiral had to swear an oath of great importance, he would swear in the name of San Fernando.[19] The cathedral at Seville, which Fernando III had built above the ruins of the old mosque, housed in Columbus's time an exquisite, larger-than-life painting of Santa María la Antigua. This four-teenth-century image is still visible in its own chapel, where the Virgin, hold-ing the Christ Child in her left hand and a single rose in her right, looks serenely out at the viewer. Above her head, two angels lower a crown to acknowledge her as Queen of Heaven. The gold tones of the painting and the serenity of the image cause it to shine out from the gloom of the cathedral. Santa María la Antigua was one of the most popular advocations at the time of the European discovery of the Americas, and this image in the ca-thedral was one that Columbus surely knew. Probably he had visited the cathedral before his first trip and between the first and second trips. At present, the remains of Columbus lie in a sarcophagus close to this image.[20] It is not surprising that Santa María la Antigua would be in his mind in November 1493 as he again sailed in the islands he believed to be the Indies.

The advocation of the Virgin of the Snows also had its origins in Rome and was associated with Santa Maria Maggiore, to this day the principal Marian church in that city and considered part of the Vatican although it is not contiguous with it. The story, in a thirteenth-century version, was that the rich and devout senator Giovanni Patricio (John the Patrician) and his wife, who had been unable to have children, decided to leave all of their worldly goods and property to the church. On the night of the Nonae of August, that is, between August 4 and August 5, in the year 358, both Giovanni and Pope Liberius dreamed that the Virgin Mary appeared to them, asking that a basilica be built for her on the site in the city where that night snow would fall. The next day, the two went to the Esquiline hill and there found the expected patch of snow. Liberius, surrounded by a crowd gathered to observe the astonishing August snowfall, immediately traced out the design of the building in the miraculous substance.[21]

That Columbus believed himself to have a messianic mission is clear. In later years, at the bottom of his signature he often wrote "Xpo ferens"—Christ-bearer. This signature, as we discussed at the beginning of this chapter, was full of his reverence for and identification with the Virgin. It is unclear when exactly he began to use the signature; Morison prints it in his edition of the *Journals and Other Documents* at the bottom of his April 1493 letter to Fernando and Isabel. If this reproduction is accurate, then well before he left on his second voyage he was signing in this way. By using this signifier of his identity, he was drawing close to the Virgin, the literal Christ-bearer. As John Fleming has pointed out, "At the most basic level Columbus's signature 'means' what any other signature means: it means a person."[22] Columbus's given name, Christopher or Cristóbal, in fact meant "Christ-bearer." In the signature, the line above "Xpo ferens" reads: "X M   Y." This line can be deciphered as X = Saint Christopher (or San Cristóbal); M = María; and Y = Yoannes, for John the Baptist. In this reading, the two Christ-bearers, San Cristóbal and María, appear with the messenger, the child who foreshadows Christ's birth. Below, "Xpo FERENS" reinforces once again Columbus's own vision of himself as Christ-bearer as well, in close proximity to the other two.[23] Whether one accepts this precise reading or not, it is difficult to escape the admiral's identification with both Saint Christopher and the Virgin. A striking visual example of the connections between the latter two may be seen in Juan de la Cosa's map of Europe and the Americas, made after his return from Columbus's second voyage. The area of Central America and the western Caribbean was obscured with a rendering of Saint Christopher, staff in hand, carrying the Christ Child across a river. On a direct line below this picture, a beautiful wind rose shows Mary and Jesus. The Virgin and her Son are located on a heavy line of latitude, marked in red, which connects the Saint Christopher picture (in the area of Central America, which Balboa would cross a few years later to get to the Pacific) directly to Africa. The wind rose, essentially a representation of the mariner's compass, once again shows the close relationship of the Virgin Mary with direction and guidance on sea voyages.[24]

Fleming has written that Columbus was "a man whose spiritual identification with the Virgin was constantly being pressed by the metaphor of Christ-bearing to the very limit of linguistic possibility." This identification included the Immaculist image of the dove, strongly associated with Saint Mary. Fleming tells us that "Columbus's own dove-ness . . . involved a blurring of the boundaries of gender." Columbus had selected the Spanish version of his name, Colón, although this was by no means the closest Castilian version of the Italian Colombo. Perhaps, as Fleming suggests, Columbus was intentionally trying to maintain an ambiguity between the Catalán *colom*, which means dove, and Castilian *colono*, which means pioneer. This play on names would not have been uncharacteristic of Columbus's spirituality.

Fernando, his son, commented in his biography of his father that "just as most of his affairs were directed by a secret Providence, so the variety of his name and surname was not without its mystery. We could cite as examples many names which a hidden cause assigned as symbols of the parts which their bearers were to play." He went on to hazard an explanation:

[T]he Admiral's name foretold the novel and wonderful deed he was to perform. If we consider the common surname of his forebears, we may say he was truly Columbus or Dove, because he carried the grace of the Holy Ghost to that New World which he discovered, showing those people who knew Him not Who was God's beloved son, as the Holy Ghost did in the figure of the dove when Saint John baptized Christ; and because over the waters of the ocean, like the dove of Noah's ark, he bore the olive branch and oil of baptism, to signify that those people who had been shut up in the ark of darkness and confusion were to en- joy peace and union with the Church. So the surname of Colón which he revived was a fitting one.[25]

And Columbus's intense devotion for Christ was played out in an intense identification with Jesus's Mother. This identification was apparent in his signature, in his sense of mission as Christ-bearer to the new lands as de- scribed in his son's words, and in his own name as he adapted it from Italian into Castilian.

One more Marian image that may well have resonated with mariners in Columbus's time and with the admiral himself was that of the Virgin tram- pling beneath her feet a serpent or a dragon. This snake or dragon, obviously, represented the devil, the old enemy. This image was based on the Woman of the Apocalypse from Revelation 12: "And there appeared a great wonder in heaven: a woman clothed with the sun, and the moon under her feet, and upon her head a crown of twelve stars." According to the fourth-century interpretation of Epithanius, this woman represented the Church and the verses that followed referred to the triumph of the Church over Satan: "And she brought forth a manchild, who was to rule all nations, And there was war in heaven: Michael and his angels fought against the dragon; and the dragon was cast out, that old serpent called the Devil, and Satan, which deceiveth the whole world. And I heard a loud voice saying in heaven, Now is come salvation." Later, in the twelfth century, Saint Bernard associated this vision with the Virgin herself and her triumph over evil. By the fourteenth century, paintings and sculpture of the Virgin frequently showed her standing on the crescent moon, "clothed with the sun," although not always with the dragon or serpent under her feet as became common later. Still, the idea of the Virgin triumphing over evil as embodied in the dragon was clear.[26] Immaculist works often leave out the serpent, but images that include all of these elements often also show her staff piercing the dragon's body as she crushes him beneath her feet.[27] This important motif, of the Virgin versus the dragon, that is, the devil, recurs in colonial Latin America, where the devil became equated with idolatry and the pre-Columbian religions. For Mexico, Fernando Cervantes sees this connection, for while the identification of the Virgin with indigenous goddesses would lead to her veneration, at the same time "the identification of the devil with the more malevolent representations of the native deities would gradually lead the Indians to repudiate the devil and his works."[28] This juxtaposition recurs as well in ceremonies today, as on the elaborate images of the Virgin paraded during Corpus Christi in Cuzco. Several of those images are accompanied by male angels thrusting lances into the mouth of a ghastly dragon located behind the Virgin on the corner of the platform on which she is carried.

Fleming suggests that the stars themselves reflect this ancient struggle. He points out that there are three constellations at the North Pole: the two bears Ursa Minor, in which Stella Maris—the North Star—appears, and Ursa Major; and Draco, the dragon. Perhaps mariners saw this image throughout the changing night sky as a sign of spiritual stability, with Mary unmoved as the heavens swirl around her, perpetually crushing the snake beneath her heel.[29]

Although Columbus became less focused on Mary than on Christ in later years, at least as reflected in such works as his *Book of Prophecies*, he wished his legacy to include works dedicated to her. In a 1498 document he instructed his son Diego to arrange for the building of a church on the island of Española. This edifice was to be named Santa María de la Concepción. Finally, in a codicil to his will in 1506, he asked that three masses be said daily in that chapel. The masses, predictably, were designated as follows: one for the Trinity, another for his soul and those of the other dead, and one to honor the Conception of Our Lady.[30]

The documents for Columbus's voyages and settlements in the Caribbean and circum-Caribbean do not tell us if he imprinted Mary's name and authority onto the sacred sites of indigenous peoples. However, in the conquest of Mexico begun in 1519 by Hernán Cortés, the pattern that had begun in Reconquest Spain of naming mosques in conquered areas for the Virgin was duplicated for indigenous altars and pyramids. Cortés's journey began less than three decades after Fernando and Isabel had expelled the Moorish rulers from Granada, completing the Reconquest of the peninsula.

The documents on the conquest of Mexico, far more extensive than those of the European discovery of America, show us the process followed as American indigenous peoples were violently subjected to Spanish control.

Cortés began his travels from southern Spain. He was familiar with the same images of the Virgin that had so impressed Columbus in the cathedral in Seville, itself on the site of a mosque converted into a temple to Mary. However, his principal devotion seems to have been directed to the Virgin of Remedios (Remedies), a devotion that would be carried to Mexico and would remain important throughout the colonial period. A recent biographer assumes that he would have been affected by the extraordinary painting of Remedios, just to the west side of the choir, in the Sevillian cathedral. This beautiful image, painted in the Sienese style about 1400, looks out at the viewer with slanted eyes. However, he may rather have been taken by the statue on the tympanum of the door to the nave of Lagarto. This statue is thought to be from the late fifteenth century, so it would have been a fairly recent addition to the adornments of the cathedral at the time of Cortés's departure for the New World. It is pure white, sculpted in the Gothic style. The Virgin of Remedies holds the child Jesus in her left hand while her right caresses his tiny foot. In any case, the Virgen de los Remedios is strongly associated with curing; stories about her miraculous intervention are linked with instances such as an outbreak of plague in fourteenth-century Valencia that abated after she appeared to one of her devotees. Documentation in the cathedral indicates that various bishops and archbishops conceded indulgences to those praying before the image.[31]

Cortés arrived in the West Indies in approximately 1506, just fourteen years after the first European encounter with the region. Although we do not have documentation about his voyage, he well may have invoked the protection of "Our Lord and the Virgin Saint Mary Our Lady, his blessed Mother," as did the famous chronicler of his conquests, Bernal Díaz del Castillo, a few years later.[32] Cortés's great conquests would not begin until 1518, when the governor of Cuba, Diego Velásquez, sent him on an expedition to Yucatán, then believed to be an island. He by this time had ingratiated himself with Velásquez, who recognized him as a leader, although they had not always gotten along comfortably. Avoiding a possible attempt by Velásquez (who seemed to be having second thoughts) to prevent his departure, Cortés would turn this commission into an opportunity to set off on his own into Mexico. Cortés went well supplied with images of the Virgin.

From the first contacts with indigenous peoples, Cortés made a habit of giving these figures to the rulers, along with a sermon delivered by himself about their significance. There is no question that the Spanish were shocked by native religious practices, especially those that involved human sacrifice. As he made his way into Mexico, his religious exhortations became increasingly insistent, and more and more images of Mary and other saints were placed on indigenous altars and sacred places. The connection with Reconquest practice is clear; Cortés had grown up in Medellín, Extremadura, a location retaken from the Moors only in 1235. He had lived within sight of a mosque and a synagogue next to churches dedicated by the Christians to Santiago and San Martín but certainly furnished with images of Saint Mary. Moreover, Medellín was only fifty miles away from the extremely important monastery of the Virgin at Guadalupe.[33] As Hugh Thomas has commented, "Like most conquistadors of his generation, he saw the Indians of the Caribbean and its littoral as if they were new Moors, to be converted and subjected."[34] He, like other Spanish in their New World, referred to native sacred altars and temples as *mezquitas*, that is, mosques, assimilating through language the complex of ideas that the Spanish held of those other sacred spaces.

When his expedition arrived at the island of Cozumel off the west coast of Yucatán, the inhabitants initially fled in terror. When contact was finally established, the Indians brought news that an earlier Spanish expedition had been shipwrecked and had left survivors, whom Cortés was eager to contact. Two were eventually found, but one had married an indigenous woman and did not wish to depart with Cortés. The other, Jerónimo Aguilar, would be extremely important to Cortés's expedition as he could speak one of the principal Middle American languages, Mayan. Their stay on the island lasted several days, during which time they discovered that Cozumel was a kind of pilgrimage site, with natives arriving from neighboring settlements to worship "very deformed figures" in a sort of chapel.[35] Díaz del Castillo reported that at that time it was common for the Indians to perform human sacrifices, leaving their altars and chapels filthy with blood and stench. A crucial moment came one morning when the Spanish discovered a large group of Indians in the patio in front of the room where the idols were kept. The smell of burning resin reminded them of their own incense. As they watched, an elderly man whom they assumed to be a priest mounted a podium. He then began to preach, according to Díaz del Castillo, a "black sermon." Cortés, able to understand the ceremony only through the imperfect translations of a native man taken prisoner on an earlier Spanish expedition, was nevertheless horrified and hastened to stop the proceedings. Ordering a mass to be held, he himself made a short speech. He told the undoubtedly astonished the natives that if they wished to be the brothers of the Spaniards, they would have to get rid of their idols, which were not gods but rather devils. Further, if they wanted their souls to avoid hell, they would have to understand truly holy matters, which he proceeded to explain. He ordered them to throw down their idols and presented them with a statue of Mary and a cross that, he said, would save their souls. The startled priest and native leaders refused, protesting that a great deal of evil would come from this action and that the Spanish, as punishment, would be lost in the sea. Nevertheless, the mass was held, and Díaz del Castillo reported that the Indians listened with attention. The room for idols and sacrifices was then cleaned and an altar built for the images Cortés provided. Cortés's speech about the virtues of Christianity would be repeated on a number of other occasions during the Conquest.[36]

Interestingly, Cortés in so doing was following a tradition of Catholic missionary practice in place for hundreds of years. In 601 Pope Gregory the Great, in a famous letter to those in the English mission field, with high practicality recommended that

[t]he idol temples of that race should by no means be destroyed, but only the idols in them. Take holy water and sprinkle it in these shrines, build altars and place relics in them . . . When this people see that their shrines are not destroyed they will be able to banish error from their hearts and be more ready to come to the places they are familiar with, but now recognizing and worshipping the true God.[37]

Though Cortés was apt later to be more destructive and perhaps was as focused on domination as conversion, he was following in a long-standing tradition of adapting other sacred spaces to the uses of Catholicism.

Shortly after this incident, the expedition departed, but a leaky ship required a return to Cozumel. The Spaniards noted with satisfaction that the cross and the image of Mary were still clean and well cared for, with incense burning before them. The problem with the ship turned out to be fortunate. Shortly after their return, a canoe arrived from Yucatán carrying, as they thought, seven natives. Andrés de Tapia, the first Spaniard to sight the group, failed to recognize the Spaniard among them because, as Díaz del Castillo wrote, he seemed "neither more nor less than an Indian." He was blackened by the sun and dressed as a slave of the natives in a breach cloth and a ragged blanket. However, as the unidentified man leapt out of the canoe, he shouted, "The Lord and St. Mary and Seville," albeit in "poorly enunciated and worse pronounced" Spanish. By this greeting, invoking the Lord and the Virgin and the common point of embarkation for the Indies, he identified himself as a Spaniard and was immediately embraced by Tapia. This individual turned out to be Jerónimo Aguilar, captured by the Maya in 1511 when returning from Panama to Santo Domingo, who would from that point forward serve as translator. Aguilar was able to inform the natives before the Spanish departure that they must take very good care of the Virgin and the cross, treating them with "reverence and devotion." If they would do so, he said, "much good would come to them."[38] Aguilar, it was said, had kept his faith after his shipwreck by constant referrals to his *Book of Hours*, including its prayers to the Virgin.[39]

In Cozumel, then, the Virgin had been implanted along with the cross as a symbol of Spanish presence, the natives had been informed of her significance and the good she could bring them, and a Spaniard so long amongst the Indians that he looked like them had been recognized through his invocation of the Christian Lord and Santa María. Other reports indicate that the people of Cozumel dressed a statue of the Virgin in indigenous clothing (as Maya communities often do to this day) and placed images of her in their boats. Although this apparent reverence is not evidence that Mary replaced native gods, at least her own presence and significance had been established.[40]

Cortés would repeat this pattern on a number of occasions as he made his way into Tenochtitlan (present-day Mexico City) and the presence of the Aztec emperor, bearing the flag of the Virgin. What is believed to be Cortés's original banner is now held in the historical museum in Mexico City's Chapultepec Park. It shows Mary, her hands together in prayer, gazing serenely out to the right of the viewer. She is wearing a crown, and rays of golden light extend around her head, which is encircled by twelve stars. Her dress is red and her cape is blue. Those familiar with the later image of the Virgin of Guadalupe will note the similarities.[41]

Cortés also named communities for the Mother of God; one in Tabasco, for example, is christened Santa María de la Victoria after a successful battle. Still in the Gulf Coast, in Cempoallan, the principal city of the Totonacs, he destroyed more idols, ordering his men to throw them from the pyramid where they stood. In doing so, he risked considerable violence, as the native leaders strongly protested and seemed prepared to fight. Cortés in turn spoke sternly to his own men, reminding them of their own "good and very sacred doctrines" and that they could "do no good if they did not turn back to honor the Lord by stopping the sacrifices to those idols." The offending images, he said, would be destroyed that day, or all would die trying.[42]

The people of the town, on seeing their idols destroyed, "wept and covered their eyes," begging forgiveness from their gods for their inability to protect them. Although some of the Cempoallans started to attack, the Spanish seized seven of their leaders and threatened to kill them if any violence broke out. Their chief then ordered them to desist. The violent destruction of the idols was an extraordinary act on the part of the Spanish, as the

Cempoallans believed themselves at this point to be their allies, not their enemies. Cortés explained to the priest, whom Díaz del Castillo described as covered with dried blood and smelling like "dead meat," that he was giving them a great lady to replace their idols. She was the Mother of Our Lord Jesus Christ, in whom the Spanish believed and whom they adored, and she would be their lady and advocate as well.[43] This time the translation would have been far better than it was at Cozumel, for Aguilar was available to translate Spanish to Maya, and doña Marina, a native woman who had joined them, from Maya into words intelligible to the Totonacs. Again, the Spanish whitewashed the temple and installed a cross and a picture of the Virgin. Flowers were sent for—Díaz del Castillo called them roses, though they were native plants—along with branches to decorate the refurbished space. Roses were especially associated with Mary, and in using the specific European term, he was invoking this connection. The Totonac priests, their long, blood-soaked hair shorn at the Spaniards' insistence, were invested with the care of the altar.[44]

Another important case in point is that of the Tlaxcalans. This group, from a region to the west of Tenochtitlan, would become allies who ultimately would help make victory against the Aztecs possible. The Tlaxcalans fought alongside the Spanish for decades and later accompanied the Coronado expedition into territory that is now the Southwest United States. Still, the advantages of an alliance were not immediately apparent to them, and they put up fierce resistance with what the Spanish described as an enormous force. The Tlaxcalans attacked the horses, killing two and wounding three more. Cortés had the dead animals buried to prevent the enemies from discovering anything more about them and possibly from eating them, as they were said to do with sacrificed captives. Previously it had been supposed that Indians thought the animals were immortal. Further battles followed that entailed the slaughter of Tlaxcalan women and children by the Spanish and/or their Cempoallan allies. Meanwhile, the Aztecs, who had long been aware of the Spanish advance, were sending emissaries and making overtures to Cortés. The Tlaxcalans were natural enemies of the Aztecs; they lived in close proximity but resisted where they could, and they came to see the possibilities of an alliance with such a powerful potential foe of their longtime enemy. Suing for peace, they permitted the Spanish to enter the city of Tlaxcala, where the Spanish would rest for almost three weeks. They also presented the Spanish with a number of slave girls, to whom they added one or two daughters of their leaders.

They gave the Spanish a convenient myth to explain their conduct. Their priests had told them, they confided, that warriors from distant lands would come from the East to work with them and govern them. If the Spaniards were indeed these warriors, they were pleased, as they could see their strength and bravery. Cortés replied that his ruler, the king of Castile, wanted the Tlaxcalans to give up their idols and their ritual of human sacrifice. He gave the slave women to Marina, the native woman who served him as interpreter and sexual partner, and sent the leaders' daughters back to their parents. Showing the Tlaxcalans images of the Virgin Mary "with her precious Son in her arms," he explained as he had on several earlier occasions to other native groups that they must accept Christianity if they wished to become brothers to the Castilians and wanted them to accept their daughters. If, however, they resisted, they would go to hell after death and burn forever. Now the translation was even smoother, as Díaz del Castillo explained that "Marina and Aguilar, our voices (tongues) were already so expert at it that they could make it well understood." From the context, it is clear that Díaz del Castillo meant by "it" not only language but also Christian doctrine according to Cortés. This time Cortés explained about the Virgin living in the heavens, about her conceiving by the grace of the Holy Spirit, and about her perpetual virginity, before, during, and after the birth of Jesus.[45]

Once again, this insistence on the acceptance of Christianity and the image of Mary must have come as a shock not only to the leaders but also to the priests, who had arrived in great numbers from temples and pyramids throughout the region. Again, the Spanish were shocked by the priests' appearance—wearing long, white robes with hoods, with their long, blood-encrusted hair hanging down their backs. Díaz del Castillo reports that the blood was running out of their ears, as they had already performed sacrifices that day. During the rest of the stay in Tlaxcala, Cortés apparently returned repeatedly to questions of religion, and the evidence shows that Saint Mary and her Son were at the center of these conversations.[46] This time, however, Cortés's own men persuaded him not to push the matter, faced with the Tlaxcalans' adamant refusal to give up their sacrifices. The indigenous leaders did agree to try to understand this new system of beliefs and especially the matters of "your God and that great Lady." They also agreed to wash the blood off one of the newest pyramids, whitewash it, and erect a cross and an image of Nuestra Señora.[47]

Intimidated by the Spanish advance, Montezuma eventually invited Cortés and his men into Tenochtitlan. Predictably, Cortés again insisted on the removal of Aztec idols and the installation of an image of the Virgin Mary and a cross at the summit of the pyramid that dominated the main plaza. This extraordinary edifice, composed of layers that had been constructed one on top of the other by the Aztecs, was approximately 150 feet high. A few days after their arrival, Montezuma had ushered the Spanish to the top, where it occurred to Cortés that it would be a good place to build a Christian church. (Later, in fact, such a church would be built on a pyramid in Cholula, through which they had passed earlier.) Cortés mentioned this possibility to the friar who was traveling with them, but as the idea seemed premature and their position delicate, the cleric discouraged him from discussing it with Montezuma. Entering the southernmost of two shrines at the summit, Cortés was horrified by the huge idols he found there.

There were apparently two altars within this room, one dedicated to Huitzilopochtli, the Aztec god of war, and the other to Tezcatlipoca, a strange figure who seemed to the Spanish the very embodiment of the devil. These idols were made, according to Cortés, of seeds held together with the blood of sacrificed victims and, according to his friend Andrés de Tapia, seeds with the blood of murdered children. These images, along with the still-warm hearts of recently sacrificed victims lying in braziers before them, distressed Cortés sufficiently that he addressed the religious issue immediately despite the danger. Turning to Montezuma, he asked how it was that such a great lord as the Aztec emperor could be so deceived as to believe that these horrible figures were gods. Obviously, they were devils. Further, he insisted that in the place of the idols, the cross and a picture of the Virgin Mary be installed. The old gods, he said, would be fearful of these true images of the Christian faith.[48]

Predictably, Montezuma and his priests were disturbed by this dishonor to their deities. Montezuma protested that the gods had brought his people good health, rain, plentiful harvests, and general well-being as long as they received the appropriate sacrifices. For the time being, Cortés built an altar with Christian images elsewhere. There, the Spanish prayed every day on their knees. Díaz del Castillo reported that Montezuma and his men were intrigued, especially when the Spanish recited the *Ave Maria*.[49] Cortés did not let the matter rest; he insisted that human sacrifice cease and that cannibalism be abandoned. He continued to request that the cross and an image of the Mother of God be placed on the Great Temple. Apparently intimidated by his unwelcome guests, Montezuma soon allowed himself to be taken a virtual prisoner by the Spanish in a failure of will that quickly began to lose him support among his own people.

Having Montezuma in their control led the Spanish to push further in various matters, including the religious. Several days after Montezuma had been taken into a kind of house arrest, Cortés and Tapia decided to walk up to the top of the Great Temple, a privilege generally reserved to Aztec rulers, priests, and sacrificial victims. Cortés and Tapia again asked the priests to put up images of Christ and Mary and insisted that they wash the walls to remove the blood of sacrificial victims. The priests laughed at them and taunted that such an act would set the whole empire against the Spanish. Cortés responded by sending a Spaniard to make sure Montezuma was well guarded and then ordering thirty or forty of his own men to come to the temple. Giving in to his growing anger, he made what Tapia described later as a "superhuman leap" onto a platform from which he could reach the offending idols. As he seized a bar and ripped the gold mask from one of the images he shouted, "Something must be done for the Lord."[50]

Montezuma, hearing of these activities, quickly requested permission to come to the site and begged that no more damage be done until his arrival. Once at the pyramid, he tried to negotiate with Cortés, suggesting that both sets of images be retained. Cortés then launched into another of his religious instructions, argued for the exclusivity of the Christian God, and refused to accept the Aztec emperor's compromise. Montezuma then shifted tactics and sought to placate the Spaniard. He indicated that since it had been many years since his people had arrived in the valley of Mexico, they might have come to err in their beliefs. Cortés, he said, should continue to explain Christian doctrine and for the time being he would do as the Spaniard wanted. The chapel was finally cleaned of the victims' blood. A few days later a group of priests rolled the idols away down the pyramid, taking care that the images not be damaged further. The Castilians never saw them again, as they remained hidden from possible destruction. After the idols were gone, effigies of the Virgin Mary and Saint Christopher were put in their place; Saint Christopher was selected, according to Cortés's companion Andrés de Tapia, because the Spanish had run out of other images.[51] It is quite likely that there was a shortage, given the way that Cortés and his men were scattering images across the Mexican sacred landscape. It is also possible that Cortés felt himself to be, as had Columbus, a Christ-bearer like Saint Christopher.

Cortés himself, writing later to the Crown, commented rather laconically and not entirely accurately that he had "the most important of their idols, and the ones in whom they most put their most faith, taken from their places and thrown down the steps . . . and I had images of Our Lady and of other saints put there, which caused Muteczuma [*sic*] and the other natives no little sorrow." He went on to say that the Aztec priests and their ruler warned him not to replace the images, as they believed that the people would rise in protest against the Spanish. They protested that "those idols gave them all their material goods, and that if they allowed them to be ill treated, they would become angry and give them nothing and take the fertility from the earth leaving the people to die of hunger. I instructed them through the interpreters that they were deceived in placing their trust in those idols which they had made with their own hands from unclean things and that they must know that there is only one God."[52]

Cortés was definitely putting the best face on the situation. Whispers of defiance grew, and pressure on Montezuma from priests and other leaders increased. Shortly after the attack on the images, a group of Aztecs came to Cortés carrying miserable and shrunken ears of corn, complaining that since the gods had been taken away there was no water and the crops were failing. Cortés assured them the rain would soon fall, and indeed the next day after the Spanish had heard mass at the Great Temple, it began to pour. Still, the whispers seem to have grown into a conspiracy, and Montezuma felt strong enough to call Cortés before him and protest the imposition of the images and the crucifix in the Aztec holy shrines. The problem, it seemed, was that his own gods had spoken to the priests and had told them that they would abandon the Aztecs if the new images were not removed. Montezuma informed Cortés that his gods had told him to make war upon the Castilians but that as he was very fond of them, he was warning them of the impending attack. Perhaps they could leave quickly and in safety. For the moment, Cortés protested that although they could leave Tenochtitlan, it would be impossible to depart from Mexico as they had no ships. A plan, however, was in place to build three new ones. Perhaps Montezuma could provide him with carpenters who would help. The Aztec ruler was eager to oblige, even though Cortés had emphasized that Montezuma himself would have to accompany the Spanish back across the ocean.[53]

Circumstances quickly changed. Cortés and his men had left Cuba just ahead of Governor Diego Velásquez's order to remain. Word now came, in early April, that a Spanish ship was just off the Mexican coast. In fact, Velásquez had sent a party under Pánfilo Narváez to pursue Cortés, whom he now knew had found treasure and allies in Mexico. Velázquez was bound for vengeance on his former protégé. Cortés was forced to leave Tenochtitlan to meet the threat.

The moment was critical. The Aztecs were assembling a large force to expel the Castilians once and for all, and the invaders would now have to fight one another. However, Cortés left a group of men under Pedro Alvarado to maintain the Spanish presence in the Mexican capital. Montezuma was concerned and, on Cortés's leave-taking, mentioned that he had heard that this new group of Christians had also set up images and crosses and said mass. Perhaps they were even more powerful and more in touch with cosmic forces than Cortés. Cortés explained that both Narváez's men and his own were vassals of the Spanish crown but that the former were bad and his were good. For this reason, Christ and the Virgin Mary would be on Cortés's side and, implicitly, would assure victory. He asked that Montezuma's priests

care for the picture of Saint Mary in the Great Temple. She should be surrounded by flowers, he insisted, and candles. Montezuma promised that it
would be done. He and Cortés then embraced, and Montezuma expressed
sadness at his departure—surely feigned, as Cortés's companion and interpreter, doña Marina, pointed out.[54]

Montezuma was correct that Narváez and his men brought images and
crosses and said mass. They also brought with them a reverence for the Virgin. When, after attempts to negotiate, Cortés and Narváez actually confronted one another in battle at the latter's encampment near Cempoallan,
Cortés's men discovered that their Spanish enemies had constructed a makeshift shrine containing a picture of the Virgin on one of the native temples.
The presence of the picture of the Virgin, however, did not deter Cortés
from battering it with Narváez's own artillery, which his forces had taken.
Narváez himself, when attacked by a pikeman, screamed "Holy Mary, protect me, for they have killed me and destroyed my eye." In fact, his right eye
had been extracted. Before the battle, Narváez had selected "Santa María" as
the password for his troops; Cortés had been forced to use the sign "Espíritu
Santo"—Holy Spirit—for his own troops. In this struggle, then, the forces
of the Holy Spirit confronted those of the Virgin, although certainly both
sides invoked her power.[55] Cortés, after bombarding the chapel, threatened to
kill all prisoners including the wounded Narváez, and his men surrendered.
This attack on a holy place was not soon forgotten and formed the substance of criticisms of him later.[56]

Most of Narváez's men then chose to throw in their lot with Cortés.
Imprisoning only their leader and one other individual, he returned their
horses and arms to the others on the proviso that they join his group. Most
of them returned with him to Tenochtitlan. A number of Narváez's officers
met with disaster on the return trip when they were captured and many of
them killed by the Aztecs. The situation in Tenochtitlan itself was disastrous; Pedro Alvarado, whom Cortés had left in charge, had murdered hundreds of Aztec warriors during an important ceremony in which they were
dancing unarmed. Apparently fearing that the Aztecs were about to capture
and kill him and his men, he had taken preemptive action, although he had
given permission for the ritual to take place.

When Cortés arrived, he found the city in mourning and the remainder of
Alvarado's men isolated and almost starving. They had even been unable to
obtain water and had been forced to dig a well that afforded them a modest
supply. When questioned about his actions, Alvarado replied that it was the
placement of the picture of Mary and the erection of the cross in the temple
that had caused the difficulty. He claimed that he had been informed by
Tlaxcalan allies that the Aztecs were intending to attack the Spanish at the end

of the ceremony. The Aztecs had been so ordered by their God, Huitzilopochtli, so as to replace the image of Mary and to rescue Montezuma. Despite their efforts to remove the picture of the Virgin, though, it had miraculously resisted. It was perhaps nailed to the wall, a system of fastening with which the Aztecs were unfamiliar. It also fit into the European tradition of the Virgin who refused to be moved, which we have observed earlier.

A shocking detail for the Spanish were the fingermarks that one of Alvarado's men had seen on the painting. They implicated the Aztec priests, who were accustomed to painting themselves black, in this affront to Our Lady. Alvarado also blamed secret contacts between the Aztecs and Narváez for having inspired the resistance. Cortés seemed to have seen these factors as sufficient reasons for Alvarado's actions; at any rate, he backed off.[57] Further evidence that Mary had not abandoned them was her appearance to the natives during the battle with Alvarado's forces. She had been seen alongside Saint James—Santiago—who was astride his white horse. It is possible that the Aztec warriors had seen María de Estrada, the only Spanish woman with the expedition, with one of Alvarado's horsemen. The white horse, they said, wounded and killed as many Indians with its mouth and feet as the rider did with his sword, while the "woman of the altar" threw powder in their eyes to blind them. Still, the Aztecs had pressed the attack, claiming that had the Virgin and Saint James not frightened them, the Spanish would have been cooked and fed to the animals and could still look forward to being killed and cooked with chocolate.[58]

Cortés's plan to dominate Tenochtitlan without fighting had failed. Montezuma's power had been irrevocably damaged by his inability to defend his people and his gods; his value as a hostage had come to an end. The Spanish found themselves confined to their compound, unable to leave without encountering hostile warriors, and the Aztecs more than once attempted to use fire to drive them out of their refuge. Stones rained into the patio, forcing the Spanish to walk close to the walls to avoid being struck. In a last attempt to use Montezuma to pacify his people, Cortés had him taken onto the roof of the palace in which he was held captive and ordered him to speak to his people. A shower of stones descended on him almost immediately, inflicting wounds from which he soon died. The Spanish then were forced to plan their escape.[59] Cortés urged his companions to maintain their faith and to pray to Our Lady of Remedios for aid while they bided their time and waited for an opportunity.[60] Meanwhile, the Aztecs terrified the Spaniards by setting loose their own gods and demons. According to a later account, Aztec priests came every night and displayed visions of human heads or legs and feet jumping around and corpses rolling on the ground, accompanied by screams and moans.[61]

The Virgin remained the antidote to these horrors. The night before the planned escape from Tenochtitlan, Cortés prayed to his preferred advocation, Remedios, although this devotion apparently did not deter him from taking a new lover, an Aztec noblewoman. The Spanish retreat started at midnight on July 1, 1520, the date that would be known in Mexican history—at least from the Spanish view—as "la Noche Triste," the Tragic Night. The retreat was complicated by the location of Tenochtitlan on a large lake with access only along causeways and bridges. Although Cortés and most of his forces were able to get across the first four bridges within the city proper, they were discovered as they were beginning to cross the lake itself. After fierce fighting in and out of the water, many of the Spanish had been killed or wounded. Accounts vary enormously, and it is by no means clear how many there were to begin with, but the Spanish force was terribly weakened. Much of the treasure of Montezuma was lost in the water, some of it later to be recovered by the Aztecs. Cortés survived, though he was wounded, and he rested the night after the retreat with his men at the temple in Otoncalpulco. This location was later known as the Virgin of Remedios "of the Divine Assistance" when a church was built to commemorate her aid on the sad

Garden area outside the basilica of the Virgin of Remedios, where construction began in the late sixteenth century. It is in Naucalpan, an industrial suburb of Mexico City. Photograph by Linda B. Hall.

night. Their rest was brief; constantly attacked, they set off again at midnight, July 2.[62]

This moment marked the lowest point in the fortunes of Cortés and his men. Though constantly harassed as they made their way west to join their allies in Tlaxcala, they were able to proceed as far as Otumba. This town, close to the northernmost pass over the mountains toward Tlaxcala, had been fortified by the Aztecs to give the coup de grace to the Spanish forces. Cuitláhuac, who had taken over as emperor after Montezuma's death, had left the army in the control of a deputy, known as the *cihuacoatl*. At first the battle went badly for the Spanish, but Cortés provided the inspiration that led to victory. Spotting the Mexican captains in their glittering war costumes at some distance behind the front lines, he led his horsemen with lances drawn right through the attacking line. Cortés immediately knocked the *cihuacoatl* to the ground, where he was killed by another Spaniard. More important, perhaps, the commander's plumes and standard were taken by the killer. These items, normally mounted on the back of leader, were used on the battlefield as a guide to indicate to the warriors where they should go. Their loss caused confusion.[63]

This encounter was arguably the most important battle fought by the Spanish in the Mexican Conquest. Cortés was later honored for the triumph, and the name Otumba decorates his statue in his hometown of Medellín. From this point forward, Spanish fortunes continued to improve as brutal Spanish victories in the countryside and the inception and rapid spread of epidemic disease weakened the Aztecs and brought more and more of their enemies into alliance with the European invaders. In August 1521, Cortés again entered Tenochtitlan, this time as a victor. The procession of conquerors followed the cross and a picture of the Virgin to a point from which the lake and the ruins of the Aztec city could be observed. A solemn mass followed. Cortés seemed more saddened than triumphant on viewing the destruction of the city.[64]

Ultimately, Cortés's success would lead to reconciliation with the Crown. Although much of the booty acquired in Mexico was looted by French pirates as it was being sent back to Spain, its intended destinations reflect both his devotion to Our Lady and his diplomatic acumen. In addition to the presents destined for nobles and high churchmen closely associated with the king, he favored churches and chapels. In Seville, he would have honored the chapel of the Virgin de la Antigua in the cathedral associated with Fernando III's Reconquest and for whom Columbus had named an island. He also meant to honor the chapel of San Ildefonso in Toledo's cathedral, so closely connected with the idea of Spanish nationalism and with the favor of the

Virgin (see Chapter II). Naturally, the monastery of Guadalupe would not have been forgotten.

The treasure itself was sent to Spain in three ships, one of which, significantly, was named Santa María de la Rábida, recalling the monastery near Palos where Columbus had first sought encouragement and refuge.[65] In 1528, when Cortés returned to Spain, he would go first to that monastery. Legend indicates that he there encountered his distant cousin Francisco Pizarro, who was just setting off for the Americas. After visiting his mother in Medellín, Cortés went on to the monastery of Guadalupe to give thanks to the Virgin of Extremadura, so important to the first generation of discoverers and conquerors. He presented her with a golden scorpion in memory of her aid in his recovery from a scorpion bite while in the Indies.[66]

Cortés, much like Columbus, received honor initially for his achievements but ultimately fell out of favor as the Crown consolidated its own control over the Spanish New World. Yet he had for some time after the fall of Tenochtitlan enjoyed the titles of *adelantado* (an explorer-warrior with governance responsibilities); *repartidor* (distributor) of indigenous peoples, which gave him great power to reward those he favored and punish those he did not; and captain-general and governor of New Spain. He had control over huge expanses of land and for a time enjoyed great wealth. Not resting content with his experiences in Mexico, he pursued further explorations—but nothing could match his accomplishments in that arena. Finally, in the latter years of his life, he returned to Spain to protect, insofar as he could, his properties and privileges by remaining in close proximity to the king. When he approached death in 1547, he was severely disillusioned and somewhat diminished in wealth. Nevertheless, his will indicates his continuing devotion to the Virgin, who he felt had favored him so generously.

Following the practice of his time, he began this document by invoking the Trinity and "the most glorious and blessed Virgin, his sainted Mother, Our Lady and Intercessor."[67] Very quickly, however, it became clear that this petition was no empty formula. On the next page, he indicated that should he die in Spain, his bones should be moved as quickly as possible to a nunnery in "my town of Coyoacán," the town near Mexico City where he had first set up his government in the wake of the Aztec defeat. The envisioned nunnery, which would be built and endowed with the resources his will provided, would be of the order of San Francisco and would be given the name of Concepción.[68] Throughout his will, in fact, he dedicated his bequests to the Immaculate Conception, that not-yet-dogma so dear to the Spanish. In another portion of his testament, he left the funds to build and maintain the convent.[69] He also indicated that in the main chapel, no one except his family and legitimate descendants should be interred. Another item indicated his bequests to found and endow a hospital in Mexico City, which had been constructed on the ruins of Tenochtitlan. The hospital would bear the same name as the convent—Our Lady of the Immaculate Conception.[70] However, his desire to have his remains brought finally to Coyoacán was never fulfilled. The convent which he had envisioned was never built. Eventually, on the death of his grandson Pedro, his remains were brought to the Church of San Francisco in Mexico City to lie with Pedro's in the main chapel. They continued to be moved until eventually they were hidden during the wars of independence.[71]

The devotion to Mary continued to be spread in Mexico and Central America as other expeditions made their way south. Bernal Díaz del Castillo tells us that as Pedro de Alvarado and Cristóbal de Olíd set off for further conquests, Cortés made sure that they had plenty of images of the Virgin Mary to take with them. Along the way, masses were heard to give thanks to God and to his Mother after particularly difficult battles. He also reported that in Guatemala, the friar accompanying them put up an image of the Virgin given to him by a dying Spaniard. She was tiny and beautiful, and he says that the Indians were enchanted with her and adored her after the friar had explained who she was.[72]

These expeditions were beginning to close the circle down to Panama, where Vasco Nuñez de Balboa had made his way to the South Sea (the Pacific) more than a decade earlier. Balboa, it was noted favorably in Spain, had repeatedly on every page of the log of his journey given thanks "the Saints of Heaven and most of all, the Virgin, Mother of God," for keeping him safe. Upon sighting the Pacific, it was further reported, he asked God and "particularly the Virgin, Mother of God," to further favor his endeavors by permitting him to continue his explorations throughout the land at his feet.[73] The Virgin did not protect him, however, from his jealous father-in-law, who later had him beheaded. It was clear from these reports that regardless of whether he actually invoked Mary's aid, his saying that he did was seen favorably in Spain.

Perhaps the growing reverence for Mary in the 1520s and 1530s had something to do with the plagues and epidemics that were beginning to sweep through the native population, moving south along with the Spanish. A letter to the Spanish emperor in 1525 from his captain-general in Panama, Pedrárias Dávila, shows that whatever the cause, a sense of her power and that of the Church in general had spread in that direction. He reported that 400,000 souls had converted voluntarily in that region because of two miracles: a cross of wood that had been erected in the region and which the natives had unsuccessfully tried to burn down, and the fact that *mezquitas* (the reader will remember that this was the word the Spanish gave to Muslim mosques, later applied as well to indigenous temples) in the region that were not protected by statues of the Virgin had been destroyed by lightning. In the same letter, he announced that an expedition headed by Francisco Pizarro was setting off for Peru.[74]

Although we do not have a source like Díaz del Castillo to describe the Conquest of Peru step by step as he had Cortés's marches through Mexico, it seems that the Virgin was with Francisco Pizarro and his men as well. Their vicissitudes are reflected in the unhappy letter of one of Pizarro's men to a royal functionary in 1527, when the expedition was stuck on Gallo Island on its way to Peru. He complained that Pizarro treated them like slaves. Indeed, he claimed that Pizarro had told them that he had bought them for money and that he could take everything they had and control them completely. Regardless of the merits of the case, this unhappy individual saw no way out of "this captivity and perpetual prison" except for the possible intervention of the Blessed Virgin, Queen of the Angels, the Mother of God.[75] He was not the only one who looked to the Virgin for deliverance. It is reported that the stranded Pizarro and his twelve companions—unwilling or not—sang at sundown the *Salve Regina*, "Hail, Holy Queen," the Marian hymn so popular at that time in the great monasteries of Europe. This hymn helped them overcome the worries of the evening and the fears of the approaching night.[76]

Despite problems with his own men and obstruction from the Spanish governor of Panama that required a trip to Spain after the Gallo Island experience, Pizarro was able to prevail on the Spanish emperor and obtain permission to continue his explorations. He occupied the coastal city of Tumbes in February 1532 and soon founded the first Spanish town in Peru, at San Miguel de Piura. He arrived at an advantageous time. The old ruler, Huayna Capac, had died in the late 1520s, and his death left a divided leadership over the Inka empire, which stretched from present-day Ecuador in the north to the Maule River in present-day Chile in the south. His two sons, Huascar and Atahualpa, tore the empire apart as they struggled to succeed their father. Atahualpa had prevailed by the time Pizarro was ready to move inland; he was camped at Cajamarca, four hundred miles from Pizarro's coastal encampment, rather than at the Inka capital of Cuzco, much farther away in the Andean highlands.

Pizarro moved quickly to a confrontation, and on Saturday, November 16, 1532, the clash occurred. Fray Vicente de Valverde approached the newly victorious Atahualpa, speaking to him through an interpreter who poorly understood both Spanish and Quechua, the Inkan language. The priest emphasized the importance of accepting the Christian God and the authority of the pope along with that of the Spanish emperor; he handed the Inka ruler a book, perhaps containing scriptures or Christian prayers. Atahualpa threw it to the ground, the Spanish attacked, and the native troops were routed with great slaughter. Atahualpa himself was taken prisoner to fulfill the famous ransom of a roomful of gold and silver and was killed by the Spanish nevertheless. No doubt the Spanish would have attacked in any case.

Still, there are reports that one of the reasons that Pizarro's men at Cajamarca reacted so violently to the confrontation between Atahualpa and the priest was that the principal topic was the Nativity of Jesus and virginity of Mary.[77] Whether this reasoning was developed after the fact or not, it is interesting that such an argument was used as a defense of Pizarro for his violent attack on the crowds accompanying Atahualpa and his taking the Inka leader prisoner.

Marian interventions also figured in Spanish victories during the conquest of Peru. When Spanish forces in Cuzco were besieged in the palace of the Suntur Huasi, an Inkan sacred building in the center of the city and later the site of the cathedral, they were attacked with incendiary projectiles. The thatched roof, however, failed to catch fire. The site already was associated with the Virgin, as the prelate Vicente de Valverde, who later would become the bishop of Cuzco, had installed himself on the premises and had set up a chapel dedicated to the Immaculate Conception. While the Inka leader claimed

The Virgin is depicted shooting dust, hail, or rain out of her fingers at indigenous warriors.
Conquista, Milagro de Santa María, en el Cuzco. *Phelipe Guaman Poma de Ayala in*
El primer nueva coronica i buen gobierno compuesto.

that the Spaniards had stationed African slaves there to put out the fire, later writers asserted that the Virgin Mary had appeared wearing her blue cloak to extinguish the flames with white blankets while Saint Michael was by her side fighting off devils.[78] Perhaps this story is reflected in the images of Mary that parade around the square in Cuzco during present-day Corpus Christi celebrations. The Virgin is almost always shown with an angel behind her, shoving a lance down into the mouth of a serpent representing the devil, as noted previously. Yet another version of the battle claims that she threw dirt in the faces of the attackers.[79]

Certainly Pizarro himself was deeply devoted to the Virgin and spread her name across the landscape in the tradition established by the Reconquest, the voyages of Columbus, and conquests of Cortés. He quickly established a church in honor of the Virgin in the Inka capital of Cuzco, some sources say dedicated to the Virgin of the Rosary, but in any case quickly rededicated to the Virgin of the Assumption. Another in Jauja was dedicated to Concepción. In Lima and in Trujillo, Peru, the latter named for his hometown in Spain, he ordered that three major Marian festivals be celebrated in perpetuity: the Immaculate Conception, that of August (perhaps the celebration of the Virgin of the Angels on August 2 but probably that of the Assumption on August 15), and that of September (perhaps September 8, which celebrated her own nativity).

The most poignant record we have of Pizarro's devotion is his will. Written in Lima in 1537, four years before his death and five years after his triumph over the Inkas at Cajamarca, it began in familiar fashion by invoking the Trinity and Mary. It went well beyond the usual formulas of the day, however, reading, "In the name of the Father and the Son and the Holy Ghost Three Persons in One True God that is the Sainted Trinity and first taking My Lady for my advocate in this task that I so desire and I am determined to carry out and affect: for the most sacred Virgin Mary Mother of God and Our Universal Lady and defender of the whole human race . . . a church and chaplaincy in the city of Trujillo."[80] Lest one think that this opening might be more the idea of the priest writing the document than of Pizarro himself, he hastened to put his money where, one might say, his mouth was. In the same paragraph as his invoking of the Trinity and of Mary, he immediately announced his intention of building a church and founding a chaplaincy in honor of the Immaculate Conception in the town of his youth, Trujillo in Spain. The portion of the document dedicated to this purpose is fully eighteen pages long and contains fifty specific clauses. The editor of his will points out that his "Andalusian and Extremaduran devotion to Our Lady of the Immaculate Conception is rooted in Pizarro's spirit with his love of his homeland, and it is the attachment that unites him with Spain and his own."[81] Interestingly, it is clear that Pizarro does not quite understand the concept of the Immaculate Conception, indicating that he believes it refers to the sainted Conception of the Son of God, but there is no question about his reverence for Mary. He declared at length his devotion to Mary and to the dogma involved, even if he did not get it quite right: "I have been very devoted and I have had and I have a special devotion and I believe and I think firmly that because of the faith and personal devotion in this sainted festival that I have had and I have and I will always have until I die, I will always have the favor and the necessary help of the most sainted Mother of God for my salvation."[82] Within the relevant clauses, he provided directions for the celebration of the liturgy, especially a singing mass every day. On Mondays these should be dedicated to souls in purgatory, probably including his own. The Virgin, with her intercessory power, was believed to have a special relationship with these souls and a powerful influence in these matters with her Son, and we have already noted similar instructions in Columbus's testament.[83] This particular day, in addition to the mass, Pizarro wanted a Response sung over his tomb and those of his descendants to be located in the main chapel of the church. Each Saturday, the *Salve*, which had consoled him and his men on Gallo Island, should be sung with candles lit on top of the principal altar and with all the chaplaincy in attendance. He also ordered that organs and an organist be obtained to provide music for the ceremonies that he had indicated. He further gave highly specific instructions for elegant vestments and decorations for the chapel. It was, quite clearly, a bequest in which he took the strongest possible personal interest.[84] To add power to the evidence of his devotion, at the end of his testament, before his signature, he had copied the words of the hymn *Ave Maria Stella*.[85]

It is interesting that although Columbus, Cortés, and Pizarro were all devoted to various advocations of Mary, in their wills it was the Immaculate Conception that drew their attention and bequests. This attention reflected, I believe, the extraordinary importance that the Spanish gave to the vision of Mary as pure and without sin. This belief reassured them when far from home in strange and dangerous lands. It also helped them justify their cruelties against native peoples; Mary would advocate their forgiveness with her Son, as she would understand their motives in spreading the message of Christianity—and a Spanishness—that she exemplified for them. The Immaculate Conception was both a belief and a celebration, one that they observed and defended in the New World and the Old. Other advocations, tied to localities and memories, might be invoked for help in particular situations, but in providing for their immortal souls it was the Immaculate Conception that was honored. And it should be emphasized again that the Immaculate Conception personified for these men, who during their lifetimes had all committed great cruelties, the purity and goodness of Mary, a human woman without stain, without sin. Further, she was for them an all-forgiving mother. As they prepared for the continued existence of their immortal souls in the afterlife, it was the Mother of God who would intercede for them with her Son. Although the Virgin was not a deity, theologically, nevertheless she was associated with a heavy and pervasive sense of the numinous. Her ability to help save them from the consequences of the horrors they had committed must have made her psychologically compelling as they neared the end of their lives. Moreover, the Virgin was closely associated with the Spanish enterprise, linking these men closely with the territory and purposes of the land of their allegiance and, in the cases of Cortés and Pizarro, with the land of their birth.

The images of the Virgin that the Spanish had with them seem to have given them a constant sense of her presence.[86] But her presence was psychological as well. In understanding the impact of the Virgin psychologically, two passages in Bernal Díaz del Castillo are worth looking at more closely. While in the documents composed by Columbus, Cortés, and Pizarro we must read between the lines, inferring from what they did the kind of feelings that they had, Díaz del Castillo makes these feelings much more explicit. After Tenochtitlan had been completely reduced, the Spanish went south, and in a battle with the Chiapanecos, Díaz del Castillo was wounded. As he expressed it:

> I was alone and badly wounded, and because they had not finished me off, and almost unconscious and with little will, I hid myself in some bushes, and pulling myself together, with a strong heart I said, 'Oh, help me, Our Lady! Is it true that I have to die while in the power of these dogs? And I regained such strength, that I leapt out of the bushes and broke through the Indians, whom I forced with strong knife and sword thrusts to yield me a passage; and although they wounded me again, I got to the canoes, where my companion Francisco Martín had already arrived with four friendly Indians.[87]

This invocation of the Virgin when faced with extremity recalls Narváez's outburst when he lost his eye to Cortés's pikeman. In that case, he was too wounded to regroup; Díaz del Castillo, in contrast, pulled himself together with, he believed, the help of Our Lady. Marshaling his strength, he was able to fight his way out of extreme danger and survive. On the one hand, these incidents recall those of wounded men in battles immemorial calling out to their mothers for comfort; on the other, the incident recounted by Díaz del Castillo adds a further dimension. In this case, the power of the Virgin was seen as aiding him to overcome both injury and seemingly overwhelming hostile forces.

A second discussion by Díaz del Castillo yields further insights. At the time of the retaking of Tenochtitlan, a group of Spaniards had been captured by the Aztecs and sacrificed within view of their compatriots. Díaz del Castillo was horrified by incident and then reflected upon it later:

> I remembered these deaths . . . for this reason fearing from this moment forward such a cruel death; and I mention this because from then on before entering afterward into battles I felt a horror and great sadness in my heart; yet putting myself in the hands of God and his Blessed Mother, and entering into battle, I was one with them, and then the terror left me; and I also must mention that that unaccustomed terror was new to me, even though I had been in many very dangerous encounters. Yet now I had toughened my heart and strength and will, and they were even more firmly rooted in my own being than I had ever experienced before.[88]

Retaining the memory of great horror, this man put it aside by asking Christ and his Mother to be present with him and found his "heart and strength and will" reinforced rather than destroyed. And the image that Díaz del Castillo probably called forth in his mind was not that of Christ on the Cross, but rather that of Christ in the arms of his mother—an image that recurs several times in his account of the Conquest.[89] It is probable that many of the conquerors also found strength with similar invocations, going into or in the midst of battle. In less perilous but still anxious times, we know that men also found strength and comfort in calling on the Virgin, as Columbus's and Pizarro's men did when singing hymns to Mary at sundown.

These men believed that the Virgin accompanied them in their travels. They had a sense of the presence of the Virgin, whether she was invoked through prayer, images, or song. She tied them firmly back to the relative safety and sense of home in Europe, as well as to the imperial project of Spain. And the presence of Mary, I would argue, often had almost the force of an apparition, as in Bernal Díaz's description of his escape from the Chiapanecos. In fact, in much reverence for the Virgin, the line between the presence felt by believers in their personal devotions and an apparition of the Virgin is very thin. This personal presence, for the warriors of the Spanish Conquest, helped them justify the cruelty of their actions and gave them an image and a vision of the sacred that made them feel spiritually fulfilled and protected as they passed it on to Native Americans. The Virgin was so important to them that they would take enormous risks to establish her presence. This point is most dramatically exemplified in Cortés's insistence on replacing the Aztec gods with her image on the Temple in Tenochtitlan.

By establishing her name on the landscape and her images in native sacred spaces, they were recreating home, in terms of space, spirituality, and family. While Nuestra Señora encouraged and protected them in battle, she accompanied them as a nurturer, healer, and comforter, a solace in loneliness and an inspiration in danger. She had a personal and present power that was immediate and near, contrasting with the remoteness of God, Father or Son. It would not be long before the Virgin would begin to be seen in some of these ways by Native Americans.

A dramatic visual image of this transference of the Virgin Mary to the consciousness of native populations can be found in the *Lienzo de Tlaxcala*, a series of paintings of the Conquest by a native artist. One scene, "The Baptism of the Lords of Tlaxcala," shows Spaniards and indigenous leaders and warriors arrayed around a central image. Only Cortés, who is holding a crucifix, and doña Marina can be absolutely identified. The people portrayed are drawn clearly and linearly in the native fashion. They are arranged around a small central image of an entirely different style. This painting, contained in a rectangular frame, swirls numinously. But it is easy to see that the painting, the focus of all those present, is a European-style representation of the Virgin Mother and Child.[90]

CHAPTER FOUR

Our Lady in Mexico
Catechisms, Confessions, Dramas, and Visions

✠ ✠ ✠

THE CULT OF OUR LADY became firmly established in Latin America during the colonial period, that time between the Discovery and Conquest in the fifteenth and sixteenth centuries and the wars of independence in Latin America in the early 1800s. At the same time, she became associated and conflated with, as well as changed by and changing, indigenous notions of the sacred. The Spanish brought the Virgin Mary to their New World as a comforting presence, a focus of reverence, an emblem of Spanish nationalism, a war leader who inspired them to victory against the Muslims. They had placed Mary's image in Muslim sacred spaces, and they did the same in native holy spaces in the Americas. But the Virgin, and Christianity more generally, had competition. In Mexico and Peru, the areas on which we will focus in the next three chapters, there were already strong notions of the sacred feminine. Yet it would be a mistake to imagine that the Virgin interacted only with notions of the feminine. Rather, reverence for Mary was intermingled with larger cosmic and sacred schemes, regardless of how or if they were gendered in the pre-Columbian world.

It should be kept in mind that several issues particularly disturbed the Spanish in regard to native culture in Mexico. In the spiritual realm, human sacrifice and the use of hallucinogens to open a window into the sacred concerned them greatly. In regard to family structure, the polygamy within the Mexica nobility was troubling. All three of these concerns are woven into the evolution of the Marian cult in Mexico.

The idea of Mary that emerged was a result not only of confrontation of spiritual systems but also of accommodations on both sides. The new forms of reverence and worship that developed out of the cultural mix of Spanish Catholicism and existing religious systems in Mexico were in no way static or uniform. The Iberian vision itself was not entirely unified and singular, of course, and both Iberians and the Africans who accompanied them brought all sorts of practices that were not strictly controlled by the principles of the Church. Moreover, the various advocations of Mary recognized by the Church had different uses, responded to different populations, and seemed to have different personalities. Although the theology was reasonably consistent, popular reverence was not. As the Virgin became an object of devotion in Mexico, the cosmic systems and visions encountered were multiple, even within the Valley of Mexico. Moreover, rural and urban contexts were quite different, including, not unimportantly, access to actual priests of the Church. As a result, the visions of Our Lady that emerged, the role she fulfilled, and the ways in which she was revered varied enormously from place to place. Nor was the system static. Rather, it was dynamic, changing over time, as it continues to change to this day.

The Church had been using the Virgin Mary in conversion attempts in Western Europe for centuries. Often she became an antidote to what churchmen viewed as magic. They redefined, reformed, and reinterpreted practices as they found them, but according to Christian principles.[1] The Virgin had a powerful influence on these changes. In the Reconquest and in the Spanish New World, Mary continued to be invoked against indigenous religions that the Spanish termed "idolatry." The Church had two techniques, with a continuum between them—repression on the one hand and toleration and incorporation of other religions and "magic" within a Christian framework on the other.[2] The Virgin figured in both techniques but was more effective in the latter. This effectiveness in the New World was enhanced by the importance of the sacred feminine in these regions and the similarities in iconography. Goddesses were associated with earth, water, mountains and high places, and serpents. Most often, the Virgin Mary herself was not directly conflated with these goddesses, which the Spanish identified, rather, with Eve, the anti-Mary. Secondly, appearances of the sacred feminine could be glossed as appearances of the Virgin and evidence that she had accompanied the Iberians, and perhaps even preceded them, to Latin America. Thirdly, she may have been more appealing than indigenous goddesses. After all, rather than being terrifying or remote, she was near, tender, human, often portrayed holding her "precious Son," the infant Christ, in her arms.[3]

In fact, the Virgin Mary was used as a major counterforce in the struggle against Satan, who was more and more identified with native religions as well as those fragmentary manifestations of those old religions as they broke down what might better be called magic. It was not uncommon for indigenous persons, faced with visions or manifestations of a diabolic nature, to invoke the Virgin, using the familiar prayers of the *Ave Maria* or the *Salve Regina*.[4] It is important to bear in mind that the figures of Mary, along with Christ and the other saints, were reworked to fit indigenous needs and religious understandings, sometimes even to replace and represent numinous beings in the native pantheon.[5]

It is unsurprising that in this endeavor they would follow the injunctions of Gregory the Great, discussed in Chapter III, to use indigenous sacred locations. They would try to rework native spaces, rituals, and beliefs so that, as Gregory suggested nine hundred years earlier, "while some outward rejoicings are preserved, they will be able more easily to share in inward rejoicings." Gregory, however, had been realistic about the resistance such replacements would face, reminding missionaries that "it is doubtless impossible to cut out everything at once from their stubborn minds: just as the man who is attempting to climb to the highest places, rises by steps and degrees and not by leaps."[6] A nagging concern throughout the colonial period in Spanish America would be just how much traditional belief and ritual could be tolerated at any given time and where the line had to be drawn, but there is no question that Spanish missionaries in this new mission field were conscious of the concerns Gregory raised in his admonitions.

Naturally, the imposition of Roman Catholicism faced significant resistance from native peoples. Still, the holocausts that followed immediately upon the conquests of Mexico and Peru, as religious and political systems were disrupted and epidemic diseases descended upon these areas, certainly gave rise as well to indigenous peoples' attempts to accommodate. Some of these attempts were sincere, recognizing the power of the Christian God and associated figures aligned behind the Spanish conquerors. Others quite likely were fraudulent, what William Taylor has called the "idols-behind-altars" strategy, that is, that of feigning worship of Christian numinous figures while in fact continuing to worship their own. In most cases, I would guess that both sorts of phenomena were involved. Of course, once idols get behind altars, the human psyche may shift its devotion to what is in front and most visible. And the conversion, conflation, and development of new forms did not happen suddenly; rather, the process was dynamic and continued and continues over the centuries.[7]

It is also very important to keep in mind that it was not just a repressive process. The Church in the early years in the Americas did not have the means to evangelize simply by force. Rather, Christians possessed "an imaginary to oppose to the indigenous imaginary, in the form of a representation of the cosmos that they tried to make accessible to the Indians of the Andes and of Mexico."[8] The Devil was useful in this endeavor, given his appearance—again, not uncommonly looking like the old gods—in dreams and other occurrences that were difficult to explain. Over and over, the Devil was targeted as responsible for manifestations like speaking idols and other visions containing elements of old religious beliefs. These problematic incidents could be decried as "inventions of the Devil." The more the native religions were seen as diabolic, the more Europeans were validated in their presence and the more they could believe in the urgency of their mission of Christianization. This issue was not one merely of expediency; the Spanish believed in the power of the Devil. However convenient it might have been to attach him to native religion, the convenience does not negate their actual horror and sense of evil at some native religious practices, especially human sacrifice. But the Devil quickly became associated with native religion more generally, and Mary, as she was represented in the Immaculate Conception stamping the serpent beneath her feet, was a major antidote to the Devil's power.[9] The Devil was also related to the use of mushrooms and other hallucinogens employed by the indigenous to access the sacred and to get the old gods to speak. As Fray Toribio de Benavente, better known as Motolinía, explained, the Nahuatl name of mind-altering mushrooms meant "the flesh of the god, or the devil whom they adore."[10] These exotic practices, which often gave rise to the most intense rejection of Christian ideas, led to what the Spanish saw as mania, not to mention lust. There was an additional fear that Europeans themselves would be seduced by these substances, and some saw them as analogous to practices common to magic and sorcery in the Old World. The Spanish horror at the use of these substances, however, did not prevent the Virgin Mary from appearing in visions thus induced in native people, as notions of Mary as part of the sacred and spiritual became infused into the native psyche.[11]

A sense of how Mary's power was conveyed, and in a way that surely would have given energy and comfort to those engaged in the conquest of Mexico, is illustrated in a story told by Pedro Mártir. Writing in 1514 about events in Cuba, Mártir told the story of the Spanish sailor who became ill and was left behind with an indigenous cacique. This sailor recovered his health and then took charge of the native troops in the frequent struggles that they endured with their mutual enemies. In all of these encounters, they were victorious. This Spaniard who, it was said, was illiterate but of good character was greatly devoted to the Blessed Virgin and always wore a beautiful painted image of her next to his chest. His assurances to the chief that Mary was responsible for these victories led the indigenous leader to throw away all the *zemis*, that is, the small sacred objects that his people worshipped. According to Mártir, "It was not difficult for the sailor to convince those naked people, and succumbing to the pleas of the chief, he made him a gift of the image that he carried." The cacique consecrated to her a chapel, where his subjects of both sexes were said to go daily, reciting the *Ave Maria*, the only prayer they knew. When the other Spanish returned, the chief proudly showed them the chapel, which was full of little gifts of jewelry and things to eat—so that the image would not become hungry and deprive the native community of food. As Mártir noted, this practice was reminiscent of the worship that they had given to the *zemis*.[12]

Although the story may well be apocryphal, it tells us much about Spanish actions and attitudes as well as about indigenous responses. The Spanish, though occasionally suffering reverses, were overwhelmingly successful. Both they and the people that they had conquered associated these victories very strongly with Santa María. Given Cortés's own deep devotion to the Virgin and his constant placement of images in native sacred spaces, this same association with Spanish power was certainly present in immediate post-Conquest Mexico.

The pre-Columbian sacred feminine in Mexico was represented by a multiplicity of goddesses, dual in nature—both nurturing and frightening—depicted either as human with accompanying splendid regalia or as frighteningly animal-like. The most prominent Aztec goddess was Coatlicue. Her gigantic stone statue had stood at the base of the pyramid in Tenochtitlan on top of which Cortés had insisted on installing the image of the Virgin in place of the male gods Huitzilopochtli and Tezcatlipoca, and it was rediscovered buried there centuries later. This massive stone carving had two serpents coming out of her neck, symbolizing, some believe, the two streams of blood that would have shot outward on decapitation. For a necklace, she wore severed hands and hearts, with a skull hanging in the center at her waistline. Twining serpents furnished her belt and skirt; her hands were bird claws and her feet jaguar paws. This terrifying image was hardly what Iberians would have regarded as maternal. Strongly associated with birth but also death, it is unlikely that the Aztec populace found her very nurturing or reassuring either.[13]

Another representation that may be of Coatlicue or of another highland goddess of birth and death appears in the Codex Borgia, a pre-Cortesian manuscript painted in the decades just before the Spanish arrived. It shows two obsidian knives at her neck where the serpents representing streams of blood appear on the stone statue. A small human being is seen disappearing into, and presumably being chopped up by, her gullet. The image of the

Mexican Goddess of Birth and Death. Codex Borgia (Folio 32), Aztec, Museo Borgiano, Vatican. Reproduced from Erich Neumann, The Great Mother *(Princeton: Princeton/Bollingen Edition, 1974), p. 154, Figure 33. Reprinted with permission from Princeton University Press.*

goddess is in the center of a square marked by a double row of obsidian knives. Other obsidian knives, decorated with exaggerated eyes and even more exaggerated teeth, are present at her elbows and knees, with small figures of Tezcatlipoca (a highland god of whom we will speak more) emerging from between the blades; these may have represented joint pain, a malady from which the Aztecs seemed to have suffered greatly. Other figures of Tezcatlipoca, a major Nahua god that we also will discuss further, may be observed—holding severed human heads—in the corners of the image between rows of obsidian knives. Another individual is shown emerging from yet another eyed, toothed knife about where her womb would be and moving through the birth canal and genitals, which are exposed and represented by a face or mask. At the bottom of the representation (or to the left, as it appears in the Codex), yet another small human is seen emerging from between two obsidian knives in the elongated body of yet another birth-death goddess with a skeletal body, perhaps being reborn into the world. It may be that the figure moving into the knives at the top, through the body of the first goddess, and emerging from the second goddess below represents Huitzilopochtli, the sun god who was reborn through his mother every night, or it may simply represent a series of hapless humans or another scenario entirely.[14] Whatever the precise story being told, it is quite clear that we are in the presence of a birth-death goddess much like Coatlicue, with the emphasis on death and pain.

According to the legends of the conception of that most important of Aztec gods—which come to us through Spanish accounts—Coatlicue conceived Huitzilopochtli virginally when a small ball of feathers fell from the sky and impregnated her. In some versions, Coatlicue was already the mother of four hundred male children and one daughter, but in others she was virgin. One even indicated that Huitzilopochtli's male siblings were created by Tezcatlipoca. The feathers resonate with a Christian idea of the Holy Spirit, so frequently depicted as a dove in Christian iconography. It does not seem too much to suggest that ideas of the virginity of Mary and of Christ's birth were already becoming conflated with Nahua myths of the sacred, at least for the Spanish reporting the stories.[15]

Another goddess revered in the Valley of Mexico was the consort of Tlaloc, the lover goddess Chalchihuitlicue. This goddess had been important at Teotihuacan, the site of a great civilization that preceded the Aztec, and was still in evidence at the time of the arrival of the Spanish. While represented as a recognizable human woman, and a beautiful one at that, she often looked distressed or perhaps just irritated and was regarded as dangerous. Symbolizing fertility and rain, she was also associated with whirlpools and floods. A younger goddess than Coatlicue, she was inconstant: appealing but dangerous, sweet and willful. She appeared as a major figure in the pre-Cortesian calendar as well as in the Mexican magic books, the Tonalamatl, codices that preserved the calendar of pre-Columbian time. A goddess of the day and week cycles of Aztec time as well as the cycles of the hours of the day, Chalchihuitlicue's pictures recur regularly in these books, which were sometimes used in astrological calculations. Although she was often conflated with other goddesses in the entangled and eclectic Mexica pantheon, she was always associated with water and with the green jewel, jade. She shared Coatlicue's association with Coatl, the serpent sign of the Aztec calendar, which itself was a symbol of flowing water, fertility, and sexual intercourse. Chalchihuitlicue represents sacrifice, sometimes shown along with a symbol of a hand holding a serpent of blood crossed by a human footprint or a heart pierced by a knife. In one image, she held a bowl containing a bloody heart, with a snake severed into pieces in front of her. Often, Chalchihuitlicue was shown along with the agave spines used by the indigenous in central Mexico to extract blood from their bodies in penance and sacrifice. Chalchihuitlicue was usually depicted wearing a blue nose ornament in a half-moon form, a snake's head at each end. She infused the strength of *teyolia*, an important life force associated with the heart, into newborns. In rituals at the time of the naming ceremony she was asked to reinforce this essence in the child. But, inconstant as were many of the Mexican deities, she was also connected to maladies of various kinds, especially those related to water—drowning, gout, rheumatism.[16] A story about her, quite possibly post-Conquest, describes her anger with human beings and her bringing a flood to destroy them. Whether the myth precedes or postdates the arrival of the Christians, it nevertheless indicates the inconstancy of her nature. Although she resembled Coatlicue and other Central Mexican goddesses in her connection with serpents and fertility, she was associated with water and change, while Coatlicue is associated with earth and solidity.[17]

Chalchihuitlicue was invoked by the midwife at the time of baptism. In the *Psalmodia Christiana*, a Nahuatl liturgical guide produced by Fray Bernardino de Sahagún in the latter part of the sixteenth century, baptismal water is described as "jade-green." The reference here is to Chalchihuitlicue and her "purifying role" as well as to the "centrality, perfection, and wholeness represented by jade."[18]

The Blessed Virgin, in contrast, was more closely associated with birth and nurturing and forgiveness than with dismemberment and punishment, although she was certainly associated with death. The association, however, was one of intercessory action to relieve sinners of the horrors of Purgatory and Hell, not of a devouring mouth of obsidian knives. Her images were not frightening but rather consoling and welcoming. According to the Spanish, she promised relief from the daily disasters and disarray of the post-Conquest: healing from disease and the preservation or reestablishment of family and even community. After all, the indigenous were faced with illness and death on all fronts. In addition to the losses of war, they also suffered "sweats and fevers, recurring every third or fourth day and which they cured with purges; some had sores . . . [and] corrupted blood" and other terrifying and mortal or chronic ailments.[19] Although estimates vary, the demographic situation reflected a horrible reality. The population of central Mexico had fallen from approximately 25 million at the time of contact to 17 million in 1532 to less than 2 million in 1585. Epidemics with ghastly symptoms and high mortality swept through the region repeatedly during the sixteenth century.[20] As Carmen Bernand and Serge Gruzinski have so vividly pointed out, "the uncertainties of the times, in addition to the changes in way of life, of food, of living arrangements, of beliefs imposed or accepted, diffuse or spectacular, led to repercussions on organisms that had already been stricken with illnesses."[21] The trauma of the bloody defeats at the hands of the Iberians is illustrated in a lament composed probably in 1523: "The cry spreads, the tears fall here in Tlatelolco; . . . we have lost the Mexica nation."[22] Faced with the disasters and cultural disintegration brought by the Spanish, it seems reasonable that the indigenous Mexicans would find the Virgin appealing. They would look for help where they could get it. But since the maladies came with the Spanish, as did the Virgin, their feelings may well have been ambivalent.

In any case, the honoring of Mary spread quickly at the level of elites, whose sons were being educated at Christian establishments. One of these was the Colegio de Santa Cruz at Tlatelolco instituted in 1536 by the Franciscans, who had been teaching the children of the nobility at less formal boarding schools since the friars' arrival several years earlier. Students at these establishments were absorbing new kinds of reverence, often without completely rejecting their older forms of worship or at least belief. Sometimes this process entailed a reinterpretation and refashioning of more traditional forms; sometimes the break was more definitive. It may be that—as among converting Jews in Spain—a special reverence for the Blessed Virgin would have marked them as pious in the eyes of the conquerors and, perhaps, in their own. After all, Cortés made it clear from his first contacts that a proper respect for Mary would be required, particularly for those who wished to ally with the Spanish. Evidence for a rapid spread of the cult of the Virgin among the popular masses, either urban or rural, is not as strong. But spread it did.

What were the mechanisms for this spread? First of all, the cult spread through images, those brought by Cortés, later by other Spanish and notably the missionary orders, and soon produced in Mexico itself. Catechisms for use in teaching and confession emphasized the nurturing role of Mary and her sufferings as the mother of the martyred Christ. Especially in confession, a one-on-one confrontation/conversation/interrogation, the opportunity for impressing Mary's purity and goodness and intercessory abilities was heightened. Sermons, theatrical productions, religious dramas, and other colorful ceremonies and rituals presented her variously as a suffering mother (with whom indigenous peoples might well identify), a powerful advocate (which they surely needed), a healer—spiritual, psychological, and physical—in the epidemic storm. Prayers for the Virgin, including the *Ave Maria* and the *Salve Regina*, were translated into Nahuatl. Jesuits, for example, produced a series of prayers to Mary in Nahuatl. The first of the cycle linked the ideas of her selection as Mother of Christ and her own Immaculate Conception. It read:

> Oh rejoice, Oh Saint Mary, oh fresh pure one who in a sacred way is a flower, for our lord God chose you, he appointed you to become his mother, before the world began. Therefore he chose you to be completely proper, he made you to be completely proper. Right when it was your being placed within someone, your conception, he took from you, he removed from you, the beginning of error, the origin of error.[23]

The initial organized transmission of Roman Catholicism to the native peoples of the Valley of Mexico was brought by the Franciscans, although they were soon followed by other orders. Three Franciscan friars were dispatched from Spain in 1523, only two years after the Spanish had retaken Tenochtitlan, though only Pedro de Gante survived long enough to make an impact; symbolically, twelve more arrived the following year. These men clearly viewed themselves as apostles. The brothers of the order founded almost three centuries earlier were vowed to poverty, spoke for the poor and the suffering, and were intensely devoted to the Virgin Mary. They saw Mary as a loving human mother, a figure close and humble, not distant and aloof.[24] This idea of her no doubt enhanced her appeal to those indigenous caught in the post-Conquest disaster. Yet the task that the early Franciscans faced was extraordinary. Charged with missionizing hundreds of thousands of people whose languages they did not yet know, they cast about for effective methods of teaching. As a participant noted, "They tried a thousand ways to attract the Indians to the knowledge of the one true God."[25]

A special concern was that although thousands of individuals were being baptized in the first years, their actual knowledge of Christian doctrine was flawed at best and nonexistent at worst. There was an urgent need for materials to convey Christian ideas in their language, which in its own visual form was graphic and pictorial. Amazingly soon, Franciscans working with the native scribe-artists developed an alphabetically written form of Nahuatl and translated that most significant of teaching documents, the catechism, into words and, most importantly, pictures. Once produced, this catechism was used in audiovisual fashion, showing the pictures, reading and teaching the text, explaining as they went along.[26]

This experience began in 1523 at Texcoco, where Fray Pedro de Gante, one of the first Franciscans to arrive, started teaching language, reading, writing, and Christian doctrine to the children of nobility in the region. To aid him in this endeavor, he directed the development of a written Nahuatl catechism and one with pictograms in vivid colors illustrating the text. This friar, noted for his linguistic abilities, apparently quickly learned the native language, but the text itself and pictograms were undoubtedly produced by a native scribe-artist, a *tlacuilo*. Highly skilled artists and writers already worked in central Mexico, where learning had two principal modes of expression—pictography and oral transmission.[27] The skills of oratory and pictographic expression were highly prized and had been taught in the *calmecac*, the pre-Conquest schools for the sons of the Aztec elite. Judging from the number of pre-Columbian glyphs and signs included, de Gante's catechism dates from his earliest years in Mexico, probably between 1527 and 1529.[28] It may well have predated the canvas on which Jacobo de Testera, a Franciscan who arrived in 1529, painted images to explain the mysteries of the faith. The methods used in the catechism, nevertheless, are widely known as Testerian.[29]

The catechism's pictograms are vivid in color and cartoonlike. Of the ten parts of this fascinating document, two were devoted to Saint Mary—the third part, "Oh, Santa María, deign to be joyous!" (the *Ave Maria*, as translated into Nahuatl), and the fifth part, "Oh, Queen, deign to be joyous!" (the *Salve Regina*).[30] These two prayers, as translated into Nahuatl in three early catechisms and back into Spanish and compared to Gante's pictorial version in a contemporary study by Justino Cortés Castellanos, vary a bit from the original versions. The major interest, however, is not so much in their variations as in the ways in which Christian ideas were conveyed in the pictures. Obviously, it would have been difficult to provide exact translations for languages developed to express entirely different cosmic systems. Native writers may also have been including their own ideas, an interesting and effective form of resistance. Or they may have been framing the texts and pictures in ways that reflected individual and/or societal concerns. In any case, the prayers depart somewhat from the Spanish originals, though much of the basic message would have been conveyed.[31]

The colors of the pictograms are vivid and primary. They are largely in the native style, executed by Gante's *tlacuilo*, that is, his native writer-artist. They are clearly designed to be used in teaching and to appeal to indigenous understandings. For example, for No. 17, the artist has chosen a hummingbird flapping its wings to represent the Holy Spirit. Cortés Castellanos suggests that this figure represented the most important of the Aztec deities, Huitzilopochtli, "the blue hummingbird on the left," or possibly Quetzalcoatl, whose associations with wind and spirit might represent the Christian context. This stylized hummingbird reappears repeatedly in other places where the Holy Spirit is mentioned.[32] Yet another native representation, that of a wasp or bee, first seen in No. 38, is intended to represent "sin" and seems to reflect the sense of damage, destruction, and pain.[33]

In Cortes Castellanos's composite versions, the Nahua version of the *Ave Maria* certainly emphasized her grace and glory and her association with the Lord and her precious Son. We cannot be absolutely sure of the form of catechism that Europeans in Mexico would have used in the early sixteenth century, as the definitive version was not designated by the Vatican until 1568, yet it is interesting to look at the emphasis placed by the friars on the renditions meant for Nahua eyes and ears. The Gante text and pictograms, unlike the Molina or Dominican texts, included a line not in the later version emphasizing her true and complete virginity—"cenquizca ychpochtle" (completely virgin). All three texts also emphasized an element of joy—"Ma ximopaquiltitie" (Deign to be joyous). Interestingly, all three also indicated "Contigo está el que habla, Díos," literally translated, "With you is he who speaks, God," reflecting the noble or divine nature of "speakers," (*tlatoani* in Nahuatl) human/divine rulers in indigenous society. Two of the texts and the pictograms called on Mary to be with them, sinners all, now and at the time the time of their deaths. Only the Gante text omitted this entreaty. Part 5, the *Salve Regina*, repeated the appeal to the Virgin to be joyous. Far darker than the *Ave Maria*, the *Salve* was a cry for mercy and consolation for them, the exiled children of Eve. The passage of exile described those who invoked her, according to Cortés Castellanos's composite translation as "we who do no more than weep, here in this desert place of lamentation," which recalls but does not exactly mirror the European version. In any case, it was a vivid cry of devastation. It is hard to imagine a more resonant message for suffering people faced with sudden disaster, epidemic disease, and drastic cultural change. Again, the focus was on death, invoking Mary as pious and merciful to speak for them with her Son so that they could attain total happiness in Heaven; this passage does not appear in the modern prayer.[34]

The pictograms that correspond to these two sections focus on the Blessed Virgin. She is shown frontally or in profile, usually wearing a red gown covered by a blue or green cape. Those for the *Ave Maria* (Nos. 49–77) are illustrative. The Virgin is seen in association with her Son, who in one extraordinary representation, No. 66, is shown on the cross, again looking almost cartoonlike but spattered with blood. To the left, in No. 65, is a triangular face with a crown, representing God the Father; to the right, No. 67, Mary appears frontally; then in No. 68, she is seen again in profile with two enlaced crosses extended from her back. The next pictogram is of Mary in profile without the crosses. In all three texts, No. 67 corresponds to the phrase, "Oh, Saint Mary," but only in the Gante text do No. 68 and No. 69

The Virgin Mary with enlaced crosses from de Gante's catechism No. 68, in Justino Cortés Castellanos, El catecismo en pictogramas de fray Pedro de Gante *(Madrid: Fundación Universitaria Española, 1988), 454.*[35]

have a correspondence. The first is "completely Virgin," and the second is "You (who are) the venerated Mother." The association of Mary with the suffering of Jesus on the cross is evident. The same depiction of the frontal Virgin next to the profiled one with the enlaced crosses appears in other places, including No. 98 and No. 99, corresponding to the Apostles' Creed. The text here invokes her name and emphasizes that she is "truly virgin."[35]

In the pictograms for the *Salve,* she is shown in No. 189 in profile, laying her hands on an individual kneeling before her, a picture of comfort. The corresponding text is "misericordia," that is, "mercy." In yet another, No. 183, a person is seen in profile, weeping into a handkerchief. Cortés Castellanos's text is "we who go weeping without cease," an image that would certainly evoke identification among the indigenous.[36] Throughout, the messages in the texts, which would have been read in Nahuatl, along with the messages of the artistic representations reinforce the Virgin Mary as a source of consolation in times of disaster and desperation.

Another interesting image appears in pictogram No. 176. A woman dressed in black and white is seen frontally and seems to be pointing away or giving an order. The next pictogram, No. 177, shows a similar image in black and white in profile with a snake hanging along her body. It seems reasonable to infer that both of these representations are of the same person. The corresponding text is "exiled, thrown out" for the first and "Eve" for the second. The two thus represented Eve in her role in the expulsion from Paradise. This passage would have reinforced Mary as the anti-Eve, the opposite and nemesis of Eve, who would be, of course, associated with the serpent. The similarity of this Eve with Coatlicue, the Nahuatl earth goddess with her obsidian knives, streams of blood, and serpent skirts, and the inconstant and dangerous Chalchihuitlicue would not have been hard for the Franciscans to point out.[37] Mary probably would not have been conflated with these goddesses, but very possibly Eve would, and it would be hard to ignore the intentional nature of these two contrasting images. It is further interesting that the Eve figures are so schematic and colorless, bland and hard to identify as a human person, while the figure of Mary is colorful, nurturing, suffering, a figure for identification and reverence.

The songs for the Nativity of Mary included in Sahagún's *Psalmodia* would have reinforced the contrast between the Virgin and Eve in terms that would have resonated with Nahua spirituality. By using the metaphors of night and day—the darkness of the disordered underworld versus the light of the heavens above—the friars emphasized Eve's connection with the former: "She, our first mother Eve, brought out upon us the sinful night. We lost the divine light; night fell upon us. In Heaven the little birds, the Angels who used to address us, who were our friends, deserted us, hated us." The Virgin brought back the light: "When the perfectly good maiden was born, Saint Mary, in the sacred way the splendor of dawn came out. Thereupon the little birds in heaven began; now they sing, now they speak."[38] With these evocative passages, Mary leads the way out of chaos into a restored order.

The Franciscans, in their use of pictorial aids along with poetic spoken messages, had come up with an effective teaching technique, given the highly visual nature of indigenous writing and documentation. The educated native population, at least, already had developed a significant sensitivity to pictographic representation. The Dominican Bartolomé de las Casas observed three decades after the Conquest that he had seen "a good part of the Christian doctrine written with their figures and their images, which they [the Indians] read thanks to them like I read what is written in our characters on the sheet."[39] This reading was feasible partly because of the inclusion of familiar signs such as glyphs, which were intelligible to those educated to understand them before and after the Conquest. Obviously, the potential for different interpretations on the parts of the Spanish and the Nahuas continued to exist and to provide flexibility for native understandings. Given the language barrier, it is not surprising that the priests in the early years after the Conquest ordered the Indians to draw their sins before confessing them. As Gruzinski observes, the signs they produced would be interpreted somewhat differently by the priests than by the natives. He notes that "misunderstanding, approximation, and confusion proliferated." Nevertheless, these drawings contributed to the penetration of Christian categories, ideas, and images into native psyches.[40]

Confession was itself an interaction with high psychological intensity. Though opportunities to confess were limited by the number of priests and their geographical locations, the friars reported enthusiastic participation by the communities that they visited. Burkhart has noted that as confession in the Nahua spiritual scheme was thought to have bodily curative powers, it is possible that similar expectations were significant in the widespread participation in the Christian rite.[41] It was certainly more consistently available and more heavily emphasized in the friars' interactions with Nahua urban elites. More frequently centered on sexual transgressions than on idolatry, it penetrated in intimate ways the lives of those confessing. The nature of marital unions was investigated, with the new Christian forms focusing on the couple and the nuclear family rather than on the marital union as part of the larger cosmic system, more characteristic of the Nahua view. The priests were particularly concerned about the polygamy of the indigenous upper classes and therefore with pushing the idea of Christian marriage. The establishment of the Christian couple as the model would also have the effect of depriving indigenous authorities of their control over "the circulation of women."[42] The issue of the nature of marriage illustrates the way in which evangelization required the restructuring of native society.

The priests were also concerned with lust. The confessional process was designed to delve deeply into thoughts and even dreams with a special focus on sexual fantasies. Taking pleasure from those fantasies, or "the filthy pleasure inside your heart," was especially condemned. Native persons cast about for ways of responding that would satisfy their interrogators and, if they were trying to be believers, that would cleanse them of their sins. Within the nuclear family, the Blessed Virgin served as a perfect, though unattainable, model. The practice, then as now, of assigning a certain number of Hail Marys certainly must have reinforced her cleansing role in this difficult endeavor.[43] If confession served as "consolation and medicine," as Alonso de Medina averred in the sixteenth century, in addition to its less attractive aspects as an example of colonial domination, then Mary would have been associated with precisely that consolation.[44] Sermons admonishing young women to take Mary as a model in protecting their virginity reinforced the messages conveyed in the confessional.[45]

Preaching provided another opportunity for slippage and reinterpretation in the transmission of Christian doctrine. Initially the friars lacked the language and trusted in their Nahua and other indigenous "disciples" as competent and well-trained translators.[46] The friars, relying on these translators, not only preached in the Valley of Mexico but also throughout the pacified areas of New Spain. Alert to the significance of music and the power of participation, the friars had the major prayers translated and set to music. According to Motolinía's report, "In order to turn them away from the error of the idols, they gave them the doctrine in many ways. At first, to provide savor, they taught them the *per signum crucis*, the *pater noster, ave Maria, credo, salve,* all sung in a very simple and pleasing manner."[47] The friars also took advantage of the Indians' pleasure in singing and other forms of oral expression to teach both plain chant and Gregorian chant. Their success in this endeavor was notable, as it had been with writing. Cantors proliferated throughout the country, and it was said that each little town had several natives who sang the Hours of Our Lady every day in the local church. Native writers also wrote poems to be sung with the great religious feasts.[48] As of 1537, according to the papal bull of that year, the indigenous were required to celebrate twelve major Church festivals. Four of these were devoted to the Virgin Mary (the Nativity of Mary, the Annunciation, the Purification, and the Assumption), and all six of those devoted to Christ (Christmas, the Circumcision, Epiphany, Easter, the Ascension, and Corpus Christi) could have strong Marian components. The other two were Pentecost and the festival of Peter and Paul. Further, native peoples celebrated the festival of their community patron saint, and in many cases this patron was one or another advocation of Mary. These festivals, though fewer in number than those required of the Spanish, nevertheless were frequently prepared elaborately and proceeded with strong demonstrations of devotion. Nahuas presented themselves as Christians who performed their own versions of religious rituals in which they worshipped God and the saints and especially the Virgin.[49] The rituals themselves would reinforce and intensify the devotion to this most sympathetic figure in the Christian pantheon.

Yet another method for presenting Christian ideas was the use of dramatic presentations in the indigenous languages, the first of these being performed in the early 1530s, reportedly to great dramatic effect.[50] As these dramas were largely written by Nahua authors, once again there was an opportunity for a kind of "creative fusion," as Burkhart has termed it. She has given intensive scrutiny to one of these plays, the earliest known script of a drama in any Native American language. Titled *Holy Wednesday* and probably written by a Nahua author who had been educated at the Franciscan

Colegio de Santa Cruz, it was based on a Spanish play, *Beacon of Our Salvation*.[51] The Spanish version was written by a Valencian bookseller, Ausías Izquierdo Zebrero, a man devoted to the Blessed Virgin.[52] Izquierdo called his play an *auto*, a form of one-act play almost always based on religious subjects. In this case, the story involves Christ's leave-taking from his mother, before his departure for Jerusalem to begin his Passion. Mary, fearing correctly that he is going to his death, tries to persuade him to stay with her, but of course he ultimately departs. Izquierdo's play was written during a period of fervor among Spain's penitential brotherhoods, focused around the Passion and the crucified Christ. In Spain's larger cities, thousands of members of these brotherhoods participated in the ritual processions of Holy Thursday and Good Friday. During these processions, they demonstrated their piety through flagellation or bearing crosses.

The devotion to Mary quite naturally developed from this fervor for the suffering Christ. Her sorrow as the mother of a martyred child led to devotion for images of the Virgin that were believed to shed tears. New sculptures of her proliferated that showed her face covered with crystalline teardrops and her hands held away from her body, palms upturned. By Izquierda's time, the Semana Santa—Holy Week—processions had borrowed from Corpus Christi the use of floats bearing images that represented scenes from the Passion. The suffering Mary was regularly included.[53] Dozens of these sorts of images still may be seen in processions in Spain during Holy Week. In present-day Semana Santa in Seville, floats carrying just such representations of the Virgin are brought along at the very end of almost all confraternity processions, furnishing a dramatic and emotional climax to these elaborate exhibitions of personal and group piety. As the images are returned to their home churches and chapels, observers often fall in behind the float carrying the Virgin and emotionally follow her for the last few hundred yards, providing a twenty-first century sense of the devotion that began hundreds of years earlier.

In Mexico, dramas designed for the indigenous were meant to inspire the same kind of intense reverence, though Nahuatl theater of the sixteenth century developed separately from Spanish colonial drama. Based on religious themes and resembling the Spanish *autos*, plays were written and performed in Nahuatl by Nahua actors for largely Nahua audiences. The early Franciscans began using these plays for the purposes of evangelization; in fact, they had discovered that the best way to attract large numbers of indigenous converts was through elaborate pageants and processions, complete with music and dancing. Nahuatl dramas not only had roots in Spanish plays, especially in content, but also could be interpreted as ritual performances related to their own pre-Columbian ceremonies. Performances, as Burkhart has pointed out, put the actors into a "liminal, 'in-between' space where they are no longer quite themselves nor are they quite the character represented."[54] For the Nahua, individuals in costume performed as deities in ritualized scenarios in which the identity of the god was seen as added to the identity of the human person; thus one was oneself and the god as well. Considered in this light, Nahua religious dramas had enormous power before the Conquest, and, I think we can safely infer, after it as well. Moreover, the Nahua term for colonial theatrical productions was *neixcuitlilli*, "something that set an example." Burkhart writes that this term came into use to indicate the importance of the performance as a kind of exemplary tale to be used as a model. It therefore functioned to provide a kind of moral instruction absent from earlier Nahua forms of drama and public speaking.[55]

Holy Wednesday, while following the Spanish version almost utterance for utterance, gives us a different picture of the Virgin Mary and particularly of the relationship between Christ and his Mother. The Spanish Christ almost brushes off his Mother's fears and suffering, focused as he is on fulfilling his own destiny.[56] At times, he seems impatient at her attempts to impede him. Although both versions show Mary as active and assertive, even authoritative, the Nahua play shows Christ's choice between the will of his Father and the all-too-human anguish of his Mother as far more difficult than Izquierdo's version. Still, the Nahua Christ has no alternative; he does not control his fate but, like indigenous Mexicans after the Conquest and like his Mother in the play, is subject to other forces. He and his Mother are bound together through love and through their subjection to another power. This emphasis may also reflect the Nahua author's relationship with his own family as he endeavored to walk a fine line between their needs and beliefs and his service to the fatherly Franciscans.[57]

The play resonated in many ways with both pre-Conquest religious practice and the Nahuas' own subjection to the Spanish. Before the fall of the Mexica empire, indigenous ritual observance included fasting, the letting of blood, and other practices of mortifying the flesh. Christ's anticipated bloody sufferings would have seemed similar. They also might have been associated with the Mexica sacrifices of humans used as *ixiptlas*, individuals who for a period of time embodied the gods they represented. The context naturally added to the possible identification of indigenous peoples with Jesus, as the injustice of Christ's treatment by the Romans might mirror, in their eyes, their own treatment by the Spanish. Burkhart states, and I firmly agree, that the Holy Week observations certainly would have inspired a "collective identification" with Christ and his Mother. Native processions and confraternities were still segregated from the Spanish ones, and concerns that there might be problems were evidenced by the armed guards who accompanied the Spanish processions. Yet although Christian practices had been brought by the oppressors, they could be adapted and interpreted by the indigenous in ways amenable to their circumstances. Christ and Mary, in this play, spoke Nahua and were played by Nahua actors. It is certainly conceivable that at some level they could have been seen as Nahua rather than as figures of European Christian reverence. This distinction was enhanced by the differences in the portrayals of their relationship in the two versions.[58]

A comparison of several passages in the Spanish and Nahua plays illustrates these differences. Early in the Spanish play, when Mary asks to speak with Jesus, he responds rather peremptorily, "I am pleased to listen." In the Nahua play, Mary first of all emphasizes much more strongly his value to her as her child, her anguish already showing in her words. Christ responds, emphasizing the familial relationship, "Oh my precious Mother, what is it you want to say? May it be that I hear it!"[59] The intimate tone and Christ's deep concern for Mary are thus established.

The Nahua version is consistently focused around the intensity of their relationship and the personal preciousness of each to the other. In yet another passage in Izquierdo's text, Mary takes Jesus to task for causing her much suffering. Querulously and almost accusatorially, she questions, "Whom do you love more than me?" In the Nahua version, rather, she poignantly cries, "Oh, how my heart is torn open to its very bottom! It is it as if you plunged a knife into it." Rather than accusing, she asks for an explanation: "My precious child, why do you afflict me so with sadness? Do tell me."[60] In this utterance Mary invokes the pre-Conquest idea of the heart as the seat of the *teyolia* life force—mentioned earlier as particularly associated with Chalchihuitlicue. Burkhart has pointed out the pervasive importance of heart imagery in Nahuatl discourse. A wide range of emotional as well as of thought processes was connected with the heart, the physical location of the *teyolia*, and thus distress, affection, memory, sentiments, attachments, and understanding were implied through this association. The reader will recognize that these symbols were associated as well with the pre-Columbian sacred feminine. Burkhart notes that through this metaphor of physical invasion, the playwright introduces a range of associations indicating "a severe disturbance in one's mental and emotional equilibrium," a sense of deep psychic disarray. The connections back to the Christian tradition are also legion, including a possible reference to the prophecy of Simeon, the Hebrew elder, at the time of Mary's post-birth purification in the temple. He warned her that her soul would be stabbed by a sword, precisely a prediction of her anguish during Christ's Passion. This suffering was one of the "seven sorrows" of the virgin, often represented as seven swords piercing her heart.[61] At the same time, the image might evoke the ritual Aztec sacrifice of ripping the heart from the body with the priests' obsidian knife, though the contexts of Aztec sacrifice and the suffering of Christ and the Virgin were very different.

It is perhaps at the end of the two plays that the most vivid differences between the two versions can be observed. In the last section that is available in both Spanish and Nahua, Christ's attitude toward his Mother is entirely different. In the Spanish version, Jesus emphasizes that her suffering fills him with anguish; in the Nahua, he grieves that she will suffer by his fault. In Spanish he blames her; in Nahua he blames himself. Then, even more tellingly, in the Spanish he rejects her embrace, saying, "Do not throw yourself into my arms. Hold onto her, Magdalene." In the Nahua his concern is that she will fall, and he urges Magdalene to embrace her so that she will not.[62] She is not rejected; rather, Christ shows his deep concern with her well-being.

Then, interestingly, the Nahua author adds two more exchanges between Christ and his Mother that have no counterpart in the Spanish text. Mary first asks to accompany her Son in death, emphasizing the horror of knowing in advance that he is to die. She compares herself to David, noting his good fortune in not having to witness the death of his son Absalom but rather only hearing of it after the fact, and to Jacob, who believed his son Joseph dead when he was shown his bloody mantle. She calls them fortunate in their lack of prior knowledge. Christ refuses her request to die with him, emphasizing that she must stay behind to console those others whom he leaves. Finally, Mary acknowledges that it is his Father's "order" that he die and indicates acceptance by saying, "May we praise him [God the Father] forever!" She then asks her Son's blessing. Christ ends the play by delivering the requested benediction: he blesses her head for remembering "what is proper and good," her womb for bearing him, her breasts for nursing him, her mouth for speaking true things, her hands for their "good and proper" work, and her soul, "which is filled with grace and truth!" The script ends with the notation, "And they encouraged each other, then they took leave of each other, they said goodbye to each other, they embraced each other." Certainly, this ending would have given a very different impression than the Spanish version in which Christ orders the Magdalene to prevent Mary from throwing herself into his arms.[63] Burkhart writes that these four speeches may have been based on another text, but the important issue for our purposes is that the passage emphasizes the wrenching nature of the loss of a child for a parent and Christ's concern, tenderness, and blessing of his Mother.[64] It may also point out the darker side of the years of Aztec domination, when huge numbers of sacrifices were carried out for religious purposes, not always with willing victims or willing families. It certainly seems possible that personal anguish caused to loved ones in the course of the sacrifices, willing or not, would be remembered, and the Christian example of taking only one to save the many could seem far preferable.

However, not all of the portrayals of the Christian cosmos provided by the evangelizers were as gentle and as poignant as those of Mary and her Son portrayed in the early Franciscan catechisms or the drama *Holy Wednesday*. Moreover, the indigenous, shocked by the Conquest and the heaps of bodies left by violence and disease, were both fragile and susceptible psychologically and spiritually. The friars, for their part, were in strange territory, concerned spiritually in the early days by the continued and open devotion of the Indians to the Devil. Motolinía described the "temples of the devil" that one entered through doors that seemed to be the very gates of Hell, there to encounter a host of terrifying idols, including snakes, frogs and toads, lions and tigers, fish, and butterflies. During the first few years after the Conquest, many of these sites continued to burn perpetual fires, night and day, simulating, in the eyes of the Spanish, the fires of Hell. Against these devilish challenges, the friars began to preach, emphasizing that there was only one God, all powerful. Also, apparently, it was necessary to straighten out for the indigenous just who Saint Mary was. As he explained, "Until this moment they only named María, or Santa María, and saying this name they thought that they named God, and all the images that they saw were called Santa María . . . then we told them that it was the devil in whom they believed and that he was tricking them; and of the evil in him and the care that he was taking that not a single soul be saved." Motolinía then went on to describe the natives' terror on hearing these explanations as so great that they came to the friars for baptism, "asking it with tears and sighs and much pleading."[65]

Many mechanisms were used to emphasize the extraordinary perils of ignoring Christianity or delaying its full acceptance. That the visual assaults on the natives by the various missionary orders would have lodged in natives' psyches is not surprising. Early native visions incorporating Christian material, as reported by the friars, clustered around visions of Hell—which must have been all too similar to their condition at that time—from which they were saved by the intervention of an angel or of Mary.[66]

The friars were not above tricks of stagecraft to impress the Indians; artificial mechanisms permitted the Virgin and Christ to ascend and angels to appear, while braziers imitated the flames of Hell. These scenes reappeared in dreams and visions, the beginning of the "Christianization of the *imaginaire*," as it has so accurately been termed by Serge Gruzinski.[67]

The Jesuits, arriving a few decades after the Franciscans, also strongly pushed the reverence for Mary. They were struck by the number of visions among their parishioners, which they attributed to the "melancholy" temperament of the Indians. Instructive is one of their techniques for reinforcing Christianity among the natives, both urban and rural. Moving into an area for a week, one or two Jesuits would organize spectacles, sermons, and penitential processions, complete with flagellations, bearing of crosses, and cries of woe and pain. The spectacles often focused around the happy intervention of Mary in clashes between Saint Michael and the Devil, combined with terrifying effects—lakes of fire, sparks, sulphurous smells, threatening darkness—against the white brightness and glitter of the Virgin, the serenity of the suffering Christ, the purple of the saints. With this introduction, they would move on to a sermon about death, the condemned soul, Hell, Purgatory, and accompanying torments.[68] The mercies of the Virgin, who might be persuaded to intercede with her Son to save them from these horrors, was an important part of the message. The vision that the Jesuits wished to impart was nothing less than the dramatic confrontation between good and evil, between Christianity and the old ways. Angels and saints and especially the Virgin faced down monsters and devils—that looked much like the old gods.[69]

Descriptions of specific visions and dreams are rare, but the consideration of a few of those that we do have is illuminating. Christian content seems to have been common from at least the end of the sixteenth century.[70] Mirroring the Spanish experience, available iconographic models appeared. For example, the Jesuits reported that an Indian of Patzcuaro had dreamed of a beautiful woman carrying a child at her breast, the description striking them as remarkably similar to an image in their church.[71]

Some visions seem to have involved native individuals associated with spirituality and healing. Two of these have to do with initiation dreams of native men claiming numinous powers. The case of Domingo Hernández, dating from the early years of the seventeenth century, is intriguing. Originally from a Nahua village in the Cuernavaca region, he had gained a reputation for holiness and healing. His vision occurred when he was stricken with a serious illness and was taken for dead. He believed that two male individuals dressed in white had taken him to visit other sick persons and also to see two roads—the wide road of the damned on one side and, on the other, which was narrow and filled with thorns and tangled bushes, the road of the Redeemer. The two men seem to have been male angels, but perhaps they were associated with the friars, who were continually pointing out such choices. The angels ordered Domingo to give up *pulque*, a drink fermented from the sap of the agave plant and associated with the indigenous numinous, on the threat of being returned to this place of death. This image may have reflected the friars' concerns with the native use of mind-altering substances to induce an opening to the sacred. Only after this warning did they teach him the words of healing. On the same night, he was visited by three women, dressed completely in white, but he could identify only two of them, the "Virgin Our Lady" and Veronica. The Virgin of the vision told him that Christ had captured him but that she wanted to save him. Veronica, on her part, waved a veil to move the air toward him. The air, which seems to be a crucial element here, revived him, and he arose healed.[72] The implication that Mary and her associate Veronica had intervened to heal Domingo himself was clear. We are dealing with a kind of shamanic initiation with clear and strong Christian elements.[73]

Jacinto de la Serna, in his "Manual de Ministros de Indias" written for the archbishop of Puebla, connected the very use of hallucinogens with the Virgin Mary, indicating that native healers used *peyote, ololuihque,* and other psychedelic substances in their cures and that at least one claimed to have received the herbs from the Virgen de los Remedios personally. In this case, from the mining district of Zacualpan, the native healer Juan de la Cruz and his mother were both ill to the point of death "with an illness that God had given them."[74] Presumably, therefore, it would take the power of God to cure it. Juan, in his vision, saw two beings in white, identified as the angels Saint Michael and Saint Gabriel, descend from the heavens. They brought with them a *lanceta,* probably some kind of small knife or surgical lancet, and instructed Juan in using it for curing illness. He was further told to bleed his mother and the others who were ill and to charge two *reales,* a fairly high price, for the service. Arising three days later, he began to follow their instructions, thereby saving his mother.

Five years later, in about 1650, Juan had another vision during illness. He saw the Virgin as a pilgrim, "una mujer peregrina," dressed in green and red as she often was in the pictorial catechisms. The nude baby Jesus was in her arms, and a golden arch soared above her head. Inscribed on the arch were the names of four herbs for Juan to use in his healing. At her side was an Indian woman with a rosy face, abundant hair, and a blue *huipil* (a native blouse). Interestingly, this woman seemed to represent the illness itself. The Virgin castigated the woman and told her to leave Juan so that he could get well and serve her own son, Jesus Christ.

The visions worried the priest who reported them. It seems at least possible that these visions were inspired by hallucinogens, as the priest mentioned that Juan had on one occasion given an ill person *ololiuhqui,* along with the rest of his family, and had lit candles as a part of the healing ceremony.

According to him, "all were robbed of their reason, which is the effect of this drink."[75] He mentioned that subsequently Juan, on entering the home of an ill person, called on God to help if it were his will. According to the priest, Juan was actually invoking Fire, the old god, not the god of Christianity. It is interesting as well that illness itself in Juan's vision was personified as an Indian woman who could be admonished and vanquished by the Virgin. The same priest further emphasized the importance of understanding the indigenous calendar so that one could do one's best to ensure that fiestas in honor of Christ, Mary, and the Christian saints were not "mixed up with the memories of their ancient gods."[76]

The Spanish priests themselves were not free of visions of Mary and the saints, with whom they sometimes engaged in serious discussions, but these visions were somewhat different in nature from the indigenous ones. Still, they could not entirely reject the possibility that natives might have authentic visions of their own, though they still had to be concerned about diabolical origins. Some, such as Fray Martín de Valencia, made major life decisions based on visions. In his case, he decided to make the trip to the Indies after seeing a beautiful woman with a child in her arms—apparently Mary holding the baby Jesus—walking across the waters and beckoning him to follow. He responded by leading the group of twelve Franciscan "apostles" to Mexico in 1524. Confrontations between the Virgin, "more resplendent than the sun," and the Devil were common in the psyches of the fathers. The Virgin was also a comfort to the religious in the strange new land; some reported tender conversations in which our Lady consoled them and healed them of their afflictions. Still others were reported to have been informed by her of the hours of their deaths, thus providing them with the time to prepare their souls for the event. Spanish nuns as well were visited by the Virgin; in 1608, for example, Mother Isabel de San José received such a visit in the convent of Santa Catalina in Mexico City, a visitation witnessed by three other nuns and two children. Another appearance in Sinaloa in 1599 brought with it a downpour that ended a severe drought.[77] But her deliverance of healing powers and direct intervention in matters between individuals and God, either Father or Son, was more characteristic of her appearances to natives. Moreover, the indigenous visions here described were much more like narratives of events or stories than they were like conversations. The Virgin, with or without the Child, was an actor among other actors within the stories, an actor who was usually seen as a support to the dreamers. Moreover, the Virgin not only saved them from life-threatening illnesses but along with the angels helped them acquire special powers.

By the beginning of the seventeenth century, then, seventy to eighty years after the Conquest, Mary was beginning to be seen as an ally of native peoples, a direct result of the teachings of the evangelizers as interpreted through native artists and authors. However, Our Lady for the indigenous peoples of Mexico was not precisely the same as she was for the Spanish. She operated in somewhat different ways, was called on for somewhat different reasons, was making herself a part of personal and group visions of the spiritual arising out of the many combinations of Spanish and native religious ideas and the needs of the times. This process was probably helped by her appearance as a recognizable human figure, often dressed simply and carrying her Child, with whom native men and women as well as the Spanish could identify.

The implantation of the Virgin in native minds was taking many forms, but there is no question that these forms were heavily influenced by the enormous number of images that began to proliferate throughout the colony. Although many of the initial images were produced by native artists, European models were usually used. Still, these images were modified in intriguing ways. The sculptures, paintings, and engravings that became available in the sixteenth and seventeenth centuries began to imprint themselves on the minds of those who observed them; some of them also began to perform miracles. Reverence for particular advocations of the Virgin began to appear and to spread. Moreover, the Virgin began to appear in various sites in Mexico. Although the line between dreams, visions, and apparitions may be subtle, apparitions in these cases may be thought of as those appearances that had an effect beyond the initial viewer or were observed by more than one person. It is to these images, miracles, and apparitions that we will turn in the next chapter.

CHAPTER FIVE

Mexico

Images, Fiestas, Miracles, and Apparitions

✝ ✝ ✝

REVERENCE FOR THE VIRGIN spread rapidly through the proliferation of her images, the almost immediate development of parades and festivals in her honor, the miracles that began to occur in relation to her images and sacred spaces, and even her appearances to indigenous peoples and to the Spanish. The sense of her presence, enhanced with images, rituals, visions with or without the use of hallucinogens, and otherwise inexplicable occurrences, might very naturally lead to a belief that she had actually physically appeared. She was already felt to be present in images and to be present with the believer, with images or without them. The figures that the Spanish carried with them, visited in shrines and churches, carried or followed in processions, or communicated with on home altars were felt to be enormously precious and efficacious. Very quickly the indigenous population would begin to interact with the Virgin Mary in similar ways. Children of nobility were being brought into the devotion through the missionary schools, and images came into the lives of ordinary people as well. Much of their earlier ritual and exposure to some of the most important indigenous images had been reserved to elites before the arrival of the Spanish. It may well be that the accessibility of Christian numinous figures to everyone, especially a representation as poignant as the lovely Virgin with or without her Child, made them even more appealing.

Images of Mary, of course, had arrived in central Mexico with Cortés. Although we do not know for sure, these seem to have been principally paintings and perhaps engravings. Certainly paintings or engravings would have been easier to carry than sculptures, but there is some doubt. Several little

Virgins of wood, including one of the Virgin of Remedies, are still known as Virgenes de Cortés or as La Conquistadora—the Woman Conqueror. Of course, we do not know that they actually came with the Conquest, but perhaps they did, and in any case sculptures of some sort probably arrived at that time. The Laws of Burgos, developed in 1512 as guidelines for interactions between the Spanish and the indigenous, required that anyone given an *encomienda*—a grant of the labor of Indians—must erect a church for the Christian instruction of their charges. This building had to have a bell and "images of Our Lady," and rapidly providing these representations in the colonized areas was a priority. Fray Pedro de Gante established a school of arts and crafts in post-Conquest Mexico to provide the various important works of reverence for the early churches.[1] It would not be long before paintings and sculptures, then engravings and frescoes spread across the land. So common were representations of the Virgin that according to Motolinía, the indigenous confused Mary with God and called all images "Santa María."[2] Especially in the period when language was a barrier to understanding, indigenous people would appreciate and identify more with the images of the human Mary than with the Christ of an abstract and figureless cross or the even more abstract and distant God the Father. The crucifix, featuring the agonizing body of Christ, was more emotionally evocative than the simple cross but certainly not as welcoming as the figure of the Virgin.

Given the need for communication across the language barrier, representations of Mary would assume a very important role in conversion. Not only were these teaching images, as in the catechisms and in the paintings and frescoes that denoted Mary's roles in the life of Christ, but also figures for veneration, beautiful and serene, a comfort not only to the indigenous but also to the friars. The need for these figures, the sculptures and paintings and frescoes, would far outdistance the ability of the local Spanish to produce them. But artists were at hand, and many of them. The Aztec world was full of them, highly skilled and available after the Conquest for new tasks. Fray Bartolomé de las Casas, a prominent Dominican with long experience in the Americas, noted approvingly that the Indian artists were excellent both at copying European models and at bringing style and poignancy to scenes of the Passion. He reported, "It is a marvel with what perfection they depict the mysteries and stories of our redemption. In particular, I have noted that many times representations of what we call the Fifth Sorrow, the descent of the body of the Savior from the cross and its reception by his Mother, have a special grace."[3]

Although earlier art historians believed that Spanish artists dominated the production of these works, current scholarship shows conclusively the

enormous involvement of native artists. The construction of Christian build-
ings and the need for the requisite art was a daunting enterprise; not only
convents but also churches and chapels proliferated throughout the land. No
fewer than six cathedrals were begun in Mexico in the sixteenth century.[4]
Constantino Reyes-Valerio has noted that these constructions, at least in the
early years, mostly took place in areas of the country that were heavily populated and were, additionally, important pre-Hispanic ceremonial centers. The
centers would have had a large group of workers specialized in the production of sculpture, painting, and architecture; the evidence of the enormous
quantity of pre-Columbian religious art that we still have, even after extensive destruction, makes this point clear. Moreover, there are many instances
of the incorporation of pre-Columbian elements into Christian art, so many
that Reyes-Valerio calls this early colonial art Indochristian. As he notes,
more than one hundred glyphs have been found in early colonial art, far
more than the usually untutored Spanish artisans would have been able to
incorporate with any meaning.[5] Of course, these non-Spanish elements raise
the issue of whether indigenous artists were communicating a hidden, non-
Christian message or perhaps at least a double message. On the other hand,
the incorporation of native elements, as we have seen in the use of glyphs in
the catechism, aided communication and understanding among the indigenous peoples under instruction. What we are seeing here, I believe, is the
construction of native versions of Christianity, with significant regional and
local and even personal variations. Very likely, conceptions of the sacred
dating from before the Spanish combined with changes in rituals, practices,
and images to produce new internal and external forms of spirituality.[6] In
the view of Reyes-Valerio, Indochristian art was "a new medium of reli-
gious-cultural integration of man with his new environment."[7]

According to art historian Hans Belting, images "reveal their meaning best
by their use."[8] It is the interaction of images with human beings that interests
me most here. How were images received, perceived, reacted to, interpreted,
understood? What kinds of rituals, emotional states, spiritual meanings, and
psychological resonances were inspired by these representations? What follows
is speculative but perhaps can get us closer to our central question of why the
Virgin Mary has been, from the early days of contact right up to the present,
such a compelling figure. There is no question that these images had enormous
power within the minds and psyches of the beholders. Marian images in particular would be used, as they had been in Europe, to distinguish true believers
from the followers of unacceptable spiritual alternatives, including most especially the Devil and other native "idolatries," that is, survivals of the traditional
religions. Well might the friars have been nervous about the accuracy and au-

thenticity of figures of the Virgin produced by native artists. Belting has pointed out, "As surrogates for what they represent, images function specifically to elicit public displays of loyalty or disloyalty."[9] They were used in just such a way for Indians to prove adherence, both political and religious, to the Spanish system. As such, they could also be particularly subversive as representative of ideas and concepts and symbols that the Spanish did not understand. Still, the priests had little choice; native artists and interpreters were available to them, and they had to communicate.

But the images were not universally well received; as emblems of Spanish dominance, they were sometimes attacked as well. Yet the very attacks indicated that the attackers already associated them with power. On the other hand, the figures could cause power inversions when, filled with the presence of Mary, they began to advocate for the indigenous or for the marginalized. They had functioned this way in Europe; they would function this way in the Spanish New World. Moreover, the representations of the Virgin were often treated as if they were the living human person of the Mother of Christ.[10]

Many of the images of Saint Mary that were revered in Mexico and elsewhere acquired their authenticity not only from their form but also from their miraculous appearances and activities, resonating with the "discoveries" of images of the Virgin during the Reconquest. Typically, again as in Spain, the figures would be found (or sometimes brought to a location), refuse to move, return to the original location, insist on their wishes until a church or chapel had been built to house them on the spot they (that is, the images) had selected. The presence of the Virgin in the image and the sense of her power were thus reinforced. Significantly, by using these figures to inspire reverence among indigenous peoples, the priests and friars were using something that was highly effective in conversion but that could also be used to circumvent their own control. The representations were available to the people and could be communicated with directly, in this way taking the connection with the sacred out of the hands of the official representatives of the Church. This tension continues today.

Probably the first images made by native craftsmen were crosses, easy to construct, certainly, in comparison with images of Mary. We know from Bernal Díaz that Cortés had ordered his ships' carpenter to make crosses of wood to place in native sacred spaces. It is likely that indigenous artists soon began to do the same. Later, when churches were constructed, temporary crosses were replaced by stone. A beautiful example, over eight feet high, can still be seen at the sixteenth-century Augustinian convent of Acolman in the Valley of Mexico near the pre-Columbian site of Teotihuacán. Possibly carved by more than one artist, given the variation between the finely wrought face of Christ at the intersection of the horizontal and vertical bar and the primitive nature of other representations, it is to this day the site of Christian popular ritual. On a recent visit, for example, I observed a priest blessing a new taxi in the shadow of the cross for an owner-driver and his wife. Important for our story is the very primitive representation of Mary carved at the foot of the cross. The advocation she most resembles is the Virgin of Sorrows, her hands crossed and her head shrouded in mourning. Although only the top half of her body is portrayed, below her figure are placed a skull, a sphere, and what may be a dragon or a serpent, looking something like a worm. While the dragon and the sphere pertain perhaps to the Immaculate Conception, the skull recalls the image of Coatlicue with the skull pendant hanging at her belt line. The Virgin's face and the skull both have gouged eyes and bulging foreheads, recalling the skulls in the Coatlicue sculpture. The dragon or snake may also refer to the indigenous association of the sacred feminine with the serpent (see Chapter IV). Also reminiscent of the Aztec sculpture are her flattened hands. Above her hands is a disk that may stand for her heart, and if it does, this element would be truly indigenous, according to Elizabeth Weismann. The complex, however, lacks style and immediacy. As Weismann has pointed out, it reflects a "falling off of both European and indigenous styles, a groping for religious magic through whatever symbols come to hand." Though she does not claim that the representation is definitively by a native artist, it seems likely. Despite its primitive appearance, or because of it, it is both evocative and mysterious, with a sense of containing more than is immediately apparent. And yet these works of Indochristian religious art were right at the center of developing native worship. As the Augustinian friar Basalenque wrote, "At *Ave Maria*, all the people come out to the Cross nearest their house (for at each street corner there is the Cross) and there they recite the catechism, and then the devout Offices . . . so that at that hour the town is like a chapel with many choirs, all praising the Lord."[11] It is not insignificant that it was at the hour of the Marian prayer, the *Ave Maria*, that the community would come together for Christian observance, resonating with the practice of Columbus's men singing the hymn at sundown.

Another fascinating image, a stone sculpture that has been dated by Constantino Reyes-Valerio to the early post-Conquest period, is a far more elegantly rendered representation of the Immaculate Conception, her heavy cape forming a triangle, her head above crowned and surmounted by a cross, surrounded by a spiked aureole.[12] Again, her face is rather masklike but with far more liveliness than on the Acolman cross. She is standing on the moon with one tiny foot emerging—a feature that appeared not infrequently in European sculptures—where it could be kissed by the faithful. Her mouth is open, quite uncharacteristically for European representations, and may have referred to speaking or singing; speaking, as we have noted before, was characteristic of the connection between the sacred and the human.[13] She greatly resembles a cornstalk-paste sculpture, La Virgen de la Salud (Health) de Pátzcuaro, an image commissioned in 1540 by Bishop Vasco de Quiroga and still revered at the Pátzcuaro basilica in Michoacán in western Mexico. Cornstalk paste was a pre-Columbian material used by Mexican artists to produce light but lasting figures. Fred Kline, the discoverer of the stone sculpture, which he has named the Virgin of the New World, hypothesizes that both were probably modeled on the same engraving or woodcut, perhaps from a fifteenth- or sixteenth-century prayer book. The four tassels that hang from the top of her cloak may be taken from the European model, or they may be bells, ubiquitous and significant in pre-Hispanic religious images. There are two dramatic striated circles on each side of her cape, with what may be flowers inside them. The circles are characteristic of Tezcatlipoca, the Smoking Mirror, the mysterious Aztec figure associated with the night wind, a trickster who introduced the random and the unexpected into the cosmos. Some authorities believe, following testimony by Aztec notables in the second half of the sixteenth century, that Tezcatlipoca was actually the "supreme power, omnipresent and omnipotent."[14] The specific iconography of the rosette is similar to that of the mirror, "a sacred means of understanding the universe and man himself."[15] The Virgin's gown drapes in what looks very much like feathers, highly reminiscent of Aztec representations of the feathered serpent Quetzalcoatl, the culture hero. The Virgin stands on a framed rectangular platform characteristic of both sixteenth-century Renaissance style and of the decoration on some of the pyramids at Teotihuacán. Probably this Virgin of the New World was carved by an indigenous artist, possibly for an outdoor niche or an open chapel, that is, a balcony from which priests delivered sermons to indigenous audiences in the early colonial period, when indoor accommodations were insufficient.

But a double message is quite likely here. Looking from the front, if the section with the Virgin's head and nimbus are obscured, the feathers of the gown and the crescent moon become a beak, with the rosette eyes forming the face of an owl. Moreover, if the image is turned to its very plain back, the spaces in the nimbus become the eyes of the owl, the striated nimbus itself the feathers of its head, the cape its wingspread. This feature is particularly noticeable in the shadow cast to its back if candles are positioned in front of it—as they would often have been reverently placed in the immediate post-Conquest period. The owl was very important among the Nahua, strongly associated with death and also with protection. Among the early missionaries, the association of the owl with native religion led them to use the word *tlacatecolotl*, meaning "owl man," to signify the Devil. It was also the term used by the indigenous for a particularly dangerous *nahualli*, that is, a shaman who,

Virgencita del Nuevo Mundo *(frontal view)*, *Mexico, ca. 1521–1550, unknown Aztec artisan. Photograph by Matthew Marston. Copyright Collection of Fred and Jann Kline. Courtesy Fred R. Kline Gallery, Santa Fe, New Mexico.*

Virgencita del Nuevo Mundo *(with owl shadow)*, *Mexico, ca. 1521–1550, unknown Aztec artisan. Photograph by Bob Wartell. Copyright Collection of Fred and Jann Kline. Courtesy Fred R. Kline Gallery, Santa Fe, New Mexico.*

Plate IV. Seventeenth-century mother-of-pearl image of the Virgin of Guadalupe. Although most of the original colors have faded, the red, white, and green of the Mexican national flag can still be observed in the wings of the cherub holding the edges of her robe. Courtesy of the Museo Franz Mayer, Mexico City.

in trance states, took the form of an animal. This being would inflict illness and death while appearing in owl shape. Moreover, the owl in Mesoamerican religion was an emissary from the underworld.[16] Interestingly, later in the colonial period blacks and mulattoes sometimes used tattoos of owls to signify a diabolical resistance to Christian and Spanish authority.[17] As this information comes from Inquisition records, and the indigenous were largely immune from its attentions, it is possible that they also used tattoos as resistance. The owl figures certainly evidence the continuing interpenetration of the indigenous, Spanish, and African cultures in Mexico.

It is tempting to read this image of the Virgin Mary, then, as the force of Christianity in opposition to the power of the old religion or as containing the power of both the Christian and the indigenous sacred, with the shadowy figure of Tezcatlipoca present in the eyes of the owl. It is also possible to read it as showing the power of Mary defeating and obliterating the traditional religion: the owl is hidden; death is inherent in the power of the Virgin. Yet

Seventeenth-century image in feather work of the Assumption of the Virgin. She is surrounded by a rosary held at the top by God the Father and below by Santo Domingo and San Francisco. Courtesy of the Museo Franz Mayer, Mexico City.

another reading is to associate Mary with the enormous death and illness brought by the Spanish, a killer rather than a nurturer. Or perhaps it implied her power to redeem the indigenous—and possibly the Spanish—from these disasters.

Two other fascinating images of Santa María produced in a post-Conquest version of a pre-Columbian art form can now be viewed in the Museo Franz Mayer in Mexico City. One of these representations is in feather work and probably dates from the seventeenth century. Although it is not as fine as earlier feather work figures, when this Aztec art form still retained its expertise and delicacy from the pre-Hispanic period, it is nevertheless intriguing. The work shows a sort of combination of the Virgin of the Rosary with the Immaculate Conception. Mary, characteristically, stands on the crescent moon—this time inverted with its points downward—and an aureole surrounds her head. She looks discreetly to the side, much like the renowned image of the Virgin of Guadalupe. However, she is completely encircled by a giant rosary, held at the top by God the Father and on the sides by Saint Francis and Saint Dominic, the founders of the Franciscan and Dominican orders so important in the Spanish evangelization. Another glowing representation, also from the Franz Meyer, shows an image that is clearly the traditional one of the Virgin of Guadalupe, this time completely represented in mother of pearl.[18] Other extraordinary images are two of Mary in ivory, contained in the Museo Nacional del Virreinato, in the old Jesuit convent of Tepotzotlan south of Mexico City. One of these figures, dated to the seventeenth century, is a classic example of an image to be dressed, with only the face and hands actually being carved. The crowned Virgin is filled out by her clothing into a triangular shape similar to the stone Virgin of the New World described earlier. The other is quite evidently a representation of the Virgin of Guadalupe, with hands and face of ivory and a body of wood. These figures almost undoubtedly were imported from the Far East, probably through the Spanish colony of the Philippines. As they are relatively small, they may have been intended for home altars. Strikingly, representations of Our Lady in Mexico were drawn from all parts of the empire.[19] The Denver Art Museum also has a collection of several of these images; some have distinctly Asian features. So the process of combining artistic, religious, and cultural traditions in the Spanish empire soon extended well beyond Spanish America.

The legitimacy and authenticity of these images and of the Virgin Mary within the emerging Indochristianity was immediately enhanced by the celebration of feast days and other ceremonies in her honor. These rituals enhanced as well the sense of her as an actual human being. Throughout Spain and Latin America today, the devoted speak about "her," not "it," when discussing her images. Further, dressing the figures for ritual presentations is a much-sought honor and done with *cariño*, that is, "great affection." These attitudes seem also to have been present in Mexico from very early times, reflecting the same sense of presence that was already common in Europe. For example, an icon of the Virgin attributed (almost certainly inaccurately) to Saint Luke was received and treated at state ceremonies as if it were a person.[20] In Latin America today, the same sense of liveliness in the image can be observed in the interaction between image and public at Corpus Christi in Cuzco, the Day of Guadalupe in Mexico, and hundreds of other yearly celebrations throughout the hemisphere.[21] As David Freedberg notes, "The sign has become the living embodiment of what it signifies." He goes on to say, "Then, wanting her to be there, to exist (because of the love we bear her), we willingly concentrate on the image, and what is represented in it becomes present again. She is, quite literally, re-presented." He discusses various ways in which an image becomes consecrated, and one of these, clearly, is through ritual use. He suggests that washing, garlanding, crowning, and parading the images reinforce the presence and the liveliness in the figures. I would suggest that the dressing and adorning of

This ivory image was purchased in Portugal, but it is similar to the images that arrived in New Spain. Note slightly East Asian cast to features. Madonna and Child. *Eighteenth century, ivory, Denver Art Museum Collection. Gift of Olive Bigelow, No. 1971.474.*

Latin American images operates similarly. Rituals that include having the images engage in human behavior, such as having the Lateran Christ from San Giovanni carried to Santa María Maggiore to meet the image of his Mother on the eve of the Feast of the Assumption (an event that is recorded in several manuscripts from the eleventh and twelfth centuries), certainly enhance the sense of personhood.[22] Similar rituals involving images in Latin America, accentuated by the dramas, teaching of the catechism, sermons, visions, and so forth, reinforce this presence. Moreover, the excitement of the rituals themselves, especially the processions of revered images, lead to a sense of the epiphany of Mary—her actual appearance and presence—when her image comes through the church door as she moves into the street or appears around a corner into the viewer's sight.

Motolinía reports that from soon after the Conquest, "fiestas and pascuas," that is, major celebrations such as Easter, Christmas, Epiphany, or Pentecost, were celebrated with great gusto in honor of Christ and his Mother. The celebrations included the days of the principal advocations of the individual communities, reinforcing the sense of the community within the protection of Mary that we have seen in the coming together to pray the *Ave Maria* at the corner cross. He reported:

> They adorn their churches very excellently with the trappings and orna-ments that they have, and what they lack in carpets, they make up for with branches, flowers, reeds, and sedges thrown on the floor, mint, which in this land has increased incredibly, and where the procession passes they build many triumphal arches, made of roses (flowers) with many wreaths and garlands; and they make many bouquets of flowers, really something to see, and for this reason they have in this land many gardens for flowers, and if they don't have enough they will send for them ten or twelve leagues to the towns of the hot country, where they almost always have some, and they have a very delicious odor.[23]

Here we see the elaborate preparations that, as they were in progress, would begin to heighten the sense of anticipation and significance of the proces-sion to follow. The color and texture and smell of the fresh flowers, leaves, and branches would have engaged the senses, along with the music and bodily movements of the procession itself.

He described the indigenous lords and notables in processions, dressed in white shifts and robes of elaborate feather work, with bouquets of flowers in their hands, dancing and singing songs translated for them by the friars and their Nahua helpers. The entire route of the procession would be covered with greenery, its odors released as feet danced across it. Heightening the drama and harking back to pre-Hispanic ceremonies, the singing and danc-ing often began at midnight. Candles lit up the large and beautiful patios where the people gathered, as the multitude was too large to be accommo-dated inside the churches. The singing, accompanied by drums and bells, would continue through the night and the next day. Christmas night, the priest noted, was especially beautiful, as the Indian and the Spanish faithful would put lights in the patios in front of the churches as well as on the terraces and roofs of their houses. As the houses extended for a league or perhaps two, "by night, it looked like a Heaven full of stars."[24]

The friar reported an incident that reflects the way in which the indig-enous had taken Christian ceremony to themselves. Entering a church some-what distant from his convent, he found that the people of the town had come together when the church bell was rung, as in other places it was rung to announce the mass. Although no priest was present to officiate, they recited the Hours of Our Lady, repeated their *doctrina cristiana*, and then sang the Pater Noster and the *Ave Maria*. Then the bells rang again, as if the host had been raised for the mass, and afterwards the worshipers struck their chests in front of the cross to indicate their devotion. They reported to Motolinía that they could hear mass with their souls, given the strength of their longing, since there was no one to say it for them.[25]

Motolinía also reported on two other feast days associated with Christmas. The first, the day of the Three Kings celebrated on January 6, now usually marks the end of the Christmas season in Latin America, and in many places it is the day the children receive their gifts. In the friar's report, it was a day of much devotion, with the Indians visiting the church to revere the images of Saint Mary with her "precious Son" in the manger. In his use of the term "precious Son," formulaic but filled with resonance, he emphasized as Bernal Díaz had the sense of her motherhood and her love for Christ, which at the same time resonated with their love and devotion to both figures at this ritual celebration of Christ's birth. The worshipers brought along wax and incense, birds such as doves and quail and others that they sought specially for that day, to offer to the Virgin and Child. As he reported, "the devotion they feel for this day has continued to grow until the present time." The second related feast day was that of the Purification or Candlemas (Candelaria), February 2, when the Christ Child was brought to the temple and his Mother was purified after childbirth. Similar to the celebration in Europe, the Indians brought their candles to the church for blessing. After having sung and walked in procession, he reported, they would save the stumps of the candles that remained to protect against illnesses and against thunder and lightning "because they have great devotion for Our Lady, and for having been blessed on her sainted day they value them [the candles] a great deal."[26]

He also described rituals he observed in Tlaxcala during Easter Week unlike any others that he had seen in Mexico. The reader will remember that the Tlaxcalans were the most important allies of the Spanish in the defeat of the Aztecs, and perhaps that fact increased their zeal for Christian ceremony and devotion. The figure of Mary was enormously significant at that time of the year as the suffering Mother of the martyred Christ. Starting on Holy Thursday, Motolinía reported, the Indians would begin to bring offerings to the church, dedicated to the Mother of God, laying them on a predella in front of the altar of the Blessed Sacrament. The number of these offerings increased through the following days, reaching a crescendo on Holy Saturday. But the offerings differed significantly from those he had described in other places; rather than birds and flowers and candles, they were pieces of cloth (*mantas*) brought by so many people that it seemed to him that no one in the region could have been left out. Some were blankets large enough to cover a person, others were much smaller, perhaps the size of scarves, and others more like handkerchiefs. They were embroidered with threads of cotton and rabbit fur. The decorations showed crosses, swords depicting the five wounds of Christ (which appeared on the coat of arms of the Franciscan order), the names of Jesus or of Mary, and beautiful flowers including roses, the European flowers so closely associated with the Virgin. He reported that the observed ritual took place in 1536, only fifteen years after the fall of Montezuma's empire.[27] The Virgin Mary, notably, was a major figure of reverence in all of these celebrations.

Saint Mary was also imprinting her name and her image importantly on the landscape. Churches and convents bearing her name spread across Mexico; significantly the celebrations in Tlaxcala in 1536, less than two decades after the initial conquest, were centered in the church dedicated to the Mother of God.[28] But many other sites also were named for the Virgin, and these included economic and political as well as sacred spaces. Homes and haciendas, indigenous and Spanish communities, and economic units such as mines were named for Santa María and her various advocations. In this way, she was invoked to protect families, economic enterprises, and communities old and new. The imprinting of the name of the Virgin on indigenous communities, of course, was a way of indicating Spanish and Christian power, but it was also a way for the indigenous to invoke that power for themselves.[29]

A fascinating illustration of this association is found in the depiction of the Adoration of the Magi dated 1669 that now is held in the Mexican national archives. The crude but complicated drawing shows the Virgin looking directly out at the viewer while the Christ Child pats the head of the kneeling king with both hands and kicks at him with his little feet. The king's crown sits shimmering in front of Saint Mary. The two other kings, richly dressed, stand behind them holding gifts, as does a small page. They are surrounded by a huge colonial church glyph, although Mary's cloak and that of one of the kings extends beyond this boundary. Around the outside of the large glyph are schematic houses—colonial glyphs indicating a settlement. This drawing is in fact a place glyph designating the tiny town of Los Reyes (the Three Kings) in the present state of Mexico. Here, although the name of the Virgin does not appear in the name of the hamlet, she is nevertheless a central figure in the way that location is considered and depicted.[30]

Mexico City itself, which grew throughout the Valley of Mexico to include the major Aztec cities and those of other groups, was soon marked by four Marian sites in the four cardinal directions. These locations reflected the significance of the four directions in all the Middle American pre-Columbian cultures; they were also significant for the Spanish. Jesuit Father Florencia, who undertook major studies of the Virgin Mary in Mexico in the late seventeenth century, exulted, "Can this presence of four miraculous images at the four poles of the city be accidents? That those of the East and West are both made similarly and of the same size . . . ? The four sides of this land are in the hands of the Lord and the Virgin." The four Virgins were prodigious indeed: in the west was the sanctuary of Our Lady of Remedios; to the east, Nuestra Señora de la Bala (Our Lady of the Bullet); to the south, Nuestra Señora de la Piedad (Our Lady of Piety); and north from the city, that prodigy of prodigies, the Virgin of Guadalupe, "the North Star of Mexico," as she was termed by Father Florencia.[31]

Miraculous images of the Virgin were securing Christianity to the landscape throughout the seventeenth and eighteenth centuries. Although Franciscans had used images for teaching and had encouraged the reverence due pre-Columbian sites to be transferred to Christ, the saints, and especially Our Lady, they soon became more cautious as the perils of this process became clear. The friars had never been particularly enthusiastic about Marian or other miracles. They were also concerned that indigenous peoples were confusing, perhaps deliberately, pre-Christian worship with Christian forms, a process enhanced with instances of the "miraculous." However, in the latter part of the sixteenth century, as secularization proceeded and the friars became less important, both Mexican church councils and the Council of Trent gave particular importance to the cult of saints. The number of images of Mary and their miraculous interventions soared thereafter. Moreover, at about the same time, the Nahua versions of Christian scriptures and prayers were suppressed by the Holy Office of the Inquisition, which had been established in Mexico in 1571. Most manuscript literature was confiscated from the indigenous at that time. Image, as a result, quickly became far more important in extending Christian spirituality than text.[32]

Many of the images of Mary began their histories of prodigies, at least as the stories developed, from the moments of their discoveries in New Spain. Indeed, the circumstances under which they were located were often miraculous. Images of the Virgin were found in the trunks of trees, floating in rivers or oceans, hidden in caves. The Mediterranean association of Mary with water had arrived in the Spanish New World with Columbus; it was reinforced in New Spain and elsewhere quite easily by the relation of the pre-Columbian sacred feminine with water and fertility. The trees and caves also reflected fertility in the close connection with the earth.

The stories themselves often duplicated or closely resembled the European models. They might be associated with high places, Mexican hills and mountains, which had had numinous significance before the Conquest. Not infrequently they were discovered by indigenous persons or those of humble background, providing the same power inversions that they had made possible, from time to time, in Europe. Again, the representations of Mary threatened to escape the control of the hierarchic Church, and not all of the miracle stories were equally acceptable to the Spanish. Miracles were useful as a tool of conversion and to solidify Christian spirituality; at the same time, particularly as long as they were associated with the Virgin Mary, they were to some degree dangerous, likely to escape ecclesiastical control, and therefore potentially controversial.

The miraculous discoveries, sometimes rediscoveries, and activities of these figures of the Virgin made up, to some degree, for the fact that actual relics of Mary were precluded by her bodily ascension into Heaven. Moreover, because the Americas were even more distant from the Holy Land than Europe, touch relics were also unlikely. Thus amazing behaviors and prodigies became legitimizing and even consecrating factors. According to art historian David Freedberg, "By means of the proper rites, the deity is induced to inhabit the piece of inanimate matter. Then it becomes an object suitable for worship and capable of bestowing help." Though Saint Mary was not strictly speaking a deity, nor was she to be worshiped but rather revered, these distinctions were not widely recognized, and she was certainly expected to bestow help. He further points out, "Consecration either turns the image into a receptacle for the sacred or confirms the sacred as already present by publicly heightening it."[33] Although no doubt rituals and ceremonies of consecration were performed for many Christian images, it seems here that the reports of the actions of the images themselves or the amazing events surrounding the discoveries were more significant in making them legitimate and believable than any formal rituals. Additionally, the circumstances of these discoveries often tied them securely to specific spots in the landscape. At the same time, the image of Mary could be seen as taking possession of the particular sacred space, in effect taking it over from the pre-Spanish deities and resanctifying it as Christian and, moreover, hers.[34] Inherent in the process was the danger that the old deities could be worshiped under the guise of Our Lady.

These images often made clear that they wanted to stay in particular places. One image of the Virgen de la Soledad, brought from Guatemala by mule, made her home in Oaxaca after she refused to move beyond the doors of a convent of Augustinian nuns.[35] The famous Virgin of Remedios also made special demands, as we will see below.[36] Frequently these demands included a request for a sanctuary to be built to house her image. Sometimes these requests were made by an apparition not yet connected to an image, as in the very special but not entirely unusual case of the Mexican Virgin of Guadalupe. Yet another case, less well known but very interesting because of its circumstances, was the carving of Mary found in the early seventeenth century in the trunk of a tree in the region of Cuautla by an Indian woman. Sold in Veracruz by an unscrupulous member of the community, the image of the Virgin managed to return to the altar where she had originally been installed. Her devotion to the town proved fortunate. During a terrible earthquake in 1712, she extended the rosary in her hand toward the trembling wall, and it was miraculously sustained. She remains in this posture today.[37]

Representations also appeared on cloth. The Virgin of the Sleeve was so called because she had appeared where tears had fallen on the sleeve of a nun who had been recalling the sorrows of Mary during Christ's Passion.[38] The miraculous Virgin of Texacic, in the valley of Toluca, was painted on a canvas of rough cotton, more typically indigenous than a nun's sleeve. This image performed many miracles from the sixteenth century on. These were prodigies particularly associated with the non-urban milieu in which they were found and involved rural workers such as mule drivers and herders, as well as natural phenomena like lightning, rushing rivers, and dangerous pools.[39]

Just as they had in Spain, Mary's miracles in Mexico often involved children. Such miracles reinforced the presence of the Virgin and her protection with special regard to these enormously valuable members of the society. Precious to the Spanish, children would establish the Spanish future in the New World; given the death from disease and other disasters among the indigenous, children were key to the continuation of anything that was familiar to them. The stories were legion. One little girl who had drowned in a well was saved when the Virgin raised the water level so that the child's body could be recovered, and then she resuscitated her. Yet another child, the daughter of fishermen, was revived by Our Lady of San Juan de los Lagos, one of the most powerful advocations outside of Mexico City, whose cult grew significantly in the seventeenth century. The same image also made an honest man out of a thief and healed illnesses, her miracles totaling three hundred by 1666.[40] Other children were cured of disease by the dozens, and images of the Virgin continued to help with fertility, that most important of issues in a rebuilding and repopulating society.[41]

The Mary of the New World was also closely associated with water, a relationship that was constantly reinforced in terms of where she was found and of the miracles she performed. In Papantla a figure of the Virgin of the Immaculate Conception was found floating in the sea in a box marked "FOR

PAPANTLA." Another Concepción was found on the banks of the River Coatzacoalcos. An image of Our Lady of Solitude was reportedly found by Cortés's men floating in the same river in 1546. The story went that a rainbow had appeared there miraculously twelve years before, denoting, according to the Spaniard who reported it, the imminent "cessation of the flood of idolatry." With the arrival of Cortés's troops, the rainbow disappeared, leaving the figure floating where the base of the rainbow had touched the river.[42] These stories were reminiscent of tales from the Canary Islands, where even before the arrival of the Iberians an image of Mary with the baby Jesus was found on the coast of Tenerife and had requested and received a sanctuary.[43] In a similar story, an image of the Virgin of the Rosary appeared off the beaches in Brazil.[44] The idea of the Virgin arriving by water and then insisting on staying close to where she was found and establishing herself on the land must have had resonance for the migrating Iberians. In fact, Mary's desire for a new home reflected their own.

Although Spanish sailors no longer had to fear sailing into the void or off the edge of the earth, water remained dangerous or, at the very least, fickle. The Virgin's power to control the significant substance was therefore extremely important. Our Lady of Izamal, one of the oldest images in the Yucatan, was brought from Guatemala in 1558. Although her trip was interrupted by a violent thunderstorm, the chest in which she was being carried remained dry. She also insisted on remaining in a certain spot, choosing the Indians of Izamal over the Spaniards of Valladolid, and immediately proved her efficacy by restoring life to a few corpses.[45] Sailors continued to be favored by Our Lady; one of them grew a new tongue after losing the original to pirates. Our Lady of Piety, whose church was founded in 1535, helped to save the shipwrecked.[46] The Virgin also helped consistently, as she had in Spain, with problems of drought and flooding. An image of Mary known as La Conquistadora, which according to a 1582 report had been given by Cortés to Tlaxcaltecan nobleman Gonzalo Axotécatl Cocomitzi, was reported as useful in bringing abundant rain.[47] According to the Jesuit Father Alegre, the Virgin was never so helpful as when she brought rainfall to the drought-plagued northern state of Sinaloa in 1599.[48] She could stop the rain as well. Guadalupe herself was invoked in 1629 in the Valley of Mexico, a region prone to disastrous flooding. On this occasion she did not prove particularly efficacious, and it took four years for the waters to recede.[49] Yet another image, in Santa Clara, went out of her sanctuary to stop a terrible storm and returned "dripping and covered with mud."[50]

From the very beginning of the Conquest, Mary was associated with Spanish victory. The various images known as La Conquistadora and linked, at least by legend, to the ones that Cortés distributed are testimony to that. The Virgin could protect herself as well. Our Lady of the Macana, that is, of the club, had received her name after a rebel Indian inspired by the Devil attacked her with such a weapon. She remained largely unharmed, but the Indian was later found hanged from a tree.[51] Remedios continued to be associated in Spanish minds, and perhaps indigenous ones as well, with Spanish victories. A later example of an image ready to protect her own was Our Lady of the Bullet, so called because she saved an unfaithful wife by moving in front of a shot aimed at the woman by her jealous spouse.[52] Not a situation of war, other than a domestic one, it was nevertheless an example of the protection the Virgin extended to her faithful. The story spread, although the message of the story went against the gender rules the Church was trying to propagate.

In fact, the Virgin intervened often to save women or female youth from sexual assault. A story recounted by Motolinía tells of a young Indian woman who was amorously approached by a young bachelor. When she resisted his blandishments, "the Devil awakened in yet another," who tried the same thing. When she turned him down as well, the two men kidnapped her from the door of her house, carried her off to a neighboring dwelling, and tried to force her to yield. Calling on God and Santa María, she defended herself valiantly. Despite being badly beaten, she successfully resisted and the next day was able to escape to a nearby school run by nuns for the daughters of noble Indians. After explaining her plight to the mother superior of the convent, she was allowed to stay and study although her family had no money or status "because God had extended his hand to her."[53] Although God himself was perceived as having saved her, it was certainly Mary's example of chastity that was invoked by the story and not at all an accident that the young woman called upon Mary, along with God, in her extremity.

The case is even clearer in Motolinía's story that immediately follows the one above in his *Historia*. In this case, a young widow was approached by a married man, who tried to press his sexual attentions on her. She reproached him, saying, "You think that because I have no husband to protect me, you can offend God by harming me? You now think of nothing else, although we are both members of the confraternity of Our Lady, although in this action we would offend her much and she would become very angry with us, and we would no longer be worthy to be called members of the confraternity or take her blessed candles in our hands; for this reason, you must leave me alone and desire me no more, as I have determined to die before committing such a terrible thing."[54] Note that although the woman, according to Motolinía, saw the offense as against God, it was in fact Our Lady who she feared would be offended and angry and whose candles they would no longer be worthy of carrying. The Virgin, in both of these cases, was the preserver of the sexual chastity of the two women, both of them besieged by men who would breach their bodily integrity. The message was as strong for the second woman as for the first, although as a widow she was certainly no longer technically virgin.

By the end of the seventeenth century, as previously noted, Mexico City was ringed by miraculous images of the Virgin at the four signs of the compass in addition to the dozens of others within the city proper. These sites not only set off the space of the city as now Spanish but safely placed it within the protection of the Virgin. As Father Florencia noted, "If we are guarded and defended by the Lord through his Mother on four sides, if the Lord put four images of his Mother as sentinels to watch out for us at its four angles, who will be able to invade and offend this city?"[55] Remedios to the west and Guadalupe in the north were by far the most important. These two would become the basis for cults that extended well beyond their areas, cults that seemed to have begun very quickly after the Spanish triumph.[56] Both advocations were closely associated with hills, significant sites in the pre-Spanish sacred landscape.

The story of Remedios, as told by various colonial authors, associated this small statue of the Virgin holding the baby Jesus with one placed in the Templo Mayor in Tenochtitlan by Juan Rodríguez de Villafuerte during the original Spanish occupation. We have already seen that there is evidence that a painting was so placed; this one may have been in addition to that one, or there may simply be confusion about the nature of that first image. Still, according to the story, during the retreat of the Noche Triste, the little statue protected the Spanish. One of them left her hidden in a maguey plant on a hill near Totoltépec west of the city, where she was found in 1540 after appearing to a recently converted Indian, Juan Ce Cuauhtli (Juan One Eagle), also known as Juan de Tobar. The reader will recognize the similarity of the story to those told about the images of the Virgin hidden during the Moorish occupation of the peninsula and recovered during the Reconquest. Juan, possibly a Christianized chief who had been among the natives during the Noche Triste, reported the incident to the Franciscan friars living nearby in Tacuba. However, the friars warned him that as a lowly Indian it was unlikely that the Blessed Mother would have appeared to him. They attributed his vision to his lively imagination. Juan, devout in his new religion, then avoided Totoltépec hill. Later, while helping construct the church at Tacuba, he fell from the scaffolding and was gravely hurt. He was given confession and taken home to die. Miraculously, at midnight, the Virgin appeared again, giving him a belt that cured him of all his injuries. A few days later, while searching for food on the mountain, he was guided into the ruins of a pre-

Columbian temple—dedicated to the wind manifestation of Quetzalcoatl, Ehecatl—and there he found under a maguey the hidden statue of the Virgin of Remedios holding her Child. Juan took the image to his home, where it was placed on the household altar. Despite careful tending, including the provision of all sorts of flowers and scented herbs and offerings of tortillas, eggs, water, fruit, and *mole*, Remedios was unhappy in her new home and kept disappearing again to the pre-Columbian ruins where she had first been found. Finally, after thirteen years of retrieving her, Juan decided to build a small chapel on the site to accommodate her visitors as they came in search of comfort and miracles. Another tradition says that Cortés himself ordered the original owner, Rodríguez de Villafuerte, to construct a small sanctuary on the hill, which was known as the Hill of the Birds.[57] Again reflecting stories that occurred through the Reconquest and Conquest, the Virgin became attached to a particular sacred spot by making her wishes known.

According to Linda Curcio-Nagy, Remedios was an important source of devotion in the locality during the sixteenth century, although a general devotion to the cult of saints characterizing native Christianity was more common in the seventeenth. She believes that it is possible that "a local native nobleman discovered an image in a pre-Columbian temple that became a major center of devotion to his constituent villagers and that through his aegis a small shrine was constructed."[58] By 1595 a shrine was in place, decorated by ten large murals relating to miracles performed by Remedios. Although, according to the murals, both the indigenous and the Spanish benefited from her help, particular attention was focused on devout natives from the immediate area and those who came as pilgrims to the church. One painting showed the Virgin presenting the staff of office to a native leader while saying in Latin, "Peace be with you. You are no longer guests or strangers but citizens of the House of God." In this way, as Curcio-Nagy points out, the indigenous were welcomed and defined as Christians. The indigenous sign of the governing staff and the ubiquitous use of images of the sun identified the murals, and at the same time the Virgin, with Native American political authority and spirituality.[59] Moreover, Remedios also quickly became associated with Mexico City and its governing *cabildo* (city council). Between 1577 and 1696, this body brought the image from her shrine into the city eighteen times. She was connected with saving the city from illnesses and epidemics, droughts and other water-related problems, and difficulties with harvests. The latter sorts of problems might seem to be more rural than urban in their implications, but harvests, of course, were crucial to feeding the cities.[60]

Another reported appearance of Mary to a devout Indian would lead to the most powerful cult of the Virgin in the Americas and, arguably, in the world:

that of Guadalupe. Her apparition, according to tradition, followed the Spanish victory in Tenochtitlan by only ten years, although the major documentary
accounts date from the middle of the seventeenth century. As the story goes, a
poor Indian named Juan Diego from the town of Cuauhtitlán was making his
way to receive religious instruction at the Franciscan establishment at Tlatelolco.
As he was passing the hill of Tepeyac just at dawn, he heard precious birds
singing on the hillside, and he wondered if he were in the land of flowers and
sunshine, that is, the Nahua version of paradise. Going up the hill toward the
east he encountered a splendid noblewoman surrounded by radiance. The ground
around her gleamed like a rainbow, and the plants on the hillside seemed to be
of jade and turquoise, their stalks and thorns of gold.[61]

As he knelt before her, she asked where he was going, addressing him as
"my youngest child." He replied, "Great Lady and my daughter, I am on my
way to Mexico Tlatelolco, to search for divine knowledge that the priests, the
delegates of Our Lord, give and teach us there." Hearing of his intention,
she revealed to him that she was the "ever Virgin Saint Mary, the Mother of
the true God . . . Lord of heaven and of the earth." Then she asked him to
see to her urgent wish that a temple to her should be built on the plain below
the hillside, a temple where she could dispense her mercy and her love to
those who sought her and confided in her. To achieve this end, she asked him
to go to the palace of the bishop in the city of Mexico to express her desire.[62]

Predictably, though Juan was received by the bishop, the prelate sent him
away with a request that he return at another time. Returning to the beautiful Lady, he protested that because of his low status—"a leaf, a person of no
account"—he was unworthy and unable to plead her case effectively.[63] She
replied that she had many followers and messengers from whom to choose
but that she wanted him to convey her message to the bishop. She ordered
him to return to the bishop's palace the next morning, a Sunday. This he did,
and this time the bishop listened more carefully, but he still requested that
Juan Diego bring him a sign of the Sainted Virgin's favor. On his way home,
he again stopped at the hill, where the Virgin appeared to him. On being told
of the bishop's request for a sign, she replied, "That's all right, my little son,
return here tomorrow so that you can take the bishop what he has asked for;
with this sign he will believe you."[64] But the next day he was unable to return,
as his uncle Juan Bernardino was gravely ill. Juan Diego hastened to find a
physician, but Juan Bernardino continued to languish. He then promised his
uncle that the next morning early he would go to Tlatelolco to find a priest
to administer the last rites.

Thus, on Tuesday morning, he set out early to call on the priest, but he
went around to the other side of the hill, fearing that he would be detained

Plate V. This image of the Virgin was over the entrance to the sacristy of the church of Guadalupe in Santa Fe, New Mexico, in 1883. Pope Benedict XIV, who officially recognized the cult of Guadalupe in 1754, is depicted on the left, while opposite him is a personification of New Spain. A view of the Mexico City sanctuary lies between them. The four episodes of the apparition story and three miracles performed by the Virgin are depicted. Our Lady of Guadalupe, Sebastian Salcedo, 1779, oil on copper, 62.9 by 47.5 cm, Denver Art Museum Collection. Funds contributed by Mr. and Mrs. George G. Anderman and an anonymous donor. No. 1976.56.

by the heavenly Lady. But then he saw her coming down from the summit of the hill to meet him. Again she asked him where he was going. Ashamed, he explained the circumstances of his uncle's illness. She assured him that she had already healed his uncle and that Juan Diego must fulfill his promise to her. To provide a sign for the bishop, she sent him to the top of the hill to collect the flowers there, flowers typical not of Mexico and certainly not of the rocky, cactus-strewn mountain, but rather roses of Spain. These he wrapped into his maguey-fiber cloak. With her reassurance that he was "her ambassador, very worthy of confidence," he set off again for Mexico City.[65]

Although this time he had a great deal of difficulty getting past the bishop's minions, he let them peek at the roses in his cloak. When they tried to take them off of the cloak, they could not, as it seemed that they were sewn or painted there. When Juan Diego was finally led in to see the bishop, he opened his cloak, the roses tumbled out, and on the inside of his cloak, or *tilma*, they found a beautiful painting of the Blessed Virgin, her skin "a bit dark."[66] Later, returning home, Juan Diego found his uncle cured by Mary's efforts. Juan Diego and Juan Bernardino then returned to spend several days in the bishop's house while the chapel was being constructed. According to this account, the people of the entire city were "much amazed that the Virgin had appeared by a divine miracle, because no one, in this world, had painted her precious image."[67]

Burkhart has noted how the version of this story with which we are familiar, a version that appeared in the middle of the seventeenth century in a series of written accounts by clerics of Spanish descent, fits well with Nahua spirituality. A Nahuatl version was published in 1649, one year after the publication of the first Spanish account, and from it we draw our summary above. It appeared under the name of the vicar of Guadalupe's chapel, Luis Lasso de la Vega, although its actual authorship has been much disputed; it has been claimed that one or more indigenous nobles were responsible for it and that the Lasso de la Vega publication largely copied their work.[68] Be that as it may, the version we have contains elements of European miracle accounts along with elements that would have been resonant with indigenous spirituality and appealing within the emerging Indochristianity. The Virgin appears at sunrise on a hilltop—a numinous place. Her arrival suffuses the area with light and beautiful sound as tropical birds sing and the rocks shimmer and appear to be jade and turquoise and gold. The Nahua idea of the sacred "flower world" filled with light and warmth and fragrance and music is evident in the setting. Indeed, Juan Diego imagines that perhaps he has been transported into a sacred world, either that of the "sunshine land" of the "grandfathers" or the heaven of the Christians. The birds named are typical of those invoked in Nahua accounts of the flower world, while roses,

European flowers associated with Mary in many Nahuatl texts, appear as well and would have been appealing and familiar by this time in a Nahua-Christian context. Moreover, it is important to note that for the Nahua, the "other world" was not an immaterial but rather a material world transformed from the ordinary to the sacred.[69] The appearance, therefore, would have been even more likely to be accepted as the actual presence of the Virgin, a sign of contact and transformation onto a spiritual plane. European Christians had the strong sense of Mary's actual presence in their communications with her; Nahua spirituality was even more open to such a possibility.

That Remedios and Guadalupe both appeared on hilltops is significant. Such locations were important and numinous in pre-Christian times and continued these associations after the arrival of the Spanish. The Aztec glyph *tepetl* signified hill, and when accompanied by the sign for water was used to designate *altepetl*, a most important communal unit described by James Lockhart as "an ethnic state . . . holding sway over a given territory."[70] Burr Brundage suggests that the elements of water and hill were the important criteria for settlement, combining as they did agricultural and defensive advantages. Brundage also suggests that this concept of "mountain" referred to "a whole environment, a homeland."[71] Mountains were sacred and dangerous, birthplaces for gods and culture heroes, sources of powerful winds that brought disease to those unfortunate enough to encounter them.[72] Typically, in central Mexico, the image of the god of the locality was kept at its home mountain. Indeed, the Aztec temple complex in Tenochtitlan seems to have been conceived of as a mountain, with the top of the temple the place where ordinary reality was transformed into the sacred, the place of sacrifice. Less extreme rituals also took place in high places, but the centrality of the mountain or its constructed surrogate, the pyramid, is clear in the spirituality of the Nahua and other central Mexican groups. Huitzilopochtli, the preeminent Aztec god, was conceived by his mother Coatlicue when she was ritually cleaning the summit of a mountain, and the sacred enclosure of temples in Tenochtitlan was dominated by the pyramid that replayed that story. This structure was known as Coatepetl, "Snake Mountain."[73] The temple faced west so the sun, Huitzilopochtli, would rise at its back and move forward to illuminate the front.[74]

The similarity with the story of Guadalupe is evident; she also appeared on the summit of the sacred hill, Tepeyac or Tepayacac, a rock associated in pre-Spanish times with the earth mother, although scholars differ about just which manifestation and what the pre-Columbian goddess was called. She came at dawn, the time of solar return associated with Huitzilopochtli. And she selected the high place, the place of the sacred.

Remedios shared the high places with Guadalupe. She appeared on the hill of Totoltépec, sacred to the ancient goddess Toci, while Guadalupe appeared at Tepeyac or Tepeyacac. Various goddess of the sun and moon—Cihuacoatl-Toci-Tonantzin, Xochiquetzal-Chalchihuitlicue-Ilamateuctli, and even Yoalticitl, related with curing, baths, and midwives—were associated with Tepeyac and the ranges nearby.[75] Tonantzin is the one most often mentioned, but this term in Nahuatl actually means "our revered mother," a title that the friars and their converted Nahua helpers were promoting as a title for the Virgin herself. The term appears to be a generic reference to other goddesses of the earth as well. Probably it was used initially as a Nahua translation for Mary, not some indigenous manifestation of the sacred feminine.[76] In any case, the site itself had long been regarded as numinous and related to pre-Columbian goddesses as well as to other sacred sites in the Quauhtepec mountain range.[77] It seems to have been associated with the sanctuary at the summit of Mount Tlaloc, of which the great pyramid of Tenochtitlan may have been a man-made representation. This connection to the powerful old god of rain and fertility is even more intriguing, considering Richard Townsend's determination that the temple complex on Mount Tlaloc was a "diagrammatic womb of the earth, containing the source of water and regenerative forces." It therefore contained strong associations with the sacred of both genders. The complex was the site of pilgrimages undertaken by the kings of Texcoco, Tenochtitlan, Tlacopan, and Xochimilco during the dry season to ensure the return of the rains. According to Townsend, "the kings, bearing offerings and sacrifices, fertilized the interior microcosm." Shortly after their pilgrimage, the storms of the rainy months would begin.[78] The pathway between Tepeyac and Yoaltecatl, another important ceremonial location, is oriented precisely to that giving access to the sanctuary at the top of Mount Tlaloc, indicating an important connection between the three sites. Tepeyac was also associated with water and fertility, and it was until recently the site of a medicinal spring.[79]

Alberro tells us that even now the Otomies and other native groups continue to call the Virgin of Guadalupe "mother moon" or "old mother," connecting the Virgin of Tepeyac to a possible Otomí origin. Remedios as well has an Otomí connection; the hill where she appeared was also known as Otomcapulco, the place of the Otomies. Later, after the episode of the Spanish retreat in Tenochtitlan and the Noche Triste, it was predictably known as the "Hill of Victory." The friar Diego Durán reported that in pre-Spanish times, a chapel to a feminine deity had been located there. Both apparitions were linked to the maguey plant, with the image of Remedios found hidden beneath one of them, while the cloak of Juan Diego on which Guadalupe appeared was made of maguey fibers. Even now, a drink extracted from the maguey that is used in rituals in San Juan Atzingo, an indigenous community in the valley of Toluca, is identified with the mother's milk of the Virgin of Guadalupe.[80] Jacques Galinier affirms this:

> The relationship between the maguey and cosmic fertility persists today in various symbols of the Christian religion. In this way, the Virgin of Remedies has been converted into the protector saint of magueys. In popular iconography, this Virgin is represented over a maguey, an image of mayahuel, the Aztec divinity of the same plant.[81]

Alberro finds further connections between the two in that they

> both appeared to indigenous men whose names were associated with the Eagle: Remedios to Juan Ce Cuauhtli, that is, Juan One Eagle, and Guadalupe to Juan Diego Cuautlatoazin, the Eagle that Sings. Juan Diego was a resident of Cuauhtitlán, a population of Otomies and Nahuas, and he may well have been Otomí. Further, the first known official pilgrimage to Tepeyac originated in the Otomí region of Querétaro, though its late date, 1886, makes the connection more tenuous. Still, in some Otomí pueblos, religious geography is still divided according to a principle of dualism—two complementary hills representing the two opposing halves. With Remedios and Guadalupe, we may be looking at sisters representing two halves of a whole.[82]

Whether or not we accept Alberro's interesting ideas about the Otomí origins of these two cults, it seems clear to me, nevertheless, that they are related to one or another or perhaps many manifestations of the pre-Columbian sacred feminine. Certainly, diverse pre-Columbian feminine deities were merged, conflated, and overridden in much the same way that the Virgin would merge, conflate with, and override sacred figures in other places, particularly the Andes. It is still unclear just when the stories about these cases became crystallized and began to circulate widely in Mexico, an issue to which we will return in Chapter VII. It is interesting, nevertheless, to see them as connected and at the same time opposed.

What seems evident to me is that following the Conquest, Marian devotion became widespread in central Mexico among the indigenous peoples and was conflated with the symbols and spaces of pre-Spanish religious belief. By the seventeenth century, her position as protector, miracle-worker, and active advocate for the Nahua and other indigenous peoples in the region was well established. Not just the Virgin of Guadalupe, but swarms of advocations and images of Mary were present and revered. Though by no means identical to or simply substituted for indigenous goddesses, she was often associated with indigenous sacred spaces. These connections, although they made the representatives of the Church nervous, were nevertheless key in establishing Christian worship in forms that were intelligible to the native peoples and served their needs.

Perhaps the clearest case that we have of the insertion of the Virgin into the realm of the indigenous sacred is that of the Virgin of Ocotlán. Studied by anthropologists Hugo Nutini and Betty Bell, it presents a fascinating case that is strikingly similar to those of Remedios and Guadalupe.[83] Her appearance is reported in a document written by the Franciscan Fray Martín de Hojacastro in Tlaxcala to his superior in Mexico City that claims to date from 1547. However, it should be noted that the first currently available manuscript that scholars have been able to locate appeared in 1662. No doubt at least partly inspired by the publication of the Guadalupe story fifteen years earlier, this Nahuatl account was written by an indigenous Tlaxcalan cacique making a claim for the Virgin's favor for his own region.[84] The date noted for the appearance is 1541, ten years later than Guadalupe, if that story is to be believed. Although the dating may be early and the document (if it is authentic at all) may actually have been produced several decades later, it nevertheless illustrates the desire of the Spanish to establish an early date for the native devotion to the Virgin. According to the report, on May 12, 1541, Juan Diego Bernardino, an indigenous resident of a small town eight kilometers south of the city of Tlaxcala, witnessed the early-morning appearance of the Virgin Mary in a wooded area on a hillside south of that city. The site was significant, less than one hundred meters from the old temple of Xochiquetzal, a mother goddess associated with flowers, arts, and games. Juan Diego Bernardino reported that she appeared within a burning *ocote* (a kind of pine tree) wearing a blue *huipil* (an indigenous blouse) and a white *titixtli* (a native wraparound skirt). The document describes the native man as a convert of humble circumstances, "pious, devoted, alert, and always anxious and willing to learn about the new religion, and with an inner glow, which ... set him apart from the other attendants at the convent."[85] Nutini supposes that the name Bernardino was significant, as it was associated with the Franciscan identification of San Bernardino and Camaxtli, the pre-Conquest tutelary god of the Tlaxcalans. Juan Diego Bernardino had been connected with the convent for more than ten years at the time of the appearance, and it was noted candidly in the document that he was as Christianized as possible, given the pagan practices that persisted among many of the Tlaxcalan Indians. The Virgin unsurprisingly was interested in having her sanctuary built nearby, over the ruins of the temple of Xochiquetzal. This goddess was the most important deity of the region after Camaxtli and was closely associated with this tribal god, whose festival took place in March, conveniently close to the Christian celebration of Easter. Xochiquetzal's own festival was observed in May, conveniently Mary's month, *el mes de María.*

News of the apparition spread rapidly, the document reported, and within a few days pilgrims had flooded to the area from all over the Tlaxcalan region. The enthusiasm among the indigenous was so strong that the presiding friar (who would have been Motolinía, who seems to have written nothing on the subject, or Fray Diego de Olarte) began the authentication of the miracle, and within three years the cult of the Virgin of Ocotlán was in place.

Nutini and Bell analyze this event in terms of what they call "guided syncretism," which they define as

> almost equivalent to religious acculturation; when two religious systems meet (in a variety of contexts which may include voluntary interaction, forced acceptance, social and political pressures, and the like) the resultant religious system is different from the two original interacting systems, because of mutual, albeit often unequal, borrowings and lendings, which are internalized and interpreted into a process of action and reaction.

They go on to analyze the "resultant religion" that developed in the Tlaxcalan region under the direction of the Franciscans of the early sixteenth century.[86]

The major points of identification between the Virgin and Xochiquetzal are quite clear, according to Nutini and Bell as well as Fray Martín. Both were regarded in their respective cosmic systems as the Mother of God; both are associated with goodness and with flowers, have the power to intercede on behalf of human individuals with more powerful entities, and are believed to have the power to grant wishes; their most important rituals take place in May; Mary appeared near Xochiquetzal's temple; the circumstances of the Virgin's appearance in terms of dress and choice of messenger were identical to those of Xochiquetzal. Still, the Virgin of Ocotlán was not identical to Xochiquetzal in the year of her appearance, nor is she today, as Nutini and Bell point out. Rather, she is a "new supernatural entity partaking of the interacting natures of both Xochiquetzalli and the Virgin Mary." According to them, when the Virgin appeared to Juan Diego Bernardino, it initiated a syncretic process (within their careful definition) in which Mary is identified with the "structural context" of the deity with which the indigenous were familiar, Xochiquetzal. Nutini and Bell identify this process as a confusion and cross-identification of the two religious figures. As the physical signs and rituals of the old religion began to disappear, and along with them the Indians' remembrance and understanding of pre-Conquest ways, they began to think more and more within the context of the Catholic order yet retained some idea of their older religious practice. Nutini and Bell find that this stage was "marked by a serious struggle at the conscious and unconscious levels between the receding and emerging structural orders." This second stage, they indicate, was so fluid and contained so many variables and possibilities that the process escaped the control of those introducing the new religion. Among the elements to be considered here would be the social and religious needs of the Tlaxcalans, the roles of the local religious hierarchies that to some degree replaced the friars, and the nature of rewards and sanctions in regard to religious devotion. Finally, a "new ideological order" emerged as the old religion as such was forgotten, with the cult of the Virgin of Ocotlán retaining elements and meanings from the earlier period. In other words, she was now structurally and functionally a "Catholic supernatural" but retained aspects—the place of her temple, the color of her clothing, and so forth—of the pre-Catholic sacred.[87]

Remedios, Guadalupe, and Ocotlán were instances, and by no means the only ones, of the Virgin's movement into the spaces of the pre-Columbian sacred, both literally and figuratively. As Fernando Cervantes notes, the Hojacastro document itself, even if it dates from the seventeenth and not the sixteenth century, "points to the existence of a strong unofficial tradition that tolerated the persistence of pre-Hispanic elements and their incorporation into the ceremonies and rituals of Christianity."[88] Sometimes these figures and spaces into which the Virgin moved were gendered feminine. As early as Cortés's conquests, the Spanish were placing the Virgin Mary in indigenous shrines and on indigenous temples. The earliest evangelizers, the friars, were devoted to the Virgin but conflicted about capitalizing on her image and especially her miracles, fearing that Santa María would be too closely conflated with pre-Spanish gods and goddesses. Later, as the friars lost their special position with the native populations and were replaced by seculars, even these reservations faded. Mary and her miracles, her active ability to help those in need, were more and more important in establishing native devotion. It is a matter of dispute how rapidly the cults of Remedios, Ocotlán, and Guadalupe spread through native populations, and virtually all of the documented discussion dates from the seventeenth century. It seems probable from the data that we do have, though, that the cult of the Virgin grew quickly during the sixteenth century among the Indians, who had been shaken by military defeat, significant cultural collapse, and high mortality rates from illness. But this Mary was one who responded to, was shaped by, and reflected and was reflected in indigenous as well as Spanish culture and in the hybrid culture that emerged in post-Conquest Mexico.

CHAPTER SIX

The Andean Virgin

✠ ✠ ✠

THE VIRGIN MARY came to the Andes with the conquerors. From the Spanish excuses for the massacre of 1532 at Cajamarca—involving the supposed unwillingness of Atahualpa to accept the story of the Virgin birth—to the Virgin's decisive appearance in battles, she soon made her mark on the victories in that region as well. After he and his men took Atahualpa prisoner at Cajamarca, Pizarro headed almost immediately for Cuzco, the center of Inka power. Entering the city on November 15, 1533, he took possession in the name of the Spanish crown but appointed Manco Inka as emperor in order to maintain authority over the indigenous peoples. Just over a year later, he founded the city of Lima on the coastal plains in the valley of the Rimac River, effectively separating the indigenous and American highlands from the more European-settled coast. At the same time, grave differences among the Spanish led them to fight among themselves and eventually to resist the imposition of imperial control. Francisco and his brothers Juan and Gonzalo would die in these struggles—Juan in battle against Manco Inka's forces after Spanish mistreatment forced the Inka leader to rebel in 1536; Francisco in Lima in 1541, assassinated by his former allies; and Gonzalo in 1548, beheaded for treason after his forces were defeated by armies supporting the establishment of Spanish imperial power.

Despite the disorder, the reverence for the Virgin—who was seen as the protector of the Spanish (on whatever side) during these struggles—began to spread, particularly in the latter half of the sixteenth century. Churches were dedicated to her in native sacred spaces, and she began to be substituted for, blended with, and understood as formerly Andean representatives of the powerful and the holy. Images of her were created by Andean artists as well as Spanish ones and proliferated throughout the region. They began to be used in the ceremonies of the conquerors, ceremonies designed to illustrate and celebrate European hegemony. But these images and rituals had an edge: they could be used to perpetuate or at least remember pre-Conquest ideas and hierarchies. In the Andes, as in Mexico, the results in art, spiritual and ceremonial life, and political power were hybrid. Just as a native Christianity developed in Mexico, so it would happen in the Andes as well, although the pre-Columbian roots remained closer to the surface in the Andes than they did in Mexico. The highly sacred region of the Andes, the extraordinary highland Lake Titicaca, became her place, as she was revered as the Virgin of Copacabana.

Andean artists were perhaps even more successful in retaining elements of the old spirituality and power structures in Christian art than the Mexicans had been. The Peruvian Conquest had been marked by strife among the conquerors themselves and with Spanish royal authority. This intra-European struggle permitted the Inka to continue to resist, and Spanish control was not securely established for more than thirty years. One result was that the immediate post-Conquest period did not see the same kind of rapid adoption of Spanish forms by the native elites as in Mexico. Still, toward the end of the sixteenth century and into the seventeenth, the adoption of at least externally Christian ways proceeded rapidly. Saint Mary was an important part of this process.

The Andean sources for the veneration of Mary were principally two. First and very important, the pan-Andean earth goddess Pachamama influenced and became integrated into many of the local and regional cults to the Virgin. In addition, Inka forms of worship had been spread throughout the Andean region in the fourteenth and into the fifteenth centuries during their conquest of the region. These forms not only included a moon goddess, Mama Quilla, who was envisioned as the consort of the sun god, but also the Coya, the living personification of the feminine sacred. She was the queen, the consort of her brother the Sapa Inka, the human embodiment of the sun. Further, the Chosen Women, a group selected for their beauty and virginity who lived in the service of the Inka king, had symbols and attributes resonant with the European symbols of the Virgin Mary.[1]

The strong associations that Andean peoples brought to the worship of Mary are made clear in the work of Garcilaso de la Vega (1539–1616), the mestizo son of a Spanish conqueror and an Inka noblewoman:

> [N]ot satisfied with learning from the priests the titles given to the Virgin in Latin and Spanish, they have tried to render them in the general language of Peru and add others so as to be able to address Her in their

own tongue and not in a foreign language when they adore Her and seek favors and mercies of Her . . . They say, Mamanchi, "our Lady and mother"; Coya, "queen"; Nusta, "princess of royal blood"; Sapay, "unique"; Yurac Amancay, "white lily"; Chasca, "morning star"; Cítoc Coillor, "shining star"; Huarcarpaña, "immaculate"; Huo Hanac, "without sin"; Mana Chancasca, "untouched, inviolate"; Tazque, "pure virgin"; Diospa Maman, "mother of God." They also say Pachacamacpa Maman, "mother of the creator and sustainer of the universe"; and Huacchac' yac, "lover and benefactor of the poor," or "mother of pity," "our advocate"; having no words with these meanings in their own language, they use what is nearest.[2]

These titles are still reflected in Andean terms for Mary; the much-revered Virgin of Bethlehem in Cuzco is referred to as Mamacha Belén, while the Virgin of Carmen in Paucartambo is Mamacha Carmen. They are also, of course, resonant with European aspects of the Virgin. It is interesting that even now the term "coyeta"—"princess" or "little queen"—applies to the Virgin of Copacabana, the most important advocation currently in the Andean highlands.

As in Mexico, native peoples quickly accepted Mary as powerful and appealing, though I would argue that Andean ideas and symbols were merging even more significantly into the reverence for her than was the case in the Mexican Conquest. And as in Mexico, elite native males were trained in schools established by Christian priests. However, the strongest of these institutions, the Jesuit-run Colegio de San Borja, was not founded until 1621, just at the conclusion of a fervent campaign against idolatry. In general, Spanish control and Christian practices came rather later to the Andes than to Mexico, possibly explaining why pre-Spanish forms are much more salient there. Nevertheless, noble natives associated themselves with the Virgin, much as converted Jews had in Spain. The coats of arms awarded to Inka nobles not only featured Andean symbols but also frequently included the words "Ave Maria." Illustrative as well is the lintel above the entrance to the Colegio de San Borja that juxtaposed the castle and lion of Castile and León with the Inka coat of arms, the latter framed by a bicephalic eagle. In the lower left-hand section of this shield is yet another bicephalic eagle, with the legend "Ave Maria" above it.[3] The significance of Mary in Christian teaching and identification could not be clearer.

Garcilaso himself was a transitional figure, and his eagerness to associate himself with Spain, where he lived most of his life, is reflected in his own homage to the Virgin. He was probably eager as well to emphasize his Spanish ties, given his choice of topic—Peru—and his subtle insistence on its importance. Therefore it is not surprising that his *Historia general del Perú*, published in Córdoba, Spain, was dedicated to "the Immaculate Virgin Mary Mother of God and Our Lady," reflecting the Spanish devotion to the idea of Mary without stain of sin. A depiction of the Immaculate Conception, with the crowned Mary ringed by the sun's rays and standing on the moon and the serpent, appears on the frontispiece. She is surrounded outside the aureole by symbols indicating the Virgin's "purity and spiritual power"—a water fountain, an enclosed garden, a mirror, a tree of life. A palm denotes the triumph of Christianity over paganism, yet again a theme closely associated with Our Lady. A moon and a sun, symbols of the sacred in both Spain and Peru, appear in the upper corners.[4]

Another transitional figure, Felipe Guaman Poma de Ayala (1534–1615), wrote an extensive illustrated history and discussion of the Peruvian region, including a series of images of twelve of the Inka queens, and a separate one of the First Queen, Lady Capac Poma Guallca. In an interesting reversal, while the Virgin Mary was accumulating attributes of the pre-Columbian sacred, powerful Andean women were being portrayed in Marylike ways. The image of Lady Capac Poma Guallca, for example, portrayed her in a Marian stance, facing forward, her hair hanging gracefully over her shoulders and down her back, her arms outstretched as if praying. She was depicted wearing a mantle over her shoulders and holding an Andean lily in one hand and a purse resembling the scapular of the Virgin of Carmen in the other.[5] An image from Guaman Poma of the tenth Coya, Mama Ocllo, shows a male attendant shading her with a parasol, an element characteristic of her rank and importance and seen in other images from Guaman Poma. Mama Ocllo is carrying a purse and is holding her hands out to the side, though the position of her feet and other figures in the image indicate forward movement. More male attendants surround her and give her pride of place.[6] The sense of the image is very similar to that of the processions of statues of the Virgin in the Spanish-era Corpus Christi celebrations, which we will discuss.

Many attributes of Andean depictions of Santa María could be related directly to native manifestations of the sacred. One of the most important was the connection with mountains, an association directly linked to Pachamama, the earth mother. A consistent feature of Andean representations of Mary is the triangular shape of her dress, a reference, according to Carol Damian, "to the shape of a mountain and, especially, her role as Pachamama, the Earth Mother."[7] In several examples from the colonial period, the Virgin as Pachamama is taken to an extreme with Mary appearing within the mountain itself. Two striking examples, now in Bolivian museums in La Paz and Potosí, show Mary's face and hands, emitting rays of light, inscribed within the mountain peak. The body of the mountain is identical

This seventeenth-century representation of the tenth Inka Coya shows her under the typical parasol representing her status. La Dezima Coia, Ocllo Reyno guanoco guayllas atpillo. *Phelipe Guaman Poma de Ayala in* El primer nueva coronica i buen gobierno compuesto.

with her body. The titles indicate that the mountain is Potosí, the mountain of silver that contributed so much to Spanish material riches. Visible on the mountain are trees, horses, Spaniards, and native rulers, all integrated within the mountain-body of the Virgin. In both, the figures of the Trinity hover above her, along with two angels, and in one God the Father and God the Son are lowering a crown onto her head. Images of the sun and moon appear on each side of the mountain in one of the paintings; in the other, the moon is visible, and at one time the painting probably contained an image of the sun as well. As the viewer faces the paintings, the moon is on the right side, the appropriate space for the feminine in the cosmic system of the Inka.[8]

Another noteworthy example can be found in a small church near the town of Urcos, a few miles from Cuzco. This image emphasizes the significance of rock, obviously part of the spiritual landscape of mountains and the connection with Mary. Rocks, in indigenous spirituality, are often *wak'as*, that is, sacred places, objects, or personages. This image, the Virgin of the Candlestick of Kaninkunka, is painted directly on rock above the altar of a church. Her blue mantle forms the characteristic triangular shape as she looks majestically out at the congregation. As Damian points out, "She is not a painted representation of a mountain . . . she is the rock of the mountain and venerated as the wak'a."⁹ Teresa Gisbert has noted the connection of Mary with rocks of a smaller size, which themselves could be *wak'as*. In the caption of an illustration in her work on iconography, she suggests that "the most usual form of representing the Virgin as Pachamama is painting her on a triangular rock in her advocation as the Virgin of Candlemas; in this way the concept of María/Mountain and María/Stone is emphasized."¹⁰

One of the most popular images in the Andes and the focus of a major festival is the Virgin of Carmen in Paucartambo. There are several versions of the story of the statue's arrival in that Peruvian town. In one of them, a miraculous image of the Virgin appeared on a rock in Pucará, near Puno. The Spanish viceroy, traveling through the area in 1667, was informed of the miraculous event and visited the site. Struck by the perfection of the picture, he first sent a painter to copy it on canvas. Then he had the canvas image duplicated in two identical statues, one destined for Pucará and one for Puno. The *puneños*, however, never picked theirs up, and it was purchased for Paucartambo by a wealthy female donor. In this case, the combination of Andean and Spanish origins is intriguing. The supernatural appearance on the rock gave the original image an Andean legitimacy, and its duplication by the Spanish provided sanction from the Europeans as well. There are a num-

Devil dancers at the Feast of the Virgin of Carmen in Paucartambo, Peru, on July 15, 1998. These diablitos hang from balconies, telephone poles, and rooftops. They hiss and snarl until the statue of the Virgin approaches, and then they cower in fear and hide their faces. Photograph by Andrea Heckmann.

Women dancers in Paucartambo, Peru, on July 15, 1998.
Photograph by Andrea Heckmann.

Plate VI. Devil dancers in Paucartambo, Peru, on July 15, 1998.
Photograph by María Elena García.

ber of other versions of the story, none of which mentions the rock, but almost all of which resonate with both Spanish and Andean systems.[11]

Gisbert has reported another striking case, that of the peak of Sabaya in the department of Oruro in Bolivia. The dormant volcano soars 3,585 meters above sea level and is the sacred mountain of the Carangas. The inhabitants called the rocks around the crater "the saliva of Tata Sabaya." The volcano seems to have erupted about 1600, wiping out the town at its foot. Today, according to Gisbert, the inhabitants of the reconstituted town recount a legend that credits an appearance of María, in the form of the Virgin of Copacabana, with the town's recovery. She appeared in a celestial fire on the peak of Pumiri, a hill somewhat west of the town. In that place they venerate a blue stone that is marked with what seem to be two footprints; they call it "Mamitan Sayt'apa," meaning in Aymara "the place where the Virgin stopped." The celestial fire that is mentioned may well correspond to volcanic activity in the region. In any case, Mary's appearance is credited with giving new life to the town and permitting its reconstruction. There is a beautiful painting of the Virgin of Copacabana become the Virgin of Sabaya in the Museo de la Moneda in Potosí in which some rays of the aureole mimic the shape of the mountain. The mountain itself is known as Apu Sabaya, linking it with the sacred masculine and with the forces of thunder and lightning. The legend further mentions a culture hero, Tata Sabaya, who may or may not be linked with Saint Martin of Tours.[12]

It is worth exploring another of the various versions of the story collected by Gisbert, as it sheds light on the intertwining of gender with the sacred and on the interaction of pre-Christian and Christian stories and elements. In none of the cases is the resulting account, or even the elements of the account, precisely European or Andean. In this telling, a young woman (probably virgin) who lived at the foot of the mountain dreamt that she was visited by a young man (Tata Sabaya). She miraculously became pregnant, eventually giving birth to a child with blond hair and blue eyes. The child was baptized Pedro Martín Capurata Condorvillca. He became a shepherd but later married a rich woman. About this time, a group of Spaniards passed through the region on the way to Potosí, and Martín went with them, returning later to found a town named Sabaya in honor of his father. He brought together various groups of people and made himself their absolute ruler. When the bishop heard about the new town he sent a priest for the purposes of evangelization. Martín Capurata and the priest came to an arrangement whereby mass would be said only after Martín had arrived on his white horse. One day he was late, and the priest began mass without him. The leader was so incensed that he imprisoned the priest, who escaped later to Sucre after excommunicating the entire town. The bishop then sent three priests to Sabaya, where they found three women who at that point disappeared, leaving only one beautiful lady in the church. Her presence led to the resurgence of the demolished town, and, simultaneously, Martín Capurata perished. His remains were divided between the various groups of the region. It is significant that a dormant volcano in the region is named Capurata.

Gisbert connects the conception of Martín, fertilized by Sabaya in a woman by the name of Asunta (related to Asunción, or the doctrine of the Assumption of Mary), with the incarnation of Christ. The bringing together of different native groups refers, she believes, to the colonial concentration of *ayllus* (Andean kinship groups). The destruction of the town resonates with the historical eruption of the volcano in 1600, providing a Christian interpretation of a geological event. The three women in the church, who become one, indicate a connection between Saint Mary and the Trinity, an idea of three in one. The dispersal of Martín's body may reflect the division among the resettled *ayllus*, an Andean reference, as is the name Sabaya.

Martín is identified both with his father, Tata Sabaya, and with the Spanish, as his coloring appears Spanish and he rides a horse. Gisbert believes that he is conflated with Saint Martin of Tours, whose image she encountered in a government office of the town listed as "Retrato del Tata Sabaya con su vidrio," that is, "a portrait of Tata Sabaya with its glass." This portrait had come from a chapel very close to the volcano. She thinks it is possible that once the picture of Saint Martin was put into the chapel, a legend grew up uniting the cult of the mountain of Sabaya with the Christian cult of Saint Martin and relating both to that of Asunta/María.[13] At the same time, the mountain/volcano/destructive force is gendered male; the reconstructive force, the Virgin, is female. In fact, in all three versions that Gisbert supplies, the male force, white horse and all, is destructive and causes the town to disappear; and in two the Virgin, or at least a beautiful lady, inspires repopulation. Martín and/or Tata Sabaya may also be associated with Santiago, the warrior saint of the Spanish, or Santiago may be named as accompanying Sabaya. Santiago is linked with the Virgin Mary throughout the Andes (as he was in Spain) and is also linked to thunder and lightning, a typical Andean association.[14]

We can, however, give other readings to these stories. The male destructive force may be seen as either Andean or Spanish or both, or as a collaboration between the two. The destruction may be either that of the volcano's eruption or the disaster and dislocation of the Conquest or both. The figure who then leads the native population to recovery is the Virgin Mary, in this case developing into Our Lady of Sabaya.

The striking painting of her by the Indian artist Luis Niño is located still in Potosí, the major city connected to Sabaya in the stories. A sumptuous canvas, it is ornately gilded and skillfully executed. Mary and the baby Jesus wear golden crowns, and the Virgin's hair is intertwined with flowers. Cherubs surround her, two of them playing musical instruments. She holds an ornate candlestick in her right hand—associating her with the Virgin of Copacabana, of whom we will speak later—and a basket in her left. The Christ Child is perched rather precariously above the basket on her forearm and holds a banner in his tiny hand. The blue of her gown forms a column down to the crescent moon on which she stands, and that in turn is located on a platform, showing that she is a statue painting. This form is typical of colonial Andean artists' representations in which a statue of the Virgin is depicted rather than the Virgin in lifelike form.[15] As in many native representations of Mary, the central column of the gown meets the crescent moon in a configuration that mimics the *tumi* or sacrificial knife of Andean ritual. It also reproduces the pin that royal Inka women used to secure their clothing.[16] The native artist signed the painting in 1737, declaring that the image was a sculpture sent to Peru by Charles V. The indigenous artist, then, was "literally painting the portrait of a dressed statue" and would have been to some degree restricted in his painterly options.[17] Despite these constraints, however, the image of the Virgin, with the sun's rays radiating around her face and wearing a crown, convincingly mimics the shape of the mountain. The Virgin in this portrait has as aloof and commanding a presence as does the mountain itself. In this case Mary, the feminine sacred, has joined the masculine sacred and is Queen of the mountain.

The association of the Virgin with Santiago in this story is not unusual. As in Spain and in Mexico, they brought the Conquest together, and both were significant in Iberian victories. The triumph for the Spanish in withstanding the native siege under Manco in 1534 at the Sunturhuasi in Cuzco was associated with both of them, and the visions of the two were credited with having so astonished the Inka attackers that they submitted to Spanish troops. Mary, it will be remembered, was variously reported to have extinguished the thatched roof of that edifice when it was set on fire by the Inka rebels and also to have shot dust and/or hail into the eyes of the attackers.[18] Unsurprisingly, given the patterns of Spanish conquest in Iberia and in Mexico, this sacred Inka location served for the first Christian church in Cuzco, and later, when the cathedral was built next door, it was turned into a chapel. The chapel was named El Triunfo, the Triumph. The cathedral was dedicated to the Virgin of the Assumption—Asunción. The triumphal apparition was celebrated annually on May 23, during Mary's month.[19]

The victory was also strongly connected with Santiago. He appeared as

*Seventeenth-century statue of Santiago with a Moor, significantly resembling an
Andean indigenous person, cowering beneath the feet of his horse. Corpus Christi, Cuzco, 1998.
Photograph by Susan Gandert.*

well, according to the accounts, preceded by an enormous thunderclap and
then a terrifying bolt of lightning that made a direct hit on the fortress of
Sacsahuaman on the outskirts of the city. The story probably gave rise to the
association of Santiago with lightning and its male supernatural force, Illapa.
Guaman Poma de Ayala and Titu Cusi Yupanqui mentioned these events in
their later chronicles. A memorial tablet in the Chapel of the Triumph states
that "Santiago, the patron of the Spains, was seen emerging . . . and the
astonished idolaters venerated him as Lightning, the Son of Thunder."[20]
According to Guaman Poma, the natives saw Santiago, mounted on a white
horse and wearing a feathered hat, descend on the lightning bolt, and from
this time forward they called him Illapa.[21] Father Pablo Joseph de Arriaga,
who spent a number of years in Peru beginning in 1585, published a book in
1621 about "idolatry," that is, the survival of native religious practice in the
colony. He described the widespread confusion of Illapa and Santiago:

They often give this name to one of the chuchus, [twins, one of which is associated with lightning] as a son of lightning, which they call Santiago. I do not think this is because of the name Boanerges, which Christ Our Lord gave to the Apostles Saint James and his brother, Saint John, calling them lightning, or sons of thunder, according to the Hebrew phrase. It is probably because the phrase has been brought here or suggested by the young Spaniards who, when it thunders, say that Saint James's horse is running. Or perhaps they have noticed that when the Spaniards wage war, they shout before shooting their arquebus, which the Indians call illapa, or lightning, "Santiago! Santiago!" However this may be, they have taken over the name Santiago and attach superstition to it. For this reason, among other rules laid down by the visitors at the end of the visit is this one: that no Indian should be named Santiago, but Diego instead."[22]

An intriguing image can be seen over the door of a small chapel in Quispicanchis near Cuzco. Santiago is shown on his white horse, sword in the air, with a dark figure, perhaps a native, cowering beneath the hooves. The figures are balanced precariously above the rainbow, and a native sun shines from beneath the rainbow. Santiago, Illapa, and domination are thus related. Illapa, in turn, was strongly associated with Viracocha and with the Sun.[23] These associations, through Mary's reported appearance with Santiago in support of the Spanish, reinforced her connection with these other native spiritual forces and with war, conquest, and victory. The Virgin of Candlemas, La Purificada, often carries a candlestick in a zigzag form, probably an Andean image relating her to Illapa and the masculine force. And the Virgin of the Candlestick is one of the most popular Andean representations, appearing most importantly as the advocations of Copacabana and the apparently related Sabaya and Cocharcas. The shrine of Copacabana is near Lake Titicaca and that of Cocharcas near Ayacucho; both advocations spread regionally and were subsumed in many local advocations and images. The Virgin of the Candlestick was often shown holding a small basket containing birds, which also had a spiritual significance for the Andeans.[24]

Birds and their feathers were highly significant in Inka and, more generally, Andean ceremony and spirituality. Warfare was associated with the eagle, as it was in Mexico, and the condor with the underworld and with fertility. The curiquenque, a highland Andean hawk, provided the two black and white feathers that were given to the Sapa Inka in acknowledgment of his position as head of state and embodiment of the Sun God on the earth.

They were worn in a headdress above the *maskapaycha*, "the distinctive scarlet-colored fringe that covered the forehead of the Inka head-of-state in the pre-Hispanic and early colonial periods." The wearing of the fringe itself was the sign that a male member of the royal family had been converted into the ruler, the Sapa Inka, "the unique Inka."[25]

Other birds were significant for various political, religious, and social positions in Inka society. Tropical birds such as parrots were associated with both men and women of high status, including royal *ñustas* (princesses) and the Chosen Women who were dedicated to the Sun and to the Inka ruler. Golden images of birds stood along with other golden animals in the Temple of the Sun.[26] Tropical birds in particular seem to have been associated with the feminine, but in precolonial times the combination of masculine and feminine was powerful. During the colonial period, however, feathers and the inclusion of the feminine in the persona of male Inka leaders was viewed as a sign of weakness or, perhaps, lack of civilization. Therefore, in male ritual dress, feathers began to disappear except when men were portraying those tribes viewed as uncivilized in dramatic reenactments of historical events or other ceremonies. The Virgin, however, took on birds or feathers in many representations. A beautiful representation of the Virgin of the Candlestick of Tenerife, painted by an anonymous artist of the School of Cuzco in the late seventeenth century, combines the candlestick (this time straight rather than jagged) and an apron of glorious feathers. A unique Peruvian image of the advocation of the Virgin worshipped in the Canary Islands, it may have been commissioned by someone bringing that devotion to the New World from this common stopping place on the voyage. Yet this image is a typical statue painting with many Andean elements. The Virgin stands on a pedestal with a platform beneath her skirt that mirrors the shape of the crescent moon, common to both the iconography of the Immaculate Conception and the Inkan feminine sacred. Rosettes resembling Andean designs circle her sleeves, with larger ones under her chin and at the lower center of her gown below the feather apron. She is surrounded by flowers, including the Andean *ñukchu* lily, the sacred flower of the Inka.[27] In this painting, then, we likely have a European patron and an advocation linked to ocean travel and the colonial enterprise. At the same time, we have a probable native artist and a wealth of Andean symbolism linking the Virgin to precolonial royal Inka women. Again, it is important to remember that the Coya herself was considered sacred. Inka princesses and the Chosen Women were also closely connected to flowers, while European depictions of the Virgin were frequently filled with them, especially the rose.

A splendid image of La Candelaria is an anonymous representation of the Virgin of Cocharcas dated 1767. Saint Mary is shown holding a bouquet of three roses in her right hand and the baby Jesus in her left, with vases of roses in front of her at each side. She is shown under a baldachino, an awning more characteristic of European processional figures than the smaller, umbrella-like coverings that usually were used in processions of the Virgin in Peru. The landscape around her, however, is clearly Peruvian, and at the base of the platform on which she stands, tiny figures go about their business. In the legend of the Virgin of Cocharcas, a young man from a village near Ayacucho injured his hand and sought out the Virgin of Copacabana on Lake Titicaca. However, in the course of the journey, his hand spontaneously healed. He continued anyway to give thanks at Copacabana's shrine. He also brought home a copy of the Copacabana statue. On his return trip, this image was welcomed along the way with celebrations, and flowers were reported to grow in its path. A shrine was built for it in Cocharcas in 1598. A satellite shrine to Copacabana, it quickly became an important pilgrimage site on its own, and numerous paintings of it were produced.[28]

Another image of the Virgin that had European antecedents and strong Andean resonance was that of the Virgin spinning. The pseudo-Gospel of Saint Matthew indicated that the Virgin learned sewing skills from her mother, Saint Anne, that she then used in performing her duties during fourteen years in the temple. Her activities, therefore, were much like those of the Chosen Women, who made the textiles and the garments for the Inka. Cuzco paintings show the child Mary, dressed in a combination of Spanish and Inka costumes, delicately holding a spindle. A small curl on her forehead extending below her headband mimics the *maskapaycha*, the Inka symbol of supreme leadership and divinity. She is shown framed in flowers, symbols of the rites of fertility and abundance presided over by the Coya.[29]

Damian notes, "In the Andes, weaving was a ritual act for ritual purposes developed over centuries." Textiles were important articles of tribute, and large quantities were used for festivals and sacrifices. One of the finest was *cumbi*, a cloth of vicuña wool and bat's fur; others were made of feathers or included threads of gold and silver. Huge quantities of cloth were used in rituals and festivals, and much of Andean tribute to the Inka came in this form.[30] In this way the young Virgin, performing domestic tasks, was conflated with the honored Chosen Women, engaged in the production of goods central to Inka ceremony. This composite vision was reflected in an eighteenth-century canvas showing the Virgin of Bethlehem—one of the advocations most revered in Cuzco—holding a needle and thread. Her crown and luxurious garments show clearly that she is the Queen of Heaven, not the humble child Mary performing her duties in the temple.[31]

Spanish representations of course continued to be very important, and some of these had elements that the Inkas could associate easily with their own religious ideas. Cuzco artists often portrayed the Immaculate Conception, that representation of Mary so significant to the Spanish. The Indian reverence for the moon, the Queen and Coya of the Inka and consort of the sun, was easy to subsume into the iconography of Concepción. The idea and the visual portrayal of the Virgin of the Immaculate Conception and of Mary as Queen coincided nicely with those of the Coya. The Cuzco representations followed the European iconography quite carefully, but they did not need to embellish. The moon on which she stands, the flowers, the elegance, the regal nature of the representations all contributed to a kind of "Double Mistaken Identity" in which mutual misunderstandings between the indigenous and the Europeans permitted each to see in the practices of the other what they themselves believed and practiced.[32]

Andean ceremonies as well were wrapped into Christian ones, and the Virgin took a prominent place in the celebrations. Father Arriaga explained that the Corpus Christi festival replaced an Andean celebration known as Oncoymita, which took place at about the same time of the year. He reported that it included the sacrifices of llamas to two lagoons from which these very important Indian animals were said to have originated. Arriaga noted with alarm that small wak'as could be hidden on the platform on which the Holy Sacrament was carried, as well as in hollow spaces in the figures of saints and below the altar. (There are still persistent rumors in Cuzco that sacred Andean objects were built into the wall behind the altar in the cathedral.) Father Arriaga also noted that in Haurochirí a festival honoring Our Lady of the Assumption was merely a mask for worshiping an idol in female form called Chupixamor or Mamayoc; elsewhere he indicated that the priest of San Damián de Checa de Huarochirí had reported that the same celebration masked the worship of Pariacaca, a local mountain deity. The deceptions were not limited to representations of Mary. In order to revere a male idol named Huayhuay, the Indians worshiped a crucifix. In another example the Andeans of Carampoma maintained a clandestine religious specialist—a rotating office to hinder discovery- —who maintained the old ways in defiance of the Christians through the nominal celebration of Christian rites, in this case to Santiago. Significantly, the day *after* the feast of Santiago (so tied in to the worship of Mary), the Carampomans congregated on a hill where there was a cross and there danced and performed their traditional ceremonies in defiance of the Spanish. Moreover, the Andean members of the brotherhood of Our Lady of the Nativity promoted the fertility of their herds through offerings to the wak'as, further integrating Christian and Andean systems to their greater spiritual and material benefit, or so they must have believed.[33]

The friars themselves continued to push the useful reverence to Mary. Father Arriaga reported the case of a priest, one Rodrigo Hernández Príncipe, who had "rendered . . . great service to Our Lord through the means and intercession of the Blessed Virgin Mary, whom he has taken for his advocate in this enterprise." As Hernández Príncipe traveled through the Andean region, Father Arriaga was zealous in providing him with rosaries for distribution to the native population. According to the itinerant priest in a letter Arriaga included in his account, he had made such progress in one Andean town that he sent to Lima to obtain permission for the establishment of a brotherhood of Our Lady of Loreto. Mary herself, he insisted, had intervened in "the discovery of the idols and the Christianization of these Indians." Continuing on his journey, he arrived in the town of Cahacay, where he preached and catechized after "a general fast to make the town ready." The people, in this somewhat altered state, agonized, he reported, by their previously insincere efforts to aid in the destruction of their sacred sites and objects, came to him afterward and promised that they would take him to find these things.

The next day, he said a mass to Our Lady, praying to her for success in weeding out these idolatrous signs of the Devil. The people of the town had all become, as he described, "slave[s] of the Mother of God according to the charter of brotherhood" and led him to the old location of the village a league and a half away over rough roads. In various spots he found idols "with such strange faces that they were horrifying to look at," stones, remnants of sacrifices, and *mallquis*, the mummies of dead leaders. In a fascinating revelation he mentioned, "This same day, on the festival of Our Lady, they told me of the location of another *huaca* and I went there personally, for I think these exercises, in which gold is not being sought but the salvation of souls, are most entertaining." Proceeding, he encountered a sacred site of a "famous huaca," Sañumama, and his female consort, Mamasañu. Another priest before him had attempted to destroy the site, but the remnants of his destruction had merely been buried under the idols, and the evidence of more sacrifices had reappeared around them. The priest continued his explorations, discovering more *mallquis*, "decked out as if for war, with plumage of various colors and dressed in garments which had become worn with time." In this day of discoveries, Hernández Príncipe continued the destruction, constantly invoking the Virgin and her Day as crucial in his success.[34]

In a further discussion of his travels the friar emphasized his intention to continue his work "until Our Lord is served and His Mother is blessed (for it is She who inspires this work)." He continued through the countryside, distributing rosaries and organizing Marian brotherhoods, concluding with

Representation of an Inka mummy, early seventeenth century. Nobiembre a La Mallqui. *Phelipe Guaman Poma de Ayala in* El primer nueva coronica i buen gobierno compuesto.

the undoing of yet another *wak'a* in the town of Chayna, burning and looting, sending the "movable huacas" to Lima and destroying the rest. The Virgin's role was once again confirmed in his words, as he concluded his letter (and the destruction of the *wak'a* of Chayna) on the day of the Immaculate Conception. He happily reported that the natives had "enrolled themselves as the slaves of Our Lady, who has so greatly favored them."[35] Still, perhaps the friar was deceived. What better way for indigenous peoples to maintain their ways of reverence than to cloak them with the figure of Mary herself.

The celebration of Corpus Christi in Cuzco, the former Inka capital, quickly became a Marian festival. A papal bull of 1537 had included it in the list of festivals that inhabitants of the Spanish New World should observe. Garcilaso tells us that it was instituted in 1550, less than two decades after the collapse of the Inka empire at Cajamarca. Forty years after the Conquest, when control of the colony was finally established by the Spanish crown, it was already acknowledged as Cuzco's most important religious celebration. Moreover, at the same time that it was a visual and dramatic assertion of Spanish power, it was also a demonstration of continuing Andean hierarchy and ritual. The Council of Trent in 1551 called the Corpus Christi festival "a triumph over heresy," appropriate as well to the triumph over idolatry in the Andes. In Cuzco, Corpus Christi seems to have had a relationship with the rescue of Andeans from what the Spanish saw as indigenous Devil-worship. Usually falling in June, it intersected with Inti Raymi, the Inka Festival of the Sun, linked to the June solstice, the agricultural cycle, and especially the harvest. It was complementary to the December solstice, when another highly important Inka celebration took place. Inti Raymi was held at the time of the small sun, the shortest day of the year, and was associated with the female and the weak, while the December festival, called Qhapaq Inti Raymi, was associated with the old male sun, the sun that was large and strong. The June solstice also corresponded to another major celestial event, the reappearance of the Pleiades.[36]

Garcilaso related that after the civil wars that followed the Conquest— "sewn by the Devil to impede the preaching of the Holy Gospel"—Corpus Christi began to be celebrated with great pomp. Each high-ranking Spaniard made sure that the ritual platforms "his Indians were to carry" were lavishly furnished with rich materials, gold, and jewels along with images of Christ, Our Lady, and other saints. The Spanish brotherhoods also mounted floats, as did the native chiefs from the districts surrounding the capital. Initially they wore extraordinary costumes, including lion skins, condor wings reminding the Spanish of wings of angels, garments of gold and silver foil, and ghastly masks. Some carried the skins of animals they had caught.[37]

But, as can be seen in Garcilaso de la Vega's telling, the native participation in the festivities might have an edge. Tribal groups proceeded according to seniority, that is, the date of their conquest by the Inkas, with the most recent first and the Inkas themselves last. However, these rituals did not always happen smoothly. On one occasion, when the Cañaris arrived, their float was painted with battle scenes of Indians and Spaniards. The Cañaris came from outside the jurisdiction of Cuzco, but they had been engaged on the Spanish side in putting down Manco Inka's rebellion a few years before. Their leader, Francisco Chilche Cañari, had slaughtered the Inka captain when the latter challenged the Spanish to single combat in the central plaza of the city. On the occasion of the 1555 celebration, Don Francisco chose to remind the celebrants of this fact and challenged the processional hierarchy. Mounting the churchyard steps, he threw open his cloak to reveal that he was wearing another blanket beneath, a defiant gesture indicating his readiness to do battle. In his right hand he held a model of a severed head, which he clutched by the hair. A near-riot ensued, with four or five Inkas attacking the Cañari leader, followed by general turmoil. When order was restored, the

Inkas protested that Chilche had exhibited the head to stir up memories of the Spanish/Cañari victory. Chilche concurred: "I cut that head off an Indian who challenged the Spaniards when they were surrounded in this square with Hernando Pizarro, Gonzalo Pizarro, and Juan Pizarro, my lords and masters, and two hundred other Spaniards. None of them would go out and accept the Indian's challenge, thinking it was a disgrace and not an honor to engage [in] a single fight with an Indian. So I asked their permission to go out and fight, and the Christians said yes, and I went out and fought the challenger, and beat him and cut his head off in this square." He went on, "Is it strange that on such an occasion as today I should take pride in the deed I did in the service of the Christians?" In so speaking, the Cañari went right to the subtext of the procession: hierarchy and power, both Spanish and native. He further challenged the Inka rights to highest native status in this Spanish ritual. He and his, after all, had joined the Spanish in vanquishing the Inka empire. His action also disputed the Inka designation of the Cañaris as outsiders and savages (aucas), although the Spanish magistrate, facing far more Inkas than Cañaris, ordered him to speak of it no more. The Cañari resistance to Inka primacy in the colonial period would not end here, however.[38]

The Cañaris, originally from the area that is now Ecuador, had been conquered and resettled throughout the southern highlands by the Inkas less than fifty years before Francisco Pizarro arrived in Peru. Like the Tlaxcalans in Mexico, they were natural enemies of the ruling group and natural allies of the Spanish, on the principle that "the enemy of my enemy is my friend." One group of the Cañaris had rebelled and been put down brutally by the Inkas in the immediate pre-Conquest period. Apparently another group of Cañaris had been almost wiped out by the Inka ruler Atahualpa. When Spanish chronicler Pedro Cieza de León encountered them, he found that women outnumbered men fifteen to one. In 1534, when Pizarro's man Sebastián de Benalcázar contacted the same group, the survivors became Spanish auxiliaries. This alliance continued through the rebellion of Gonzalo Pizarro, and the Cañaris also participated in the campaign to defeat the unpacified Inkas of Vilcabamba. According to Spanish lore, they were fierce and faithful allies against the Inkas and Spanish rebels alike, and they developed an early devotion to the Catholic religion.[39]

The Cañaris, along with other non-Inka ethnic groups who were brought to Cuzco to serve the Inka state, were settled on the hill of Qarmenqa. After the conquest, the neighborhood was renamed Santa Ana, for the Mother of the Virgin, and it was here that Chilche resided. It may be that the indigenous leaders selected this affiliation with the Virgin purposefully, thus reinforcing their Spanish connection, as Chilche had reinforced it more confrontationally during the Corpus Christi celebration. Or perhaps the Spanish themselves wished to emphasize this allegiance between conquered peoples and the triumphant Virgin as they had during the Reconquest in Spain. Santa Ana parish was further connected with Spanish power in that it furnished the entry point into Cuzco from the viceregal capital at Lima. When important visitors arrived in what had been the Inka imperial capital, Santa Ana parish was where they entered and witnessed dances of welcome that recalled the pre-Spanish past.[40] And it was in this parish that a remarkable series of paintings illustrating the colonial Corpus Christi celebration—commissioned by Indian parishes, a Spanish nun, and brotherhoods and religious orders—would be housed. These twelve canvases, which give us a fascinating but not always accurate picture of the Corpus Christi celebration in the late seventeenth century, seem to have been produced during the tenure of Manuel de Mollinedo y Angulo, bishop of Cuzco from 1673 to 1699; we will refer to them often below.[41]

The Virgin was quickly imprinted on Cuzco's landscape. The first Cuzqueño church was built on the spot where she appeared to save the Spanish from Manco Inka's forces. It was in fact practically the only building in Cuzco standing during Manco's siege, and the Spanish worshiped there daily during those hard times.[42] Later, in the mid-seventeenth century when the cathedral was completed next door, the original building became the Chapel of the Triumph, as noted earlier. The cathedral itself was dedicated to the Virgen de la Asunción. It continues to dominate what had been the Inka's central plaza, the *haukaypata*, which was converted into the somewhat smaller Spanish Plaza de Armas. Streets such as the Calle Loreto were named for the Virgin and her advocations, although Loreto has now been renamed the Intik'ijllu.[43] Parishes, especially native ones, aligned themselves with her images. The spatial, spiritual, and ritual significance of Mary in colonial Cuzco is strikingly portrayed in the colonial Corpus Christi festival.

The ceremony consisted of the procession of the major Christian images from various parishes and religious establishments around Cuzco. It continued throughout the colonial period and continues until the present, gaining and losing luster and elegance, adding images from time to time. The Spanish seem to have meant it to submerge and replace the great Inka holiday of Inti Raymi, in which the mummies of previous rulers and their consorts were brought out by the priests and placed on platforms around the *huaycapata*. There these images could enjoy the festivities and be venerated. The iconography associated with Christian images resonated with that of the mummies. For example, the aureole worn by the image La Linda, the Immaculate Conception, according to Carol Damian, shows the same pattern as that of the

La Linda de la Catedral in Cuzco, Peru, 1998. She has the moon at her feet, and her aureole resembles the solar radiances worn by the Inka in worshipping the sun. Photograph by Susan Gandert.

solar radiance in colonial drawings of the Inka worshiping the sun and the royal headdresses of the Sapa Inka and his solar priests. It also recalls an aureole worn by the image of Santa Ana.[44]

From early days, the ceremony seems to have had an emphasis on the Virgin Mary. By the seventeenth century images of Mary predominated in those that made processions to the cathedral and around the Plaza de Armas. The native parishes in particular seem to have focused on reverence for Santa María. Of the seven Indian parishes or pseudo-parishes—Santa Ana (mentioned above), Santiago, San Sebastián, San Blas, San Cristóbal, Hospital de los Naturales (now San Pedro), and La Catedral—four were associated with the Virgin. Santa Ana's image depicts the Virgin as a baby in her mother's arms; Santiago was securely connected to the Virgin in both native and Spanish eyes. The Hospital parish procession carried a beautiful image of the Virgen de la Candelaria, so important in other parts of the Andean region.

Also most important was the image of the Immaculate Conception known as La Linda, who processed with the pseudo-parish of natives affiliated with the cathedral.[45]

The image of La Linda enjoyed enormous reverence in Cuzco. Dating from the sixteenth century, she is a dressed statue of great beauty, her face serene and her hands held together in prayer. In one seventeenth-century painting she is shown being carried reverently on a platform of silver just behind the image of Saint Rose of Lima. La Linda is richly dressed in white bordered in gold, emphasizing her purity and freedom from stain. (She is also frequently depicted in a celestial blue, blue and white being the colors most often associated with the Virgin of the Immaculate Conception.) Her position in the painting relative to that of Santa Rosa is significant. The saint from Lima, only canonized in 1671, precedes La Linda; this placement puts Santa Rosa farther from the host, which in the seventeenth century came last and gave La Linda pride of place. The figures pass before one of the temporary altars in the plaza that were reminiscent of the platforms previously occupied by the mummies. A *custodia* for the host is displayed at the top, along with a figure of Carlos II, the contemporary Spanish monarch, a Castilian lion at his side. He is shown sparring with a Turk; Turks seem to have been used often as a kind of substitute or replacement for indigenous warriors when the display of Spanish power was desired. The relative importance of the two images is underlined by their *andas*, the platforms on which they are carried. Saint Rose's is of wood, La Linda's of heavily worked silver. Indeed, this platform is very similar to the one used today, although it is of only one level, while the current version has three. Native bearers carry both images, but the second is accompanied by a high-ranking Inka in elegant indigenous regalia, carrying the Virgin's blue banner. He is joined by his father, identified as "don Baltazar Tupa Puma." The painting, therefore, accomplishes many purposes. It privileges the *cuzqueña* over the *limeña*; it links the Spanish monarch with victory over the infidel Turk, which can be read as the indigenous peoples of Peru; it associates high-status Inka descendants with the Virgin of the Cathedral and of the Triumph; and it possibly also reasserts Inka power and hierarchy, as the accompanying young man displays Inka garments—combined, to be sure, with European elements—and symbols of Inka power.[46]

A second vitally important representation of the Virgin is that of La Candelaria associated with the native parish of Hospital de los Naturales, now known as San Pedro. At the present time, this image retains its high status in the Corpus Christi procession. It is always richly dressed and possesses a trove of jewels; it is the patroness of the market women, whose stalls are located just in front of this church. Also known as the Virgen de la Purificación and as La Purificada, her association with the advocations of the Virgin of Copacabana and the Virgin of Cocharcas are obvious. In the seventeenth-century paintings, she appears twice, in a processional representation and later standing among other images outside the cathedral. In the first image she is seen atop a fanciful processional cart, certainly copied from prints of the Corpus Christi procession in Seville. The image itself, however, seems to be the one used today. She is crowned, her long, dark hair flowing over her shoulders. Her dress is decorated with crescent-moonlike ropes of pearls attached with Andean rosettes. She also is preceded by a noble Inka wearing a *suntur pakar*, an elaborate headdress denoting nobility, which contained two images of the Inkan *mayskapacha*, one of normal size over his forehead and another within the framework of the headdress. The *suntur pakar* also contained birds, feathers, fringed staffs, ax-scepters, flowers, and a rainbow, and his other garments were covered with indigenous symbols. The ax-scepters are tiny versions of a weapon known as a *conga cunchona*, a "beheader," while the rainbow is a highly powerful Andean symbol that could indicate either good or bad fortune. The end of a rainbow was a sacred place. The Sapa Inka's correlation with the rainbow indicated his mediativity; when he stood under the rainbow in the Qorikancha, the Temple of the Sun, he formed the link between the upper and lower worlds and this one.[47] The nobleman accompanying La Candelaria also displayed many of these same symbols of Inka spirituality and power. His *suntur pakar* included flowers, a rainbow, the fringed staffs, and the large and small *maskaypachas*; a bearer carried it ahead of him to indicate reverence for the altar of the host that the entourage is passing.[48]

The individual thus attired was claiming status and power, combining Andean symbolism with reverence to the Virgin. He appears with another high-status Inka who is wearing more Spanish attire. Two parrots hover near the spectators in the windows and balconies; they are portrayed as larger than the human beings next to them. These creatures invoke the sacred, as they are associated with tropical birds, as well as with the feminine.[49] In addition, an arrangement of white feathers circles the Virgin's feet. Most striking, she carries a zigzag candlestick reminiscent of Illapa in her right hand, opposite the baby Jesus in her left.[50] This image, then, combines many Andean elements with the European figure of La Purificada. The Virgin of Candelaria appears again in the last painting of the series, dressed richly in red and carrying a zigzag candlestick, but this time she appears on a wooden carrying platform with a rainbow-colored parasol over her head. Thus, she is pictured as a *ñusta*, an Inka princess. In both paintings, her robe forms a V as it approaches the crescent-moon curve of the bottom of her dress, creating again the *tumi*-knife form.[51] Further, in displaying their reverence for the Virgin, the Andean men leading each group of her devotees were themselves performing a mediating role. They were at once asserting Andean spiritual symbolism, paying homage to Spanish spiritual and political power, performing in ways meaningful to both cultures, and claiming their own high status.

In the seventeenth-century paintings of Corpus Christi still present in Cuzco, only one other representation of the Virgin appears, although two more are part of the contemporary ceremony. This last image is associated not with an Andean but with a Spanish parish, the first to be established in Cuzco. She is the Virgin of Bethlehem, La Virgen de Belén, now the most important of all the images of Mary in the modern Corpus Christi procession. She is known locally as Mamacha Belén, an appellation that corresponds to the Andean earth deity, Pachamama. Her iconography is that of the Queen of Heaven, recalling the Inka Coya. She carries the baby Jesus in her arms but stares impassively out at the viewer, aloof and self-contained. The numerous paintings of her in Cuzco style are all statue paintings, as she was in fact a dressed statue. She too is depicted with ropes of pearl draped in moonlike crescents across her robes and with the ubiquitous Andean rosettes, flowers, and birds.[52] In the representation we have of her in the seventeenth-century series of paintings, she is dressed in white and gold, her long black hair woven with flowers.[53]

The popularity of this figure may be related to the legend of her miraculous arrival in Cuzco. The claim is that fishermen from the town of San Miguel, outside the walls of the fort of Callao near the Spanish capital of Lima, discovered a box floating in the ocean. Inside they found the image of the Virgin of Belén, with a note inside saying "For Cuzco." The viceroy, the archbishop, and the royal council, faced with this miraculous discovery, determined that Cuzco indeed should be her destination. On arrival, lots were drawn to decide in which church she should reside. The neighborhood of Three Kings won, and there she was installed, giving her own name to the parish. Another tradition indicates that she was a gift of Emperor Carlos V of Spain.[54] A painting commissioned by Bishop Mollinedo, mentioned before as significant in inspiring the Corpus Christi paintings, recounts the first miracle and two others: a procession of the image that resulted in relieving a severe drought and salvation from the Devil of the soul of an individual who helped carry her image and then gave the first coin he earned to her church.[55] In present-day Cuzco, Mamacha Belén is closely tied to Taytacha Temblores (*Padrecito*, or "Little Father" Earthquakes), a beautiful image of Christ on the cross that is said to have saved Cuzco from these terrible acts of nature.

Plate VII. Procession in front of cathedral from the late-seventeenth-century series of the Corpus Christi celebration in Cuzco. Note the Virgin of Belén in ivory robe to the right of the door of the cathedral, facing the viewer, and the Virgen de la Candelaria with parasol between Belén and San Sebastián. Unknown artist. Unknown photographer.

It is worth analyzing in detail the amazing canvas from the Corpus Christi series showing the return of the procession to the cathedral. The patron is believed to be the individual portrayed in the lower right-hand corner of the canvas. He is recognizably native by hairstyle and dress, probably a resident of Santa Ana parish and very likely either ethnically Cañari or Chachapoya. No Inka nobles are pictured here, despite the presence of La Candelaria. The entire processional line, which cuts diagonally across the bottom right-hand portion of the painting and ending in the center, is Hispanic, but the Spanish magistrate's elite guard, composed of Cañaris and Chachapoyas, is prominently featured at the front of the left side of the canvas. Further, the figure of Saint Anne with the baby Mary is located to the left of the host in the position of honor, an honor which would not normally have been extended to the image or the parish and is almost certainly a fictional representation. In these ways, the Cañari/Chachapoya presence is privileged over that of the Inka.[56]

A further point may be made in observing this canvas, however. Of the six images portrayed—Santiago, San Cristóbal with the Christ Child on his shoulder, Santa Ana and the Virgin, the Virgin of Belén, the Virgin of Candelaria, and San Sebastián—the Virgin is central. She herself appears in three images: as a child in her mother's arms and as the Virgins of Belén and Candelaria. Santiago was closely connected with her in the Andean cult of the Virgin. Only San Sebastián and San Cristóbal have no direct connections to her, although San Cristóbal has long been linked with her in the sense that they were both bearers of Christ. Santa Ana, connected with the non-Inka indigenous groups of the hill of Qarmenqa, stands to the immediate left (from the viewer's perspective) of the door of the cathedral, and the Virgin of Belén is on the right, shown significantly larger than they actually are in proportion to the other figures. In this way, the Cañari, the Chachapoya, and the Spanish are linked in the center of the canvas through images of the child Virgin and her Mother and of Mary with the infant Jesus. La Candelaria, arguably the most important of the Inka-related images, is smaller and to the right of the Virgin of Belén, and much smaller than Santa Ana. The painting is laden with Andean images; white plumage with red Andean rosettes surround the feet of each image except for that of Santiago on the extreme left. However, white plumage adorns his hat, and red rosettes decorate the canopy under which he stands. Indian natives dressed in largely Spanish garb stand in a row in front of the images in the line that stretches horizontally across the canvas, intersecting the diagonal processional line of Hispanic clerics and political elites. The Cañari and Chachapoya guards wear elaborate Andean headbands adorned with abundant white plumage, and in several the bands boast additional ornamentation: in five they bear silver new moons, in four more what seems to be silver *mayskapacha* fringes, and on one a small badge of gold with a cross on it. All of these ornaments are associated with the Cañaris and with either nobility or service to the Spanish. Therefore, in this extraordinary ritual display of the power of the Spanish sacred over that of the native, the Virgin Mary is central in a canvas commissioned by descendants of native allies of the Spanish who had helped the Iberians put down the Inkas. And this fictionalized display was represented in the very center of what had been the Inka empire. Fictionalized or not, moreover, the placement of Mary and her mother indicated the Virgin's centrality and significance.

The sacred spaces of Cuzco were by no means the only locations that became dominated by an association with the Virgin Mary. Nor were the advocations of Mary that were so important locally in Cuzco ever generalized regionally. By far the most important of the single Andean advocations would arise at Lake Titicaca, described by one author as a "paradigmatic sacred space."[57] Almost 4,000 meters above sea level, it is South America's largest lake at almost 8,300 square kilometers. Throughout centuries before the arrival of the Spanish, this place was holy for Andeans and indeed for at least two cultures considered the origin point of the world. The Island of Titicaca has been seen as the *sanctum sanctorum*, the center of the world.[58] In appropriating this space, Christians were arrogating to themselves and their spiritual system a location from which power and life radiated. By associating it further with the Virgin, they made it appealing both emotionally and psychologically while symbolically establishing European spiritual power.

Veronica Salles-Reese has analyzed three cycles of stories associated with the region, all of which, including the Christian, imply some kind of darkness and chaos into which an organizing principle is inserted. The first, originating with the Aymara-speaking ethnic groups dominant in the region before the Inka conquest, emphasizes that Viracocha, a culture hero and creation god who emerged at Titicaca to bring light and order out of cosmic chaos. He created the astral bodies—sun, moon, and stars—and then created human beings and gave them culture. Moving out through the Andes, he announced himself in those regions as the creator as well. When his earth mission was completed, he vanished into the ocean.[59]

Sometime during the fifteenth century, ethnic rivalries among the Andeans in the region left them vulnerable to conquests by the Inkas, who were moving south. Stories of these conquests, which had likely taken place only a couple of generations before Pizarro arrived at Cajamarca, were recounted to many of the Spaniards as they traveled through the region.[60] And the Inkas, of course, developed their own story. It is a tribute to the power and beauty of the region that they also chose it for their origin point, an interesting displacement from Cuzco. According to their story, Manco Capac was the culture hero who, following divine instructions, arrived and established order. As the master narrative went, the Sun, a glowing figure in the form of a man, adopted the Inkas as his own and gave them a civilizing task. Appearing to them on the Island of Titicaca, he sent them north, where they emerged out of a cave near Cuzco. One of these emissaries, Manco Capac, took with him a rod of gold that would sink into the ground at the spot where they should settle. This spot is alternately indicated as either Cuzco or as the cave of emergence. The other males in the group were turned into *wak'as*, while Manco Capac survived to engender a son with one of his sisters, founding the Inka dynasty.[61]

One of the Christian stories associated with the region is similar, but in this case the chaos is not primordial but moral, as the devil has intervened to corrupt the people. Before the Spanish conquerors arrived, according to this legend, the Apostle Thomas had come on a Christian evangelical mission to restore moral order. But the culminating point of this story is the creation of the image of the Virgin of Copacabana and the miracles she performed, bringing nurturing, regeneration, and goodness with her. The interest in Saint Thomas soon fell way, but the Virgin of Copacabana has remained at the center of a remarkable devotion until this day.[62]

The standard story is recounted by Alonso Ramos Gavilán, an Augustinian, the order that took over the sanctuary in 1589, less than a decade after the image was produced and brought to Copacabana. The account was published in 1621, at the height of a vicious anti-idolatry campaign that had largely been pushed and prosecuted by the Jesuits. By 1619 thousands of native *wak'as* had been destroyed, and 25,000 cases of idolatry had been investigated. The latter often led to imprisonment, loss of property, and burning the homes of those found guilty. Ramos Gavilán's account was in a sense an Augustinian and humanitarian challenge to this Jesuit zeal, as he defended the notion of complete conversion under the guidance of the Virgin for those indigenous peoples in this highly numinous location.

The image was one of the Virgen de la Candelaria carved in about 1582 by an Indian from the Copacabana area, a man named Francisco Tito Yupanqui. The circumstances were these. In about 1580, with the region suffering from a severe drought, the native inhabitants decided to put their fate in the hands of the Christian god and call upon his Mother for relief. To accomplish this end, they decided to form a brotherhood. However, two rival groups in the community could not agree on a patron saint, the Urinsaya arguing for San Sebastián and the Anansaya choosing instead the Virgen de la Candelaria. The governor of the Anansaya, in the midst of the dispute, made a visit to Potosí, the community near the great silver mines, where his kinsman Tito Yupanqui had already begun sculpting a statue of the Virgin. According to Ramos Gavilán, this artistic task was an expression of devotion, and the artist fasted and prayed throughout the process to the Virgin for her guidance. Though this first image was initially placed on the altar, when a new priest arrived he did not find it aesthetically pleasing and had it taken down. Tito Yupanqui then resolved to apprentice himself to a Spanish artist named Diego Ortiz, and with hard work he was able to produce the second statue that has now become so famous. The entire community was involved in the design; residents went from church to church until they found an image they felt was a worthy model. Tito Yupanqui began work on June 4, 1582, and while he worked, other community members continued to try to get permission to found a brotherhood in honor of the Virgin. The two goals were achieved when the statue was completed and the bishop, pleased with the results, gave permission for the establishment of the brotherhood.

However, the jealous Urinsayas objected to the native artist's sculpture and insisted on finding a substitute from either Spain or Lima. At this point, the Virgin herself intervened. Fray Francisco Navarrete, in whose care the sculpture had been left, was dazzled one evening by rays of fire emanating from the sainted image. Ramos Gavilán interpreted this event as a miraculous sign and noted, "Before the Virgin performed miracles in their town, the people of Copacabana were subsumed in their idolatry since the place had been the capital of Idolatry, which still persisted there." The Virgin's voice, directed through the holy image, led them out of error, and henceforth they went regularly to confession.[63] His work, therefore, was a defense of the native peoples of the region from the charges of idolatry being pushed so relentlessly at that time in the Andean highlands. The many miracles that were publicized by Ramos Gavilán's work were crucial to the subsequent success of the image. It is worth noting that he used a treatise to the Virgin to protect the natives and reasonable that they should seek protection (or perhaps camouflage) in her worship. The Virgin of Copacabana quickly became an object of great reverence and the center of a pilgrimage cult in the Andes, in a region that had already served that function for centuries and had been reconfigured by the Inka only a few years before the arrival of the Spanish to serve the cult of the sun. The very fact of the miraculous image's production by a previously unskilled native artist was considered a miracle in itself. Most of the second part of Ramos Gavilán's lengthy work dealt with her subsequent miracles, which included curing the insane, protecting women from abusive husbands, resuscitating dying children and drowning adults, and exposing criminals. Sabine MacCormack has noted that the pattern of Copacabana's miracles and the way she was perceived to provide them made her very similar to Andean wa'kas and that the image "behaves as an independent agent: it has power, it lives, just as the huacas of the Inkas had power and lived."[64]

The similarities are obvious between the Copacabana story and those of Guadalupe and Remedios in Mexico, not to mention earlier European stories, but the miracle is on a more human scale and more immediately believable. The image was not originally Spanish nor was it miraculously created, except in the sense that perhaps a divine power guided the hand of the artist. Ramos Gavilán recorded the story only a generation after the historical events occurred, and the details are largely plausible. In fact, this story gives a picture of the way that the reverence for the Virgin may have been spread to conquered peoples. The initial concern, even disdain, of Europeans for the statue reveal a different aesthetic, but the acceptance of it by the towns-people of Copacabana and eventually throughout an enormous region of the Andes was not impeded by their displeasure and perhaps was even en-hanced. The selection of the Virgen de la Candelaria by the artist indicates a certain acceptance of European spiritual ways, but at the same time he in-sisted on creating the image himself and providing a native vision.

Yet the story is more complicated than that. The region of Copacabana had only been controlled by the Inka a few decades before, and they had moved settlers in from all over the empire, as they had moved many of the original inhabitants out. The initial purpose was to integrate "the newly conquered region and its people into the overall framework of the Inka empire" and, further, "was formulated to bring together the very diverse populations of this empire in a shared ritual and shared allegiance, which comprised the Sun and the Inkas in one entity."[65] In this process, they were functioning very much as Alfonso X had in southern Spain three centuries earlier, attempting to unify a conquered region through the establishment of powerful religious ideas. Such an overlay had by no means completely wiped out the former purposes of the site, however. The newcomers, who were dominant and were crucial in the reorganization and construction of the area as an Inka cult site, were in fact the above-mentioned Anansaya, who after the arrival of the Spanish favored the Virgin over another saint. The old inhabitants, the Urinsaya, resisted. Moreover, the region was under the con-trol of an ally of Paullu Topa Inka, who had been at odds with Atahualpa before the Spanish arrived and had fled to the region of Copacabana. He joined the Spanish in 1535 during their campaign against the indigenous in-habitants of what is now Chile, along with Apuchalco Yupanqui, at the time the *curaca*, or indigenous leader, of the Copacabana region. In other words, the Inkas at Copacabana had been allied with the Inka allies of the Spanish in Cuzco at an early stage of the Conquest. Paullu survived the period of conflict and died in 1549, a convert to Christianity. Though Apuchalco, ally in Copacabana to both Paullu and the Spanish, was killed by Inkas opposed to the Spanish, his two grandsons were the governors of the Anansaya at Copacabana at the time of the controversy about whether the Virgin would be selected as the community's patron. By 1582, MacCormack tells us, Saint Mary was understood in the highlands as the "patron and protector" of the Spanish. By choosing the Virgin, the Anansaya were aligning themselves openly with the Spanish in a new attempt to unify the region, but with the Virgin rather than the Sun as the principal cult figure.[66] Here, once again, we see the entwining of political with religious purposes and the use of Mary as a symbol of religious and political alliance.

Ultimately, however, the Virgin of Copacabana, though enjoying extended reverence throughout the region, would not become the totally dominant force that the Virgin of Guadalupe would come to be in Mexico. Local and even neighborhood advocations continued to have enormous power. Within Peru the signs and symbols of the previous religions and cultures would be woven into the reverence for Mary. MacCormack tells us that even now the Aymara, descendants of those dominated centuries ago by first the Inkas and then the Spanish, come to Copacabana in pilgrimage, go into the church, and watch the procession of the image, but then go on to perform other rituals at a site of their own below a rocky mountain near the lake.[67]

The extraordinary dispersal of sacred sites and objects, not to mention the striking ruggedness of the Andean highlands, have made the persistence of distinguishably native religious practice much easier than in Mexico and almost inevitable. Spanish control was more difficult to impose; native political and spiritual resistance was easier to sustain. Ethnic diversity also contributed to a kind of competition between different images of the Virgin, who became woven into ethnic identifications and conflicts, ideological or otherwise.

While the Virgin remained a surrogate for other Andean practices and figures of reverence, nevertheless the Spanish vision of Mary was becoming intertwined in indigenous religiosity. It is likewise clear that Saint Mary— while a mother figure for Indians and Spanish alike—continued as a significant marker of political power and affiliation. She also continued to be associated with issues of regional and personal identity as well as with war, as we will see in the next chapter.

The fame of Copacabana continued to grow throughout the Andean highlands. Into the nineteenth century, her popularity increased, and her help was invoked in struggles large and small. The Spanish had defined themselves as the people of one or another advocation of the Virgin. This phenomenon had two salient aspects: the familial belonging to one nation or people with the same Mother and the incorporation of others—either by peaceful means or by coercion—into that national family. Guadalupe was the advocation that surged forward in Mexico, and both Guadalupe and Copacabana became important in the definitions of Latin American nations that would emerge after independence from Spain. Other advocations of the Virgin in other regions would go through similar processes. It is to these developments that we turn in the next chapter.

CHAPTER SEVEN

The Virgin as National Symbol

The Cases of Bolivia, Mexico, and Argentina

✠ ✠ ✠

DURING THE THREE HUNDRED YEARS of Spanish rule in Latin America, the advocations of Guadalupe in Mexico and of Candelaria, especially Copacabana, in the region of the Andes that would become Bolivia, gained power and reverence. By the time of the independence movements at the beginning of the nineteenth century, both were strong, both were centers for pilgrimage, and both would be invoked for their aid in the wars on the insurgent side as well as on the Spanish side. In fact, these advocations would be contested between opponents. The Virgin as warrior had returned vividly to the struggles. When these regions gained their independence, Copacabana and Guadalupe as symbols of the new nations became important unifying factors, rallying points that gave comfort and legitimacy in the disturbing flux of political, social, and economic changes. The case of Argentina was somewhat different. Though the arrival of the Virgin of Luján was dated from the early colonial period, her significance as a political symbol and as a warrior did not emerge strongly until the early twentieth century. Still, the purposes of national unity and cohesion that the advocation served in Argentine politics, though not perhaps as successful, were strikingly similar to those of Copacabana in Bolivia and Guadalupe in Mexico. In essence, these countries were using a "sacred language," in Benedict Anderson's phrase, of signs and symbols focused on advocations of the Virgin rather than a shared "written script" to create a sense of nation.[1]

Both the Copacabana and Guadalupe advocations became true regional devotions, centers of pilgrimage, associated with miracles in individual and larger contexts. Though popular religion and sanctioned belief have it that the Virgin of Guadalupe appeared very early, in 1531, documentation on the apparition to Juan Diego, as we have seen, dates from the middle of the seventeenth century. In contrast, the statue of Copacabana was created in 1582, and the documentation is closer in time to the beginning of the cult and its development much easier to trace. Two Augustinians—Alonso Ramos Gavilán, noted earlier, whose work was published in Europe in 1621, and Antonio de la Calancha, whose volumes appeared in 1638—have given us a good picture of events surrounding the image and of the widespread popularity of the cult.[2] Copacabana was located at Lake Titicaca, the sacred lake not only of the Inkas but also of Aymara-speaking populations. It was prime territory for evangelization, both around the lake and also throughout the highlands. As noted in the previous chapter, reports of miracles began immediately, to the point that even before the end of the sixteenth century, the native population is said to have feared that some wealthier or more powerful community would remove the statue.[3]

She was not removed, though; the location was far too useful to the Spanish for purposes of evangelization to permit such a fate. Her chapel and her image were located at the very heart of the sacred landscape of the Andean highlands, while the Guadalupe site, though certainly used in the pre-Columbian period, was not nearly so central. Thus Copacabana has continued to be a pilgrimage destination throughout the colonial period and into the twenty-first century. The rites conducted there combined Christian and native elements, as they do today.

The image of Our Lady of Copacabana was securely grounded in the landscape very quickly after its production and associated with the Spanish political as well as religious project. The Spanish, taking advantage of the location on a peninsula leading out into the sacred Lake Titicaca, found it a convenient destination for those coming into the region for Andean as well as for Christian religious purposes. The nature of the lake might well make native populations more willing to believe that the Virgin, now firmly established in this holy place, had miraculous powers. The conflation of Andean and Christian religion in this deep-rooted "contact point with the sacred" was convenient for the Church and for the Crown.[4]

The statue of the Virgin produced by Francisco Tito Yupanqui in the late sixteenth century was quickly provided with ceremony, miracles, and an edifice to mark its importance. The image and the site were soon given into the care of the Augustinians (1588), a move that the political authorities believed would guarantee a large number of priests in attendance.[5] In less than twenty years, a new chapel was begun to accommodate the growing reverence; it was completed and inaugurated in 1614. The pomp and ceremony that marked its inauguration, twenty-six years after the image had been brought to the town, highlighted its importance. Our Lady of Copacabana was removed from her old chapel, put on a carrying platform (*andas*), dressed in a beautiful white robe embroidered and covered with "jewels and pearls of much value," and taken by four Augustinians to the door of her new sanctuary. A number of groups of native dancers accompanied the image, among them reportedly a group of Inkas who were very well dressed and who brought along their weapons of war. Jesuits from Juli also attended with their musicians, adding to the festive and regional nature of the occasion. The governor of the area attended, as well as "persons of rank," the dignitaries of church, state, and society numbering two hundred. The celebration did not ignore native Andeans by any means. Two thousand "Indians—men and women—from elsewhere" were said to have attended. Though that number may well have been exaggerated, it nevertheless indicated that the cult of the Virgin of Copacabana was already spreading outside of the immediate area. The nature of the celebration and variety of those attending illustrates as well that the cult served the purposes of both religion and empire.[6] The Spanish had spectacularly claimed possession of yet another sacred site, but its use and meaning would simultaneously maintain its Andean context and heritage.

The authorities had already established a brotherhood in her honor made up of indigenous folk and linked with the image. Approved on August 14, 1604, in a bull from Pope Clement VIII, the *cofradía* of La Candelaria immediately began to function. The brothers erected a hospital to care for the sick who came to ask for the Virgin's mercy and aided pilgrims who stayed in its guest house. The Augustinians reported that with the help of the *cofradía*, they were feeding one hundred people a day, including the poor from the town and from outside it.

Donations to the Virgin were both large and small, ranging from white wax and oil to endowments and funds to improve the sanctuary. In 1669 the viceroy from Lima, the Conde de Lemos, visited La Paz, the administrative and religious center of highland Alto (Upper) Peru, and then went to Copacabana as well. He reportedly spent several days praying before the statue of Our Lady. Recognizing that the churches of Cuzco far surpassed those of Copacabana, he donated a large sum to replace the altarpiece. The new, more sumptuous version was installed in 1687. This representative of the Spanish state might perhaps have been moved by piety. Still, he was surely also conscious that a richly adorned sanctuary in a place so regularly visited by the indigenous inhabitants of the southern highlands would be an impressive and memorable marker of Spanish spiritual and temporal power.

Print of the silver mountain of Potosí, showing native Andeans in highly stylized European form. Potosi, unknown artist, eighteenth century, print on paper, 37.1 by 46.4 cm, Denver Art Museum Collection. Gift of Seymour Rubenfeld, No. 1985.672.

The Virgin and the Catholic religion were tied to the extension of European control. At this point, the cult of Copacabana seems to have spread widely throughout Alto Peru. It was particularly connected to Potosí, the mountain of silver where many Andeans served rotating but grueling stints in the mines.

The Augustinians apparently did all they could to promote the cult of Copacabana throughout the highlands, making copies of Tito Yupanqui's image and disseminating them. By the middle of the seventeenth century, throughout present-day Bolivia and beyond, the images spread along with the reverence. Travelers felt protected by her kindness and generosity and acknowledged her help by commissioning images and then installing them in their home communities. One mule driver, it is recounted, was gravely injured in 1634 while bringing a load of fish into Copacabana. Saved by the mercy of the Virgin, he sold his mules and used the money to commission a copy of the image. When it was completed, he took it to the Augustinian convent in Lima, where it was installed in 1635. He entered as a lay brother at the same time and dedicated the rest of his life to serving God and his Mother.[7] The Franciscans in Salta, the Jesuits and Augustinians in Cuzco and the cathedral, and the Dominicans in Cocharcas, Huancavelica, Callao, and Lima all had statues of Copacabana. In the other direction, the reverence arrived in Buenos Aires and got as far as Rio de Janeiro in Brazil. One of the Augustinian friars took an image back to Madrid; it was placed in the Colegio of Our Lady of the Incarnation, and Copacabana's feast day and the weeklong ceremonies that accompanied it were being celebrated by 1652. Three years later, an altar in Copacabana's honor was installed in the Augustinian church in Rome.[8]

The significance of the Virgin, though not always in her advocation as Copacabana, was highlighted during the widespread indigenous rebellions in the highlands during the latter part of the eighteenth century. These devastating movements were led in the northern Quechua-speaking region by José Gabriel Tupac Amaru. In a separate but possibly related movement in the South, the Aymara-speaking area, Tómas Katari was the first leader until his death and then was succeeded by Julián Apasa, who took the name Tupac Katari, claiming that Tómas lived again in his body. Both rebellions were brutal and bloody, turning into a kind of race war against the Spanish, their Europeanized Andean collaborators, and Hispanic culture. However, the natives in the bitter fight against all the Spanish and those associated with them did not reject some aspects of that culture, most particularly aspects of Catholicism.[9] In both northern and southern rebellions the indigenous leaders claimed noble succession and had appealed to Spanish authorities for redress of their grievances before rebelling. In both cases, however, they also maintained that they were Christians and denied that the Spaniards, given their behavior, could be so. (This theme, interestingly, was reiterated during the wars for independence when insurgents identified themselves as Christians and their Spanish opponents as "sarracens.") When captured and tortured, Tupac Amaru called upon Jesus and the Virgin for aid; during the rebellion, however, he was seen as a kind of new Andean messiah, "a figure equivalent to Jesus Christ." He based his rebellion on both Inka and Christian ideological elements. The myth of Inkarri told of a creator-figure who would return to restore harmony and justice, and the idea that this resurrection was at hand had spread throughout the Andean region in the years just before the violence broke out. On the other hand, both rebellions also self-legitimized their attacks on officials in Peru by claiming connections directly to Spain.[10]

The rebels, then, saw themselves as being more loyal to Spain—about which most of them had only a vague idea—than were the Spanish authorities in the New World. The line of cultural and political loyalty was flexible, however. As the rebellions grew and spread, Andean elements came more to the fore. Leaders delivered speeches in native languages, not in Spanish, and locations they selected for these exhortations were likely to be Andean sacred spaces rather than Spanish churches. Yet native leaders called upon the Virgin for protection. A painting in the church of Yanaoca shows an Andean family, possibly Tupac Amaru's own, beneath the protecting arms of the Virgen del Carmen. Another suggestive painting is now lost but for years was located in the chapel of Nuestra Señora de los Dolores, which had been the Chapel of the Indians, in the church at Tinta. It showed the final battle of Tupac Amaru's rebellion, in which his native forces were defeated by the loyalists. In the center of the picture one saw the Virgin in the town plaza clasping a man by the hand. She was depicted as almost twice his size, indicating her power, with no other figures appearing in the square. This painting recounted the miracle of Illatinta. The story was as follows: at the conclusion of the battle, the victors brought seventy-five of Tupac Amaru's supporters before a firing squad. One man, identified as Josep Illatinta, died in the execution but was later resurrected by Our Lady and was able to move about the town and the encampment without being detected. He died for the second and final time, according to the legend on the painting, twelve years to the day later.[11]

Spanish loyalists, including Andeans, similarly invoked the Virgin in the struggle and acknowledged her aid in their successes. Teresa Gisbert has noted that virtually all Spanish military men had their portraits painted in front of a particular object of their devotion, usually a representation of Mary (as Tupac Amaru seems to have done).[12] Andeans on the Spanish side were likewise devout and grateful to the Virgin. The Pumacahua clan, which had supported the Spanish in the earliest struggles with the Inka, remained faithful two centuries later. Their leader, Diego Mateo Pumacahua, was important in Tupac Amaru's defeat, taking part in the decisive battle of Tinta. Pumacahua appears in one image with his wife, both of them kneeling and praying to the Virgin of Montserrat, the patroness of Chincheros, where his family's estates were located. He is dressed in the Spanish fashion with a long coat, a vest, and tight trousers; his wife wears the characteristic petticoats of an Indian woman and the high hat of a female ruler. It is significant that Pumacahua's wife was included, reflecting the gender complementarity of indigenous society. Another painting was produced after Tupac Amaru was captured to celebrate the occasion. This image showed a puma killing a snake while the approving Virgin of Montserrat looked on, an interesting mixture of Andean and European elements. The puma represents Pumacahua; the serpent is Tupac Amaru, a reflection of an ancient Andean feud. Both Amaru (in Quechua) and Katari (in Aymara) refer to serpents, creatures of cosmic power associated with the mountains. To the Virgin's right, one sees the battle between Pumacahua and Tupac Amaru depicted; on her left, the Pumacahua family moves in procession, all praying together.[13]

The rebellion of Tupac Katari in the Aymara area of the South was perhaps even more insistent on the elimination of the Spanish and their culture than that of Tupac Amaru in the Quechua-speaking North. Still, Catholicism was by no means completely suppressed. A remarkable report from a priest at the sanctuary of Copacabana who managed to survive the violence gives us evidence of the continued significance of the European religion and of the Virgin. It illustrates the confusion that the leaders of the rebellion and the indigenous peoples they were trying to lead felt in regard to issues of spirituality.

On March 19, 1781, while Fray Matías de la Borda was performing mass for a number of the Spanish who had taken refuge in the church of Copacabana, an Indian named Tomás Kallisaya appeared in the town, claiming to be the representative of "Tomás Tupac Catari Ynga Rey." He wore a rope around his neck and carried a string tied with a knot. The rope, he said, indicated that he would hang anyone who did not tell the truth. The string, reminiscent of the *quipus* Andeans had used to transmit information since the pre-Spanish period, signified the authority conferred on him by Tupac Katari. Armed with these credentials, Kallisaya made his way around town screaming announcements and orders to the inhabitants; then he called a meeting of the natives of the community, who "had already congregated."[14]

Tupac Katari's emissary announced his leader's wishes: that all Spanish officials and their retainers, including women and children of both sexes, and "all persons who were or seemed to be Spanish, or that at least dressed in imitation of the Spaniards," were to be put to the knife. Those who took refuge in the church or with a priest or anyone else would be killed immediately, along with their protectors. His exhortation brought the excitement and fury of his native listeners to a fever pitch. As Fray Matías was in the process of saying mass for a group of people seeking refuge, the frenzied Indians stormed into the Copacabana church. When de la Borda reproached them for such irreverence against the Holy Sacrament, they replied heatedly that they were carrying out the orders of the Inka king. Further, they would no longer hold *their* ceremonies anywhere but in the mountains—those spaces so sacred to Andean spirituality—and would reject other Spanish practices, such as eating bread. Then Kallisaya undid the knot in the string he was carrying, shrieking as he incited the Indians to begin the assault on the church. De la Borda's entreaties that God would punish the attackers seemed to slow the action for a moment, but the fury soon began again. It became clear that the Indians meant to burn the church with all the refugees inside.

Understanding this purpose, the priest was forced to lead his flock out of the sanctuary. Each carried some Christian image—a crucifix, a cross, or some other token. Yet there was to be no mercy. As soon as they were outside, they were fallen upon and murdered, the men by the men and the women by women, indicating, perhaps, Andean gender reciprocity and the sharing of religious and political tasks including killing. De la Borda, somehow, was spared. He estimated that one hundred people were slaughtered, including children, and the plaza filled with a "horrible lake of blood."[15] Even the priest's pleas for aid in burying the dead were ignored; the rebels insisted that it was the express will of the Inka King that the bodies be thrown out into the fields, "as all of the Spanish were nothing but excommunicated creatures, and some of them demons."[16] Again, the Andeans claimed that they themselves were the true Christians.

The twenty-fourth of the month saw an even more frantic and bloody tumult, though the priests were still spared. The religious began flagellating themselves and performing other penitential practices, all the while pleading with the rebels to desist and threatening them with divine vengeance. These efforts served for nothing. The violence continued, now with the leaders demanding that the Fathers be killed, the sanctuary destroyed, and the "miraculous image of our Lady of Copacabana be carried off to another place."[17] At this point, something startling occurred. Two of the rebel leaders, who called themselves Reyes Fiscales (native ecclesiastical authorities), entered "very irreverently" first into the sanctuary of Our Lord and then into the recamarín—the dressing room—of Our Lady of Copacabana, "without the least respect or veneration."[18] As they were prowling about looking in all the nooks and crannies, "other Indians who had not totally lost their Devotion to the Divine Image" met together and sentenced the two to death.[19] They were executed immediately. As de la Borda reported, "at that instant they were Souls of which God would dispose."[20] Having killed the offending pair, the rebels returned to killing the Spanish.

The incident is telling. Although the insurgents were determined to wipe out the Spanish, their culture, and their acculturated indigenous allies, the Virgin herself was not to be dishonored. Not only did they not intend to destroy the image of the Virgin—which they considered taking to another place for safety—they executed two men, leaders of the uprising, who they felt had in some way dishonored her. As Christianity to them was no longer strictly Spanish, neither was the Virgin. Copacabana retained her power for them; the rebels wished only to respect and safeguard her. Threats to her or irreverence toward her were not be tolerated, even from within their own ranks.

This blurring of what was Spanish and what was native extended to their leader, Tupac Katari. Fearful of continuing his struggle without the services of Catholic priests, he had gathered several of these unfortunate individuals around him. They had been taken from towns around La Paz, which his forces had surrounded. Not having enough religious practitioners, apparently, he sent to Copacabana for yet another. On this occasion, Father Matías

himself was chosen and was escorted directly into Katari's camp. He remained there for several weeks until he was able to escape into the besieged
city. De la Borda noted that Katari constantly reiterated his opposition to
the Spanish and everything to do with them, even refusing to permit Spanish
to be spoken in his presence on pain of death. But that did not include
religion—not exactly. Rather, he insisted on regular masses, but with a difference. During these events he would pull out a little box of silver he kept
with him at all times, look inside it, close it, and then hold it to his ear. In
this way, he said, he would receive messages about everything that he needed
to know to carry out his purposes, as God was speaking to him through the
little container. After the conclusion of mass, Katari's people sang (sometimes religious verses) and danced in the church. However, they refused confession. In a remarkable combination of Catholicism and the native religion,
Katari removed the Sun from the monstrance where the Host had been placed
and began to wear it around his neck. Though this action shocked Fray Matías,
it was not entirely unprecedented; such a pendant would have resembled
those used in the Corpus Christi ceremonies in Cuzco by Inka leaders after
the Conquest. It is not unlikely that such pendants, combining as they did
Andean and Christian symbols, had continued to be used by Andean elites
throughout the colonial period.

Further, Katari treated the priests as his servants rather than spiritual
advisers, executing one who denied him absolution after he had confessed.
He demanded that the captive clergymen say mass every day in the makeshift
church he had created and adorned with looted religious treasure, including
an organ. He used these occasions to promote himself as almost divine, not
only consulting his little silver box but also looking at himself in a mirror in
search of revelation. He also claimed to converse with the Virgin, who, he
said, helped him make his life and death judgments regarding his prisoners.[21]

The indigenous threat was finally put down, but less than thirty years
later, Upper Peru was thrown into a new conflagration. This region became
the first center of an independence movement against Spain, as local elites
divided among themselves to support either separation from or loyalty to
the metropolis. In fact, the first declaration of Latin American independence from Spain came from local leaders in La Paz, when in July 1809 they
seized the local governor and the bishop, declared themselves a governing
junta, proclaimed an independent American republic in the name of King
Fernando VII (who was actually in the custody of the French), and refused
to recognize the Spanish junta that was governing in Fernando's absence.
Although this initiative was short-lived, Alto Peru would become an area of
turmoil for the next sixteen years, caught between the generally loyalist government in Lima and the strong independence movement coming out of

Buenos Aires. The Virgin was present for those conflicts as well, again invoked for her aid by both sides. It was not uncommon, in fact, for uprisings to take place on feast days dedicated to the Virgin.[22]

General Manuel Belgrano, who led an insurgent army from northern Argentina into Upper Peru in the early years of the conflict, was well known for his devotion to the Virgin of Mercies. He proclaimed Nuestra Señora de las Mercedes to be a General of the Army in thanks for her aid in his victories. A contemporary observer noted the astuteness of this action, as it associated the revolutionary movement and the "patriot army" with the "consciences of the people."[23] The Virgin not only served as military leader but also as protector in these conflicts. In her advocation of Our Lady of the Rosary, she was sometimes called upon to provide mercy. In 1814 rebel leaders Juana Azurduy de Padilla and her husband, Manuel Asencio Padilla, extended amnesty to royalists found hiding in the priest's quarters in Pombabamba, as they felt they could not harm them in the presence of her image. Juana Azurduy herself was often equated with both Pachamama and the Virgin Mary, a conflation of spiritual and political power in the person of this charismatic female leader.[24]

Less successfully, royalists in Sasari who had fallen into rebel hands were executed, although the priest tried to bring out the image of Nuestra Señora del Rosario to intercede for their lives. The native forces who had taken the priest prisoner said that this was no time for the Virgin to be removed from her throne. They put her back in the church and declared that the men should die.[25]

The "consciences of the people" and the way in which revolutionary forces related to them were extremely important. A case in point is the way Simón Bolívar, the great liberator of South America, attempted to establish a civic culture and set of symbols resonant with those already in place in the Andes. In one example, the constitutional assembly in August 1825 authorized Bolívar to present a gold medal to the great hero of the battle of Ayacucho, Marshal Antonio José Sucre. A few months earlier Sucre had soundly defeated the loyalists and assured the independence of Upper and Lower Peru. The medal would show the silver mountain of Potosí, the mining center that had been the mainstay of Spanish economic activity in the Andean region, with Bolívar himself at the top of a ladder "formed by guns, swords, cannons and flags." That Great Liberator would be shown placing the cap of Liberty on the summit of the mountain.[26]

The revolutionaries in general were no friends to the Roman Catholic Church. In this particular case, they were appropriating Andean and Christian symbols to their own cause. The mountain Potosí, known locally as Sumaj Urqu (the beautiful mountain), and the hill Huayna Capac just in front of it where indigenous people were brought to provide tribute labor to the Spanish-run mines were symbolically powerful in Andean spirituality. The whole process was further related to Andean rights to land within the Spanish system. Potosí was tied to the idea of Pachamama (Mother Earth) and to the Virgin Mary; Huayna Capac was associated with the child Jesus. The tribute work that Andeans performed in the mines is still commemorated today in local fiestas as a claim on rights to land. Coinage itself was symbolic and significant, and the medal reflected the importance of the Potosí mint, which was "also the object of ritual libations and invocations." Here, Andeans might believe, was Bolívar promising the return of lands and at the same time honoring both Pachamama and Mary. According to Tristan Platt, the Andeans could also read the image as a promise to aid in increasing Indian harvests, as Mary (and Pachamama) were sources of fertility. The association with both the Virgin and Pachamama—shown as the mountain that Bolívar could be seen crowning—seemed to be designed to provide legitimacy for the new republic in Andean eyes.

Potosí also was linked with the Virgin of Copacabana. From the earliest development of the cult, miracles in Potosí were attributed to her benevolent sponsorship. Tito Yupanqui had worked for a time with a master sculptor in that city. Ramos Gavilán reported that the image was credited with many miracles involving *mitayos* (native workers who had been rotated from their homes to the mines), saving them from cave-ins, the loss of animals, and severe illnesses and injuries.[27]

The wars of independence resulted in the separation of Upper Peru from the northern and coastal area that became the nation of Peru, as the independence movement had been far more active there than in conservative Lima. On August 6, 1825, insurgent leaders in Upper Peru declared it to be the new state of Bolivia. It was to the Bolivian nation rather than the Peruvian one that Our Lady of Copacabana became attached, geographically and spiritually, although the native reverence for La Candelaria in general and for Copacabana in particular remains significant throughout the highlands. However, the sanctuary itself fell on evil times.

The revolutionary years had not been kind to the church complex, as the region was roiled by the struggle between loyalists and rebels. The early years of the republic were not much better. The Augustinians were ejected in March 1826, following Bolivar's and Sucre's decrees suppressing religious convents in December 1825 and early 1826. Gold and silver collected in the colonial epoch were melted down at Sucre's order; he used the funds to pay the Colombian army that had swept down the Andes with him.[28] The struggles between Peru and Bolivia impacted the sanctuary negatively, given its location almost on the border between the two countries. Liberal leaders attacked the Church; venal ones demanded money. The pilgrimages and ceremonies never completely stopped, but without a religious community to care for the image and its popular following, Copacabana's sanctuary and cult struggled. Throughout the nineteenth century, conflicts between church and state made it difficult to reestablish the presence of a responsible religious order at the site. Not until 1894, when at last it was delivered into the hands of the Franciscans, was restoration and rebuilding of the complex possible.[29]

As Bolivia moved into the twentieth century, the turbulence characteristic of the previous period began to diminish. The resurgence and development of a significant mining industry, this time focused not only on silver but also on tin, gave elites good reason to desist from continuing conflict in the highlands. At the same time, economic connections within the country became stronger, centered around the mines. The increasing wealth, the developing sense of being Bolivian, and an easing of political conflict around the Roman Catholic Church gave the Franciscans an opportunity to rebuild Copacabana. This opportunity they seized.

The *recamarín* of the Virgin—the room violated during the Tupac Katari rebellion, leading to the immediate execution of the two violators by their fellow rebels—was enlarged in 1910–1913. This space would contain her special altar, and here local inhabitants would come to dress the image for her processions and ceremonies. The improvements to and especially the enlarging of this area demonstrate that the very personal reverence in the relationship of a given population with Our Lady was still present in the Copacabana of the

Plate VIII. Exterior of the Sanctuary of Copacabana, 2000. Photograph by Susan Gandert.

Plate IX. Altar of the Sanctuary of Copacabana, 2000. Photograph by Susan Gandert.

early twentieth century. The interior of the church building was completely renovated for ceremonies in 1925 to celebrate the centennial of Bolivian independence, thus emphasizing a relationship with the Bolivian sense of nation. At the same time, the Virgin of Copacabana received a canonical coronation, although she had regularly been exhibited with a crown before that time. The Franciscans had prepared the way and persuaded the Vatican to authorize this honor. On August 1, 1925, the image now more than three centuries old was put on an altar erected outside the Church, where she would be visible to the pilgrims in attendance. In the presence of the papal nuncio, three Bolivian bishops, the president of the country and his wife, and the ambassadors of Peru and Argentina, Our Lady of Copacabana was crowned Queen of Heaven. Church and civil authorities had again joined in the name of the Virgin Mary. The crown, however, was not a new one. It had been donated by the women of Arequipa, Peru, in gratitude for her saving that city in February 1600 when the volcano Misti erupted.[30]

The honors and the connection of Copacabana to the Bolivian nation, albeit with a nod to Peru, did not end there. In 1940 the church was named a basilica, with General Enrique Peñaranda, the president of Bolivia, serving as patron for the event. Once more, religion and nation coincided in the figure of the Virgin.[31] In 1948 a Marian congress was held in conjunction with the fourth centenary of the founding of the city of La Paz. Yet the plans to bring the Virgin of Copacabana into that city for the festivities were thwarted when the native population of the peninsula rose up in resistance to even the temporary removal of the image from its sanctuary. The dismayed secretary of the La Paz organizing committee complained that the protestors were charging that the committee wished to profane the image, when in fact they only wished to honor her. The plan to move her was immediately abandoned, with the secretary asserting nevertheless that she was "as loved as she was venerated."[32] The image was still contested between the indigenous and the Europeanized populations; yet her connection with civil and political as well as religious purposes, all facets of being Bolivian, continued. In another example of her connection with politics—as well as with potential violence and protection—in 1954 she was named patron and general of the National Police and Carabineros. On this occasion she was presented with a sword with a hilt of gold—the gift of the widow of a deceased general.[33] The navy, not to be outdone, named her its patron and admiral. The naval decree read, "The sainted Virgin of Copacabana is declared to be the principal patron before God, of the entire Navy of Bolivia, with the High Rank of Admiral of the Navy, with all the corresponding rights and privileges of her high station, as an act of Christian faith of the Armed Forces of the Nation."[34] The Virgin continued as warrior.

Pilgrimages never ceased, and today worshipers stream into Copacabana to honor the patroness of Bolivia. Significantly, the two major days for pilgrims are February 2, the feast of Candlemas, and August 6, Bolivian Independence Day. Bolivian and Peruvian brotherhoods still compete to honor her, as they vie for the privilege of carrying her statue during the celebrations. The different culture groups express their devotion to Mamita de Copacabana in different ways and in different languages; those from Cochabamba, for example, sing in Quechua in their processions, while those from the southern highlands sing in Aymara, accompanied by traditional Andean instruments. Worshipers from major urban centers usually express themselves in Spanish.[35] Within the populations, the meaning, apparatus, and content of the celebrations continue to differ.

Northern Argentina, particularly the three states just south of Bolivia and along the Andean ridge, has also been affected by the devotion to the

Images of the Virgin of Copacabana for sale near her sanctuary, 2000.
Photograph by Susan Gandert.

Virgen de la Candelaria and to Copacabana.[36] The cult of Candelaria was spread in the area during the colonial period, and Copacabana is a prominent example of generalized devotion linked with a specific location. There are still numerous celebrations in honor of La Candelaria in the provinces of Jujuy, Salta, and Catamarca. The cult is also present in Chile, not only in the highlands but on the coast, where an image of La Candelaria, said to have been rescued from Dutch pirates during the colonial period, attracts mariners and especially their wives to her protection.[37]

Devotion to Copacabana is also significant in these countries to the South. An interesting fiesta in her honor is that of the Virgen de Punta Corral in Jujuy, Argentina. According to the tradition, the Virgin of Copacabana appeared to the shepherd Pablo Méndez on the 12,000-foot peak of Punta Corral. The reader will recognize the similarities to European stories in which a shepherd—a poor, marginalized, and often solitary person—is honored by Mary; additionally, her appearance on a mountain reiterates that European tradition. However, given the significance of herding in the Andes and the imposing Andean mountain peaks, the story is consonant with Andean spirituality as well.

The Virgin asked Méndez to return the next day, and so he marked the location with a pile of stones. On his return he found that this sign had been replaced by a single small rock on which an image of the Virgin of Copacabana appeared. Méndez left the marvelous stone in the care of a priest in a nearby town, and the priest then placed it in the local church. The Virgin, however, was not content in this location, and the rock disappeared. It was rediscovered, of course, on the site of the Virgin's original appearance. A small chapel was constructed to house it, and in 1889 a grateful believer had that structure rebuilt.[38]

As the cult of Copacabana was renewed by the authority and efforts of both Church and State, it spread even farther. In the first decades of the twentieth century, Bolivians began to move in larger and larger numbers into Argentina to work in agriculture. At first a rural-to-rural migration, by mid-century it was shifting to a rural-to-urban pattern as Bolivians began working in construction and industry. Even as early as the 1950s, the presence of Bolivians in Buenos Aires was more evident. In that city, *villas de emergencia*, that is, urban communities of shacks, grew up around the periphery of the city. Several of these sheltered substantial numbers of Bolivian migrants. Over time, some of these areas were transformed into working-class neighborhoods that acquired certain amenities. In Villa Soldati, for example, a chapel and a primary school were built, and some of the streets were paved. Still, the situation for the migrants was insecure, as they were exposed to economic problems, cultural differences, and outright prejudice. Survival depended on cooperation with family members and other Bolivians, and the development of community took place, at least in part, around popular religion. One way they reinforced ties was in celebrating religious festivities, notably those dedicated to the Virgin of Copacabana.[39]

According to Laumonier, the devotions originated within the family. The typical pattern would be as follows: a family with an image, be that a statue, picture, or print, would erect a small household altar. Soon, they would begin to invite the neighbors to share their moments of reverence. Other individuals and families from the same neighborhoods in Bolivia moved in and would be included regardless of where they lived in Buenos Aires. The *dueños* or "owners" of the image would "lend the saint," permitting it to visit houses nearby or farther away for prayer and other observances. The original household altars also began to expand into something more open and more permanent, with the images receiving gifts of candles and flowers the year round. The fiesta for the Virgin of Copacabana in Villa Soldati was one of the first of these Bolivian celebrations and continues to be the largest and most elaborate.[40] Throughout these Christian observances, Andean forms are very much in evidence, providing an abundance of sources for Bolivian national identity through the worship of the national patroness.

The intensely personal nature of aspects of the celebration blends with the larger community observance. Each year, new outfits specially made in Bolivia are brought to dress the Virgin. Sometimes, devout Bolivian women living in Buenos Aires embroider and decorate the clothes on the basis of their personal promises. The Friday night before the fiesta, a group of women led by the wife of the *pasante*—the man who has taken on the responsibility of directing the festivities—gathers in the chapel to dress the image. They surround it to protect it from indiscreet gazes, and the director's wife takes the old dress off the statue and replaces it with the new one. The image of Copacabana is then adorned with jewels donated by the faithful. On the day itself she is placed in the atrium of the chapel, where believers bring flowers and candles as well as strings of Bolivian and Argentine money, either real or miniaturized. Celebrations continue with banquets, dances in honor of the Virgin, and processions, complete with decorated resting points where she can stop to enjoy the spectacle and prayers can be said in her honor. Houses chosen for such visits are considered especially blessed. Comments among the observers illustrate their sense of the Virgin as a real person, with needs and feelings like their own. For example, they say, "She has to rest from such a long walk," "She enjoys the fiesta," or "After all, she gets tired, too."[41] Dancing groups from various regions in Bolivia illustrate the widespread support for the Virgin and the sense of nation and national community. The youth of these groups show that the reverence is not simply a nostalgic remembrance but rather a vital part of continuing immigrant life; most of the dancers are between fifteen and twenty years old, though there are also troops of younger children. When the procession arrives at the church and the Virgin is again enthroned on her altar, the invited guests form a circle, and the organizers of the festival dance in the middle. On successive dances, other important members of the community and future organizers are brought into the places of honor. Finally, the orchestra begins to play all sorts of music, and all participants begin to dance in a less structured fashion. Toasts take place at various times during the festivities, to the Virgin and, with a few drops of each drink sprinkled on the earth, in an offering to Pachamama.[42]

A spectacular part of the celebration is the procession of the *cargamentos,* cars or trucks decorated in honor of the Virgin. These reflect the old customs of the mining zones, where mules and other animals used for transport were covered with an abundance of items of silver or of other metals. The intention was to honor the Virgin (and Pachamama) by giving thanks for the riches provided from the earth. In the immigrant celebrations, the vehicles come covered with pictures ranging from the Sacred Heart and the Virgin to Bolivian and Argentine national heroes such as Sucre and San Martín. In addition to the pictures, they are covered with mirrors, flowers, dolls, and other colorfully decorated household items. Again, the personal, the spiritual, the political, and the national are mixed in an extravagant material form of reverence.[43]

For Mexicans, the Virgin of Guadalupe is the outstanding national symbol. As with Copacabana, the reverence to Guadalupe developed around a pre-Columbian sacred site that became a Christian pilgrimage center. Likewise, the reverence spread widely as travelers and migrants moved out from the city of Mexico. However, despite the legend, at the beginning she was revered far more by the Spanish and then the *criollos* (those of Spanish descent born in the New World) than by the Indians. The devotion was largely restricted to the environs of the Mexican capital city until the late seventeenth century, when it began to spread.

Important factors differentiated the two cases. The first involved the proximity of Spanish power to the native sacred site. Spanish administration was centered in Lima on the coast of Peru, far in distance and time from Lake Titicaca. Therefore, elements of indigenous worship remained more strongly a part of the devotion, as Spanish control of all kinds was significantly weaker than it was near Mexico City. In Mexico, the devotion developed under the scrutiny of both the Church and civil authority. Further, a rival cult existed in Mexico. This competing reverence was to the advocation so significant to Cortés, the cult of the Virgen de los Remedios, La Conquistadora, who had come with the Spanish. In fact, the first major impetus to the Guadalupan devotion does not seem to have come until the middle of the seventeenth century, with the publication of the story of her apparition by the *criollo* prelate Miguel Sánchez. We know, however, that devotion of some sort to Guadalupe existed at Tepeyac as early as 1555, when a resident priest was appointed there. The archbishop of that time, Alonso de Montúfar, was devoted to Guadalupe's developing cult and helped sponsor it, an effort that drew the ire of the Franciscan provincial, Francisco de Bustamante. This friar was well known as a teacher of the indigenous population. In a sermon on September 8, 1556—the feast day of the Nativity of the Virgin and of Our Lady of Guadalupe of Spain—he denounced the devotion at the chapel and the miracles already attributed to the image, whatever it may have been, as false and misleading to the Indians. Montúfar only two days earlier had praised the same devotion and mentioned the miracles.[44] Despite the controversy, no record exists of the apparition story until the Sánchez account.

A respected diocesan priest, Sánchez served at least for a while as the chaplain to the nunnery of San Jerónimo in Mexico City. This convent was the one occupied somewhat later by Sor Juana Inés de la Cruz, the Mexican nun and writer who gained such prominence and who wrote many poems of praise to the Virgin. Sánchez also, importantly, had served as the chaplain of the *ermita* (chapel) of Remedios, and later retired to Guadalupe. His work on the Guadalupe apparition was published in 1648, 117 years after that apparition was supposed to have occurred. It furnishes the first clear document we have of the version that is now widely accepted. Significantly, he addressed both the Remedios and the Guadalupe advocations, explicitly using oral tradition rather than documents as his sources. Remedios, he averred, reiterated the connection with Spain, as she was from that country and had come with the conquerors. Guadalupe, in contrast, had appeared in Mexico, among the flowers, to "signify this land as her own, not simply as a possession but as her own homeland." The inhabitants of Mexico, then, were related to the Virgin Mary through the image of Guadalupe, "reborn miraculously in the city of their own births, and the homeland, while mother to all, is a Mother dearly loved." According to Sánchez, Guadalupe's appearance united Mary and the Mexican nation in the same way that the Virgin and the Church were united in the figure of the Woman of the Apocalypse, noted earlier in this work as directly connected with the Immaculate Conception. Sánchez was drawing on powerful traditions and beliefs to assert the significance of the appearance of the Virgin in the Spanish New World and thus to assert the significance of the Mexican nation and its people. Mexican nationalism was securely planted in this early account.[45] Sánchez justified the conquest in his document and related Guadalupe to the evangelization project: "The very public miracle of Guadalupe engendered in all the Indians an affectionate devotion to the miraculous image . . . The Virgin Mary from the beginning of the conversion of this New World showered her favors on the Indians, in order to attract, teach, and draw them to the Catholic faith and the support of her intercession, as we see that the two miraculous images that we now enjoy here in Mexico, were delivered to and discovered by two Indians; one is in the sanctuary of Guadalupe, the other in that of Remedios."[46]

The stories of Remedios and Guadalupe were regularly conflated, and both devotions were centered in the city of Mexico, but in the early years of that capital, it was Remedios who was most often called on for aid. According to Linda Curcio-Nagy, by the seventeenth century Remedios had lost

An eagle—an important symbol of Mexican nationalism—stands at the base of a statue of Christ outside of the basilica of the Virgin of Remedios, Mexico City. Photograph by Linda B. Hall.

her connection to the Conquest and had taken on "the persona of the Madonna, of protectress of Mexico City and environs. She became the premiere urban image." Curcio-Nagy points out that Remedios was the image normally called upon to ease the disasters, "epidemics, drought, and famine," that befell the city.[47]

Still, as we have seen, Sánchez was re-emphasizing the connection of Remedios to the Spanish and not to the Mexicans, that is, the citizens of New Spain. And the path indicated by Sánchez is confirmed by Curcio-Nagy as she traces the increasing appropriation of Remedios for Spanish authority. In 1692 a general uprising of the poor in the city frightened officials. Remedios was brought from her sanctuary in the indigenous countryside to aid in ending the famine, and she was kept in the cathedral within the city until 1695. When she was next brought in procession to the capital, in 1696, it was not for the general welfare of the residents of New Spain but to advocate for the safe arrival of the Spanish fleet. Returning to Spain, the same fleet took one of the Virgin of

Remedios's dresses along and found it an efficacious protection. Between 1700 and 1810, her image was brought to the city thirty-two times, and almost half of these had to do with royal concerns including the protection of the fleet during arrivals and departures. She was even called upon to safeguard the health of royal officials.[48] Guadalupe enjoyed personal patronage from Spanish officials as well. The Marquis de Mancera, the viceroy of New Spain between the years 1664 and 1673, was said to visit the church and sanctuary of Guadalupe each Saturday, and he was present in March 1666 when a panel of experts examined the *tilma*, the maguey-fiber cloak said to have belonged to Juan Diego, on which the image still appears. The conclusion of these experts was that no human hand could have produced such a fine image on the difficult surface; therefore, it had to be of divine origin.[49]

The idea that the Virgin produced her own image was an extraordinary boost to Mexican nationalism. As early as 1678, an engraving of the Mexican Virgin included on its border the legend *Non fecit taliter omni natione*, words from Psalm 147 meaning, "It was not done thus to any other nation." Stated differently, Mexico had been specifically selected by the Virgin for her special favor. Father Florencia, who wrote *Estrella del Norte*, mentioned in Chapter V of this volume, ordered a medal struck in Antwerp in the same year and had it inscribed with the same phrase. Florencia, a Jesuit who headed schools in Puebla and Mexico City, averred that although he had visited the Holy House of the Virgin at Loreto in Italy, Tepeyac stirred his reverence more. He directly linked this sentiment to his own Mexican patriotism.[50]

Almost forty years passed before a major epidemic of *matlazahuatl* hit Mexico City and brought Guadalupe's significance to new heights. The disease was believed to be the same, still not precisely identified, that killed hundreds of thousands of indigenous people in the late 1500s. In this case, Remedios was first invoked and her image brought to the city in January 1737. After a novena between January 10 and 19 failed to slow the spread of the illness, the council of the city suggested to the archbishop that the image of Guadalupe be brought as well. The archbishop, concerned about possible damage to the *tilma*, turned down this suggestion, and the council then suggested that Guadalupe be selected and honored as the foremost patroness of the city. The archbishop countered by suggesting a procession to Tepeyac, which was held later in the month. Still the epidemic raged, and on February 11, the council at last insisted on an oath to Guadalupe as patroness of the city. The ceremonies were carried out on April 27, and at the same time the council swore that the city would observe December 12 as her feast day. A procession on May 26, followed by mass at the cathedral, publicly celebrated these decisions. The epidemic began to abate.[51]

In the eighteenth century the advocation of Guadalupe rapidly gained significance, particularly for Creoles, encouraged by Mexican archbishops, Jesuits, and diocesan clergy who had either been born in the colony or identified with it. The Spanish also asked for her help in military endeavors and in guarding the fleet.[52] Still, the devotion was taking on an increasingly Mexican character. Reverence for the Virgin of Guadalupe was spreading beyond the region of Mexico City and into the countryside, where she became important to farmers and their guild. In the first half of the eighteenth century, Guadalupan sermons were preached at Sombrerete, at Guanajuato, at Antequera (preached by the bishop of Oaxaca), and in Zacatecas at the Colegio de Nuestra Señora de Guadalupe, the Franciscan seminary where missionaries received training for the northern frontier of New Spain, from which point her significance spread even further.[53]

Virtually all of these sermons focused on establishing the significance of the unique character of the Guadalupe image; however, one went considerably beyond this concept and moved boldly into the area of prophecy. It was delivered in 1748 at Querétaro, where one of the first Guadalupan sanctuaries outside of Mexico City was located. Preaching on December 12, Guadalupe's Day, Jesuit Francisco Javier Carranza followed the usual argument that the image on the *tilma* had been produced miraculously by Mary herself, not, as in the case of other images, by human or angelic hands. He went on, however, to insist that therefore Tepeyac was her principal sanctuary on earth and that although the Church would be crushed by the great dragon in the Old World, the Mexican Virgin (obviously, he declared, the Woman of the Apocalypse) would defend the Americas. The pope would flee Rome for Tepeyac, and the Church would remain at that location until the final judgment. Thus, the Jesuit had firmly linked Guadalupe to ideas of the millennium.[54]

The diffusion of the devotion was aided by the acceptance of the *patronato* (that is, the principal patronage of the Virgin of Guadalupe) by other cities in New Spain and Guatemala. By 1746, sufficient responses had been received for the archbishop to declare Guadalupe as patroness over the nation. In 1757 the *patronato* was also accepted by city council of Ponce, Puerto Rico. Thus even very early on, Guadalupe was established in an extended area.[55] The pope approved the *patronato* and the mass and office in 1754, and in 1757 the feast and office were extended to all Spanish dominions. Guadalupan sermons, processions, and ceremonies began to occur widely through New Spain and contiguous areas.[56]

The reverence and millennial associations of the devotion extended to native peoples as well, but here her figure was ambiguous. William Taylor has pointed out that although most scholars in recent years have seen the Virgin in indigenous Mexico as carrying "revolutionary and messianic messages," she has also been a "model of acceptance and legitimation of colonial authority." Certainly she maintained this ambivalence, but as New Spain moved through the eighteenth century, her messages of "accommodation and liberation" moved toward the latter. In legal struggles between indigenous and Creole adversaries, she might be called on to help the native litigants. For example, in 1783 the scribe of the Indians of Zacoalco, the Afro-mestizo Toribio Ruiz, proclaimed that "Most Holy Mary is praying for us" in a land dispute. When the high court in Guadalajara ruled against the Indians, a Spanish resident remarked that Holy Mary must no longer be pleading the case. Ruiz, undeterred, portentously answered, "Consider the temporal and eternal judgments." Here the Virgin was being invoked as a protector and ultimate moral arbiter, an active and assertive stance in favor of the indigenous over the Spanish. Further, Mary might actually protect the native population from their local priests; a complaint by one of these groups in Veracruz to the viceroy about their curate's excessive fees called upon the Virgin Mary "to free us from these many oppressions."[57]

As in Peru, the idea of a "millennial reconquest" circulated in the years leading up to the independence movement. This idea was apparently even more closely tied to the Virgin of Guadalupe than the Peruvian movements were to any of their own cults of the Virgin. A regional insurrection in Tulancingo in 1769 called for the creation of a priesthood of natives and death to Spanish officials. The leader of this movement was called the New Savior, his consort the Virgin of Guadalupe. Another uprising, plotted between indigenous peoples in Tlaxcala and Nayarit and a Spanish aristocrat in Mexico City, was scheduled for December 12, 1800, the day of the Virgin of Guadalupe. The significance was ambiguous, however, at least in terms of its connection to the Mexican Virgin. The first act was to be the burning of the church at Tepeyac, which would have put the sacred painting in peril; while the church was burning, explosions were to be set off at the viceregal palace in Mexico City. It is unclear whether the attempt sought Guadalupe's aid and rescue from Spanish authority or her destruction.[58] In either case, she was associated with political and religious power. The sense of her power likewise can be seen in the messianic movement of an Indian named Mariano, who turned up in the town of Tepic in late 1800. He claimed to be the son and heir of the last governor of Tlaxcala and said he had traveled to Spain, where King Carlos IV had confirmed his right to rule. His coronation was to take place on January 6, 1801, Three Kings Day, and he would be presented by the Spanish and indigenous authorities along with men carrying banners of the Virgin of Guadalupe. His plan had two elements: land restitution to the Indian villages and relief from tribute payments. His crown was to be of neither gold nor silver but rather the one that was used to crown Jesus Christ on the local religious image.[59]

During the independence movement beginning in 1810, the Virgin of Guadalupe was repeatedly called on to aid insurgent forces. Father Miguel Hidalgo y Costilla invoked her in inciting the indigenous in central Mexico to rebellion in September 1810, giving his followers a banner of the Virgin of Guadalupe to follow. He would later inscribe on their flags the following slogans: "Long live religion! Long live our most Holy Mother of Guadalupe! Long live Ferdinand VII! Long live America and death to bad government!" The Creole writer and insurgent Carlos María de Bustamante wrote in 1813 that when the Virgin appeared to Juan Diego, he heard her say, "You shall call me Mother and I will be yours; and you shall call upon me in your tribulations and I will hear you; you shall plead with me for liberty and I will loose your chains."[60] José María Morelos, another priest who led the movement in the South during its second phase, proclaimed her "the patron of our liberty" and her feast day a national holiday. His flags bore the colors of the Virgin's dress, blue and white, and his troops used her name as a countersign, as Pánfilo Narváez's men had used "Santa María" centuries earlier. The man destined to be the first constitutional president of independent Mexico, Manuel Félix Fernández, changed his name during the war of independence to Guadalupe Victoria.[61]

Guadalupe was by no means appropriated exclusively to insurgent forces in the struggle. From early on, the Spanish invoked her name as well, often with considerable horror that the Blessed Virgin would be profaned by association with murderers and criminals—that is, the rebels. During the conflict, prelates came forward to claim Guadalupe for the Spanish cause. In 1811 a Creole priest and canon of the cathedral in Mexico City, José Mariano Beristain de Souza, preached a sermon that is instructive. This priest, along with several others who wrote preambles to his published work, objected strongly to the appropriation of Guadalupe by the insurrection. One of these introductions, authored by an honorary inquisitor of the Holy Office in New Spain and rector of the church of San Ildefonso, protested that the taking "of the sweet name of María of Guadalupe to promote insubordination, theft, homicide, and all the other things that the revolution has brought with it, is a horrible sacrilege that tries to claim the Mother of God as protector of the excesses and horrors prohibited and condemned by the sainted law of her Son, which she came to these kingdoms to establish."[62] In a commentary, the vicar general of the religious convents of the archbishopric viewed with equal alarm the "invocation of the august name of Sainted Mary of Guadalupe to protect a project which itself involves a mass of the most destructive evils aimed at religion, at the State, at the lives, at the estates, and at the public and private peace of all the inhabitants of this new world."[63]

Beristain's sermon reflected these ideas as well. "Are we not all in agreement that it has been blasphemy, insult, and contempt to call upon the sainted and sweet name of Mary to authorize, legitimate, and sanctify the disorders which have afflicted and still afflict our towns?" he queried. Speaking to a group of Spanish military men who had come to honor the Virgin, he emphasized that it was Mary of Guadalupe who had brought the Mexicans out of the shadows of paganism and into the light of the true religion. Her instruments had been precisely Spanish military and religious institutions. The result had been three centuries of peace, faith, and greatness. "Only a terrestrial paradise could compare with our land." He then recounted at length the ways in which Holy Mary had aided the Spanish: at Zaragoza, when she had encouraged Saint James to continue in his quest to convert the Spanish; when she had inspired them to victory over the Moors at Covadonga; when as Remedios she had protected and aided them during the struggle against the Aztecs; and finally, when she descended at Tepeyac. (It is interesting to remember that at this same time, the Spanish themselves had been struggling against French invaders and calling on Pilar, their own national advocation, for assistance, as it was the French invasion and the imprisonment of the Spanish king that had given initial impetus to the Latin American independence movements.) Thus, for Beristain, the Virgin Mary's advocations of Pilar, Covadonga, Remedios, and Guadalupe were all linked, were all the same, and never would the Virgin, the same marvelous human woman despite her various advocations, support the barbarous masses ranged against the Spanish. In this assertion he was fighting the pronounced and continuing tendency that we have observed to see Mary as divided into many advocations, with different attributes, supporting various groups. Mary the Mother of God, he pronounced, was the symbol of peace and order and obedience, not of violence against authority. She was, he concluded, the Mother of Indians only if they were united with the Spanish.[64]

Beristain was not the only prelate who objected to the use of Guadalupe by the forces of the insurrection. In June 1812 Fray Diego Miguel Bringas delivered a sermon on the issue to a Spanish division after their victory at Tenango del Valle. He quite specifically derided the claims to Guadalupe made by Hidalgo and other revolutionary leaders. In his opinion, "The manifest injustice of their cause is not, nor ever will be, a project worthy of the protection of Mary." As he saw it, recent losses by the revolutionaries at

Zitáquaro, Lerma, Quautla, and Tenango were evidence that those adhering to the Spanish side were the ones who enjoyed God's protection "through the mediation of Mary."[65]

Not only Spanish priests objected to the attempt by Hidalgo to appropriate Guadalupe for the insurrection. When they discovered that Hidalgo, whom they opposed, was using her name in favor of his cause, the Zacapoaxtla Indians claimed her as their own protector and patroness against his forces and gave her credit for their own victories. In 1813, when they requested permission to construct a church to honor Guadalupe, they explained that she had protected them in 1810 and 1811. It also seems likely that members of Hidalgo's movement were probably reverent toward other advocations of the Virgin—such as that of Our Lady of San Juan de los Lagos—and to the generalized devotion to the Immaculate Conception to which the Guadalupe image was linked. As the war waned and as Mexican independence was ultimately achieved, the Virgin of Guadalupe emerged as the preeminent Mexican national symbol. It seems to me, as it does to William Taylor, that the war itself was the most significant factor in dispersing and universalizing the association of Guadalupe with the Mexican nation and its new-won independence.[66]

The primacy of the advocation of Guadalupe during and after the independence wars was by no means uncontested. Remedios continued to be important with indigenous and Spanish devotees. During the struggle, a number of treatises recalled her significance in bringing religion and civilization to New Spain. She was called upon again by Spanish supporters to rally against the threats to continued Spanish rule. She herself was named General of the royalist forces, and the nuns of San Jerónimo dressed her statue in military attire—including a small gold baton and a sword. A procession and novena in February 1811 gave thanks to Remedios for saving Mexico City from Hidalgo's threatening hordes. Once again, as Linda Curcio-Nagy points out, she "had become the Conquistadora, patroness of the political heirs of Hernán Cortés."[67] Yet similar reverence for Guadalupe continued to be significant on the royalist side. Nevertheless, with the Spanish withdrawal, Guadalupe prevailed in Mexico as the heroine of independence and as a marker of the Mexican nation.

As with Copacabana and Bolivia, throughout the nineteenth century the association between Guadalupe and nation of Mexico continued to strengthen, though political struggles between pro- and anti-church forces complicated the issue. When Agustín Iturbide, a latecomer to the insurgent cause, took over Mexico City in 1821, his triumphant entrance was followed by a sermon at Tepeyac offering thanks to the Virgin for the independence of the country. Iturbide later proclaimed himself emperor of Mexico and tried to legitimize his claim by founding the Imperial Order of Guadalupe, naming him-

Tortilleras *and children with image of the Virgin of Guadalupe in the 1860s.*
Aubert & Cia., ca. 1864–1867, Center for Southwest Research, General Library,
University of New Mexico, No. 997-013-0049.

self grand master. In 1831 the third centenary of the Virgin's apparition was
observed with four days of celebrations. In the wake of enormous Mexican
military and territorial losses to the United States in the late 1840s, Guadalupe
was called on as an icon of national unity. Even during the long years of
strife between Church and State in the second half of the nineteenth century, Guadalupe continued to be very important in popular reverence. Finally, in 1895 the Virgin of Guadalupe was crowned in an event described by
the editor of the Catholic newspaper, *The Times,* as "the most important and
transcendental . . . in the history of our country."[68] Better was yet to come. In
1910 Pope Pius X proclaimed Our Lady of Guadalupe as the patroness of all
Latin America. Despite the tensions between long-term dictator Porfirio
Díaz and the Church, just a few weeks after this proclamation a banner of
Guadalupe thought to have belonged to Hidalgo's army was carried in honor
through the streets of Mexico City along with the uniforms, recently re-
turned from Spain, of that other major hero of independence, José María
Morelos.[69] These demonstrations strongly affirmed the connection of the
Virgin with other icons of Mexican nationhood.

Within just a few months, however, Mexico would be thrown into a decade of turmoil with the violent events of the Mexican Revolution. Díaz was quickly driven into exile, and the victors, liberal and relatively anti-clerical leaders from the Mexican North, had little interest in Guadalupe. At the same time, the Mexican hierarchy itself seemed interested in moving to a more modern and European Catholicism and attempted to push the cult of the Sacred Heart of Jesus in place of that of the dark Virgin. Yet Guadalupe prevailed and moreover was significant to other revolutionary forces, regardless of the ideologies of northern leaders or the modernizing desires of the hierarchical Church. In November 1914 Zapatista revolutionaries from the South carried her banners through the streets of Mexico City. Nevertheless, reflecting the wishes of the Northerners, the 1917 Constitution removed the Catholic Church from its former educational mission and deeply restricted its privileges. Despite the relatively mild attitudes toward the Church that President Alvaro Obregón (1920–1924) held, the issue rankled, illustrated by a deeply shocking event. On November 14, 1921, a bomb exploded before the high altar of the Tepeyac sanctuary, damaging altarpieces including a crucifix, which was bent dramatically backward. The *tilma* with the image of the Virgin, however, was unharmed. A member of Obregón's own presidential secretariat was implicated in the event.[70] As one might expect, the bombing merely increased devotion to Guadalupe, with her followers perceiving the survival of the image as a miracle.

The tensions between Church and State erupted in 1926 during the presidency of Plutarco Elías Calles, significantly more anti-clerical and repressive than Obregón. Carrying banners of Guadalupe inscribed "Viva Cristo Rey!" (Long Live Christ the King!), rural Catholics moved to rebellion, supported by urban, middle-class Catholics. The struggle lasted three years and was costly in human lives and bitterness, and it largely achieved its objectives. The willingness of Catholics to fight for their religious rights led to an accommodation, and the Church was able to rebuild its institutions. This time, however, the Church chose to focus its efforts around the already powerful image of Guadalupe by renovating her basilica at Tepeyac at a cost of over two million pesos. Celebrations in 1933 at Saint Peter's in Rome, attended by the Pope as well as prelates from all over Central and South America, at last ritually acknowledged her patronage over all of Latin America.[71]

As the Mexican state continued to consolidate in the wake of the Revolution and the Cristero conflict, the Virgin of Guadalupe further reestablished her symbolic national and international position, sponsored now by the Vatican. In 1935 her patronage was extended to the Philippines. Church-state tensions within Mexico were considerably relieved in 1940 when President Manuel Avila Camacho announced, "I am a believer." In 1945, on the fiftieth anniversary of her coronation, Pius XII, his voice broadcast to the ceremo-

Pilgrims carrying the Mexican flag and an image of the Virgin of Guadalupe as they arrive at the Basilica of Guadalupe on December 11, 1999, Mexico City. Photograph by Linda B. Hall.

Virgin of Guadalupe images against truck in Chihuahua on December 12, 1998. Photograph by Jacqueline Orsini Dunnington.

nies in her basilica, referred to her as "the noble Indian Mother of God" as well as "the Queen of Mexico and Empress of the Americas."[72] The acknowledgment of Guadalupe's special status by Rome and the extension of her dominions in establishing her as patroness of the continent not only enhanced her cult but also Mexican national pride.[73] Millions of pilgrims come annually to her basilica in Mexico City; it is the most visited Catholic site in the world, with the exception of the Vatican (see Chapter IX). Thus, similarly to Copacabana in Bolivia but in a more intense and extended fashion, the Virgin of Guadalupe has become "the most powerful religious and national symbol in Mexico today."[74] In 1990 Juan Diego, whose very human existence was somewhat in doubt, was beatified; in 2002 he was canonized. Devotion to Guadalupe has spread well beyond Mexico into the United States, into Central America, and back to Europe. Certainly, this Mexican image is the most widely reproduced and worshiped advocation of the Virgin in the world today. Moreover, she gives Mexicans outside of their country a strong sense of connection with and pride in the homeland.

The case of the Virgin of Luján in Argentina is at once similar to and yet considerably different from the prior two cases. Both the images of Copacabana and of Guadalupe were created—either miraculously or by human hands—near the sites in the New World that they would sanctify, but that of the patroness of Argentina was brought from a neighboring country, Brazil. Moreover, the devotions to Copacabana and Guadalupe, though no doubt sponsored by both the Roman Catholic Church and Spanish State in the colonial period, were closely connected to indigenous sacred sites where they developed more organically than would be the case in Argentina. Most importantly, the Copacabana and Guadalupe devotions became strong in the colonial period, while that of Luján grew most significantly after 1930, as several regimes associated with the Argentine military brought the image forward and affiliated it with a project of nation-building.[75]

According to the discovery story, the clay statue of the Virgin of Luján arrived in Argentina in 1630. Antonio Farías de Sáa, a Portuguese *estanciero* (estate owner) of Sumampa, Argentina, had asked a sailor to bring him an image of the Immaculate Conception of Sainted Mary from Brazil. The sailor brought not just one but two images of Our Lady, which arrived safely at the port of Buenos Aires. Loaded onto an oxcart, the images initiated their journey north to Farías de Sáa, but on arrival at the Río Luján, the cart came to a stop and could not be budged. Removal of the box containing one of the images failed to correct the problem, but when the boxes were switched, the cart easily moved forward. It was determined that the second box contained the image of the Immaculate Conception, which, it seemed, had elected to stay in that particular location. It was carried to a nearby estate, while the sister image, of the Mother of God, was taken on to Farías de Sáa at Sumampa. The owners of the estate where the first image had chosen to remain initially constructed a small altar to provide for her, and over time, larger and larger chapels were built. Eventually a basilica was constructed alongside the river, approximately where she had originally prevented the movement of the oxcart.[76]

The Luján site became a pilgrimage destination as word of miracles associated with the image began to spread. It was nevertheless much different from those of Copacabana and Guadalupe. Rather than being established on an indigenous spiritual site, it was the site of an Indian attack on Spanish troops in the year 1536—on the date of Corpus Christi. Several were wounded, among them one Captain Pedro Luján, who was brought to die on the riverbank. The location was marked by a solitary tree and later was known by that landmark. There were no native sites nearby.[77]

Although interest in the shrine grew in ways similar to those of Guadalupe and Copacabana, with word of La Lujánera's miracles spreading in the eighteenth century and the devotion reaching into the capital of Buenos Aires, the cult was always clearly Spanish and Creole. Argentina's native population was not sedentary, and much of it was wiped out early in the colonial period. As a result, the cult of the Virgin had little to do with any kind of indigenous content and was largely constructed in keeping with the needs of the populace of European descent.

The interest in and influence of the Virgin of Luján may have grown during the independence movement, as Argentina struggled to separate itself from Spain and to resist takeovers by other foreign powers. Some of the events, however, may be more legendary than actual. Symbolic actions, either then or later, became associated with the image or with the Villa de Luján, the town that had grown up around the sacred site. Juan Martín de Pueyrredón and other Argentine patriots met in the Villa—located near Buenos Aires—to plan the expulsion of the British from the capital city in 1806. According to the received wisdom, in 1813 General Manuel Belgrano offered Our Lady of Luján two flags that he had taken from Spanish forces in the battle of Salta, though as noted earlier, his armies were dedicated to Our Lady of Mercies. Also, the story goes, José de San Martín, the liberator of Argentina, visited her sanctuary after the key independence victories of Chacabuco and Maipú.[78] The association of these two heroes with Luján has perhaps reflected more about twentieth-century commentators than about actual nineteenth-century events.

As with Guadalupe, the sainted image received a pontifical coronation in the late nineteenth century; this honor occurred in 1887, while Copacabana would have to wait until 1925. But only after the Virgin of Luján was named patroness of Argentina, Paraguay, and Uruguay in 1930 did her cult begin to grow rapidly and become clearly associated with the Argentine state.

The events of September and October 1930 were important to the devotion to Our Lady of Luján. On September 6, the liberal government of President Hipólito Yrigoyen fell to a military coup. He was replaced in power by a general, and quickly the ceremonies naming her as patroness of the country were organized and carried out. It was not that the military as individuals were devout Catholics; rather, they were "Catholics by tradition and that did not imply a particular kind of social comportment." The army was still substantially "aconfessional" but definitely conservative and opposed to the social and labor activism that was arriving with immigration and industrialization. The army and the Church were brought together through their "common invocation of tradition" and their mutual claims to be repositories of that tradition; they were also united in their opposition to a socialism that they saw as "anti-patriotic" and destructive.[79]

The connection between naming the Virgin of Luján as patroness of Argentina in 1930 and a state project of constructing a homogeneous national identity around Catholicism is made clear by the rhetoric of the ceremony itself. Monsignor Miguel De Andrea declared on this occasion: "To establish the Patronato of the Virgin of Luján is, from the national perspective, to pledge our honor before God and our Country to maintain the security of the tradition that she embodies and that is both religious and patriotic ... without whose cardinal principles the historical identity of the country, which should be indivisible and unique, will perish. And what are these cardinal principles which at all costs and in spite of any developments we must maintain? God, Country, Family, and Property."[80]

The State in making these connections was clearly involved in both legitimation and militarization, processes that had begun a decade earlier. Argentina would see, from this point forward, the development of an "integral Catholicism," based on an intense identification between Church and State. According to Eloisa Martín, the concern of the Church had to do with unifying and homogenizing the enormous number of immigrants pouring into the country, especially from Spain and Italy, during the early years of the century. Moreover, a substantial internal migration from the interior into Buenos Aires province, the capital city, and the coastal littoral had further accentuated the need to foster a sense of what it was to be Argentine. All of this movement of diverse peoples into a single space had created a number of "catholicisms" that needed focus and unity and that would be tied to the needs of the State. This unity of Church and State was further emphasized by the 1934 Eucharistic Congress, for which La Lujánera also served as patroness. Another Argentine Eucharistic Congress was held in 1937, this time actually in the city of Luján. The Church emphasized that the reason for choosing that location was to associate the congress with the fiftieth anniversary of the coronation of the image. The same year, when Line D of the subway of Buenos Aires was opened, a mural in the Ninth of July station—so named for Argentine Independence Day—featured the Virgin of Luján close to the "solitary tree" and the river, with her basilica nearby. La Lujánera was moving into Argentine public space, specifically that public space associated with Argentine nationhood.[81]

The role of the Virgin of Luján in this centralizing, homogenizing mis-

Virgin of Lujan prayer card. Courtesy of the Marian Library, University of Dayton, Ohio. Photography by Teresa Eckmann.

sion was intensified after the next military coup, which took place in June 1943. At this point, many of the government officials who came to power with the coup were either priests or devout lay Catholics. In 1945 devotees of the Virgin of Luján began "Embajadas de la Virgen"—"embassies" undertaken around the country to disseminate the devotion. A group of priests headed by the bishop would take a copy of the image of La Lujánera around the country, usually by train, stopping at each station to leave an image of the Virgin. These trips were made also by automobile and naval vessels. Juan Perón, soon to become president of Argentina, emphasized the connection between "the Gospel and the Sword" in a June 1944 speech; during his presidential campaign, the bishops of the Church prohibited their flock from voting for candidates who advocated making divorce legal, maintaining secular education, and further separating Church and State. This stance, in effect, was an endorsement of Perón, as his major rivals had announced these principles in their published platforms.[82]

The movement of the Virgin of Luján beyond her sanctuary out into public space continued rapidly in the period after 1943. The Federal Police, the national highway system, the railroads, and the National Council of Education were all dedicated to La Lujánera. Particularly important in this connection were the railroads. The nationalization of these most important infrastructural connections—long owned by the British—took place during the first Perón administration; he dedicated the railroad lines to her and continued to place images of her in the stations. It was at this time, too, that the connections between the Virgin of Luján and the heroes of Argentine history—particularly Belgrano and San Martín—began to be publicly emphasized. In fact, as the stations were graced by the presence of María of Luján, many of them were renamed for the heroes of Argentine history. Medallions of Our Lady were also placed in all the locomotives.[83] In 1947, both Juan and Evita Perón made an appearance at the First National Marian Congress in Luján; in 1948, the Virgin continued her embassies around the country, a copy of her image traveling 4000 kilometers by road and railroad, including a visit to her sister image at Sumampa.[84]

Perón in the later years of his presidency became less interested in pushing any advocation of the Virgin, as his own wife, Evita, became strongly identified with Mary, as we will see in the next chapter. In fact, he broke with the hierarchical Church and was ultimately excommunicated as he strove to replace Roman Catholicism with his own secular Peronist religion.[85] Concerns about Perón's intentions in this regard led Catholics, during the last days of his presidency, to remove the statue from the sanctuary and to hide it away until his government collapsed.[86] After his fall in 1955, however, the Argentine State renewed the emphasis on the devotion to the Virgin of Luján. In 1956 she was named patroness of the Central Division of the Argentine National Gendarmerie, and her images began to appear in police stations throughout the country, particularly at border crossings—a clear association with protecting and defining national frontiers. And although the patroness of the Argentine army was another advocation—La Merced—in 1958 Our Lady of Luján was linked to that institution as well when she was named patroness of the military vicarate, established only the year before. She also undertook new travels; in 1957 images of her were taken into Uruguay and into the far northeast of Argentina in an effort to combat secularizing tendencies and to spread her cult. She continued to be associated with the military; in 1958 she enjoyed her first helicopter flight, and in 1960 air cadets from Spanish-speaking nations around the world, including Spain, Mexico, and the nearby countries of Chile, Uruguay, and Bolivia, paid their respects to her in her sanctuary.[87] Also in 1960 the original image of Luján was brought to Buenos Aires to preside over the so-called Great Mission, an effort by the Church to reinvigorate Argentine religious observance. It was the first time the image had left Luján to be brought into the capital. At this time Catholicism itself was undergoing a process of liberalization, with new tendencies in many directions, including greater social activism. The Virgin of Luján, in her new mission, was reassuring to those seeking instead to shore up conservative integral Catholicism.[88] Moreover, the next year her martial and national nature was reemphasized when U.S. Air Force head Chaplain Terence Patrick Finnegan arrived by helicopter to celebrate mass in the basilica.[89]

The Virgin was not ignored by sports figures, either. In 1963 she was visited by Boca Juniors, one of Buenos Aires's two preeminent soccer teams. The team had come to thank her for saving them from a serious accident on the road between Rosario and the capital and also for helping them win the national championship. The following year the Argentine middle-weight boxing champion came with his wife and children to present to La Lujánera the gloves with which he had won the South American championship. Boca Juniors' major rival, the River team, visited her in 1967, and in the same year the teams of Rosario, Independiente, Lanús, Quilmes, San Telmo, and Racing came as well. Perhaps they were inspired by Boca Juniors' success.[90] In 1978, a time of great political difficulty and of government and military repression, the Argentine national soccer team triumphed in the World Cup. Subsequently, many of the members of the team visited La Lujánera to thank her for her aid in the triumph. As one of the players reported, "We did nothing more than come to fulfill a promise made in the most difficult moments. The Virgin of Luján helped us, and it is only just that we come to thank her."[91] Although the circumstances were not so dire as those that inspired Columbus and his men to visit various advocations of the Virgin after their perilous return from the Spanish New World, the process and the emotion seem to have been similar.

The repressive military government that Argentina suffered between 1976 and 1983 continued to push reverence for the Virgin of Luján as part of a centralizing and homogenizing effort. While hundreds of Argentines were disappearing from around the country as the government bitterly attacked the political left, La Lujánera continued to be at the center of its nation-building iconography. For Argentines 1980 was the National Marian Year, as the 350th anniversary of the miracle was celebrated with everything from pilgrimages to postage stamps. In his state of the union speech that year, the president, General Jorge Rafael Videla, referred to her as the "patroness of the Argentine people," the designation confirmed by the Church itself; the Argentine Conference of Bishops declared her "the Patroness and Mother of the Argentine people." The same year, this association of the Virgin with national identity was underlined by the inauguration of the Crypt of the National Sanctuary of Luján. The permanent exhibit in this underground space contained images of the Virgin in her advocations as national patroness of countries around the world, and many of them had come as special gifts to the Church of Argentina. Two years later, the Argentine military attacked the Falkland Islands in an attempt to rally the Argentine people behind another national symbol. A statue of the Virgin of Luján was carried to the Falklands and enthroned there by the bishop of Lomas de Zamora, Desiderio Collino, while thousands of rosaries, medals, and printed images of Luján circulated throughout the country. After the British roundly defeated the Argentine military and retained control of the islands, many of the returning soldiers reportedly made pilgrimages to the basilica. One of these was José Fernández, a well-known military chaplain who had taken part in the losing struggle. However, in another twist in the use of Luján for national purposes, the Church called on La Lujánera to aid in a public dialogue of national reconciliation in the wake of the defeat and of the harsh internal military repression.[92] At the same time, the Mothers of the Plaza de Mayo—women who had lost their children and other loved ones in the wave of illegal arrests, tortures, and disappearances sponsored by the military government—invoked the Virgin in their rhetoric, though usually not the advocation of Luján by then so closely associated with the military. They compared the martyrdom of their children with that of Christ and their own sorrow with that of Mary.[93] We will explore this movement further in the next chapter.

The change in the attitude of the Church had likely been inspired by Pope John Paul II, who visited Argentina in June 1982 and called on the Argentines to unite around La Lujánera, the Mother of God. The pope found the streets full of posters and flags carrying the words *Todo tuyo* (All yours) flying throughout the country. The theme was his own and revealed his devoted commitment to the Virgin Mary. On his arrival at the Luján basilica, the image was brought out to the front of the building to welcome him. He prayed for a few minutes in front of the image and then presented her with the Rose of Gold, a papal medal signifying great honor. Throughout his visits, he called repeatedly for "justice, love, and peace." Later that year, in a visit to the Virgin of Pilar, the national patroness of Spain, the Pope connected Pilar and Luján in his remarks.[94]

Although the military government was replaced in December 1983 by a civilian president, the Virgin of Luján continues to be associated with the Argentine military. The yearly pilgrimages from Buenos Aires out to the basilica are accompanied by military bands. The march played is the same one that was used to introduce government proclamations and announcements on the radio during the Proceso, as the years of the repression are known in Argentina. The sounds of this march still stimulate considerable emotion, often quite negative, in those who hear it. Two side chapels in the basilica are dedicated to the military and one to the national police; these include huge lugubrious messages invoking the protection of the Virgin. The lettering in these appeals is formed from hundreds of small ex-votos of legs, torsos, heads, and other body parts that are presumably imperiled by the dangerous duties of the military and the police. Yet another side chapel is, startlingly, dedicated to sports.

The Virgin is a powerful unifier, as the image of spiritual Mother draws the people of a nation together as a symbolic family; the use of Mary for national identification and integration is compelling. In Latin America in the colonial and national periods, up to and including the present, advocations of Nuestra Señora, with the emphasis here on *Nuestra*—"*Our*"—have been used sincerely and cynically, spiritually and politically, to produce new sensibilities and identifications. In Mexico and Bolivia, these new understandings have drawn together diverse populations, initially enhancing Spanish control of indigenous peoples but ultimately being reconfigured into a sense of Mary for all, an equalizer, an inspiration, and a benefactress for new and independent nations. The belief that Guadalupe constructed her own image miraculously has led to the idea of Mexico as uniquely favored. The repeated insistence by the current pope that she is the patroness and benefactress of all the Americas has been a source of enormous pride for Mexicans and those of Mexican heritage, both inside Mexico and in other countries. Mexican devotion has expanded into an enormously powerful cult, spread throughout the hemisphere and into other areas. However, the direct association of Guadalupe with the Mexican State, much less with the military, has been avoided by the extreme anti-clericalism and insistence on secular institutions by the immediate postrevolutionary governments and then by the official party, the Partido Revolucionario Institucional, the PRI, which grew out of those administrations in the late 1920s. Now, with the defeat of the PRI for the presidency in 2000, it seems that a closer relationship between the Virgin and the State in that country may be emerging, an issue we will explore in the tenth chapter of this work.

Bolivia has resembled Mexico in the early and strong acceptance of an advocation of the Virgin in the Andean sacred space of Lake Titicaca and throughout a large regional area. Similarly appropriated for state-building purposes in the nineteenth century, the association of Copacabana with the government continued strongly in the twentieth, with the Virgin linked to institutions of control such as the military and the police. The advocation of Copacabana functions for those Bolivians traveling and living elsewhere to link back emotionally and spiritually to their own homeland, as the images and ideas of Mary permitted Cortés and Pizarro to do centuries earlier. At the same time, the cult is widespread in adjacent countries because Bolivians and other devotees have moved there and preserved her celebrations, as in Buenos Aires; because the devotion already existed, as in Peru; or because she is believed to have performed miracles in these places as well. In the colonial period, it seems clear the sacred nature of the lake and the region it served as a numinous site were largely preserved by the shift to a devotion acceptable to the Spanish, that is, devotion to the Virgin. This reverence was appropriated by the Bolivian State in the nineteenth century, and this connection between Copacabana and the State has continued to the present.

The case of the Virgin of Luján combines aspects of Copacabana and Guadalupe but is nevertheless considerably different. The colonial story did not involve the indigenous; it was Spanish from the start and underlined Spanish victory and the heroic sacrifice of Spanish life. It seems as well that the devotion was not widespread or pan-Argentine until it began to be pushed by military governments after 1930. This twentieth-century association with the State was very similar to the Bolivian one but quite different from the Mexican. The use of Luján for unification and state building seems to me the most calculated of the three cases, as the military men who invoked her were not always particularly devout Catholics. Rather, the devotion was a useful way to appeal to new immigrants, themselves from southern Europe and especially Spain and Italy, where the reverence for the Virgin was strong, while also uniting native Argentines, many of them internal migrants. By presenting migrants with a nearby national advocation of a spiritual Mother with whom they were already familiar and from whom they could draw solace and a sense of home in a new location, Argentine leaders explicitly tried to homogenize and better integrate the populace behind their own rule. The figure of Our Lady of Luján was at once familiar and new, an entry point to a new land, new loyalties, and a new sense of nation.

But the Virgin of Luján in the middle to late twentieth century was not the only feminine icon around which Argentines and immigrants, especially laborers in the Buenos Aires area, could come together. A resonant and present image—a living woman, Eva Perón—emerged to eclipse Our Lady of Luján as a rallying point for Argentine nationality among those born in the country and outside it. Though she enjoyed political power for less than a decade, her image is still vivid and effective. Brought into the public eye through her radio programs and films, she married Juan Perón at a time of turmoil, just as he was rising to supreme political power. As first lady she constantly invoked images, gestures, and sentiments associated with the Virgin Mary and made this association into a potent political tool. However, it was not a role that was, in my opinion, fraudulent and contrived, but rather one in which she felt completely absorbed and committed, a sincere emulation of the purest and most admirable female model available to her. It was one in which she, dishonored from the time of her illegitimate birth, rose to honor and legitimacy. At the same time, she was able to give the working classes of Argentina, native and foreign-born, a spiritual mother and hero around whom to rally.

CHAPTER EIGHT

Evita and María

Religious Reverence and Political Resonance in Argentina

✠ ✠ ✠

ALTHOUGH THE DEVOTION toward the Virgin of Luján had been heavily and perhaps rather cynically oriented toward state building, state power, and the deliberate construction of national identity, that did not mean that devotion to the Virgin and a sense of her nurturing goodness did not exist apart from that project. On the contrary, Argentina was a Catholic nation in which heavy immigration from Spain and Italy in the late nineteenth century and the beginning of the twentieth reinforced Mary's significance. The same kinds of family separation, of feeling out of place and endangered, existed for these immigrants as they had for the Spanish in the colonial world as well as the Bolivians who came later for work. Though the contexts were very different, the idea of having a kind and concerned Mother as a presence in one's travels and adjustments was again powerful.

As we have seen, Argentine governments had promoted the cult of the Virgin of Luján, particularly since the 1930s. It may be that there was a conscious understanding of the need for such a unifying image, given the changes brought by industrialization and immigration, or perhaps the image was psychologically satisfying to leaders themselves in a way that was more felt or intuited than intellectualized. Probably both factors were involved. Certainly it seemed to work, and pilgrimages to the Virgin of Luján and her basilica on her day remain popular and important in religious observance in the area around Buenos Aires. Even Juan Perón, during the first period of his rule (1946–1955), continued to put statues of this advocation in public places, often train stations. But it was his wife, Evita, who made best use of Marian symbols, rhetoric, gestures, and evocative acts and performances to establish a resonance with the Argentine people. During her lifetime this connection had enormous power, and the devotion to her personally since she died in 1952 has remained strong. Remarkably, in the months before her death of cancer, her identification with Mary extended to an identification with the martyred and dying Christ as He suffered the Passion. However, Peronist attempts to continue the political use of the dual Evita/María image without the living Evita largely failed. I am not arguing here that Argentines in any sense confused Evita with or adopted her as a substitute for the Virgin. Rather, I believe that her behaviors had strong Marian resonances that evoked highly positive responses in the Argentine masses and contributed significantly to her political power and personal charisma. Moreover, I believe that the motherly, nurturing, giving, caring Marian persona that she took on as the wife of the president was psychologically satisfactory to her and helped make it possible for her to feel whole despite her dishonored past.

Eva Perón was born illegitimate (certainly) in the town of Los Toldos (certainly) on May 7, 1919 (possibly), and died in 1952, at the symbolic age of thirty-three. Her birthdate is in question because no documents, either civil or religious, are known to exist—they seem to have been destroyed. According to sources who claim to have viewed these documents, she and one of her older sisters, Erminda, and her only brother, Juan, were baptized at the same time—November 21, 1919. Her baptismal name was Eva María Ibarguren. Interestingly, Erminda's middle name was Luján.[1] No name was listed on Evita's record for her father, perhaps because, as village gossip would have it, her parents had had a dispute about what names should be used for the children. Her mother was Juana Ibargueren. Her father, Juan Duarte, may have wanted to conceal the children's parentage, and perhaps his affair with Juana had entered difficult times; he reconciled with his legitimate wife in a neighboring town just months after Evita's birth. Thus ended a liaison of almost two decades and five children including Evita. Along with it died any hope of status for Juana and her children in Los Toldos, a small town in the pampa west of Buenos Aires. The family had enjoyed some regard, dressing well and employing a maid before Juan Duarte's departure, but he left Juana and her children in reduced circumstances. Regardless of the name on the baptismal certificate, Evita and her siblings always used the name Duarte, aspiring to the status they had lost.

When Evita was six her father died, and Juana and her five children, dressed in mourning, tried to attend the funeral. A terrible argument with the legitimate wife followed, and only after the intervention of the wife's brother were the children permitted to enter the house. During the walk to the cemetery, they were relegated to the back of the line of mourners, away from the family members immediately behind the hearse. These events must have been shaming and distressing to Evita and her mother and siblings; in any event, Evita and her sisters were never willing to admit their illegitimacy.[2] It seems clear, however, that the shame of her birth and the stain on her mother's honor and her own weighed heavily on Evita, as a child and as an adult. Paco Jamandreu, her designer during her early years as presidential wife, reported that he went with her to a shantytown for a political appearance. Over and over, she asked obsessively the women, "Where is this child's father?" When informed that he was gone or that the child was fatherless, she bit her lower lip in distress.[3] The issue of illegitimacy and fatherlessness seems to have distressed the entire family, who, within a few years after her father's death, moved to a larger town a few miles away, Junín, a way station on the road to Buenos Aires.

Even Junín, however, was too small for Evita, who left on her own for the capital city in 1935, and rumors have it that she left in the company of the tango singer Agustín Magaldi. However, there is no evidence that he was in Junín in the year that she moved, and the rumors may have had to do with the consistent attempts by her later political opponents to attribute her success to her sexual availability. Some accounts even claim that she was a prostitute, and while she was by no means chaste while unmarried, these accounts are false. Nevertheless, and remarkably, she went to live on her own in Buenos Aires when she was possibly only fifteen years old.[4] She had arrived in a city of one and one-half million people, at that time the third largest in the Americas after New York and Chicago. Her first years there were no doubt hard, but she apparently quickly got work playing the role of a maid in a theater company and shortly thereafter toured with another. Most of the time she lived in one small pension or another. She began to get radio parts; amazingly, by 1939 at age twenty she already was successful. Her pictures appeared in magazines, and she began working in soap operas. She turned out to be quite suited to these stories that focused on love, initially unrequited or thwarted and later marvelously fulfilled. Her brother Juan had moved to Buenos Aires and was working for Radical Soap, which soon began to sponsor Eva's radio programs. She had bit parts in movies. At some point she formed her own company, and Juan facilitated her contracts with his own employer. By 1943, at twenty-three years old, she was earning between five thousand and six thousand pesos a month, making her one of the best-paid actresses in the Argentine radio world.[5] In June 1943 the Argentine military under General Arturo Rawson took over the country, along with the regulation of communications and especially radio. Those military officers responsible for broadcasting seemed to have liked Evita and facilitated an idea of hers, a radio series called "Heroines of History," of course featuring her. The quickly produced series presented episodes about women who were significant either because of connections with important men or, occasionally, on their own. Evita was preparing for her own greatest role.[6]

A natural disaster provided the opportunity for the deciding event in Evita's life. An earthquake that barely disturbed Buenos Aires devastated the Andean town of San Juan, killing 6,000, and the military government soon began a major campaign to aid the victims. The fund for this purpose was administered by the secretary of labor in Rawson's administration, Colonel Juan Domingo Perón. Juan and Evita met at a benefit he had organized for the victims, and they left together. She referred to it as her "marvelous day," while Perón himself called it "destiny." From that time forward until Evita's death nine years later, they were together. Within a few months Evita was the president of the union of the broadcasting agency. She also participated in propaganda programs three times a week that the secretary of labor and public welfare sponsored. She was not yet a blond.[7]

A role in a film called *Circus Cavalcade* brought about that major change. Bleaching her hair for the part, she discovered her new golden hair suited her pale skin and differentiated her from other, mostly brunette, actresses. The change provided her a kind of ethereal quality and made her visible from a distance. In fact, in photographs of the era, her light hair gives the appearance of a halo or an aureole, a feature later emphasized in paintings of her promoted by the Peronists. But she was far from ethereal. She took great interest in Perón's activities and attended meetings he held with political associates. Some of those present at these meetings were surprised at her strong interventions on those occasions. At the same time, their public affair was fodder for Perón's enemies and Evita's as well. His position within the military began to erode.[8]

By September 1945 the military government was under pressure. Perón, meanwhile, was associated with pro-Nazi sentiments at a time when Germany had just capitulated to the Allies. At the same time that opposition demonstrations against the military were accelerating, Perón was addressing rallies of workers with raucous and rousing speeches, emphasizing the connection between the military and laborers. The labor opposition to the military government remained active, however. On September 19, 1945, a huge anti-government rally marched right past Perón's office while he, it was said, took a nap. Although most of the unions were not involved, the hostility was significant toward the government though not toward Juan Perón, and the unions were a serious threat. Perón and his lover, given his reputation as labor's champion, were seen as liabilities or even potential traitors, as many within the government saw him as using the unions to enhance his personal political power. Perón became the object of criticism within the army and outside of it. Perón's own support from workers and workers' groups remained strong.

A movement to force Perón to resign from his government positions—extraordinarily, by now he was vice president as well as secretary of war and secretary of labor—quickly developed in the powerful Campo de Mayo garrison a few miles outside the city. One of the officers involved later complained, "We were convinced that it was our duty to stop the nation from falling into the hands of that woman, as in fact ultimately happened." The garrison threatened to march on the city, the president called Perón and asked him to resign, and on October 9, 1945, Perón did so. Evita was immediately fired from her job at Radio Belgrano. When Perón made a public appearance to bid farewell to the employees of the Secretariat of Labor, a crowd of fifteen thousand showed up, among them Evita. On October 13 Perón was arrested and taken to Martín García Island, but the immediate outbreak of strikes and mass demonstrations forced the frightened government to release him four days later. On October 17, 1945, Perón made a dramatic address to a mass demonstration led by the laborers in the Plaza de Mayo, the open square in downtown Buenos Aires. He spoke from the balcony of the Casa Rosada, the presidential palace, and he and the president, General Edelmiro Farrell, repeatedly embraced. The government had been forced by the people to bring Perón back, and the political landscape of Argentina changed.

For Evita, the most important transformation was in her marital status. While it was unlikely that Perón under other circumstances would have chosen to make her his wife, given her questionable reputation, the strains of the arrest led him closer to her. Their public affair had put her in considerable peril during the time he was detained, and she could have moved on to another, safer lover rather than maintain loyalty in that perilous political climate. Some Argentines, perhaps those from "good families" who disapproved of her sexual conduct, demonstrated outside her apartment, and one woman spat on her doorstep. Nevertheless, she did what she could, searching for someone who would help him. It was not accurate that she herself had led the laborers to demonstrate in Perón's behalf; she did not have the proper contacts, while those in the Secretariat of Labor did, as did some of his supporters in the labor movement. She did try unsuccessfully to obtain permission for him to leave the country, returning repeatedly to a labor lawyer who was a friend of Perón's to get him to file the necessary paperwork. She did not appear at the Casa Rosada on October 17.[9]

But her ambiguous status was about to change. Perón wrote to her from his prison on Martín García Island about his feelings. Addressing her as "my adored treasure," he declared, "Only when we are separated from those we love can we know how much we love them . . . Now I know how much I love you and that I cannot live without you . . . [A]s soon as I get out we'll get married." The ceremony took place on October 21.[10]

Immediately she was transformed from a famous woman with a shady reputation into the wife of Argentina's new leader. The shift coincided with the extraordinary emergence of the working class as an important factor in the Argentine political system. Eva quickly became active on the campaign trail for Perón's presidential bid. Soon after he won the presidency in 1946, Perón gave her a special status in his government. He put her in the Secretariat of Labor as his own personal representative, although another individual took the job as labor secretary. Later she founded the María Eva Duarte de Perón Foundation, and she personally attended hundreds of individuals who came to her for help. Evita took her responsibilities seriously, and she very quickly became a personal and accessible mediator between her husband and the people of Argentina. She was the source of financial help and other favors for union members or their families as well as more marginal members of society who came to her directly to seek help. She was already moving into a Marian role, furnishing aid to those in extremity in a way that the poor of Argentina saw as close to miraculous. I am not suggesting, of course, that she was anything other than a human woman doing what she could to help others or that the beneficiaries believed differently; nevertheless, the help she was providing was not available from any other source and was extraordinary in nature, and it was remembered as such by the many whom she favored. Many of those she helped became Peronists. At the same time, she was emphasizing her role as mother, taking special interest in issues that involved children and the family, a stance entirely consistent with well-bred Catholic womanhood, though the public way in which she was doing these things was highly unusual. I see no reason to believe that these efforts were insincere; indeed, she seems to have found enormous solace and perhaps a special form of legitimacy in her ability to help. From a shamed child, she had become an effective and legitimate adult, protected and empowered by her marriage to the most powerful man in the country. Further, this man did not keep her in the background but brought her forward into an active role in his political life.

Biographer Marysa Navarro has pointed out the significance of Evita's charisma to Perón's own charismatic power. Drawing from Max Weber's definition of charisma, that is, "a certain quality of individual personality by virtue of which he is set apart from ordinary men and treated as endowed with supernatural, superhuman, or at least specifically exceptional powers or qualities," Navarro guides us to an understanding of the way in which Evita's power would be realized. As Weber described these qualities, they were "not accessible to the ordinary person but . . . regarded as of divine origin or as exemplary, and on the basis of them the individual concerned is treated as a leader." Weber, however, never explored this possibility of a "shared" charisma, that is, charisma extending beyond more than one leader.[11] With Evita, however, ascribed status as the wife of the president—combined with her beauty, force of personality, and acting ability—made it possible for her to share in his power and in his own charismatic force. I am in no way suggesting that Evita was using the role she would assume—a role with strong Marian overtones—cynically, or that it was just an acting job. On the contrary, I believe that it was effective precisely because it was such a good fit with her own desires, social concerns, and psychological needs. And, I believe, the charismatic power of this role was enormously enhanced by her ability to use, consciously or otherwise, an identification with the nurturing, giving, mother-ness of the Virgin. In this way, she acquired by association the "supernatural, superhuman, or...specifically exceptional powers or qualities" associated with charismatic power. Further, these qualities were "not accessible to the ordinary person," and they were accessible to her only through Perón's position.

Indeed, her very rhetoric implied that Juan Perón was all-powerful, a human stand-in for God the Father, with herself as intercessor. Strangely, she would take on the role of the martyred child during her prolonged final illness, her own Christlike passion, at the age of thirty-three. Her husband was always the superior and the source of power, she the intermediary whose presence would guarantee that "the people and above all the workers would always find the way to their Leader unimpeded," as she put it in her autobiography.[12] The very structure of her speeches reflected her position between the *descamisados*—the shirtless ones, the poor, the people of Argentina who needed her and her husband—and Perón himself. Her favorite metaphor of herself, and one repeated often, was as the "bridge of love between Perón and the people." And, in fact, it was a role she played.[13] Another metaphor of which she was fond was of herself as a rainbow, in this case not only between Perón and the Argentines but also from Argentina back to Europe. When in 1947 she visited the old continent as the representative of the new, she described it as "stretching a rainbow of beauty" between the two.[14] Authors would use it regularly to refer to her and her activities.[15]

In portraying herself as entirely subordinate and devoted to Perón, she maintained the fiction that she was an ordinary wife forced into activism by her support for her husband and his causes. Thus she sought to avoid a direct conflict with the gender ideologies of her time, and she took a stance, at least rhetorically, similar to that of the handmaiden of the Lord, the submissive and compliant Mary. Yet she was recognized as a leader even when she portrayed herself as "this humble woman who works trying to interpret the patriotic dreams of General Perón" or "I who am the most inconsequential of General Perón's collaborators."[16] Meanwhile, she was speaking constantly on Perón's behalf at political gatherings and meetings of the labor movement—far from traditional activities for an Argentine woman. In taking on a role as supporter and interpreter of Perón to the people, she became a striking power in her own right. Her fanatical devotion to both sides—Perón and the people—was expressed in terms of love, caring, commitment, and even physical self-destruction. Evita was willing to sacrifice her life for them, as Christ had to save all peoples. Her rhetoric of "burning" her life for others soon became fact.

Evita's Marylike persona was reinforced by her constant appearances and accessibility. David Kertzer has described the process of establishing "ritual as symbolic behavior":

The caption on this political poster for the Peronist movement in the 1980s, decades after her death, translates as "The era of privileges and elite minorities has ended, because the hour of the people has arrived." Evita 1952—26 de julio—1983. Offset lithograph, 38 by 56 cm. Sam L. Slick Collection of Latin American and Iberian Posters, Center for Southwest Research, General Library, University of New Mexico. Photography by Teresa Eckmann.

A ritual helps give meaning to our world in part by linking the past to the present and the present to the future . . . But even though there are certain psychological and even physiological bases of ritual, understanding its political importance depends on recognizing the ways ritual serves to link the individual to society . . . Even where individuals invent new rituals, they create them largely out of a stockpile of pre-existing symbols, and the rituals become established not because of the psychic processes of the inventor but because of the social circumstances of the people who participate in the new rite.[17]

Her speeches from the balcony of the Casa Rosada, particularly on the October 17 anniversaries of Juan Perón's dramatic appearance after his imprisonment in 1945, indeed linked that important past event to the political triumphs of the present. The physical presence of thousands of people in the Plaza de Mayo, along with the presence of the Peróns themselves, provided strong individual physiological experiences—that of standing in an immense crowd, usually in beautiful weather known as "Peronist days," and being in the presence of the adored leaders/benefactors and able to see and hear them, albeit often with difficulty and at a distance. Psychologically, one's presence among other believers reinforced the importance and drama of the occasion. Those who attended were further linked to the people around them and to the Peróns themselves. The occasions were linked to "pre-existing symbols," in the sense that Evita evoked the strong, loving, nurturing Virgin. And the "social circumstances" of the participants were significant: they were people without power absent the Peróns, and powerful with them, much as believers thought themselves to be powerful with the help and the presence of the Virgin and desperate without her.

These appearances took on the aura of epiphanies, of the appearance of the sacred, as in the use of images and religious ritual. In this case, they were dual epiphanies, as Juan himself spoke as well. More and more, however, it was Evita, who used the loving language of soap operas and of nurturing mothers, who established the deepest emotional resonance with the crowd. Her striking blond hair and feminine (though increasingly tailored) clothing made her visible and distinguishable even at a distance. She could be heard as well; she was quite familiar with the best way to use a microphone. Evita speaking from the balcony might evoke a sense of Mary miraculously speaking to believers.

She also was accessible in one-on-one situations, open to personal appeals, as the Virgin was perceived to be. When receiving petitioners at the Secretariat of Labor or at her own foundation, she received them kindly, frequently coming from behind her desk to embrace or kiss even the visibly ill. Often she gave them more than they asked, because she liked to and she could. Once she had ordered the petitioner's wish granted, the actual delivery of whatever was necessary was handled by social workers. For the parent of a sick child, access to a hospital could seem a miracle; so could the provision of a house of one's own for the very poor. Though recipients certainly realized that these were not miracles in any theological sense, the actual reception of desperately needed benefits went stunningly beyond what, without Evita, would have been normal expectations. Beyond the giving of these gifts, she showed that she understood the practical difficulties of those coming in to see her. She kept fifty-peso notes on her desk to hand out to all who sought her help, knowing that they often needed money to get home. If they lived in Buenos Aires, she sometimes sent them in her own limousine, waiting in the early hours of the morning for it to arrive back to take her home. She became thinner and thinner, surrounded in her office by pictures of her husband and herself and of religious figures. Those who were visiting noticed her pallor, her loss of weight, her exhausting schedule. All of these activities and occupations were punctuated by her own declaration that she herself was a woman of the people, a declaration that was credible, given her humble background and what seems to have been her evident sincerity.[18] Moreover, her epiphanies and miracles were not confined to Buenos Aires and were long remembered. Scholar of religion María Julia Carozzi reports that in a recent conversation with a taxi driver, he recounted to her that his mother had thrown a letter into Evita's train when she passed through the town of Mendoza, at the foot of the Andes far from the capital. The communication told of his sister's need for medical care that her husband, a railroad worker, could not afford. Evita answered in a letter that the taxi driver remembered vividly more than fifty years later, and the government paid for his sister's trip to the capital and for the three surgical interventions that returned her to health. Though he was not a Peronist, he said, he nevertheless felt that no other politician had done as much for the country as Juan Perón, here identified with the good works of his wife.[19]

Evita's devotion to the Virgin became manifest during her 1947 visit to Europe. She was extremely fearful about the trip, and on embarking she wrote a letter to Juan, reiterating her strong connection to him as well as her concerns. She dwelt on his redemptive role in her life: "you have purified me, your wife with all her faults, because I live in you, feel for you and think through you." She then urged him, "Juan if I die take care of mother please she is alone and has suffered a lot." She proceeded to indicate her wishes about what should happen to her personal things in the event of her death. It was a peculiar foreshadowing of her death five years later.[20]

Her first stop was in the highly Catholic Spain; Juan Perón was an admirer of its leader, Francisco Franco. There she received the Grand Cross of Isabel the Catholic of Spain and then received the acclaim of a cheering crowd of thousands when Franco presented her on a balcony above Madrid's Plaza de Oriente. Later she went to the shrine of the Virgen del Pilar, where she prayed and, dramatically but touchingly, left her own gold and diamond earrings.[21] The advocation was familiar to her, as the Los Toldos church had held a copy of the statue.[22] Similarly, she visited the Virgen de la Macarena in her sanctuary in Seville, where she probably observed the jeweled medal that had been presented to La Macarena for her help by General Gonzalo Quiepo y Llano, the commander of the forces that had taken the town for Franco several years earlier. Evita was even given the title of Handmaiden of Honor of the Virgen de la Esperanza Macarena, a title that seemed to please her.[23] After her visit, she sent a present to the brotherhood of La Macarena, a picture of the Virgin of Luján hovering in the sky surrounded by blond and brunette angels. The blonds looked very like Evita herself. In fact, the Francoist state had taken the Virgin as its patroness, much as in Argentina, and La Macarena was the advocation of choice for many Franco supporters.[24] In Seville, Evita also visited the *camarín*, the special room, of the Virgin of Buen Aire—the Good Winds—who was closely associated with mariners and the discovery of the Spanish New World. A painting of this advocation, also known as the Madonna of the Navigators, showing her sheltering King Fernando to her right and Columbus, the Pinzón brothers, and Americo Vespucci on her left, hangs in the Alcazar in Seville, with the ships of the Spanish discovery at her feet. It was from this advocation of the Virgin that the city of Buenos Aires got its name. It is said that this painting belonged to Fernando and Isabel, and it is a powerful representation of the Marian connection between Europe and the Americas (see Figure 3.1).[25]

So significant were her attentions to images of Mary in this most Catholic and most Marian of countries that one biographer has described her visit there as one of "the banquets, the Virgins, the reviews of troops, and the speeches."[26] These activities made clear the connections between religion, religious symbolism, and the state in Spain and probably in Evita's sensibilities as well. She herself reflected her understanding of these connections and, not least important, her own potential power, in the talk she gave on receiving the Grand Cross of Isabel. "This is the legacy of a queen who gave her energies to the universal, the Catholic faith, and the expansion of her Christian realms. This is the legacy of Isabel, the woman who was closest to God in the most sacred period of Spain, when to be near God was to do battle and to pray."[27]

In Italy she was received by the Pope, and she wore the Grand Cross of Isabel to that meeting. He gave her the Great Cross of the Order of Pius IX to take to her husband. Speculation had it that she herself had hoped for a papal decoration, perhaps a Pontifical Marquisate, a recognition that would have neutralized still further her illegitimate birth and would have permitted her to confront more effectively the conservative society of Buenos Aires.[28] If that is what she wished, she was disappointed, but her meeting seems to have impressed her greatly; the rosary of gold that he gave her on that occasion was in her hands when she died five years later and then was interred with her corpse.[29]

Similarly, the high point of her trip to Paris was described as her visit to the Cathedral of Notre Dame. In an appearance well planned by her confessor, Father Hernán Benítez, she arrived wearing a simple white suit and hat, was greeted by a prelate, and then went immediately to kneel at the altar of the Virgin. Observers noted that she was moved to tears by the cathedral organ booming the Argentine national anthem. They were moved in turn by her dignity and emotion. One among them, Monsignor Angelo Roncalli, the papal nuncio to France who would become Pope John XXIII, remarked, "Empress Eugenie has returned." He and Evita spoke later about her charity projects, which she insisted were simple justice. He provided two ideas that she applied to her later founding of the Eva Perón Foundation: avoid bureaucracy and devote yourself completely.[30]

Her work with the foundation and in the Secretariat of Labor was indeed tireless, leading to concern on the part of her husband and others close to her. Despite signs of illness as early as 1950, her work accelerated as time went on. By 1950 and 1951, Perón wrote, they barely saw each other. She ate little, slept less; union officials who accompanied her back from the Secretariat of Labor reported that she often worked all night, arriving home as Perón was eating breakfast. She would sleep a couple of hours and then return to work. Perón disapproved, but he was powerless to stop her. Meanwhile, her idealization and sanctification in the popular eye continued and grew. She became more and more Marian, inverting the social order as she attended to the hundreds of the poor—mostly women and children—who came to her for aid, while male government officials dressed in their elegant suits were forced to wait.[31] Meanwhile, she continued to lose weight, her naturally white skin became even more pallid, her eyes developed heavy dark circles beneath them. As one of her biographies has suggested, "Of all the many distortions surrounding her life the least outrageous and the closest to the truth is the suggestion that she elected to die for Perón and Peronism."[32]

The first public sign of trouble came in January 1950, when she fainted during a ceremony celebrating the opening of a branch of the taxi drivers union. She underwent an appendectomy and then quickly resumed her normal schedule. Her problem, however, was not only appendicitis: she had uterine cancer. The circumstances of its discovery are much under dispute, but it seems clear that she avoided tests that might have saved her, despite pain, weakness, and bleeding. And, strangely, the illness coincided with granting the vote to the women of Argentina, a cause for which she had long pressed, along with a movement to have her named vice-presidential candidate on the ticket with her husband in the 1952 election. She was reluctant to give up this possibility, although her health was more and more an issue.

This combination of events led to an extraordinary series of epiphanies that would continue almost until her death. On August 2, 1951, two hundred unionists visited Perón, asking him to accept renomination with Evita as vice president on his ticket. When he did not immediately refuse to consider her candidacy and said nothing to Evita, she apparently thought the opportunity might be open to her. She herself was reluctant to refuse.

The date of August 22 was set for the declaration of the candidacies. This time, the events would transpire on the Avenida 9 de Julio, not at the Casa Rosada, since the Plaza de Mayo was thought, correctly, to be too small to hold the crowds. The day dawned radiant, a typical Peronist day, despite the fact that the sky is often overcast at that time of year in Buenos Aires. Even the sun, it seemed, shone for the Peróns. Close to one million people gathered facing the enormous stage where two huge portraits of Juan and Evita, each sixty feet high, dominated the display behind the speakers' platform. A connecting arc, like a rainbow, tied the two portraits together and bore the inscription "Perón-Eva Perón, the combination for the fatherland." But Perón surely never intended that Evita run for office. In any case, she was far too ill. What probably was planned was that Evita would appear and refuse decorously, thus putting the issue to rest. What happened was quite different.

Perón began the event by entering with politicians and union officials—all of them male—but without Evita. When José Espejo, the president of the C.G.T., the over-arching Peronist union, began to speak, he was repeatedly interrupted by the clamoring crowd calling for Evita. So far, things seemed to be going as planned. The speaker left the dais and returned with the First Lady. She delivered a long and emotional speech, her hands held out at her sides palms up, a stance often used in images of the Virgin, or her left hand raised militantly in front of her face. She was visibly thinner than in her last appearance, carefully tailored in a black suit with her blond hair pulled severely back into a knotted braid, but she still seemed vigorous. Nevertheless, her hands trembled. She did not immediately address the vice-presidential nomination, saying only that she would rather be Evita than the wife of the president, a strange distinction and claim to an identity separate from her connection to the presidency that she had begun to elaborate in the autobiography that she was simultaneously writing. The crowd took this statement as a refusal, continually interrupted her husband's speech, which followed hers, and began to chant her name. Espejo himself then went to the microphone and asked Evita to accept. She declined more directly and force-fully, leading to protests and calls for a general strike—a potent threat and one that cannot have pleased her husband. She repeatedly asked for more time, but the crowd shouted "No." Finally, she declared that she would do what the people said, and the crowd, believing that she had accepted, peace-fully dispersed. The emotion of the afternoon was intense. Perón himself was left on the sidelines, virtually shouted off the platform in favor of his wife. Her charisma, her connection and identification with the people and their hopes, now eclipsed his own.

If he had wavered before, now he would be resolute. Nine days later, undoubtedly at his insistence, she announced on the radio that she would decline the honor of the vice-presidential nomination.[33] Still, the intensity of devotion and the interaction of Evita with the crowd was resonant with the rituals in which images of the Virgin were brought into the streets on Mary's special days. Moreover, her declared subordination to her husband and to the Peronist cause recalled the Virgin's own self-abnegating stance. Once again, she was the handmaiden to Perón. The event was known in Argentina as "El Renunciamiento," the renunciation, the title recalling those important Marian events, the Annunciation and the Assumption.

The distinction between "Evita" and "the wife of the president" was one that she was developing in her autobiography, a ghost-written opus with which she was nevertheless very much involved. Entitled *La razón de mi vida*, translated, I think, most appropriately as *The Meaning of My Life*, it was a ram-bling but fascinating self-view. In Chapter 16, entitled "Eva Perón and Evita," she averred that she had a double personality, that of Eva Perón, the wife of the president, with her ceremonial tasks of appearances on holidays, of re-ceiving honors, and of gala functions. The other was that of Evita, "the wife of the Leader of the people which has entrusted to him all of its faith, all of its hope, and all of its love." Sometimes she played the first role, which was easy and agreeable. Most days, however, she was "Evita, the bridge stretched between the hopes of the people and the enabling hands of Perón," a difficult role and one in which she continually found herself wanting. Eva Perón was of little interest, but Evita was different. Through an understanding of Evita, she declared, would come an understanding of the *descamisados*, of the very people themselves.[34] In this way, she differentiated the Eva Perón of ceremonial and ascribed power, the distant Eva, from the human Evita, completely at one with her people. She was not the secular god of the Peronist political movement, which was surely Juan Perón himself; she was the near and fully human Mother of the Argentine people, with whom "Evita" was entirely identified. A few pages later, she emphasized, "When a child calls me 'Evita' I feel I am the Mother of all children and of all the weak and humble of my country."[35]

In my opinion, this sentence precisely expressed her true sentiments. The dishonored child, Evita herself, had moved into a queenlike role and then had stepped out of the office—or down from the altar. She had become a real and giving presence in the lives of many individuals and especially the poor and the needy. They in turn fed her own deep need to give and to make a difference for them. By occupying no official office, she remained for them a real human being, unlike her Godlike husband, the president. Perón had made the same mistake in denying her office that the fathers of the Church had made when they insisted on Mary's full humanity; he had left her free to be the beautiful Mother of those who chose her. Hundreds of thousands did. That Mother was dying, and quickly the people of Argentina would know that. At the same time, she was identifying herself with those she regarded as true members of the Argentine nation—the poor, the descamisados—and framing the idea of political nation within a language of kinship and family.[36]

Evita fainted again the night after the tumultuous August 22 meeting on the Avenida 9 de Julio. She suffered from acute abdominal pain and was unable to resume work. Her husband and others begged her to permit medical tests, but she continued to refuse. Finally, a month later, she agreed. The diagnosis was an advanced case of uterine cancer. Perón, according to observers, was devastated, having lost his first wife to uterine cancer as well. In accordance with the usual cancer treatment of the time, Evita was not told the diagnosis. Meanwhile, the obvious and growing popularity of the Peróns frightened many in the power structure. On September 28, the first military uprising against Perón took place. It failed, and Perón appeared on the balcony of the Casa Rosada without Evita to reassure the populace that the rebellion had been contained. However, Evita's absence caused about as much anxiety as the rebellion had. The government was forced to acknowledge her illness, blaming it on weakness due to anemia and overwork. Later that evening she insisted on going on the radio to ask the people of Argentina to pray for her health on behalf of Perón and the descamisados. Sobbing, she promised to return quickly to public life. Meanwhile, she ordered a cache of arms, meant for her workers, to be paid for with foundation funds. She did not inform Perón, possibly because she anticipated his opposition to such militant and potentially risky action.[37]

Workers and other Peronist supporters began holding masses to pray for the first lady's health, and there were continuing spontaneous exhibitions of personal and group concern and piety, many of them associated with petitions to the Virgin of Luján. Thousands came in pilgrimage to the sanctuary there carrying the Virgin's image with the inscription "For Evita's health." Altars proliferated on the streets and in homes, with flowers and candles surrounding images of Evita and the Virgin. Father Hernán Benítez, her confessor, reported that the secular Argentines, unaccustomed to attending Church and even unfamiliar with the appropriate prayers, sought out the holy places of the city and repeated invocations not spoken since childhood. In a more secular but still impressive demonstration, the trucking union assembled one thousand vehicles and drove them slowly around the park of Palermo to show concern and support. Meanwhile, her autobiography was published, though she was too ill to attend the reception in her honor. Sales passed the half-million mark within a month, making it the fastest-selling popular book ever before in Argentina.[38]

Another epiphany would take place on the balcony of the Casa Rosada a few days later. The ceremonies of October 17, 1951, were dedicated by the unions to Evita's renunciation, and she was given two medals—one from the C.G.T. and one from Perón himself, the Grand Peronist Medal, Extraordinary Grade, the only time it had been awarded. She appeared at the podium, but, weak and emotional in the face of the huge number of people crowded into the Plaza de Mayo and the honors she was receiving, she was at first unable to speak. After a bit of confusion, she was lifted away and Perón came to the microphone. His oration was a tribute to his wife, in particular to her contributions to the unions, to the foundation, and to the new Peronist Women's Party. In tone it was somber, almost funereal; in content, it was adulatory. Evita, overwhelmed, staggered to his side and fell against him, weeping and embracing him. The crowd was silent. At this point, re-energized by her husband's tribute, she was able to speak, and her message was intense. She promised to be present with Perón and the *descamisados* every October, "even if I have to shed the tatters of my life to do so." Her words expressed her gratitude to Perón and to her supporters. As the crowd continued to stand in silence, she declared, "All that I have, I have in my heart, it hurts my soul, it hurts my flesh and it burns on my nerves, and that is my love for this people and for Perón . . . Were the people to ask me for my life, I would give it to them singing, for the happiness of one descamisado is worth more than my own life." She ended her speech by shouting "La vida

*The poster of this famous moment illustrates the use of Evita's image by the Peronist
Justicialista movement in the 1980s. It announces a meeting in the Plaza de Mayo, with
a religious service and a march with flaming torches. The bold print at the top announces,
"Evita Lives" (Evita Vive). Offset lithograph, 83.5 by 58 cm. Sam L. Slick Collection of
Latin American and Iberian Posters, Center for Southwest Research, General Library,
University of New Mexico. Photography by Teresa Eckmann.*

por Perón!"—My life for Perón. Her words were echoed by the crowd as she
fell sobbing into her husband's arms.[39]

Despite what was becoming incessant pain and debility, Evita was still unin-
formed, at least officially, about the nature of her illness. Obviously she must
have known that something was wrong with her reproductive system. Quite
likely she feared—as most women would—the loss of her female organs and
any hope of actual, physical motherhood. Symbolically, her connection with
the people of Argentina was as Mother. Losing that physical capacity must
have been very threatening, and there are rumors that she refused treatment.
Perón, of course, feared losing her as he had lost his first wife. Not only did all
accounts insist on his deep love for her, but the events surrounding her two

public appearances in September and October had made clear her extraordinary importance to his own political popularity. While keeping the nature of her illness secret from the Argentine people, Perón arranged for a Manhattan cancer specialist, Dr. George T. Pack, to fly to Argentina. Pack examined her while she was anesthetized and was able to confirm the earlier diagnosis of cervical cancer; she never knew he was there. Further secret arrangements were made for him to fly back the following month, November, when the first lady was again anesthetized, and this time he performed extensive surgery on the cancer that had spread through the pelvic area. At no time was the patient ever officially informed about her illness, nor did she know that Dr. Pack had examined her or performed the operation.[40] Father Benítez, however, knew that she was not completely deceived. She told him that she believed her doctors were lying to her and that she was lying to them in turn. It was a charade that in some measure all understood.[41]

After the operation she began to improve a bit, though she was still weak. On November 11, after a bad night with an attack of some kind that led her to believe she was dying, she was able to cast her ballot for the Peronist ticket in the first Argentine election in which women were permitted to vote. The young man who came to her bedside to take her vote remembered the women kneeling outside on the sidewalk who touched and kissed the box that contained it when he left the residence. They treated it as if it were a sacred object.[42] Perón won, a victory largely delivered by the female vote.

Her temporary recovery made several other appearances possible, although she remained very ill. In early December she thanked the Argentine people for voting for her husband as she had asked them to do, thus appropriating a large part of the victory for herself. By February 1952, she was again in a great deal of pain. At this point she was beyond medical help. A flood of images, amulets, and other items purported to have curative powers poured into the Casa Rosada, along with huge numbers of flowers. She sent these along to local churches, particularly the shrine of the Virgin at Nueva Pompeya. She told her nurse that she believed in the Virgin but that she was not a *chupacirios*, that is, a "candle licker."[43] She was still able, on May 1, Labor Day, to walk without assistance on the balcony at the Casa Rosada, but on this occasion her demeanor became almost frenzied. Her rhetoric was increasingly violent, possessed with warnings of potential destruction, filled with messianic overtones, all made more dramatic by her obvious physical anguish. Again she emphasized her willingness and that of her people, *mi pueblo*, to die for Perón. She and her people, she said, did not merely show up to provide a presence in support of Perón, but rather to dispense justice. Combining threat, judgment, and call to action, she said, "We will take justice into our own hands."[44] A month later, meeting with Peronist governors, she declared, "Those who believe in sweetness and love forget that Christ said, 'I have come to earth to bring fire, so that it may burn more.'"[45] She continued her rhetoric of burning her life for Perón, now associating herself with Christ as a fellow martyr for a higher purpose.

On the day of Perón's inauguration she determined to participate, despite the attempts of those around her to dissuade her. An aide put together a frame of plaster and wire to hold her upright in the convertible from which she and her husband would greet the crowd. Dressed in a full-length fur coat, bejeweled and with one of her heavy medals around her neck, she drove with her husband through the streets of Buenos Aires waving at the crowd. She was more beautiful than ever, pale and ethereal; the crowd responded. A triple dose of painkillers made it possible for her to appear, and she received a double dose when she returned to the residence.[46] Evita's own sense of her importance and mission was reflected in her plans for a monument to herself and to the October 17 Revolution, a huge structure with an image of a *descamisado* on top. These plans would never be realized. She died on July 26, 1952, and official reports claimed that the hour of death was 8:25 P.M., the time of her marriage to Perón. This time was probably not accurate but rather was used for its symbolic power, perhaps at her insistence.[47] Even her death must reinforce her destiny, her redemption from shame, her connection with Juan Perón, her acceptance of her mission to the people of Argentina. At 8:26 an official from the Secretariat of Information announced on the radio that the spiritual leader of the nation was dead. Outside the residence mourners braved the intense cold to kneel and say their rosaries.[48] Before her death she had confessed to a friend, in front of an image of Mary, that she believed in God and the Virgin but not in priests. And a day or two before she died she asked Juan Perón to construct a chapel in honor of the Virgin of Fatima, a devotion he confirmed later. Her body would later lie, at Juan Perón's request, with a representation of the Virgin of Luján watching over it.[49]

Plans were in place to embalm the body without delay. Perón's advisers already filled the residence in expectation of the death. Also nearby was Dr. Pedro Ara, a professor of anatomy who had studied in Vienna and had worked in Madrid. Known as discreet and highly competent, he also had the ability to turn the dead body into an aesthetic work. Lugubriously, he had been alerted several hours earlier and arrived at the residence almost at the time of death. He was quickly taken to Perón, who gave him the keys to Evita's bedroom and insisted that he keep the doors locked against everyone, including himself. Ara's later comment on first viewing the body was, "On her deathbed lay the shadow of a rare, tranquil beauty, liberated, at last, from the cruel torment of a body eroded to its limit, and from the cruel torture sustained by a science that, hoping for a miracle, had prolonged its treatments." He found the family gathered at the foot of her bed, being led in prayer by Father Benítez. When he entered, the members of the family quickly rose and began to leave the room. As Father Benítez passed Ara, he prayed, "Que Díos le ilumine"—May God guide you.[50] Ara summoned not only his assistants but also dressmakers and Evita's hairdresser and quickly began to work. The final embalming would take much longer, of course, but by morning the body had been temporarily preserved against decay. A final detail reflecting Evita's own consciousness of her postmortem image was her concern that her manicurist remove her bright red nail polish and replace it with something more fitting for death—a clear polish. Her wishes were carried out.[51] The hands now manicured discreetly, her body was placed in a cedar coffin with her rosary between her crossed hands. The Argentine flag was placed over her. Thus, devotion to religion and nation were symbolized in the presentation of her remains. Her face and upper body remained visible through the glass of the casket.[52] Evita's corpse was ready to become the sanctified relic of the Peronist state.

After the initial embalming, the casket was transported to the Ministry of Labor, where it would lie in state for almost two weeks. Later, it would go to the C.G.T. headquarters, as Evita had wished, to await the building of the monument that she had envisioned.[53] Meanwhile, Argentines had crowded around the residence and the streets were congested for a radius of ten blocks. Just moving the casket from the ambulance into the ministry caused such a crush that eight people were killed. During the following twenty-four hours more than two thousand people were treated for injuries. Flower shops sold out, the virginal white flowers going especially rapidly.

Lines immediately formed for viewing the body. Adding to the enormous and spontaneous public display of grief, the Peronists made sure that giant photographs of Evita were placed throughout the city. These images, too, gave rise to emotional scenes as people gathered beneath them with lighted torches and candles. Each evening these were symbolically extinguished at 8:25 P.M. The churches were filled with those praying for the departed Mother.[54] For the next thirteen days the Peronist weather changed to reflect the loss: it rained almost constantly. Those waiting to see the body stood for up to ten hours, chilled and hungry. The foundation and the Red Cross provided coffee and food to some of those waiting. Mourners touched or kissed the coffin when they said their farewells, much as they might touch or kiss the hem of the Virgin's gown or her foot. Finally, with concerns for the permanent preservation of the body paramount, on August 9 the casket was placed on a gun carriage, moved through the crowd of two million to the Congress, and then taken at last to the C.G.T.[55]

An extraordinary campaign by Perón and the Peronist party to equate

Evita with the Virgin followed immediately, although, as we have seen, the image of her as a loving, Marian sort of mother long preceded her death. Still, the heavy-handedness of this campaign reflected the problems of the regime and the need to resurrect their most effective standard-bearer. In particular, declining economic conditions threatened their compact with the workers, and political problems immediately became evident. Trying to take advantage of the mystical nature of the charismatic connection that Evita had established with the people of Argentina, they emphasized her immortality, her spiritual Motherhood, her presence in Heaven. But without the figure of the living Evita to provide actual benefits and personal appeal, this attempt to appropriate her charisma posthumously failed as a political project. The Peronist government fell in 1955. The image of Evita as Mary and as Mother continued, nevertheless, to provide a center of popular reverence.

Neither of the Peróns had been active in specifically Catholic causes before Juan Perón's presidency, but during the first years he was in the presidential office he conciliated the Church, primarily before 1949. He reinforced its priorities in several ways: strengthening Catholic religious instruction in the schools with the Religious Education Decree in 1947, increasing state monies going into the ecclesiastical budget, appointing individuals known for their Catholic stance in his administration, and adopting Christian social thinking as the "official" doctrine of government before the Peronists adopted their own doctrine of *justicialismo* in 1949. *Justicialismo* increasingly came to imply an idea of "spiritual unity" with his own government rather than the Catholic Church or some abstract idea of Argentine nation. Still, he maintained a relationship of open communication with leaders of the Church.[56] This relationship had begun to change by the early 1950s and would shift toward an emphasis on a kind of secular or civic religion identified with Peronism in the years immediately following Evita's death. Given the enormous reverence she had generated during her active years and prolonged dying, including the almost hysterical grief that followed her death, Evita became a central figure in this Peronist effort. Given these tensions, the administration of Juan Perón quickly came into conflict with the hierarchical Church.

Interestingly, Evita had penned a stinging indictment of the Church hierarchy in the months before her death. In a document titled *Mi mensaje* (My message) she bitterly pointed out the lack of connection between the clerical hierarchy and the people of Argentina. Calling them "cold men" and pointing out their "inconceivable indifference to the harsh reality of the people," she asserted that she had rarely seen "love and generosity" among their numbers.[57] Specifically denying Lenin's assertion that religion was the opiate of the masses, she insisted that religion instead should be the liberation of the people, that in God all were equal. "Religion," she declared, "will recover its prestige among the people when it is taught as a force of rebellion and equality, not as an instrument of oppression."[58] She distinguished between the priests who worked directly with the people to "assuage their thirst" for God from the prelates of the hierarchy. She insisted that God would make the latter pay for their "betrayals," while judging much less harshly those who, though less trained in theology, instead had "decided to give all for the people . . . with all our souls, with all our hearts."[59] She was beginning to articulate the need for a new Church, a Peronist Church, with a newfound focus on the poor; in fact, in regard to religion as in regard to her political stance, she was arguing for power to be shifted to her people, her Argentines, to the *descamisados*. This theme would be taken up by the Peronists after her death.[60] Again, in these words, we see her own suffering over her much-criticized and shaming past and her vivid self-justification in terms of the works and caring of her own life. These words would make her spiritual self whole, in fact redeemed, while her dishonored body was destroyed in the effort. Her self-abnegating, loving rhetoric is clearly Marian, but her words are fiery and confrontational. In the same short work she also attacked the military, thereby taking on another powerful institution within Argentine society that she and her husband had good reason to fear and within whose ranks she had been denigrated. It is unsurprising, given the uncompromising tone of her message, that Juan Perón did not publish it. It would have been an open declaration of war against two of the most powerful institutions in the country, the Church and the military, a war he was still hoping to avoid.

In the wake of her death, he needed to invoke her powerful image, and this need would lead him toward confrontation with the Church. Evita's secular sanctification and her identification with the Virgin Mary, as well as with the martyred Christ, was overdrawn from the beginning. Even before her death, the vision of her being presented officially and the one she herself projected in her last public appearances were significantly at odds. She was militant and confrontational; Peronist propaganda presented her as mild and self-effacing. The first edition of *The Meaning of My Life*, published the year before her death, shows her on the cover smiling benignly but already thin and pale, discreetly and conservatively dressed but with a large rose, so closely associated with the Virgin, on her left shoulder. The frontispiece reproduces the same image, but the mottled background has given way to landscape of trees and mountains, over which rise pale yellow clouds. These clouds include lighter portions which seem to be rays of light emanating from her head and her neck. The effect is altogether ethereal and Virginal. The portrait of Perón that follows two pages later, on the other hand, shows him dressed formally and presidentially, with one of his many medals hanging around his neck. This picture seems to be a colored photograph rather than a painting; in any case, it is a much more lifelike representation of the president than the one of his wife. It appears opposite the short prologue to the work, in which Evita dedicates the book to him and insists on her devotion, "body, soul, and life," to Perón and his cause. Evita remains a "humble woman," while Perón is the "giant condor who flies high and sure above the mountain peaks close to God."[61] In the book, at least, she is the embodiment of wifely submission and Marian humility, subservient to her lord, Juan Perón. This vision is in great contrast to what was actually occurring, as her own popularity and charisma soared, and her frantic rhetoric and delivery poured out a revolutionary message to the people of Argentina. In fact, as a passage in *Mi mensaje* makes clear, she was seeing herself as an active partner, not just a menial helpmeet to the great Perón. As she wrote, "I knew that like him, condors flew high and solitary—yet nevertheless, I had to fly with him!"[62] The tranquil image of Evita that the Peronists pushed before and in the wake of her death was therefore at odds with her own self-image—and self-knowledge—as she was dying and with the powerful figure that dying had helped her become.

Pictorial images after her death routinely depicted her surrounded by flowers and smiling benignly or lifting her eyes piously toward Heaven. A copy of *Mundo Peronista*, a popular slick magazine produced by the regime, had on its cover a painting emphasizing her pallor and the dark shadings under her eyes, which are looking up reverently. She is shown without jewelry, which in life she would never have omitted, and her blond hair is pulled back severely from her face. Swirls of yellow and blue surround her head, producing a kind of halo. Inside, the introduction to an adulatory poem by a reader insists, "Evita, your name will never be forgotten" and goes on to say, "The work of Love and sublime sacrifice of the Immortal Evita has an eternal presence in the heart of her People." Later in the same magazine, there is a portrait of Evita looking directly out of the canvas and smiling. She is surrounded by flames and stars—a more dramatic halo—and the sides of the page, alongside a sonnet in her praise, show the columns of state to the left and the roses of the Virgin Mary to the right. The sonnet itself speaks of her "fire of Love" for her people and her eternal life "outside Time and Space."[63] Yet another, which coincided with a 1952 request for her canonization by the Newspaper Vendors Union, showed her head surrounded by an austere halo and stars, a Marian shawl draped around her, blue robes covering her red gown, her hands crossed on her chest. Her suffering face is turned in profile. Except for the recognizable features of Evita, the tranquil image could be of the Virgin Mary.[64]

Probably hundreds of poems and other forms of verbal tributes linked Evita with sainthood, martyrdom, and the Virgin, as well as with Juan Perón and the Argentine state. In the *Songbook of Juan Perón and Eva Perón*, published in 1966 but with most of the entries written long before, these themes intertwined. Immediately following a poem entitled "God-Fatherland-Perón," we find another entitled "Eva Perón Has Not Died." The next, "To Eva Perón," insists, "In the sublime sphere your song vibrates. The music of light is your eternal halo. In your essential purity you adorn the sacrosanct Empire and make it more splendid." And yet another, "Redeemer of Peoples," declares, "Under your advocation the Fatherland dreams, Redeemer of peoples, light of the poor, to say your name, oh illuminated one, a time of bells and flowers." The association with Christ is even more explicit in the last stanza, "Enlighten us, Señora, from among the nails; your image is a field of hopes. Under the Southern Cross your glory is born: Saint Eva Perón, banner and Martyr!"[65]

The efforts toward a secular religion centered around Evita were particularly noticeable in the field of education. The Perón government had already made significant changes in the way education was administered in Argentina; in 1948 a Secretariat was created, and in 1949 after a constitutional change it became an autonomous Ministry of Education. A well-known surgeon, Oscar Ivanissevich, was put in charge. During his term in office, the Peronists used the school system to legitimize their ideologies and political stances, associating them with overarching national or religious values.[66] Ivanissevich would later claim that he had conducted the initial tests that had had revealed Evita's cancer. According to his account, he immediately suggested a hysterectomy but she refused with fury. She apparently doubted his motives, and, thinking that he might be a tool of her political enemies, asserted, "All of them want me out of politics, but they won't succeed."[67] One implication here is that Evita knew that she had adversaries who would stop at nothing, not even threats to her health or unnecessary physical mutilations, to hinder her political work. Another, however, was that the physical possibility of motherhood and her identification as spiritual mother were so important to her sense of herself and her political resonance with the Argentines that a hysterectomy would have been devastating.

In any case, education as indoctrination had been an important part of the Peronist project from the beginning. From 1951 forward, it was clear that education would become an instrument for the secular religion Juan Perón wished to create. Of course, religious themes had appeared in pre-Peronist texts, but these had been extremely general. The Virgin Mary only appeared in traditional legends or songs. In the Peronist book, in contrast, there were many images of the Virgin, especially the Virgin of Luján, along with Christ and the saints. These figures were used to illustrate all sorts of topics. Particularly after Evita's death, she herself was the major focus of these religious connections.[68] Law 14.126 of 1952 required that Evita's biography be used as an obligatory text for all grade levels under the ministry's control—as a reading in all the primary grades and as the only text for grades five and six. It was also assigned for upper grades in courses ranging from literature to civics.[69] The most striking example, however, of the deliberate association of Evita with Mary was a first-grade primer published shortly after the first lady's death. Entitled simply "Evita," it was an invocation of Evita Perón as Spiritual Mother of the Argentines, the Love that she continued to hold for her People, and the devotion that all were expected to show for her. One page showed three children kneeling to pray at bedtime before an image of the Virgin on the wall. The caption, extraordinarily, read, "Mommy taught me to pray. In my prayers, I never forget Eva Perón, our Spiritual Mother."[70]

Perón and Evita were further identified with the readers' own parents. Another page showed Juan Perón shaking hands with a group of young female athletes dressed in uniforms. The caption read, "Perón loves children.

Mamita me enseñó a rezar.
En mis oraciones, nunca
olvido a Eva Perón,

nuestra Madre Espiritual

*Children are shown praying to the Virgin at bedtime. The text translates as "My mommy taught me to pray. In my prayers, I never forget Eva Perón, our Spiritual Mother" (*Nuestra Madre Espiritual*). Print courtesy UCLA Special Collections. From Graciela Albornoz de Videla,* Evita: Libro de Lectura para Primer Grado Inferior, *Buenos Aires: Editorial Luis Lasserre SRL, 1953, 10.*

My mother. My father. Perón. Evita."[71] Right in the middle of the book, juxtaposed among the images of Perón as Father and Evita as Mother and Virgin, is a brief illustrated version of the visit of the Three Kings to the Holy Family and a discussion of Christ's visit to the temple, where he startled the sages with his knowledge. The text further emphasizes that nevertheless, "He was a model son, obedient and submissive." The picture illustrating the latter is one of Mary walking tranquilly with her young son, both holding flowers. The following page contains a poem entitled "Evita," which reads: "Our Fatherland is a nest, our Fatherland is a home, all the little ones, brothers, and Evita is the mother."[72] The Peronist project, reinforced with Catholic references, is further emphasized on the vocabulary sheet included with the primer. Words like *renunciamiento* (renunciation), *presidente*, (president), *Nación* (nation), Evita, Juan, Eva, *fundación* (foundation), and Perón are interspersed with Virgen, Jesús, Luján, and Dios.[73]

Meanwhile, Dr. Ara proceeded with the preservation—or mummification—of Evita's body. This process took place on the second floor of the C.G.T. building, where Ara was provided with complete freedom to work. Even direct telephone lines were provided so that he did not have to go through the C.G.T. operators. There the doctor worked devotedly for a year, while a cross in front of the building with Evita's picture on it continued to be the focus of prayers and to receive floral offerings.[74] At the same time, the construction of her tomb—which she had envisioned as a tribute to the workers of Argentina—was delayed by a dispute over the statue that would be placed on it. She had expected that it would be a huge representation of one of her *descamisados*, but others felt that it should be, more appropriately, a statue of her. When the body was ready, the tomb was no more than a huge hole in the ground, and so the body remained with the C.G.T. and in Ara's hands. Perón visited only three times and was amazed by the sight. According to him, it was so lifelike that he expected her to arise living, which of course corresponds with Christ's own rising from the dead. He further emphasized that "she shone with a special radiance."[75] He was not so forward as to compare her with the Virgin Mother herself, but the reader will understand the significance of the light that, according to him, surrounded the body. His presidency would survive his wife for only three years.

Meanwhile, as Perón's political difficulties mounted, his own attitude toward the Church began to mirror Evita's own, though he still did not permit publication of *Mi mensaje*. The Church, certainly, did not watch the secular sanctification of Evita with comfort, and the strains between it and the government continued to fester and grow. The year 1955 saw even further Peronist attacks on the Church's prerogatives. Fewer religious holidays were permitted, and divorce and prostitution were legalized. Perón sought to silence Church authorities and lay Catholics alike, expelling the latter from the civil service and the former from teaching in the schools. The legal status of Catholic Action was withdrawn after a major demonstration in Córdoba, and some of its organizers were arrested. Leaders from the Church and from Catholic organizations were banned from communicating through newspapers and the radio; some publications were closed, while others saw their paper supplies curtailed or had to cope with disruptions in their distribution. Catholics fought back by circulating pamphlets, pastoral letters, news of arrests, and other important information, an effort that led to professional newsletters that were widely available, despite the opposition of the Peronists, through press offices, unions, hospitals, and even government offices and army units.[76] On June 11, 1955, Corpus Christi processions in front of the cathedral turned into anti-Perón demonstrations. Catholic protests led to defections within the military. Five days after Corpus Christi, the same day the Peronist state decided to expropriate and secularize the cathedral, naval aircraft taking part in a military show flew over the city and dropped bombs near the Casa Rosada. They missed their target, but a number of bystanders in the Plaza de Mayo were killed. Later a naval unit attacked Perón's palace, although he was no longer there. In the fighting, a number of C.G.T. members who had come to the center of Buenos Aires to support Perón were killed.[77]

Despite Perón's last-minute attempts to reconcile with his enemies, by August 31 these attempts had ceased. On that date he made a fiery speech of his own, much in the spirit of Evita's last public communications to the people of Argentina. In mid-September, units of the army and navy rose against him, and he left the country on September 20, 1955. He left no instructions about Evita's cadaver.[78] Evita's power, as evidenced by the subsequent treatment of her body by the military government, continued to be significant.

The incoming regime was very concerned that the cadaver might become a center of a religious/political cult and soon took it under control. The body itself was not seized until the original government of General Eduardo Lonardi was replaced by that of General Pedro Eugenio Aramburu shortly after the coup. At that point the C.G.T. building was taken over by the army, and a number of military visitors descended on the room where she was kept. Even when representatives of the military government saw the cadaver, however, they were a bit unsure that they were seeing the actual body, so statue-like and perfect did it seem. After a medical examination, which included the removal of part of one of her fingers for further analysis, they were convinced. Throughout, it was clear that these men were nervous in the presence of the corpse and sometimes even reverent. Few were unaffected by the sense of sanctity that seemed to emanate from Evita's remains. According to Captain Francisco Manrique, "She was the size of a twelve-year-old girl. Her skin looked like wax, artificial. Her lips were painted red. If you tapped her finger, it sounded hollow. Ara, the embalmer, did not part from it as if he loved it."[79] The body, they felt, had to disappear, and some hoped it would be destroyed. Apparently, the strong Catholic convictions of some of the leaders including Aramburu preserved it from this fate.[80]

Strikingly, the cadaver seemed strongly connected to the most pure aspects of the Virgin, even for some members of the military. Ara tells the story of Lieutenant Colonel Manuel Reimúndez, who visited the sanctuary on November 4. The officer prayed before the image of the Virgin of Luján that hung above the body, wept, and kissed the rosary in Evita's hands. He commented, "This little medallion should be that of the Immaculate. Poor little thing! Surely God has pardoned her." Apparently, for him, the stain of her illegitimacy, her sexual history, and her political activities had been expunged by her works. The next day, the little sanctuary on the second floor was closed to all, including Ara, except with permission of Reimúndez himself and in his presence.[81] By the end of the month, the body had been removed and was then sent into its own exile, but not until it had been kept for awhile as a kind of trophy or icon by the head of military intelligence, a man named Carlos Eugenio Moori Koenig. Moori Koenig had been in charge of its removal from the C.G.T. building, and, according to him, it had been placed first in a military vehicle. The next morning, he said, a mysterious offering of flowers and a candle were found beside the truck. The coffin was transferred to another truck, this time not marked as military, and the same sort of thing happened. The process was repeated several times with the same results, so Moori Koenig decided not to bury it at all. He ordered it put into a box previously used for radio transmission equipment and stored, feet down, in the attic above his office. Evita's body remained in his keeping for the next two years, although it may have been buried during a portion of this time. Eventually, it was taken away from him when it was determined that he had lost his reason. Rumors claimed that he would murmur, "She is mine. That woman is mine," and he later insisted that all associated with the body were mysteriously struck by disasters. What he said later was that he had buried her standing up "because she was a man!" Later, when the body was finally returned to the family, it was damaged in ways that were consistent with such a burial.[82]

In 1956 or 1957, after the body had been taken from the obsessed Moori Koenig, the government decided, in consultation with the Church, to remove it from the country. The ultimate location in which it would be secured was to be secret, even from the highest Argentine officials. It was sent to Italy in the possession of an Italian priest, who returned six weeks later and gave President Aramburu a sealed envelope with information about where the cadaver was located. Aramburu, with consequences that would later be fatal to himself, did not open the letter but rather gave it to a notary. The instructions he gave were to deliver it four weeks after Aramburu's death to whoever was Argentine president at that time.[83] Perón seemed little interested in keeping track of the body; he had visited it at the C.G.T. headquarters only rarely and does not seem to have tried to search it down. Some reports indicated that he had been so horrified by her wasting away during her illness that he was disinclined to maintain access to the lifeless body, perhaps preferring to remember her in good health.[84] Having known her as a living being and aware of her humanity, it was unlikely that he would deify her after her death. Others, however, did. Her death led to the sanctification of her body in similar ways to relics of the saints and to the objects associated with the Virgin. More than forty years after her death, a sample of her blood drawn by a physician was offered for sale on the open market.[85]

The extraordinary political and emotional significance of her corpse became clear in 1970, eighteen years after her death and thirteen years after its secret burial. The Peronist movement had never died in Argentina, and in the late 1960s it began to resurge with the Montonero movement, so called to relate its members to nineteenth-century revolutionaries. This movement, generally of middle-class young people (often university students), took Evita as their standard-bearer and tapped into the energy of her memory in favor, they proclaimed, of social justice. As violence and civil strife broke out once again in Argentina, they determined to recover the body by whatever means necessary. Believing that Aramburu, long since out of office, was the most likely person to know of the body's whereabouts, they kidnapped him on May 29, 1970, and threatened his life if he did not reveal the location of the cadaver. Aramburu refused "for reasons of honor." He, of course, did not actually know where it was. Condemned and executed, his body was later found by the police. The notary in question gave the envelope four weeks later to the president, General Alejandro Lanusse, and the body was found in an Italian cemetery. It was soon returned to Perón, who was living in Spain with his third wife, Isabel. In the presence of Isabel, Perón, and Perón's mysterious adviser, José López Rega, who was also known as El Brujo (the Warlock), the casket was opened. Perón is reported to have exclaimed, "Those bastards!" Then he began to weep.[86]

The condition of the body has long been in dispute. According to some, the body had been mutilated, and a statement by her sisters in 1985 listed a number of problems, including an assertion that her neck had been practically severed. However, Dr. Ara, who seems to have been living in Spain, was summoned immediately to verify that it was her body. He has stated that there was little damage that could not be explained by the frequent transport and rather rough handling of the remains, including what appeared to be a cut at the neck. It was, according to him, no more than a narrow break in the plastic surface that had broken in the same blow to the casket, reported years earlier, that had also caused the greatest damage to the body—the flattening of her nose. So, it seems that the implication that someone had tried symbolically to kill Evita again after her death or to gain power over the body through mutilation was inaccurate. Nevertheless, the cadaver continued to exert the symbolic if not necessarily mystical nature of charismatic power. Isabel, at the time of the opening of the casket, took a tender interest in the body and immediately began trying to arrange the hair, which had become wet and matted.[87] The body was moved to a room on the second floor, perhaps to keep it safe from yet another disappearance, and rumor had it that López Rega instructed Isabel to lie on top of the casket while he muttered incantations designed to help the first wife's spirit rise into the body of the second.[88] If that indeed happened, however, the attempts failed, as Isabel, despite efforts, never became politically effective.

Perón returned to Argentina in 1973 to be greeted by a huge Peronist crowd. This time, however, unity was impossible. His supporters came from the extremes of the right and left, he was well past the point of being able to manipulate opposing political forces as he had in the past, and the uncharismatic Isabel, rather than Evita, was at his side. Still, Evita's presence was invoked in enormous signs showing Perón's portrait in the middle of those of the two women. In fact, from the time in 1971 when Peronism was once again officially sanctioned, the cult of Evita was immediately visible in Argentina in posters, in records of her speeches, and even in comic-strip versions of her life. The return of Juan Perón intensified the public yearning for the woman they had identified as the Lady of Hope. The crowds called on her to be with them, intoning, "Se siente, se siente, Evita está presente" (We feel it, we feel it, Evita is present) in the same manner that other martyrs are invoked in political movements throughout Latin America, and "¡Evita vive!" (Evita lives!) appeared on walls throughout the country. The Montoneros in particular called on her memory, stealing Aramburu's own corpse and threatening to keep it until Evita's body was returned to Argentina. Perón lost patience with these young people, ridiculing them as "beardless youth" in a speech at the Plaza de Mayo, although, in the manner of the Cuban revolutionaries whom many of them admired, the males were in fact mostly bearded. Perón was out of touch and out of control. He survived only briefly, and after his death on July 1, 1974, political chaos erupted.

Isabel, who had been permitted to serve as vice-president as Evita had not, assumed the presidency, but she was thrown out by the military in March 1976. In October of that year, Evita's body was finally returned to her sisters, who buried it deep in an unprepossessing family vault in Buenos Aires' Recoleta cemetery.[89] The travels and travails of Evita's powerful remains were over, and the horror of the military government to follow, during which thirty thousand Argentines disappeared, distracted the attention of the Argentine people. The vault has not become a center of popular reverence. In fact, during that military government as well as during the one that overthrew Perón, overt reverence for Evita might have been dangerous. Certainly the repression had a smothering effect on any kind of opposition political expression.

Nicholas Fraser and Marysa Navarro have indicated their belief that, although "a real and persistent cult of Evita" developed in Argentina after her death, particularly in regard to the resistance to military rule, it did not constitute a "popular canonization." The altars to her in the homes of Argentines, they say, were remembrances, similar to those that might be constructed of photographs of family members. Both these authors and Julie Taylor have suggested that the reverence for Evita, especially among working-class people, was particularly tied to the real benefits that she provided to themselves or to people whom they knew; they also revered her willingness to fight for them at great cost to herself.[90] These observations, it seems to me, link her even more strongly to the kind of reverence that we have observed for the Virgin Mary. For many individuals, for families, and even larger groups, the relationship with Mary is infused with the same sense of familiarity and presence that we see here in the case of Evita. Mary, like Evita, is seen as a friend, a mother, a passionate but intimate advocate. In these ways, Evita's altars resembled the ones to Mary, and in Argentina they frequently included images of Mary and Evita side by side. I am not arguing that a cult to Evita rivaling that of the Virgin developed in Argentina; rather, the image and idea of the Virgin and the ways in which Evita seemed similar heightened Evita's appeal and permitted it to continue posthumously.

A sense of that spiritual resonance is seen in another encounter that Carozzi has described. In a recent interview conducted by researcher Pablo Semán with an evangelical pastor in Buenos Aires named Isabel, the woman reported, "When I go up to the pulpit and face the congregation, I have in my mind all that Evita did. She was . . . incredible. Because she brought much for women. She was the first to play football, to engage in politics . . . She didn't let anyone ignore her. And I do what she did. When some male preacher tells me that I am a woman and that I shouldn't be a pastor, I tell them that was before. But not now. *That I am like Evita.*"[91] For this woman, Evita's actions and leadership were still encouraging her, by example, to accept a role both spiritual and public.

Evita's memory is preserved in thousands of paintings, photographs, amulets, and even relics, the largest of which, of course, is her carefully protected body. Her name invokes ideas of the good, the beneficial, the generous, the powerful. It is seen as a paradox to some that a woman with a shady sexual past, a lower-class woman carrying the stigma of illegitimacy, would be so strongly associated with the Virgin Mary. However, many real human beings of Argentina, knowing the impossibility of perfection, have forgiven Evita her faults and applauded her for her goodness, her passion in their behalf, and her very humanity. After all, was not *Mary herself* dishonored and misunderstood for conceiving a child in mysterious circumstances, and was she not then a model wife? Moreover, if Evita could be honored and whole, so could they. Her faults, if such they be, brought her closer to them and magnified her virtues. Her great beauty and her extraordinary accessibility intensified these bonds. She was a figure they could relate to and could hope to emulate and at the same time could admire. Even her need for jewels and beautiful clothes could be understood by those who had little. Besides, is the Virgin not honored with rich robes, titles, and jewels? Further, as we have seen with the image of the Virgin throughout this volume, Eva Perón was both mother and warrior, powerful in her own right while claiming that right, at least rhetorically, through a man, Juan Perón. Yet, it was for Evita that the Argentine masses felt a personal closeness and loyalty, a reverence, and a sense of presence, even after her death.

Her loyalty to them, her sense of unity with them, her demands for power for them, were Marian on the one hand and challenged the gender order on the other. Eva, strangely, was operating without institutional position, from behind the throne, so to speak, but was nevertheless operating publicly and strongly. While declaring her secondary position and subservience, she was moving clearly into a position of equality with her husband and even preeminence. And I believe strongly that it was her sincerity and her faith in the role she was playing and the deep satisfaction that it brought her that made it work. When the Peronists attempted to use her image cynically after her death, they failed. Perón himself was unable to sustain the coalition that brought him back to politics in Argentina in the 1970s. Perhaps with Evita's help, the Peronists would not have failed so quickly; in any case, it seems likely that she would have had more connection with that segment of supporters concerned with social justice and against the concentration of power in the hands of economic and military elites. It is hard to believe that the repression exercised by these latter groups could have been so intense had she been a part of Perón's return.

The Marian image has continued to be significant in Argentine politics. During the so-called Proceso, the "dirty war" of military repression lasting from the fall of Isabel Perón in 1976 until 1983, when civilian rule was restored, the Virgin Mary was invoked by both right and left for opposite political purposes. Even before the return of Juan Perón, the military government of President Juan Carlos Onganía had consecrated the nation to the Immaculate Heart of Mary. In November 1969, the president, surrounded by two thousand bodyguards, led civilian and military authorities to the shrine of Luján. There he prayed, "Our flag has the same color as your tunic and mantle . . . Patroness of the Argentinean people and their military regiments; Virgin of Loreto, Patroness of the Air Force; Stella Maris, Patroness of the Navy; and Virgin of Mercy, General of our Army." The Virgin as warrior was clearly present among the Argentine military. Officers in training in 1975, just prior to the coup against Isabel Perón, are said to have prayed a special "campaign rosary" (recalling the Spanish in the Reconquest praying to the Virgin before battle) and to have kept images of the Virgin in their desks alongside swastikas.[92] An image of Our Lady of Luján had been installed in Port Stanley in the Falkland/Malvinas Islands in 1974, perhaps an assertion of Argentine identity against the reality of British control. Eight years later, Argentine officers led the troops in saying the rosary during the brief occupation of these islands. It has even been reported that torturers in the concentration camps during the repression came together to pray beneath an image of Our Lady. In the wake of the fall of the military juntas, officers have continued to unify around the figure of the Blessed Virgin. In 1984, shortly after the end of military rule, some 1,500 right-wing supporters including cadets and retired and serving officers came together at the sanctuary of the Virgin of Luján to hear Father Julio Triviño preach in favor of a "holy war" against "the radical synagogue."[93] That basilica currently houses two separate chapels dedicated to the military.

During the Proceso, many students, union leaders, and other opposition activists disappeared, victims of the military repression. The powerful movement that came to be known as the Mothers of the Plaza de Mayo arose out of a group of bereaved mothers joined together hoping to bring attention to the disappearances and to commemorate their lost children. Most of the women had been traditional housewives, unaccustomed to political activity and often with little schooling. Brought to their activism by their frantic searches for their disappeared family members, many of whom they knew had been taken by the military and then had vanished, they invoked a vision of Marian motherhood. Their resolve was strong, despite the danger and the lack of involvement and even opposition on the part of much of the hierarchical Roman Catholic Church. They began to meet regularly in the Plaza de Mayo after they had been regularly rebuffed by government officials who refused to clarify the fates of their loved ones. They would circle the pyramid in the center of the plaza, walking arm in arm to demonstrate solidarity and counterclockwise to demonstrate defiance. As they began to attract attention, they decided to adopt a way of identifying themselves to one another and to outsiders and passersby. The idea of using mantillas or shawls, which had clear Marian associations, developed when they decided in September 1977 to accompany the yearly procession from Buenos Aires to the Cathedral of the Virgin of Luján. However, since not all the women owned such garments, they decided on white gauze shawls or diapers, thinking that such a symbol would make them feel closer to their children and emphasize their motherhood.[94]

As the procession that year moved toward Luján, a town at a considerable distance from Buenos Aires, the Mothers and their white shawls joined in at various points. As they grew in numbers, the police began to follow them, and they mixed in with the Marist priests for protection. When the police moved closer, they began to pray the Lord's Prayer and the Hail Mary. On reaching the basilica, the mothers joined together to recite the rosary. When approached by the curious, they responded that they were praying for their children, who had disappeared. While the message inside the church was one of world peace, the mothers sat together with their rosaries, bearing courageous witness to their losses. Attempts to repress them began soon afterward; spies were in their midst, and violent attacks took place on the Mothers themselves, but their demonstrations continued and outlasted the military government.[95] They continue today and will doubtless continue as long as these women are alive to commemorate their children.

Despite the attempts of the military government to stigmatize the women as "the crazy ladies," *las locas*, they began to attract national and international attention as they extended their motherly efforts to discover what had happened to their children and to emphasize the horror of the repression. These activities were conducted within a Marian framework. A beautiful publication appeared in 1983 in English, just before the fall of the military junta—*Selection of Poems of the Mothers of the Plaza de Mayo*. The illustrations and the poems emphasize the connection of the women's suffering with that of the Virgin. A drawing of a suffering mother before the cross has the caption "Terrible Cross without Calvary, a way which leads nowhere, only to the Plaza de Mayo." The figure of a woman at the black abyss of an open tomb is captioned "Where have you put his body? Tell me where you have put it." Another shows a woman with a shawl embracing her son behind a window covered with a geometrical, schematic cross.[96] In one of the poems, "Conversation in the Cathedral," one of the mothers confronts the monsignor over the closing by the police of that holy place. The monsignor explains that it is the presence of the mothers that requires him to lock the doors, as "they take refuge in the church, and this is not a hiding-place." The Mother protests, "In that case, I suggest that, instead of closing the doors, you cover the Cross and Jesus with a great black cloth, so He will not have to suffer the indignity of seeing the Beating of the Mothers. Mary was on the mountain, at the foot of the holy cross . . . With what pain must the good Jesus, suffering on the Cross, look down on this Calvary! He will think: It was all in vain; men are still the same!"[97]

The vision of the Virgin has continued to have the same kinds of power in Argentina that it had in Reconquest Spain and in the Conquest of Mexico and the Andes. She is seen as the protectress and patroness of the country, closely associated with what it is to be Argentine. Her image is used and her sheltering presence invoked for political as well as spiritual projects by the powerful and by the powerless. The Virgin is ambivalent, ambidextrous, and ambiguous, used to justify and absolve horrible violence, to give courage and solidarity to those who protest this repression, and to illuminate the justness of their cause. Her resonant image continues to inspire, across the political spectrum, from Evita Perón speaking to the *descamisados* to the generals of the military repression to the Mothers of the Plaza de Mayo commemorating their children.

CHAPTER NINE

Marian Celebrations at the Turn of the Millennium

✠   ✠   ✠

AS THE TWENTIETH CENTURY has drawn to a close and the twenty-first has begun, Marian devotion continues as strong as ever. Celebrations of the Virgin's majesty are widespread, especially in Spain, Italy, and Latin America but also in Spanish-speaking areas of the United States and among other populations elsewhere in the world. The connection between the celebrations of Mary and issues of identity are just as clear as they were in the time of Bernal Díaz del Castillo and Hernán Cortés; these identities may be national, local, or highly personal. The rituals are beautiful and affecting, even for those who are not personally devoted to the Virgin in one or another of her advocations.

I have been present for four of these in recent years: Corpus Christi in Cuzco, Peru, in 1995 and 1998; Semana Santa in Seville, Spain, in 1999; and the Día de Guadalupe in Mexico City in 1999. In these ceremonies I have observed the intense identification of the crowd with the figures of Mary; the shared understanding that she is a person and that she is personally present within the image, despite what the theology dictates; and the interaction between the observant, believing crowd and Our Lady. There are a number of important points to make about these ceremonies. First of all, they are popular in several senses: they are largely organized by the people of those communities, not exclusively and sometimes not even primarily by the hierarchical Church; they are heavily attended; they are enjoyed and are meant to be enjoyed, in that they are arresting and psychologically satisfying spectacles. Moreover, they are highly engaging, the living participants and spectators interacting with the images of this uniquely revered human being. Further, despite their various ostensible purposes, they are all heavily focused on the Virgin Mary herself. The reason for this emphasis is evident in Guadalupe's Day but certainly not obvious for Corpus Christi, which is supposed to be centered around the Eucharist, or for Semana Santa, which recounts Christ's passion and resurrection. However, of the fifteen images in Cuzco's recent Corpus Christi celebrations, five are of Santa María, and one is of her mother, Santa Anna, with the baby Mary in her arms. Further, the five major images of Mary are located at the end of the procession around the Plaza de Armas; one would expect the Eucharist to take that pride of place. However, members of the crowd around the Plaza freely offer the information that in earlier years when the images of Mary came at the beginning, the crowd departed after they had appeared, leaving the Eucharist and its attendant priests to march around the empty square. During Semana Santa in Seville, virtually every brotherhood carries an image of the Virgin. It almost always comes at the very end of the brotherhood's procession through the streets of Seville, and it is the Virgin's appearance that evokes the most emotional response from the crowd. Probably the reason for having her come last is the same as in Cuzco—some people would leave otherwise—but perhaps there are additional appeals. Her suffering, as the Mother of the martyred Christ, is deeply intense and deeply understandable to the crowd. Her appearance is a dramatic ending, and in my opinion a life-affirming one, to the message of sorrow and sacrifice that has preceded it. The Virgin becomes the symbol of hope, redemption, life, and joy—the Mother who sees her child overcome death.[1] Yet another possibility is reflected in the 1578 Rule Book of the Confraternity of Jesus the Nazarene and the Holy Cross in Jerusalem. It deemed that in every Good Friday procession, the members would carry images of Christ and Our Lady through the streets of Seville, so that by "carrying Jesus Christ as captain before our eyes, and our backs protected by his divine mother, we will be free of the demon in this procession."[2] Thus, the power and protection of Mary are present at the location where humans are most vulnerable—behind their backs.

These rituals have much in common, but they are greatly different in form. Corpus Christi in Cuzco is a movable feast and takes place, as a rule, in June. It initially was a Spanish replacement for the Inka ceremony of Inti Raymi, at which the *mallquis* (mummies) of the deceased rulers and their wives were brought into the sacred space in Cuzco that is now the Plaza de Armas. Carol Ann Fiedler has also pointed out its similarities to the Inka festival of Capacocha, in which idols and sacrifices from the holy sites of the Inka empire were brought to the capital city, and in return, gifts were sent back to those locations. In this way, the Andean deities were centered on the Inka capital in a relationship of mutual responsibilities and sacrifice. She indicates, and I have observed, that while the images are en route to the plaza, they are greeted with celebratory rites near the church of Santa Clara, and they stop frequently at churches and other sacred locations as they leave the city after the Corpus Christi week is over. Fiedler writes that certain features of Capacocha, such as the gathering in the central plaza of the city of sacred images representing various geographical and social units, the competition inherent between groups in the rituals in favor of the various figures, the expression of "socio-ethnic identities" through costume and dance, and even a prophecy that emerges in the meeting of the idols and involves the Virgin of Belén, are characteristic also of the modern Corpus Christi celebrations.[3] Now, the ritual involves parishes inside and close to Cuzco who bring fourteen images to join the Virgin of the Immaculate Conception, known as La Linda de la Catedral (the Beautiful Woman of the Cathedral), to the center of the city. The images, and the parishioners, spend the week in various activities, including processions around the plaza. Naturally, this ritual involves large numbers of Peruvians of the Cuzco area in planning, preparing, transporting, and moving through the ceremonial drama that is unfolding. The images, all of saints or of the Virgin, are like houseguests at a weeklong party; La Linda is even known as *la anfitriona*, "the hostess."

Semana Santa, of course, takes place in the week between Palm Sunday and Easter, so it is in late March or in April. This timing coincides with the beginning of spring in Seville and with it the flowering of the orange trees, whose beauty and fragrance enhance the festival. The major events of the week are the parades of the most important brotherhoods of that city; fifty-seven of them took part in 1999. They begin in various locations, usually at the church where the images are normally housed, and take several hours to move through the city. All pilgrims wind up passing the bell tower known as the Campana in downtown Seville, proceeding along Calle Sierpes, and moving through the cathedral. Each procession is made up of hundreds and often thousands of members of the *cofradía* carrying crosses or candles, with two or even three large *pasos* (processional platforms containing one or more images), one of them usually devoted exclusively to the Virgin. Most have bands and orchestras—commonly more than one—to provide the music that guides the participants and gives rhythm and emotion to the ritual. Several of these parades are going on simultaneously every afternoon and evening, and elaborate schedules are published in the local newspapers every day letting the populace know where any procession will be at any given time.

The total time that each brotherhood takes to process varies from five or six hours to the extraordinary thirteen of the brotherhood of La Macarena, which is the longest and most lavish in terms of costuming and spectacle. Normal routines in the entire city come to a stop during this week, and several local television stations cancel their regular programming to cover the events almost around the clock. Several processions are going on at once in various parts of the city, so that any one person can only sample the events, but the devout who attend regularly have purchased seats in the best spots—the same ones year after year—in the center of the city where they can see all of the brotherhoods passing by the landmarks mentioned above. Participants and observers are aware of the difficult points—the corner in front of the Campana, for instance—and murmur or otherwise show approval when they are negotiated well.

The celebration of the Day of the Virgin of Guadalupe, December 12, is likewise more than just one day. Pilgrims begin arriving, singly or in groups, several days before the twelfth and visiting the Virgin in her basilica at Tepeyac. In 1999 the estimated total of individuals coming through her church during that week was six million, although it would have been impossible to get any sort of accurate count. Still, we know that huge numbers of the faithful come to see her in the days just before December 12. It is easier to observe them than in the other cases, since the major action takes place in one location, and all pilgrims arrive there. Cuzco and Seville, though focused on the central area, have activities that are citywide and even regional. It would be a mistake, however, to see Guadalupe's celebration as taking place in only one location; in addition to the movement of the pilgrims, celebrations with dancing and other kinds of festivities take place all over the country, and the children often appear in costumes—Juan Diego for the little boys, for example—whether or not they intend to participate in any public event. Even in highly secular places, such as Ciudad Juárez, dancing takes place in front of the cathedral all day long on December 11. The Mexico City festivities, moreover, are now heavily televised and thus available to those who cannot attend in person.

All of these celebrations, notably, are focused on some sort of return to a central home. During Semana Santa in Seville, *sevillanos* come back in droves; the hotels are filled with regular returnees year after year, making it difficult for others to find a hotel room, and homes are full of relatives. In Cuzco the statues themselves come each year for a kind of cosmic reunion, accompanied by hundreds of the faithful who bring them into the cathedral at the center of the city. Millions of people crowd into Mexico City during the week before Guadalupe's Day, file through the grounds of her sanctuary into the basilica, and wait in line to view her image. On the night of December 11, just at midnight, a huge crowd gathers to honor her and sings "Las Mañanitas," the Mexican birthday greeting. The sentiment and emotion of the song, however, go beyond a birthday wish; this serenade, in Mexican society, is offered to women particularly dear to those offering the musical tribute.

The spectacles are full of emotion, visually and spiritually moving, but there is more here than spectacle. It is a time of reunion and filled with the joy of

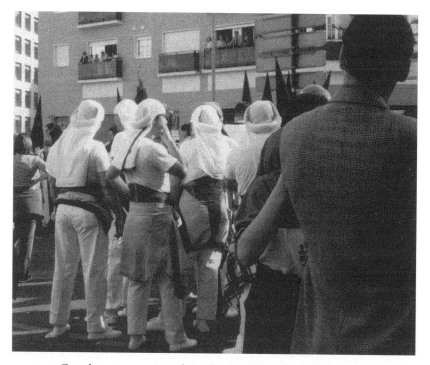

Costaleros *in a procession during Semana Santa in Seville, Spain, 1999.*
They are resting while another crew carries the paso. *Photograph by Linda B. Hall.*

seeing family members, or of joining with others in the common purpose of
returning the sacred images to a special location, or of traveling together to
honor the Mother in her house and at her special place. It is a regular, anticipated time of return. The celebrations are reaffirmations of family as well as
of individual, neighborhood, regional, and even national loyalties.

The visual and auditory spectacle is enhanced by the kinds of sacrifices
and penances and tasks of devotion that are implied and witnessed in producing them. The bearers of Cuzco's *andas*, the *costaleros* who carry Seville's
pasos, the pilgrims to Guadalupe's sanctuary all experience various kinds of
rigors, given as a tribute to the Blessed Mother. In Cuzco and Seville the
images of the Virgin are adorned with dresses, jewels, and other accoutre-
ments that are gifts from the faithful. The donors of the dresses of the
Virgin in Cuzco are often acknowledged by their having the names of their
donors embroidered on the garments, or perhaps detailed in sequins, along
with the dates of the gifts. In Seville and elsewhere, the various images of
the Virgin may even have treasure rooms where the most significant of these
items may be observed when they are not being used. The effort in-

volved in these offerings seems to be more important than their monetary value, though their worth can be considerable. The Peruvian gifts are sometimes made, at least in part, by the donors themselves, and the elaborate embroidery and the other decorations surely entail significant work and expense. The mantles of the Virgin of La Macarena and the Virgin of La Triana, the two most important images in modern Seville, are far too elaborate to be produced in any reasonable length of time by only one person, but other treasures certainly illustrate personal effort and sacrifice. Among the riches of La Macarena is a beautiful medal given her by General Gonzalo Quiepo y Llano that he received for taking Seville during the Spanish Civil War. He, in turn, presented it to her to acknowledge her help in the victory. The story is even more complicated, however; earlier *she* had given him *her* crown, they say, to be used for the cause of General Francisco Franco during the early days of the Civil War. Certainly the contribution was made by the brotherhood of La Macarena and by the Church, but the perception was that it was *her* gift. Unsurprisingly, the general could not bring himself to sell it and gave it back to her a year later.[4] Further illustrating the political importance and identification of La Macarena with the government of General Franco, Evita Perón was brought to her sanctuary in 1947 for an official visit and later, as we have discussed before, presented a painting for the treasure room (see Chapter VIII).

The Virgin of Guadalupe, of course, is painted on the *tilma* so that it cannot wear adornments of this sort, although for awhile it sported a crown, and statue replicas may well have their own special embellishments. The urge to ornamentation, however, seems to be discouraged by the clergy in favor of uniform images, but the paintings often have beautiful handmade frames that may be embellished with flowers or ribbons. Statue replicas will often be carefully protected with wrappings of various kinds that are removed before entering Guadalupe's church. Moreover, La Guadalupana has recently inspired a kind of sequin art in which the familiar image is covered with sequins, pieces of jewelry, bangles, ribbons, and other ornaments. She is also an extremely popular motif for recent Chicano and Mexican art, although these images are not, as a rule, brought to the basilica. These efforts and adornments lead us to another issue in regard to what *is* brought before her at Tepeyac: the sense of the Virgin Mary's personal presence and humanity. The gifts are for *her*, the attention is for *her*, the efforts and physical rigors are for *her*. And there is a real sense that she is present in the image and in her special space, appreciates these labors, and reciprocates with her loving concern, regardless of any theological principles that may be infringed. Here, surely, is what Hans Belting refers to when he says that "the image . . . not only represented a person but also was treated like a person."[5]

*Here the richness of the embroidery of the Virgin of La Triana's robe and of the decoration
of her balanchine and flowers are evident, as well as the crystal tears on her face.
Semana Santa, Seville, Spain, 1999. Photograph by Linda B. Hall.*

Usually the gifts do not represent a quid pro quo, a payment up-front for
a favor that is being requested; rather, they are in thanks for something specific that the Virgin has already provided, or for a lifetime of help and comfort, or they may simply be a sign of reverence. Sometimes they fulfill a vow
made when seeking a favor from the Virgin—the recovery from an illness or
the safe return of a loved one, perhaps. After all, one does not buy her favor,
but one can promise her ahead of time that her help will be appreciated.
Another aspect of this personal relationship with a presence and human
spirit in the image is the pleasure and honor that individuals and groups take
in being able to dress and otherwise prepare the image for her important
appearances. In the case of Guadalupe, the same kind of dressing and preparing does not take place, but individuals can carry and attend the communal and personal representations of Guadalupe as they are being brought to

the sanctuary. These personal services constitute an important part of the interaction with the image. Many churches throughout Latin America have dressing rooms, *camarines*, for their statues of Mary, and the honor of being selected as the person or as part of the team to whom the duty of dressing the image falls is highly sought out.

In these celebrations the Virgin Mary in her various advocations is intertwined with questions of identity, again personal, local, regional, or national. In Cuzco the population is divided in its reverence among the various figures of the Virgin that process. The two most important—La Linda of the Cathedral and the Virgin of Bethlehem (Mamacha Belén)—have overarching associations for the entire community: La Linda in particular is a kind of female spiritual metaphor for the city itself, and most *cuzqueños* revere Mamacha Belén, whose miraculous arrival in Peru we discussed earlier.[6] Still, all of the Virgin's images have important followings and, with the exception of La Linda, are associated with specific parts of the city or region or with social or economic groups; the members of these groups are the most important organizers and workers for the festivities surrounding the week of Corpus Christi. The Virgin of Remedios, an image of some antiquity, only began to appear in the Corpus Christi processions in 1980. Apparently, the upper middle classes were eager to have a statue of their own included in the ritual; though tiny compared to the other images, she is opulently dressed although not particularly well attended.[7] La Purificada, an image of the Virgen de la Candelaria, is also extremely well dressed, fussed over, and rearranged; she is the advocation favored and sponsored by the vendors in the market, many of them women, who attend her well and spend a great deal of money on her part of the ritual. It seems likely that the choice of La Candelaria has to do with its popularity in highland Peru and Bolivia, as exemplified by Copacabana, and the fact that market vendors have contacts throughout the region. In 1998 she was the only statue of the Virgin to have her outfit changed during the course of the week, displaying in this way more of her ritual finery. Moreover, she had the best orchestra, both in terms of their musicianship and of their appearance, though the latter was a bit incongruous. The band members dressed in crisp khaki pants, meticulously ironed blue dress shirts, and ties featuring Walt Disney characters.

The elaborate attentions of the devotees of the various images cost money and reflect differences within the community; the Virgins compete as the groups compete. The goal is to have one's own preferred Virgin as the best dressed, best adorned, and best attended of all. Stories and gossip reflect this competition and reinforce the sense of each of them as almost separate persons; though the participants know that the Virgin Mary is one and overarching and that all the images represent her, still they operate as if they did not.

This competition is played out in the intense efforts to honor the specific image and reinforce her status by dressing her well. Several years ago the Virgen de la Almudena, a beautiful statue carved in the round (rather than as a framework for dressing with carved head and hands, as are La Linda, Mamacha Belén, and La Purificada), was restored with funds from the government. At that time, her supporters were enjoined from dressing her in other garments so that the restoration work would not be damaged. Those devoted to her were outraged; this prohibition meant that they were unable to express their reverence and intimacy with the image at the time of dressing, but it also meant that they could not compete in providing lavish adornments.[8] The various images of Mary are even said to compete sexually; Almudena is said to be the biggest flirt, while all the male saints are said to be in love with the Virgin of Belén. One story tells of La Almudena offending Belén, who then attacked Almudena in turn, blaming her for "insulting the poor." In another story Belén is said to accuse La Almudena of appearing "naked," since she wears no dress over her statue. Fiedler believes that these warring images may stem from rivalries dating from the pre-Spanish and

A close-up view of La Macarena adorned for Semana Santa, behind the candles of her paso de palio, 1999. She holds a rosary, and emerald flowers adorn her lace mantilla and blouse. Photograph by Linda B. Hall.

early colonial years, and well they may, but there are certainly competitive images of the Virgin in other areas, including Seville.[9]

In Seville the most prominent competition is between two representations of the Virgin of Hope: la Virgen de la Esperanza de la Macarena and la Virgen de la Esperanza de Triana. Both are exquisite images of the Virgen Dolorosa, the sorrowful Virgin, with crystal tears shining on their faces. They are *imagenes de vestir*, that is, images for dressing, as are the three principal Marian images in the Peruvian Corpus Christi celebration. The Macarena is the older of the images, produced by an anonymous artist in the seventeenth century. The Virgin of La Triana, in contrast, dates from the beginning of the nineteenth century and is attributed to Juan de Astorga. The style of the sculpture, however, is very similar. It is not insignificant that they are images of Esperanza (Hope), for though they are weeping, their purpose, it seems to me, is to inspire precisely that emotion. La Macarena is from a central location in Seville proper, her rival from across the river, which gives the former a bit of an advantage. Still, devotees of the latter are pleased to cross the river for her, if they do not already live on that side, and she enjoys enormous reverence. La Macarena has an elaborate basilica; the Virgin of La Triana is located in the Chapel of the Sailors (la Capilla de la Marina), close to the Spanish naval headquarters, significantly on the Calle Pureza—Purity Street.[10] Both images are about the same size, 1.7 meters tall. In the days before they leave their sanctuaries to move through the streets of Seville, hundreds of people come to view them. It is fairly easy to get into the basilica of La Macarena, as it is spacious, but the Triana chapel is small. The traditional day to visit the Virgin of La Triana is Holy Thursday; women dressed in black with the traditional Sevillian high combs and mantillas and men in elegant suits, along with families with babies in strollers, line up for hours, chatting as they wait patiently for their moments inside the chapel. Both brotherhoods process on the Madrugá, the early morning hours of Holy Friday—the most emotional and psychologically effective time as the participants move with candles through the darkness among throngs of sleep-deprived spectators. It is also the most prestigious time of the week. Thus the two *cofradías*—and the two Virgins—are competing directly, separated in the center of Seville by the procession of only one other brotherhood.

The description of the Virgin of La Triana by Juan Martínez Alcalde, in his encyclopedic compendium on the representations of the Virgin Mary in Seville, is fascinating; he says that she has "a pure grace, as is typical of her neighborhood," and "a dark, womanly bearing." She is, in this way, identified directly with and seen as exemplary of the women of Triana, distinguishing her from other representations of the Virgin. The handkerchief she uses to dry her tears is "not a tragic relic but a certain signal of Hope, which announces the Co-redemption obtained through her own Sorrow." It is from this Hope, he tells us, that "the happiness that surrounds her procession" stems. He claims that by her presence in Triana she is doubly Sevillian, a claim perhaps not accepted by the devotees of La Macarena. The Virgin of La Triana's importance for sailors is clear in Martínez Alcalde's description; she is "*Captain of the eternal seas that have no ports*, the anchor of salvation, the radiant lighthouse of the sailors' day."[11] She therefore often reflects the connection of the Virgin with the dangers of the sea, a connection that in the area of the Mediterranean stretches back to Columbus and before (see chapters II and III).

Both brotherhoods stem from the late sixteenth or early seventeenth century, and both are associated not only with the specific advocations of the Virgin that they honor but also with scenes from the Passion of Christ and other doctrines and saints. However, in modern times the schedules of the processions are presented under the names of their advocations, indicating their precedence in popular reverence over the other figures.[12] The rivalry is of long standing and has to do with what part of the city and what side of the river one happens to come from but also with one's position in society and with one's occupation, family associations and allegiances (spiritual and otherwise), and the efficacy of one's own appeals to one or the other image in times of need.

Despite the enormous fervor for La Triana's Virgin, it must be admitted that La Macarena is the Sevillian representation of the Virgin par excellence. Again according to Martínez Alcalde, she is "the most universal expression of Spanish Marianism," although this statement would surely be disputed in Triana and in other parts of Spain. She received a canonical coronation in 1964, during the Franco years, and her sanctuary became a basilica in 1966. Both of these events reflect her political importance to that regime and the significance of Spanish Catholicism to the Vatican. The Virgin of La Triana's canonical coronation came only in 1984, well after the restoration of democracy. The relative importance of the two images is reflected in Martínez Alcalde's enormous book on the images of the Virgins of Seville. La Macarena rates four full-sized plates, including one complete with her impressive, bejeweled crown; her rival has two, still more than any other image of the several hundred that he catalogues. The same author also discusses the fact that both images have satellite or subordinate versions of themselves in other churches and chapels around Seville. The author is not atypical in his views in regard to La Macarena, and his emphasis would probably reflect the judgment of the majority of Sevillanos. He hyperbolically sees in her the point at which "earth and sky, the human and the divine, the sob and the smile, the torment and the forgiveness" come together.[13] However, his hyperbole does not exceed that of media commentators, participants in her procession, and many others devoted to her.

The competition continues year after year, and the areas of contention range from the length of time it takes their processions to pass any one point—La Macarena wins here, as hers is almost two hours, while that of Triana is less than an hour and a half, the former with 2,300 *nazarenos* (Nazarenes, that is, participants), the latter with 1,600—to the quality of the music to the sumptuousness of the *pasos* that accompany them to the way in which their *costaleros* (bearers) carry them through the streets. These days the *costaleros* are drawn from *cofradía* members who practice for months before Semana Santa, work out so as to be strong enough to carry the heavy platforms through the streets, and often suffer real physical problems as a result of these efforts. The music is also very important, and here often Triana wins, able as she is to take advantage of the musical organizations of the navy. Of concern and much remarked in the crowd is the coordination between the music and the *costaleros*, how rhythmically the *costaleros* are bearing their precious burden, how well they maneuver around corners, how well the Virgin's *paso* moves from side to side and seems to be dancing, even how well they lift the *paso* after the rests that they must take frequently, given the size and weight of their burden. What is being witnessed is a drama in real time, and as the *costaleros* make a special move at a dramatic point in the music, the crowd will respond with a gasp or a sigh. The lifting move after a rest is known as the *levantá*, and it should be quick and direct but not too abrupt so that the Virgin (or other images on a given *paso*) will not be too shaken. The move is requested when the individuals directing the procession call "to the heavens with her" (*¡Al cielo con ella!*).[14] The crowd will remark on how well this lifting is done. A further point of contention is the emotionality and excellence of delivery of the *saetas*, those typically Andalusian songs designed, in the words of Timothy Mitchell, to "strike contrition into the hearts of their hearers."[15] They are, however, meant to do more than that; sung in a nasal, almost gypsy or North African style, they evoke deep emotional responses and empathy from the spectators in reverence to the Virgin or to the other figures on the processional platforms that are passing. Susan Webster defines a *saeta* as a "sung poem" that is "vocalized by a member of the audience during the course of a procession." These individuals will usually appear dramatically on a nearby balcony to honor her with their songs when she stops for a rest. A *saeta* in honor of La Macarena will convey the idea:

The Virgin who is in heaven
will not have a face of sorrow,
but she will surely have your face
Virgin of the Macarena.[16]

Another *saeta* illustrates the competition to which we have referred:

My Mother of Hope,
honor of the trianeros,
your face is prettier
than (the Mother) of the macarenos.[17]

In 1999 all of Seville was talking of the captivating *saeta* sung to the Virgin of Triana just as she was leaving her chapel. The emotion involved and the power of the musical message caused the singer and some of the spectators to fall to their knees at its conclusion. In that year, at least, she seems to have prevailed over La Macarena in that specific arena of contention. Excellent *saeteros* are in great demand; in 1999 the *saetero* known as Perejil reported that he would be singing several times each day, including for his own brotherhood, Museo, but he would not be marching in the procession. As he explained, "I don't dress as a Nazarene because I'd suffocate." Still, his talent contributed to the honoring and the spectacle of many of the images. He emphasizes that the applause is for Christ and the Virgin, not for himself.[18]

In other years, competition has centered around which images have actually appeared in processions. When the weather is bad, one or the other may be kept inside while the other is taken out. When this occurs, the image that actually appears on the streets is rated as more *guapa*, that is, not only more attractive but stronger and more courageous. The crowd is witnessing a drama, and those who are processing and carrying the *pasos* are participating in it, but it is a drama in which a flow between "action and awareness," to use Turners' formulation, may be present in those involved.[19] Those moments are the most satisfying to all concerned.

The Virgin of Guadalupe does not have to compete in the same way, having long since won her competition with the Virgin of Remedios (see Chapter VII). Her affective presence is national and international, not local. The groups who come to see her, however, identify closely with their communities. Although they do not compete in the same way as the devotees of one or another Cuzcan or Sevillian image do, they nevertheless reinforce their sense of community by arriving together, often from far away, on foot, in decorated buses or commonly shared trucks, or even by bicycle convoys.

Young men walking down the aisle in the Basilica of Guadalupe in Mexico City.
They wear "Recuerdo de mi visita a Tepeyac" T-shirts as they carry an image of the Virgin
to be blessed, December 1999. Photograph by Linda B. Hall.

When they arrive at the basilica to greet the Virgin, they often dress alike—most frequently, at least in 1999, in warm-up suits of red or white or green, the Mexican national colors, with the name of the town or the parish from which they came printed on the backs of their T-shirts or sweatshirts.

Victor Turner has spoken of the "communitas" that stems from ritual enactments, "a relational quality of full unmediated communication, even communion, between definite and determinate identities." It is a quality that "has something magical about it." He sees it as "associated with ideas of purity and pollution" and asserts that those who experience it "have a feeling of endless power."[20] It seems to me that his concepts are extremely useful in understanding what is occurring in these Marian rituals. All involve coming together around a central set of symbols that have enormous affective power, a power accessed through shared and often strenuous effort, in an atmosphere of visual, auditory, and even muscular stimuli all directed toward reverence for a superhuman woman, a shared Mother. In the Mexican case, the appeal is national; in the cases of Cuzco and Seville, the appeals are more local and divided in various ways. But even in the Mexican case, the process of pilgrimage and shared exertions reinforces local solidarities. At the same time it binds these loyalties into a sense of nation, of Mexicanness as well, given that all of these different efforts, though originating locally, are ultimately focused on the Virgin of Guadalupe. Although Turner and Turner emphasize the significance of the individual, not the group, as the "moral unit" of pilgrimage, it seems to me that both local and national communities—not to mention Christian communities—are reinforced in these Marian celebrations.[21]

Anna Rita Valero defines pilgrimage as "a journey directed to a sacred place with the intention of having an encounter with divine," an intention that sets the trip apart and provides an emotional charge from the beginning. Thus, the pilgrim sets out for Tepeyac with the expectation that she or he will be able to communicate directly with the Virgin of Guadalupe in her house, that one's own presence in the sanctuary where the Virgin is felt to live will provide a special intimacy and a special opportunity for reverence. Many pilgrims come in groups that gather in home communities and set out together. This experience of travel may last only a few hours or it may be days, and along the way the travelers stop in schools, parish houses, or other public spaces, with little opportunity for privacy or even comfort. But they share a camaraderie and a sense of community.[22] Most of these groups carry an image of Guadalupe that they wish to have blessed; sometimes they have more than one. At the same time, the ultimate goal is to arrive at Guadalupe's

Women pilgrims arrive on their knees at the Basilica of Guadalupe in December 1999. Photograph by Linda B. Hall.

basilica at Tepeyac, a place profoundly connected with a sense of Mexican national identity (see Chapter VII).

On arrival at the sanctuary, the group usually enters together, waiting in line to make their way down the aisles past the altar to the area where the *tilma* is hung. At that point there are moving sidewalks running in opposite directions in front of the images of Guadalupe, so that the traffic never stops. Individuals often kneel on these electrically powered paths as they sail sideways past the *tilma*. Members of the group may return to the sanctuary in ones and twos and threes after viewing the image to linger for a while longer. Of course, many people come by themselves or with only their families, either to view the image or simply to spend a while reverently in the basilica. Some people, in a sign of devotion, cross the plaza in front of the basilica on their knees; others drop to their knees as they are going down the aisles. One father I observed fell to his knees on entering, put his small son on his shoulders, and, with his wife at his side, proceeded in this way up to the altar. We can only speculate about the power that this experience might have for the child in regard to the connection of family bonds with the reverence for the Virgin, but it seems reasonable to assume that it must be profound. Many of the reverent bring candles to light; another young man I witnessed came into the basilica, knelt behind the last row of pews, and carefully lit the three votive candles that he had brought along. Despite the crowding, he was able to establish his own special ritual space, and those around him gave him room to do so. The crowd is gentle, joined in a shared purpose of reverence, unlike the jostling crowds of similar size that go into and come out of the subway just a block or two away. The feeling of solidarity is strong; after all, had Guadalupe not chosen Mexico for her very own? The candles are closely associated with the Virgin; though they may be lit for other figures, they are particularly connected with her reverence, as they were in the time of Motolinía in the decades following the Conquest and before that in Spain.

This connection seems to be particularly associated with hope and light. The relationship of the Virgin to light, it seems to me, probably has a great deal to do with the fear of the dark stemming from childhood, a dark that could be relieved by the presence of the mother. Recent popular images that connect the Virgin and light are the widely available Virgin Mary nightlights for placing in children's rooms. Moreover, in the past few years, strings of Christmas lights in the form of the Virgin of Guadalupe have been available both in the United States and in Mexico, and illuminated statues of the Virgin are available throughout Latin America. In a story about the energy crisis in Brazil in 2001, a Brazilian woman who was described as a "jittery 81-

year-old," reported in distress, "I've even disconnected the lights illuminating the little statue of the Virgin Mary in my living room."[23] For this woman,
one of the most important functions of electricity was to provide the Virgin's
light to her household.

   This connection of the Virgin with light is embodied in the presentation
of many of the images of the Virgin on the *pasos de palio*, platforms covered by
elaborate canopies with banks of lighted candles in front of her figure, that
parade during Semana Santa in Seville. These rituals are planned and carried
out by the brotherhoods, and the system has been mirrored in organizations
in the Spanish New World. In Seville the brotherhoods are usually groups
formed around a particular reverence for one of the events in Christ's passion, as well as for Saint Mary. Mitchell has made the point that the
identification of an individual with the brotherhood is not necessarily a function of formal membership; it is "the loyal attachment to the images of
Jesus and María that magnetizes the emotion and devotion of the cofradía
and its public alike."[24] This reverence for Mary is embodied in a richly dressed
and ornamented image, which will be carried during the week, as noted above,
almost always at the very end of the brotherhood's procession. Most of
these statues—and the Virgins of La Macarena and La Triana are particularly lovely examples of the genre—are sorrowful Virgins, *dolorosas*. Many of
these images date from the late sixteenth century, and the iconography has
remained virtually the same. Although some statues were not actually produced that early, they are all very similar: the Virgin stands upright with her
hands to her sides, palms forward in an imploring gesture, or they are a bit
closer to her face, still imploring, or they are clasped as if in distress or in
prayer. The arms are usually articulated so that they can be moved around.
Obviously, since the statues represent the mother of an adult Christ in the
case of Semana Santa, there is no child associated with them. Frequently
they carry a white cloth, the "handkerchief" that we spoke of earlier, or a
crown of thorns, or perhaps both. The white cloth, presumably, would be
used to tend to her injured Son or for drying her own tears. Her face reflects
intense sorrow and often anxiety, with her brows knitted in distress and
crystal tears streaming down her face. Although the faces differ significantly,
the major features of the images are very much the same, although with La
Macarena, anguish is the most important visible emotion, her face lined and
tightened, while in La Triana, a sorrowful serenity predominates. Indeed, the
former seems a more human woman, the latter goddess-like in the austerity
of her gaze. There are numerous other examples of the grieving Mothers on
display during Holy Week, differing slightly from one another but very similar in major features. Another iconographic type also appears, the *soledad*

(solitude), a representation of the solitary Virgin alone at the foot of the cross after the removal of Christ's body. She is grasping a crown of thorns and nails, and a sword hilt protrudes from her breast to indicate her desperate suffering, an element that also appears in the *dolorosas* and connects Mary to her Son's sacrifice. Strangely, the iconography of La Soledad seems from an early time to have been considered inappropriate for the *pasos de palio*, and at present the two penitential brotherhoods of Our Lady of Solitude, along with a few *pasos* showing the Virgin with Christ, are the only ones that do not place their images under canopies.[25] In spite of this differing treatment, the Soledad and the Dolorosa are very similar to one another, and the dominant emotion of both is sorrow. The emergence in the distance or around the corner of the *pasos* of the Virgin, with their swaying and elaborate baldachins and their shimmering banks of candles are emotional events for the crowd, recognized in sighs or gasps or shouts of "*¡Guapa!*"—that utterance for which there is no good English equivalent but indicates, I have observed, beauty, courage, and power all at once. As the Virgin's *paso* returns to her home church or chapel, the waiting crowd often follows reverently for the last block or two. When she is returned home, the devout and silent train breaks into random movement and noise, as penitents are reunited with family members and friends recognize one another. If the penitents lack a ride, they can be seen waiting in their processional garb on the corner for the bus.

The confraternities themselves, it is important is to note, create the final image, particularly in these *imagenes de vestir*, images to be dressed. It is in this dressing process that these representations are distinguished one from another. The details of the ornamentation are of great interest to the public and reported extensively in the press, as are all the details of the ornamentation of the *pasos*. Interestingly, the "dresser," the *vestidor* of the Virgin, is listed separately; La Triana's in 1999 was José M. Jiménez Ortiz. Descriptions of the new embroidery on her skirt and train also acknowledge the artists (Fernández y Henríquez—no first names given—and Benjamín Pérez) and the dates (1997 and 1990, respectively) that work was completed.[26] The repairs and enhancements to maintain and improve the images are ongoing, and the enormous need for this kind of work supports a whole industry in the environs of the city. These details are also much discussed by the Sevillian public, not only because of the competition between the brotherhoods and social and spatial groups within the city who identify with and claim devotion to the images, but also because of the personal identification with and personalization of the figures themselves.

The dress of the figures is of interest here. Basically, they are dressed as queens, with skirts and huge mantles heavily embroidered, white lace blouses

*Penitents wait under a Sprite sign after La Macarena's procession in Seville, 1999.
Photograph by Linda B. Hall.*

full of ruffles, especially around the face and wrists, mantillas also of heavily ruffled white lace, crowns with elaborate aureoles of precious metals and jewels. This sort of splendid dress, chosen and commissioned by the brotherhoods, developed in the late sixteenth century, while at the same time paintings of the Virgin, commissioned instead by Church authorities, showed the Virgin in the traditional—and far simpler—white headdress and black cloak. The clothing selected for her by the brotherhoods was the current fashion for the royalty, and the connection was decried occasionally, but without effect, by church authorities. Again, the concern was that the Virgin was, as Webster states, "becoming too 'immanent': she was being treated like an ordinary woman, or, in other words, was too humanized for comfort."[27]

Isidoro Moreno Navarro has shown the increasing tendency over the years to move to *pasos de palio* with their single images of the Virgin instead of including her in the *pasos de misterio*, which show scenes of Christ's Passion. By the late nineteenth century, more than half of the processions had these special floats; only five brotherhoods out of fifteen processing in 1875 did not have such *pasos*, and in 1890, seven of eighteen lacked them. In the 1920s and 1930s and continuing to the present, the percentage has gradually gone up, so that in 1982, only five of fifty-five brotherhoods did not have *pasos de palio*. Moreno Navarro points out that these platforms unlink Mary from the specific scenes of the Passion of her Son and center attention on the Virgin herself. He sees a similar tendency with the images of the crucifixion, as the focus now is on Christ as a suffering individual rather than as part of the action. The narrative scenes of the Passion become less significant, while the Virgin and her Son become more important. As he notes, this process "extraordinarily individualizes the central figure."[28] At the same time, it reinforces the significance of Christ and his Mother that Mitchell emphasizes as well, rather than the events of the Passion. For that author, *cofradía* membership means "to belong to *Him* and to *Her*."[29] And, I think, Mitchell is correct that belonging to one implies belonging to the other, or, at the very least, through a strong identification with one, a believer has a strong psychological, almost familial connection with the other. He emphasizes the significance of the power of the Mother in southern Spain—which, the reader should remember, furnished the individuals involved in the initial encounter with the Spanish New World and many of the Spanish migrants to that area. Mitchell claims, accurately I think, "In southern Spain, whenever there is needed group affirmation at any level—*hermandad*, city, county, or region— some icon of the Virgin is likely to be involved." He speculates, "It is not the virginal as much as the maternal aspect of Maria that makes this possible, a result of the early childhood identification with a real nurturing female and subsequent projection of same onto a given Marian cult until the end of one's days." He also points out that the selection of a *cofradía* for identification by a given child usually follows the loyalties of her or his mother, reinforcing my own observations of the way in which the reverence for Mary serves as a major connection in mother-child bonds, even when the child is not a practicing Catholic.[30] Sons readying themselves for the processions still often return to the homes of their mothers to put on their penitential garb. Even in the creation of the images, at least some of the artists seem to have used their own mothers as models, adding a strong affective tie to the creative process.[31] I would suggest as well that using a live human mother as a model might well add to the liveliness of the image, the sense of dealing directly with a real and accessible human being. Again we see an aspect of reverence about which the hierarchical church has long been concerned—the personalization of the representations of María.

The five images of Mary in the Corpus Christi celebrations in Cuzco— La Linda de la Catedral, the Virgin of Belén, La Purificada, Remedios, and

La Almudena—are likewise highly personalized. Most of those figures date from the late sixteenth or early seventeenth centuries, approximately the same period as many of the Semana Santa images in Seville; three of them are very similar to the ones that we have been discussing—La Purificada, Belén, and La Linda. They are dressed images, and the same kind of time and attention are lavished on them as on their Spanish counterparts. In fact, several of the images are believed to have come originally from Spain. La Almudena, as noted before, is a lovely image carved from a single piece of wood, and there are legends indicating that the wood itself grew miraculously into the form of the Virgin and then needed only to be trimmed and polished by the artist. One story says that she was brought from Madrid sometime in the seventeenth century by the Bishop of Cuzco; another attributes the figure to an Andean artist named Juan Tomás. Belén is said to have made the journey from Spain in the miraculous fashion described in Chapter VI; the origins of La Purificada and La Linda are even less clear. Remedios, however, seems to have come to Cuzco with a community of Dominican nuns in the early years of the seventeenth century. A tiny carved statue, she is dwarfed by the other figures of the Virgin, and her place within the cathedral, in the back facing the altar, removes her somewhat from the conversation group—and so it is referred to in Cuzco—of the other images. Some say that she is also originally from Spain, but it is difficult to tell.[32]

The attentions to the dress and arrangement of the images continue throughout the eight days that they spend in the center of Cuzco, and throughout their peregrinations to and from the plaza. Even during the time when they are brought out of the cathedral to parade around the plaza, devotees may be seen climbing onto the *andas* to rearrange a skirt, replace a crown more firmly on the head of an image, or readjust a piece of jewelry when the float stops to permit the bearers a moment of rest. The faces and identities of the members of the entourage are well known to the observers, very different from those in Seville, where the participants in the processions are hooded and, in theory, anonymous. One assumes, therefore, that the authority of the individual or individuals clambering around on the *andas* is established and recognized by the participants.

The costumes of the Marian images are also almost identical to those of Seville, though the embroidery reflects Andean rather than Spanish flowers and is considerably less refined than the Spanish version, and the textiles involved are somewhat less expensive and elegant; one sees more satins and fewer velvets, for example. But the ornate skirts, the voluminous mantles, the crowns with aureoles, the lacy mantillas and blouses are very similar in style. The *andas* also are similar, though less grand, to the processional platforms used in Seville; they are constructions of precious metals, especially silver, and/or carved wood, and they are also extremely heavy, making it a significant personal effort to serve as a bearer. But here the similarities end.

Four of the five figures of the Blessed Mother, all except La Linda, process under canopies, but these canopies are much more like the parasols used at the time of the arrival of the Spanish to shelter the Coya, the Inka Queen, than they are like the Spanish baldachins. These images of the Virgin are not alone on their platforms; in back of each of these four, there is a male angel holding the parasol in one hand and energetically thrusting a lance into the mouth of an ugly dragon with the other. Huayhuaca suggests that it may be Saint Michael, and perhaps it is, but in any case he is aiding the Virgin in her fight against her adversary, the devil. The dragon here may well represent the Andean religions that Christianity and the Virgin have come to replace; they were, after all, depicted as errors foisted on the local populace precisely by Satan and condemned and persecuted as idolatry by the colonial Church. Bouncing along incongruously behind this complex of Virgin, angel, and dragon, on a flexible though sturdy piece of metal emerging from the back of the *anda*, is a little doll known as a *killkito*. No one could explain to me exactly the purpose of the strange little figures, and they vary from year to year. Most of them seem to be little boys or little girls dressed in frilly costumes, and as such they may be the *angelitos* or little angels that some observers claimed them to be. It seems to me that they may be, then, symbolizing the souls of dead children, for *angelito* is the term used commonly in Spanish to mean children who die before reaching the age of reason and then enjoy an eternity of innocence.[33] But a *killkito* that I observed in 1995 calls this interpretation into question and adds an ominous note as well: it was a doll representing a young man in combat fatigues. Perhaps it also represented a lost child, but lost as an adult in the violent struggles between the Peruvian military and the Shining Path guerrilla movement that flourished for a number of years and was only just being brought under control at that time. The connection with the Virgin would be reasonable, as it is Mary who in her mercy sees to the souls of those who die through intercession with her Son. In any case, by 1998 this particular little figure had disappeared from the Virgin's float.

The peregrinations of the images are similar to those of Seville in that they are brought from outlying but not distant sacred spaces to the center of worship. Yet they are very different in that they arrive and stay for a period of time and are visualized as consulting with one another. The above-mentioned conversation group, that is, the arrangement of the figures within the cathedral on the two sides and at the back of the sanctuary, is seen by some scholars as reflecting former arrangements of the mummies of Inka rulers or

San José with the child Jesus is carried in procession, Corpus Christi, Cuzco, 1998.
This image is closely associated with the Virgen de Belén. Photograph by Susan Gandert.

of particular spaces for Andean deities within the Coricancha, and so they may be.[34] This discussion is connected with the issue of prophecy, and the saints are supposed to discuss the auguries for the coming year. The prophecy is revealed at the time of the ritual circuit around the Plaza de Armas, when the Virgin of Belén emerges into the sunlight in front of the cathedral from the darkness of the interior. If she appears to be tan, the future looks good; if she is pale, bad times may lie ahead. The prophecy is also associated with the time that she spends in the convent of Santa Clara immediately before she is brought to the cathedral. While there, she is taken out to the interior patio, undressed, and left for a while in the sun. Fiedler believes that this practice may reflect the pre-Spanish practice by the *mamaconas*, the Inka Virgins of the Sun, who tended the sacred fires that, Garcilaso de la Vega

San José is often shown in Latin American art in tender scenes with the Christ Child. Saint Joseph with Child, *Melchor Pérez Holguin, ca. 1690, oil on canvas, Denver Art Museum Collection. Gift of Mr. Robert J. Stroessner, No. 1992.67.*

informs us, were taken directly from the sun's rays.[35] Jorge Flores Ochoa sees the male saints San José, San Pedro, and San Antonio as having significance as they relate to three of the figures of the Virgin: the Virgin of Belén, La Purificada, and La Linda, respectively. The feminine principle, he believes, accords status to the accompanying male. He sees this relationship mirrored in present-day Cuzcan society, in which the maternal line determines the family status of the married pair and their children.[36] Spanish forms and practices have been mixed with the Andean, yielding a hybrid celebration in which advocations of the Virgin perform functions that are neither precisely early Andean nor Spanish.

Mexico was also the site of many pilgrimages during the pre-Spanish era. Tepeyac itself was reported by the Spanish to be a place of reverence for indigenous peoples, and Friar Bernardino de Sahagún reported in the 1570s that it was the site of a pre-Columbian temple dedicated to the "mother of the gods," where "the gathering of people in those days was great and everyone would say 'let us go to the feast of Tonantzin,'" the latter term being the word for "Our Lady" in Nahua. Sahagún's concern was that the devotion for Guadalupe that had developed by that time was simply a cover-up for the earlier devotion and therefore highly "suspect." He viewed with alarm the fact that "they come from distant lands to this Tonantzin, as they did in former times."[37] Though the reverence for Guadalupe seems to have been primarily Spanish in the sixteenth and seventeenth centuries, it is certainly possible that pilgrimages to her site are in some way related to that earlier reverence. In any case, both modern-day Cuzco and Tepeyac are ritual "fields" in the sense that Victor Turner describes them and exhibit "the same picture of a multiplicity of routes converging on a great shrine, each lined with sacred way stations. It is as though such shrines exerted a magnetic effect on the whole communications system, charging up with sacredness many of its geographical features and attributes and fostering the construction of sacred and secular edifices to service the needs of the human stream passing along its arterial routes."[38] However, Cuzco's Corpus Christi involves the arrival not only of humans but also of saints and is devoted not only to Mary but also to those saints and most importantly to the Holy Eucharist, at least in terms of the Church. If Corpus Christi is indeed reflective of the Andean celebration of Capacocha, as Fiedler believes, and ritually acts out religious and political loyalties to the center, the pilgrimages to Tepeyac are now and seem to have been far more exclusively religious in nature. The current celebration of Guadalupe's Day, of course, often reflects a century of secularism in the political realm, although in Mexico, as we will see, the political is being reinserted into the worship of Guadalupe.

The *tilma*, of course, is quite different from the images in Seville and Cuzco, and its origins, either human or divine, are heavily disputed. An appendix to the *Nican Mopohua*, the Nahuatl account of the Guadalupe story that was published in the mid-seventeenth century, describes the *tilma* as a "rather stiff" maguey cloak, "well woven because at that time the maguey cloak was the clothing and covering of all the common people."[39] Whatever its origins, it was certainly not European. The figure, in iconographic terms, is the well-known Immaculate Conception, closely related to the Woman of the Apocalypse. However, she crushes no serpent beneath her feet; she stands on the moon and on a pillow while a cherub supports the whole from below. Her expression is peaceful and benign; her robes, covered with stars, are striking but in no way as elaborate as the clothing in her Sevillian and Cuzcan representations. In fact she has been difficult to embellish because of the nature of the image, yet copies of the image itself have been enormously dispersed throughout the hemisphere and back to Europe, and now throughout the world.

The celebration of Guadalupe's Day in 1999 was marked by an enormous fervor as the city was crowded with the faithful there to celebrate her birth-

The tilma *of the Virgin of Guadalupe in her basilica, July 2003. Two moving sidewalks going in opposite directions carry worshipers past the image. Photograph by Teresa Eckmann.*

day. This celebration was of very special importance, as it was considered the last of the twentieth century, the end of the millennium, and marked the beginning of a year dedicated to her. Accounts in the local newspapers discussed the devotion of police precincts, soccer players and boxers, bullfighters, and ordinary people, while photographs showed her altars in the dressing rooms of sports arenas and in government offices.[40] An enormous student strike was in progress at this time at the national university, and in this supposedly secular nation, a newsletter distributed by some of the strikers called on the Virgin of Guadalupe, "Patrona de la Insurgencia" (Patroness of the Insurgency) to help them prevail. A huge picture of Guadalupe graced the fiftieth issue of this publication, and a double-page drawing in the center showed Guadalupe under an eagle (a strong national symbol drawn from the ancient symbol for Tenochtitlan), a pyramid, a church, a middle-class apartment house, a truck, an earth mover, an Aztec warrior, and a feathered serpent. The drawing evoked an enormous number of symbolic associations—the working and middle classes, the Aztec past, the Catholic heritage of the country, all centered on the Virgin Mother.[41] Among Guadalupe's worshipers at the basilica, the use of the colors red, white, and green constantly evoked the Mexican flag. Often the flag itself appeared in proximity to the image of Guadalupe. Dancers dressed in native costumes mirrored the iconography used in the flyer passed out by the students.

Still, in 1999 the Guadalupe celebration was laden with controversy, and it came from within the Church and from within her very basilica. It related to a long-standing attempt to get Juan Diego, the Indian to whom she appeared, canonized. In the midst of the outpouring of public sentiment in Guadalupe's favor, the news broke that Guillermo Schulenburg, the retired abbot of the basilica, had contacted the Vatican to insist that there was no evidence that Juan Diego had ever existed and, by implication, that Guadalupe had miraculously appeared. Schulenburg had made similar statements several years earlier, also causing great commotion, but in the context of Guadalupan devotion at the turn of the millennium, the uproar was even greater. Stories condemning or supporting or forgiving Schulenburg were ubiquitous in the press but as a rule more negative than positive. His German origins were widely pointed out, and support for his position by another official of the basilica, Carlos Warnholz—also of German descent—did not slow the controversy at all. Even the papal nuncio attacked Schulenberg, saying that a "person who lives as he has lived has no right to make these accusations. If he converts and asks pardon, God will pardon him, and in my confessional, I would pardon him as well." He further criticized Schulenberg for having lived a life more secular than clerical, for doubting the judgment of the pope, and even for possibly having manipulated the finances of the basilica for his own private gain. The Vatican quickly authorized an audit of the accounts of the basilica, citing possible irregularities during Schulenburg's tenure.[42] Even musician Carlos Santana, in Mexico City for a concert on December 11, became embroiled in the controversy. In an interview he reported that he had gone to visit La Guadalupana in his hometown of Autlán, and recalled that while on his knees before her, "my heart was converted into a bird of fire that flew toward her, I began to weep as never before, and she said to me, 'be calm, breathe deeply and I am with you.'" The interview emphasized the spiritual content of his prize-winning album, *Supernatural*. When asked about Schulenburg's assertions, Santana reaffirmed, "We are all of the Virgin of Guadalupe and Juan Diego."[43]

All of these events took place within a political system that had strongly suppressed the role of the Church in education and politics almost eighty-three years before in the Constitution of 1917. These prohibitions had continued in force and largely unchallenged—though not always observed in the realm of education, at least—for the remainder of the century. In the year 2000, that situation would change dramatically as the entire political system experienced major upheaval.

Signs were already appearing by the time of Guadalupe's Day in 1999. A new president would be elected in 2000, and concerns were rampant that the official party, the PRI, might finally lose the presidency for the first time since its founding in the 1920s. The campaign had already begun, and the PRI candidate, who was speaking in the Yucatan, was asked about the Schulenburg controversy. His comment was that Schulenburg's actions had distressed and offended Catholics and that he was now negating something that he had spent years defending.[44] Though this comment reflected no particular position on the issue, that the PRI candidate would speak about this matter at all was remarkable and gained mention in the newspapers. However, the ante was upped considerably when Vicente Fox, the candidate of the opposition PAN party, waved a banner of the Virgin of Guadalupe during his campaign visit to the town of Guadalupe Hidalgo, where the independence movement against the Spanish under the Virgin's banner had begun in 1810. The uproar was immediate, and he did not bring Guadalupe back into his campaign. At the same time, the Mexican Cardinal Norberto Rivera kept attention focused on La Guadalupana when he announced that a digital reproduction, $5\frac{1}{2}$ feet by almost $3\frac{1}{2}$ feet, of the Guadalupe image had been created that would preserve it for posterity.[45] When Fox was elected in June, the Church seemed poised to return more visibly to Mexican politics at the national level; it had, of course, never been completely absent, despite the anti-clerical nature of the Revolution.

The controversy continued when Fox took communion at the basilica of Guadalupe on the day of his inauguration in December and invoked God in his speech before the Mexican Congress. One of the female senators accused him of a lack of respect for members of Congress when he not only mentioned the supreme deity but also greeted his four children from the podium.[46] The controversy steamed up considerably when his incoming secretary of labor, Carlos Abascal Carranza, closed a meeting appointing his new collaborators, including labor leaders and employers' representatives, by saying, "May the Virgin of Guadalupe, patroness of the workers of Mexico, bless you." One commentator noted that San Judas Tadeo was more properly the patron of laborers, while one of the labor leaders pungently noted that "the only saint is the saint of the collective contract." Later, Abascal said it

Ester Hernández's powerful image shows the Virgin of Guadalupe as Warrior.
The Virgin of Guadalupe Defending the Rights of the Xicanos,
© *Ester Hernández, 1976, Aquatint Etching, 35.5 by 40.5 cm.*

was only a personal wish for whoever was open to receive it, a response that mollified no one.[47] Six months later, Abascal and his wife were present among one hundred elected officials at a special mass at Guadalupe's basilica in honor of Saint Thomas More, known as the Roman Catholic patron of politicians. The media immediately objected, and one headline screamed, "Caesar in the House of God." The sermon was given by Cardinal Rivera, who is now considered such an important power that reporters regularly cover his masses. According to a report in the U.S. press, the cardinal said, "Christ, on the one hand, affirmed the healthy autonomy of the worldly from the spiritual. But on the other hand, in numerous pronouncements by Christ himself, he obligated conscientious Christians to protect the values of the Gospel above the demands of civil society. Men cannot be separated from God, nor can politics be separated from what is moral."[48] The debate seemed certain to continue.

For Mexican critic Carlos Monsivais, writing in the 1990s, the devotion to Guadalupe had its dangers. He acknowledged, "Historically, Guadalupismo is the most embodied form of nationalism, signifying belonging and continuity . . . But at the end of the twentieth century, one finds condensed in Guadalupe the experiences of marginality and suffering that are concealed by the pride in being Mexican. Present in the childhood of all Mexicans (be they Catholic or not), she constitutes the landscape of tutelary convictions and is the sign of normality in poverty, the formidable pretext for the exercise of intolerance."[49] For others, Guadalupe is a sign of liberation and empowerment, both in Mexico and among Chicanos in the United States. This latter view is well illustrated by Ester Hernández's powerful image, showing Guadalupe emerging out of her aureole of sun's rays, dressed for karate, hands clenched, and foot kicking out. The controversy continues over just what the Virgin means.

CHAPTER TEN

Mary Moves North

Aspects of National Identity and Cultural Dissemination

✝ ✝ ✝

FOR CENTURIES, as we have discussed, the Virgin Mary has been associated with Spanish Christian imperial projects, in Reconquest Spain, then in the Spanish discovery and conquest of Latin America, and later in combating independence movements in that continent; the leaders of those movements also invoked María. The Virgin has also accompanied Latinos into the United States, and the identification of migrating populations with several advocations of the Virgin associated with countries or regions of origin is rising along with their numbers. International agreements such as NAFTA, the North American Free Trade Agreement, which increase contact between the United States and Latin American nations, and U.S. immigration policies, such as favoring Cuban migration into the United States in the period since Fidel Castro took over in 1959, have accentuated and accelerated the significance of this cultural and religious icon in the United States. Turmoil in Central America in the 1980s, the continuing drug war in Colombia, and economic problems throughout Latin America have further driven Latino migration north. The 2000 U.S. census shows that more than 50 percent of U.S. residents born outside the country come from Latin America, up from 44 percent in 1990.[1] Comparisons of the 1990 and 2000 censuses showed that Hispanics in the United States had increased from almost 22 million to more than 36 million; the percentage boost, in terms of total U.S. population, was from 9.8 percent to 12.5 percent. As President Vicente Fox in Mexico continues to push George W. Bush for a smoother and more regularized Mexican immigration to the United States and despite the problems for all immigrants caused by the destruction of the World Trade Center on September 11, 2001, the movement of individuals from that country seems likely to continue at a high level. Given the intense devotion for the Virgin of Guadalupe in Mexico, the reverence for her on this side of the border is growing as well. However, a crucial difference separates the current migration from the ones we looked at earlier in this work, those of the Reconquest and the Conquest. In those two cases, the image of Mary was used along with military force to impose new political, economic, and social systems in the dominated areas. It should be kept in mind that though the Virgin became a, and perhaps the, major figure of reverence, she was no longer only the European Mary. European ideas and images interacted with indigenous and even African ones, leading to new, hybrid versions of the Blessed Mother. These, in turn, changed as the context did; the ideas of Mary corresponded to the needs—psychological, social, economic—of those invoking her. These have varied from nurturing to militant; and these traits may be combined and emphasis shifted as the occasion arises. The needs of Latino immigrants to the United States have been quite different from those of the Spanish as they moved into Moorish territory or into their New World, and the images and ideas of the Virgin have changed according to those needs.

The situations of Latin Americans moving to the United States are far different from the position of power that the Spanish were able to establish in southern Spain and in the Americas. These immigrants have most often been relatively disadvantaged in relation to Anglo, Protestant, U.S. citizen populations. Nevertheless, the image of the Virgin has been significant in maintaining a sense of identity, protection, and even power among Latinos in the United States. The mechanisms and significance of Mary's travels are similar over the centuries, as current migrants bring with them images and a sense of her presence, much as did Fernando III and Cortés. But there are significant power differences. In Reconquest Spain, the Virgin became closely associated with differentiation between Christians and people of other faiths, particularly Muslims and Jews. The fact that Muslims held peninsular territory that Christian princes desired made this distinction more significant, as Nuestra Señora developed into a kind of warrior goddess leading Christian forces forward. The figure of Mary likewise divided the Christian Spanish from the idolatrous indigenous. The Virgin Mother of God, in various manifestations and advocations, also was seen as bringing a nurturing and protective presence into the dangerous, liminal areas retaken from the Moors or taken from native groups. Mary's churches replaced mosques in Spain and preempted sacred spaces in the Americas. A more direct assertion of Christian power is difficult to imagine. Latino immigrants to the United States could not so forcefully and centrally impose their, and her, presence.

The movement of Latin Americans into the United States, as well as the

Nuestra Señora de la Caridad del Cobre prayer card. Courtesy of the Marian Library, University of Dayton, Ohio. Photography by Teresa Eckmann.

absorption of a significant Mexican population into the U.S. Southwest after the Mexican-American War, has given the Virgin, and particularly La Guadalupana, a presence on this side of the border for a very long time; indeed, images of the Blessed Mother and the reverence for her arrived centuries before U.S. forces took over the American Southwest in 1848. The devotion to Guadalupe in the United States has had a long life of its own, and it is constantly renewed by incoming migration from Mexico. In fact, in recent years it seems to be intensifying significantly. But Guadalupe has not been the only Mexican reverence to come north. The Virgen de San Juan de los Lagos is also significant to migrants in maintaining the connection with the homes they have left behind and with their families there, and she is important in the thoughts of those who remain in Mexico as they express prayerful concern for their absent loved ones. She has been especially important among migrants from western Mexico into the United States, a wave that began during the Mexican Revolution (1910–1920) and continues to the present. Many of those sustained by her help, as they believe, have returned in gratitude to her sanctuary.

The Virgen de la Caridad (Charity) del Cobre (Copper) has been of enormous significance to Cuban immigrants to United States in the period after Fidel Castro's takeover of the island in 1959. The Cuban case is the most clearcut in linking the Virgin with issues of national identity and politics, and we will treat it first. The Virgin of San Juan de los Lagos is an excellent example of regional connections, in this case between western Mexico and South Texas, and we will explore it next. The third, the Virgin of Guadalupe, is the most complicated of the cases, far more widespread and more diffuse than the other two, and therefore I will leave it for last. The Virgin of Guadalupe is developing a pan-Latino and even a worldwide following, but her presence remains strong and personal in the individual context as well. The effort to canonize Juan Diego, the indigenous man to whom she is believed to have appeared, has been supported by letters from throughout Latin America, not just from Mexico, and her image in the Cathedral of Notre Dame in Paris is often surrounded by Latin Americans from all over the continent, including the Caribbean and Brazil.[2] However, it is important to remember that it is not just a group identification; it is a personal devotion as well.

The psychological benefits for migrants of believing that their Blessed Mother accompanies them in their travels and vicissitudes are obvious. This multivalent image or presence provides both power and protection, help in adversity, renewed health from illness or injury. In the liminal and highly surreal atmosphere of a movement, legal or illegal, into a new, often hostile, culture, such a figure provides reassurance and energy. In the case of the Virgen de la Caridad, for Cubans, she provides additionally a strong and close tie with their unattainable homeland, so close to Florida spatially but so inaccessible. This bond transcends loyalties to the hierarchical Roman Catholic Church; Cubans, both in Cuba and in Miami, do not have a high level of participation as practicing Catholics but believe in the Virgin. A characteristic comment is this one recorded by a woman praying outside the Virgin of Charity's shrine in Miami: "I take communion not in my mouth but directly from God . . . and I take it alone . . . The Virgin, not the Church, helped me leave Cuba last year."[3] The association of this advocation of the Virgin with the flight from Cuba is clear in the minds of many of the migrants. For example, several years ago when a bus carrying those who wished to migrate to the United States smashed through the gates of the Peruvian embassy in Havana, the driver was wearing an image of the Virgen de la Caridad. He attributes his success in eventually making it to the United States to her.[4]

One of the most important events seen as crucial by Cubans fleeing Castro was bringing an image of Our Lady of Charity to Miami in 1961. Even though it was not the original image, it was a statue that had long been revered in a parish church in Havana. Her "escape" was dramatic. In August of that year, Cubans in Miami contacted Italy's ambassador to Cuba. He agreed to harbor the image, which been taken from the church. He then arranged with a member of the diplomatic corps of Panama to smuggle the image to Miami. This woman managed to get the image to a friend's son, who did not know the contents of the satchel he was carrying. Meanwhile, 25,000 Cuban exiles congregated in a baseball stadium to celebrate her feast day. The young man who was unknowingly carrying the little figure delivered her to a church in Miami Beach, from which location she was rushed to the stadium. At 6:50 P.M., just before the rosary was to begin, she arrived and was prepared by the priest for the festival mass. When the Cubans in attendance realized that the image was present with them, they sang, shouted, wept, and celebrated.[5] The Virgin was now an exile, just as they were.

Since that time, she has presided over many similar masses. In addition, the Cuban exile community has built a shrine to house her. Ceremonies at the shrine may take on a political tone and often demonstrate opposition to the government of Fidel Castro. An example, on July 13, 1999, was the gathering five years to the day after Cuban patrol boats had rammed a tug they believed to be escaping for the United States. Reports claimed that the patrols had blasted it with streams of water, sinking rather than trying to right the boat. There were forty-one drowning deaths. As one of the participants in the prayer service commented, "This is one of the biggest crimes of Castro's tyranny. We cannot let it slip into oblivion."[6] The political message was clear.

The location of the shrine is significant: beside the water, aligned with the island approximately 200 miles away. Migrants interviewed at the site indicated that the place was "frente a Cuba" (facing Cuba) or "cerca de la patria" (close to the homeland). The mural inside makes the connection even clearer. The Virgin of Charity and her child are front and center, closest to the viewer, with José Martí, the intellectual patriot of Cuban independence, in a large portrait to the viewer's right. Other individuals important in Cuban history, particularly in the independence struggle, are shown in portraits throughout the mural. Scenes of the Cuban landscape occupy the background. At the bottom of the mural, the scene of her initial discovery is pictured; she is shown in the middle of a canoe with her discoverers, a slave and two Indians, recalling the image of Fernando III leading the Reconquest with the Virgin on his saddle.[7] Thomas Tweed notes, "Almost all Cuban American visitors to the shrine see it as a place to express diasporic nationalism, to make sense of themselves as a displaced people." He further suggests that "through transtemporal and translocative symbols at the shrine the diaspora imaginatively constructs its collective identity and transports itself to the Cuba of memory and desire."[8]

An extraordinary opportunity for Cubans in Miami to demonstrate their connection with the island was the arrival from the sea of Elián González, the child saved when eleven other rafters, including his mother, died on the perilous trip from the island to the coast of Florida. As his father, who had not known about the escape, desperately tried to secure his return to Cuba, the struggles by his relatives in the United States to prevent that from happening became more and more surrounded with religious rhetoric. Very quickly Elián became "the miracle child," "the angel," and what were believed to be images of the Virgin—taken as signs that the child should remain in the United States—appeared on the window of a nearby Miami bank and on a mirror inside the house where he was staying with his relatives. Thousands of postcards were sold in Miami showing Elián either with the dolphins who were supposed to have saved him, or the Virgin of Charity—who was also supposed to have saved him. Some of the demonstrators who gathered every day by the house where he was staying carried images of the Virgin, usually the Virgin of Charity but even, sometimes, the Virgin of Guadalupe—perhaps in solidarity or perhaps because an image of Guadalupe was what they had. Prayer vigils were held outside the house, with demonstrators holding candles aloft and praying to the Virgin; inside, Elián's relatives had special prayer services of their own, with an image of the Virgin of Charity on the home altar that they had put together. Finally Elián's father had to come to the United States and take the issue to court, but ultimately the child was returned to him and to Cuba. Once that occurred, the incident quickly faded from the news, though it was by no means forgotten in the Miami Cuban community. It had been an occasion of remarkable intertwining of personal, family, political, and religious purposes and concerns.[9]

Another instructive case is that of the Virgen de San Juan de los Lagos, an advocation of the Virgin from the Los Altos area of Jalisco, Mexico. Migration to the United States from this area was extensive in the twentieth century, largely during and after the Mexican Revolution of 1910–1920 and the Cristero rebellion of the 1920s. The second is particularly significant, as it marked a peasant reaction defending Catholicism against the secularizing tendencies of the Mexican state in the wake of the Revolution. Similar to many of the other New World legends of the Virgin, the image was said to have been brought to San Juan in 1542 by a Spanish priest. However, we know very little about it before 1623, when the daughter of an indigenous couple was saved from a grave illness by the fervent prayers of her devoted parents to the figure. The reverence spread to Spanish, Amerindian, and mestizo devotees throughout the region, and a market fair was begun on the supposed date of the image's installation, November 30. By 1840, approximately 100,000 persons attended, but the reverence fell off after that date. Yet in the twentieth and twenty-first centuries, she has remained a figure of devotion in the region, and migrants carried this devotion with them on the challenging and dangerous trek to the U.S. border. The situation of Mexican migrants was even more difficult than that of the Cubans; while Cubans received significant aid from the U.S. government, Mexicans usually arrived and crossed in an undocumented status. As such, their situation was perilous, and they were subject to exploitation in jobs and difficult encounters in legal and immigration matters.

This devotion has been studied by Jorge Durand and Douglas S. Massey, who have investigated the tin paintings left as offerings in the region by returning migrants or by their families in gratitude for the special favor of the Virgin. Durand and Massey have shown that of the fifteen images (including four other images of the Virgin Mary and five of Christ) that attract attention from migrants in this part of Mexico and that received these votive offerings, the Virgen de San Juan received almost 50 percent of the total. The paintings they analyze reflect a number of concerns: the difficulties of making the trip and finding one's way, legal and medical problems, getting by economically in the United States, and gratitude at homecomings and reunions. A satellite shrine of the Virgin of San Juan was established in the late 1940s in the town of San Juan, Texas, by Mexican immigrants in the area. Now known as the Virgin of San Juan del Valle, the new statue quickly attracted reverence and donations. In 1952 work on the church to house her began, and it was inaugurated in 1954. Money and pilgrims flooded in, in response to radio appeals. A school, a home for the aged, and eventually a ninety-room hotel were built in the complex. All this success upset a disturbed fundamentalist preacher from the nearby area who was also a pilot. In 1970, enraged by the success of the shrine, he crashed his plane into the church while ninety-two priests were celebrating a special mass. In what was seen as a miracle, only the pilot was killed in the inferno that resulted. This tragic incident spread the fame of the Virgin of San Juan, and the insurance provided for an increase in the size of the rebuilt church from an 800-person chapel to a 4,000-person sanctuary.[10] These extraordinary events must have enhanced the view of the Virgen de San Juan as both powerful and protective.

A replica of the Virgin from Jalisco now regularly visits churches in San Antonio, Los Angeles, Chicago, and other cities with large communities of Mexican migrants. Masses during her visits are said to be "standing room only."[11] It seems fair to conclude with Durand and Massey that "icons such as the Virgin of San Juan provide a reassuring source of solace that enables migrants to construct an inner Mexico within the alien material culture of the United States."[12]

The Virgin of Guadalupe has a longer and more complex history on the northern side of what is now the U.S.-Mexican border. The devotion to

Virgin of San Juan de Los Lagos Sanctuary, San Juan, Texas. Photograph by Aaron A. Anaya.

Guadalupe in New Mexico, for example, dates at least from the first part of the nineteenth century. Father Thomas J. Steele, who has made an extensive study of religious folk art in New Mexico, believes that this advocation was extremely popular prior to 1850. In fact, he has found almost as many images of Guadalupe for this period as of Nuestra Señora de los Dolores, an advocation that was extremely important to the regional sect of the Penitentes. Yet another study cited by Father Steele indicates that among place names in the region honoring the Mother of God, the largest number honoring any one advocation (eight) are known as Guadalupe. This devotion was renewed in New Mexico, as indeed it was throughout the Southwest, during the period of the Mexican Revolution, when more than one million Mexicans spent a significant amount of time on the U.S. side of the border, and during the 1920s, when many more came and stayed.[13]

Other waves of Mexican migration have continued this renewal, up to and including the present. Images of Guadalupe abound throughout the

U.S.-Mexican borderlands and wherever there are large Mexican and Mexican-American populations. These images appear in art and in literature; Chicana artists especially have begun to use Guadalupe as a major theme in their work. Some of these images reflect the nurturing and protection that we have discussed; others are clearly directed toward power. In a vivid example, at the Chávez Gym in the South Valley in Albuquerque, New Mexico, teenagers both male and female engage in rigorous physical training in front of the image of the Virgin. At the same time, youth programs reinforce her connection with physical power. Some representations are even inscribed on the bodies of the faithful; images of Guadalupe are now popular in tattoos (almost always on males). The Chicano boxer Johnny Tapia protects his torso with a representation of this advocation of the Virgin.

In a more troubling development, Guadalupe has become a symbol and a presence for some prison and street gangs and important in prison art. Only further research can clarify this point, but I suspect that both her power and her protection are being invoked in these latter cases. I believe that the Virgin of Guadalupe indicates not only a strong connection among gang members but also underlines their emotional links with Mexico and perhaps with Latin America more generally.

At the same time, identification with her differentiates them from Anglos and other groups, although even some Anglos are adopting the devotion. In

Plate X. La Guadalupana, patron saint of the Chávez Gym in Albuquerque's South Valley, New Mexico, 2003. Photograph by Teresa Eckmann.

fact, it does not seem to be only Mexicans who are attracted to her image. A sort of pan–Latin American nationalism among Latinos in the United States, particularly in large cities such as Los Angeles that harbor immigrants from many nations of origin, seems to be developing around this figure.

Jeanette Rodríguez, in her remarkable study of the reverence for Guadalupe among Mexican-American women, emphasizes the sense that these women have of the power of the image. Despite the falling off of direct connections with the hierarchical church within the second generation, the tie to Guadalupe seems to remain very strong.[14] And strength, precisely, is what these women characteristically draw from her:

> Assumptions are tied to beliefs. For these women, the world is ordered. There is a God. God cares for them. God works through Mary/Our Lady of Guadalupe. More importantly, Mary is accessible. She is approachable, and because we can approach her, we can approach God.[15]

Rodríguez's informants emphasize the connection with mother, with power, with loyalty and support for family, with the strength to stand up for oneself, with light, with one's identity as Mexican. They say: "She has more leverage . . . Well, I pray to the Virgin like I say the 'Our Father,' but I speak to the Virgin, and you know, like as if she's my mother"; "She's always been there for me, but then again she's always been there for God, she's always represented him"; "When I pray to her I feel like she's really listening to me"; "Because she was Mexican and I am Mexican"; "I think that I have always had her like a torch in my life, the torch that keeps burning, and there is nothing that can turn it off"; "I feel proud that we have the Virgin of Guadalupe on our side"; "Our Lady of Guadalupe represents to me everything we as a people should strive to be: strong yet humble, warm and compassionate, yet courageous enough to stand up for what we believe in." Rodríguez continues, and I agree, that "Our Lady of Guadalupe is viewed as having achieved something, as being competent, as in control, and as having power." She emphasizes that she is "a 'felt presence.'"[16] These women reflect a powerful, assertive view of Mary. An article several years ago in *The New York Times* gives an indication of what Mexican men in the United States think as well. As a group of Mexican runners in Brooklyn was about to undertake "a speed workout of laps and sprints," one of them crossed himself and asked the Blessed Mother to take care of his legs.[17] For him, as for the women, the Virgin is associated with strength, power, and endurance, not passivity.

A popular venue for images of Guadalupe in recent years has been in public murals in Mexican-American neighborhoods in the United States.

These murals have been appearing at least since the 1970s, although the earliest murals seem to have fewer representations of Guadalupe than more recent ones. Of course, this proportion is difficult to measure. The murals of El Paso are instructive. Situated directly on the border with Mexico, it is in the neighborhoods closest to the border that the largest numbers of murals—and the largest proportion of Mexicans among the residents—occur. Most of these are the usual more or less accurate duplications of the famous representation on the *tilma* of Juan Diego hanging in the basilica of Guadalupe in Mexico City. A particularly large one that appears in a housing project just at the edge of the border shows the scene of the apparition of Mary with Juan Diego kneeling below in reverence. Another appears at the side of a house, framed in stones with plastic flowers in front of the image, a site clearly meant as a private shrine but available for public use.

The association of the Virgin Mary with the deceased is shown in another, which was created by Felipe Adame in memory of his son, Felipe Adame Jr., after the younger man's untimely death in his twenties. This image appears in the Spaghetti Bowl area of the city, underneath the freeway, close to the Chamizal. The murals in this area are painted on the supports of the freeway. The location is significant. The Chamizal is an area where the Rio Grande River shifted course, adding territory to the United States and taking it away from Mexico. This area was restored to Mexico during the administration of Lyndon Johnson, so this part of El Paso is very close to that previously disputed territory. The most powerful of the El Paso images that I was able to observe appears just across the street from the one commemorating the life and death of Adame's son. This second image was painted during the summer of 1999 and was the work of high school students participating in a mural program organized and directed by Carlos Callejo. The design is Callejo's.[18] It occupies the entire freeway support, both the central upright and two flying panels at each side. In this mural, Guadalupe's power shows as she emerges boldly out of her blue cloak, clad in bright red rather than the muted pink of the original *tilma*, her hands spread wide apart rather than together in prayer. The relationship to Mexican nationality, but at the same time expressing a dual loyalty, is shown on the two panels: on one side, a cherub unfurls a Mexican flag, while on the other, another cherub unfurls the Stars and Stripes of the United States. Below Guadalupe's feet is written, "Nuestra Reina de El Paso Ombligo de Aztlán" (Our Queen of El Paso Navel of Aztlán). This mural, it seems to me, indicates a number of shifting loyalties. It connects Mexican Americans clearly with Guadalupe and at the same time asserts a particular Chicano identity, Aztlán being the mythical homeland in the North (the U.S. Southwest) from which the Mexica (Az-

Plate XI. Nuestra Reina de El Paso, Ombligo de Aztlán. *This representation, in the Spaghetti Bowl area of El Paso, Texas, close to the Chamizal, was painted by high school students in a 1999 summer program directed by El Paso artist Carlos Callejo. The design is Callejo's. Photograph by Gabriel Cardona.*

tec) people originated. At the same time, Mexican Americans—devoted to Guadalupe—are no longer seen as being only Mexican or some kind of subset of Mexican, but also as American, with loyalties on both sides of border. Pride in both is indicated here.

But the image of Guadalupe, as other images of Mary, carries different meanings for different people, and the use and interpretation of the image continues to be contested. An example was the Guadalupe T-shirt controversy that erupted in April 1998 in Santa Fe, New Mexico, when elementary school principal Bobbie Gutiérrez sent a letter to parents reminding them that "any outerwear that is deemed gang-related, for example, Our Lady of Guadalupe shirts" would not be tolerated. One parent, Leonard Gómez, protested that he was outraged, as it was "basically violating my freedom of religion." Gutiérrez, who is Catholic, responded that experts had informed her that the T-shirts were gang attire, as were sagging pants and the like. Although she said she had never sent home an elementary school student, in her former position as a teacher at De Vargas High School, she knew of students either being sent home or forced to turn their Guadalupe shirts inside out.[19] Both the American Civil Liberties Union of New Mexico and Archbishop of Santa Fe Michael Sheehan immediately objected. The ACLU offered to represent any student told to change clothing; the archbishop demanded that Gutiérrez apologize. The spokesperson for the ACLU opined that the policy was "terrible for those little kids who just love the Virgin"; Archbishop Sheehan offered that "Mary is Our Lady of Peace, not Our Lady of the Gang, and I think we shouldn't allow gang members or anyone else to take away the symbols that are sacred. I don't think that this sacred image, which is so important to Catholics, should be discouraged because a few people abuse it."[20] Though police spoke in favor of the policy, warning the Santa Fe public of a "rude awakening" if they continued to permit the wearing of T-shirt images of Guadalupe, public school authorities hastened to plan a meeting with the archbishop, and the policy was quickly rescinded.[21]

A more divisive incident occurred in the same community not very long after and resulted in a confrontation that illustrates strongly the variations in the way that the figure of the Virgin can be used and revered in conflicting ways. It also illustrates competing claims of ownership.

On February 25, 2001, the Cyber Arte exhibit opened in the Museum of International Folk Art in Santa Fe. Featuring works by Chicana artists, the exhibits contained a number of representations of the Virgin of Guadalupe, ranging from digital collages to works created with pieces of computer hardware. A digital representation by artist Alma López—who was born in Mexico and was raised and now lives in Los Angeles—caused an immediate storm of controversy. The print was entitled "Our Lady" and featured the photograph of an assertive Hispanic woman standing on a half-moon, one hip slightly forward and an expression of pride and defiance on her face. Wearing a blue mantle similar to Guadalupe's, she is shown surrounded by an aureole of light and the roses so commonly associated with the Virgin. However, this representation did not show her in her usual red gown; rather, she wore garlands of flowers, especially roses, around her breasts and hips, with the legs and mid-section of her body left exposed. A bare-breasted women emerging out of a butterfly replaced the usual cherub holding up the moon beneath her feet. Her mantle of blue was covered with Aztec iconography, in particular that of the stone image of Coatlicue's dissected daughter, Coyolxuahqui, that was discovered several years ago during the building of the Mexico City subway.

The controversy developed momentum over the next five weeks, though many of those disturbed had not viewed the image. On March 17, the artist received an e-mail from Santa Fe resident José Villegas expressing his distress at what he felt was a disrespectful presentation of the Virgin, but most importantly questioning López's right to portray Guadalupe at all. A week later, he organized a rally of New Mexicans against the image. On March 26, three days after Archbishop Sheehan returned from a pilgrimage to Fatima and Lourdes, he issued a statement calling the image a "trashing," characterizing her garb as a "floral bikini" and indicating that the depiction was "insulting, even sacrilegious, to the many thousands of New Mexicans who have deep religious devotion to Guadalupe." He urged the museum board to remove the image and to demand an apology from those responsible for displaying it. A public meeting to discuss the issue was scheduled by the museum board for April 4. Despite the presence of professional mediators in attendance to guide the meeting, a hostile crowd of about six hundred people, only about half of whom were able to get inside the hall, disrupted attempts to speak and frightened the meeting's organizers. Many of the protesters carried traditional images of the Virgin of Guadalupe and prayed the rosary, and some shouted, "¡Que viva la raza!" (Long live our race!), raising the issue of the just who "our race" or "our people" might be but clearly excluding López. Protestors led by Villegas, many of whom were bused in from local churches, interrupted curator Tey Mariana Nunn, herself a native New Mexican of Hispanic descent, as she was about to speak. A number of people attending the event characterized it as frightening. Security guards quickly took López and Nunn out of the building because of fears for their safety. Although obviously most of the protesters did not have violence in mind, the passions aroused by the interpretation of the image were fervent and heartfelt. The protests illustrated the power of the emotions of New Mexicans devoted to the traditional image. Another meeting twelve days later attracted approximately six hundred people, and though López herself did not attend, other artists with works in the exhibition who spoke were "intimidated and harassed."[22]

The matter was eventually taken up by the New Mexico Museum's Committee on Sensitive Materials, which recommended on May 22 that the complete Cyber Arte exhibition be kept on display. On June 16, opponents of the image appealed to the New Mexico Museum, giving Director Thomas Wilson thirty days to reply. Wilson, stalling for the full thirty days, responded by denying the appeal. Further appeals and protests continued, with Villegas and Deacon Anthony Trujillo of Our Lady of Guadalupe Parish of Santa Fe announcing that they were embarking on alternating weeks of a holy fast until the image was taken down. The public protests began to peter out, although the controversy continued in the press.

The issues were several, but important was what seemed to be a sense of ownership among Villegas and his supporters that led to his strong and near-threatening response. He wrote López in his March 17 e-mail, "You may find yourself in some serious trouble with our raza in Northern New Mexico."

Referring to López's New Mexico supporters, he said, "We will find out who they are and when we do, we will do whatever it takes to admonish them in the public forum and hold their actions accountable. They have no clue on what a controversy is in New Mexico, especially when you mess with an image that does not belong to you." Even more ominously, he continued, "You started a firestorm in New Mexico, and we are going to put it out."

Nunn herself strongly defended the artist's right to her vision, saying publicly, "All the artists who have reimaged Guadalupe speak eloquently that they want the Virgin to be strong. They needed to see a reflection of themselves in her." And Chicana writer Sandra Cisneros, whose own work had to some degree influenced López, said that "For her [the Virgin of Guadalupe] to approach me, for me to finally open the door and accept her, she had to be a woman like me." López herself, shocked by the threatening nature of the response, indicated her resentment of Villegas's sense of ownership, declaring that "She is everyone's Virgin, not just Mr. Villegas' Virgin . . . I really wish he would understand I'm not coming from a place of disrespect at all. This is an image I have grown up with. She is everywhere—in my home and community. The idea for me was to relate to her in a way that was empowering."[23]

The controversy continued sporadically until the closing of the exhibit, and comments in the local and national press continued to investigate the roots of this shocking and, at least in the views of some, potentially violent confrontation around the Blessed Mother. Columnist Patricia Gonzales discussed the background of the digital collage, bringing to light the significance of the model—Raquel Salinas—and her attempts through posing as Guadalupe to "heal herself as a rape survivor." She recounted that one of her readers had written about her eighty-three-year-old grandmother, who, she implies, had initially been disturbed by the work but who had come to accept it when she was told Salinas's circumstances. "Now I understand," the grandmother had responded. "The artwork should stay in the museum." Gonzales herself revealed her own deep yearnings toward the sacred feminine, poignantly writing, "By honoring the feminine energies, I honor myself as a woman." But for others, women and men alike, their protest against the image was their way of honoring the feminine energies, which they saw in another way. Although I agree with Gonzales that "government must be open to all viewpoints 'in a society of difference' lest we return to inquisitions against the likes of me," the protesters as well as the artist were honoring the Virgin, but in their own ways.[24] It is unlikely that now or ever one vision will be satisfactory to all, and the strength of the controversy is a testimony to the power inherent in reverence for Mary. And, perhaps, it was the Virgin's power that was under dispute here, a question of who had the right to appropriate that power and how. Surely the impossible model of virgin motherhood was being challenged, and the rights of real women in situations of peril and violence to claim identification with Mary was being asserted. But real men and women were also seeking to invoke her power by recourse to the traditional image. A belief in the Virgin's strength was inherent in the attitudes of both sides, and the perception of her strength was part of what made the conflict about how that should be accessed so heated.

Plates XII. La Línea (special thanks to Melissa López),
by Alma López, Iris print on paper, © 1998.

The controversy about the image overshadowed another that López had on exhibit, more subtle and far more arresting, at least for this observer, on careful examination. Entitled *La Línea* (The Line), the obvious reference was to the U.S.-Mexican border. It shows a young girl dressed in T-shirt and blue jeans teetering on a graffiti-covered fence shaped as a half-moon. Beneath the fence, a dirt road and a rocky cliff lead downward to a map of Mexico depicting the U.S.-Mexican War, which determined the boundaries between the two countries in 1848 and delivered half of Mexico's claimed territory to the country to the North. A strong red line tracing the current boundaries between the two countries overlies the fence and the road and rocky cliff beneath it, while a traditional image of the Virgin of Guadalupe hovers in the lower right-hand portion of the image, with "Manifest Destiny" in bold white print running in front of her. Just in back of the fence is the ocean, with waves washing on the beach, increasing the sense of peril for the child seesawing happily between the two worlds with the mountains of Los Angeles in the background. A line of text above the fence reads, "This is my home. This thin *línea.*" The child herself, Melissa López, is Alma López's niece, the first generation of the family to be born in the United States and raised in California.

This image emphasizes both the innocence and the peril of the child, teetering between the United States and Mexico, literally and figuratively, not quite accepted in either country or culture, yet belonging, enigmatically, to both. Simultaneously, it shows her strength, her cheerful optimism, her ability to balance, anchored by a representation of Guadalupe on one corner and the massiveness of the Los Angeles skyline at the top of the image. Yet storm clouds hover in the background, and a U.S. border patrol vehicle moves across the image toward the ocean and toward the fence. At the same time, it shows the richness of the cultures on which the child draws and will draw. And the underlying symbol of the Immaculate Conception and of the Virgin of Guadalupe, with the young girl poised on the half-moon, emphasizes the powerful identity of the child, not her teetering peril, within her "this thin *línea*" and the image of the Virgin.

In this representation, I see the connection and strength that, for me, are the most important aspects of the reverence for Mary in the Hispanic world. Melissa's situation, and the richness of the heritages and contemporary cultures on which she draws, are shown as exemplary of those balancing precariously between two worlds. She personifies millions of Latinos in the United States, faced with hazard and ambiguity, but full of possibility.

CHAPTER ELEVEN

Conclusion

✠ ✠ ✠

A NUMBER OF THEMES EMERGE, it seems to me, from the discussion above. Perhaps the most important is that the Virgin, throughout the regions and historical times that we have investigated, is a figure of identity and relation. Whether she links migrants to their country of origin, or individuals within the family, or members of a community, or children to their mothers or the memory of their mothers, she dissipates solitude, provides strength, and reinforces connection. Those who feel alone feel her presence in situations of unfamiliarity or danger; those in trouble call on her for help.

She may be invoked for power, or resistance, or endurance. She may be called by both sides in a conflict, by the oppressor against the oppressed or vice versa, by those inflicting great cruelties or those fighting such cruelties. She may be invoked to reinforce specific notions of national identities and state boundaries, or she may be called upon by individuals or groups or communities within a given nation to challenge ideas of identity and to seek their own inclusion or to define their solidarities and differences.

The role of the Virgin in migration is instructive. The image, and the presence for believers, of Mary, the Mother of God, has been spur, solace, and expression of identity—both national and transnational—to migrants for centuries. The Virgin Mary was a powerful and reassuring presence in Spanish expansion during the Reconquest and Conquest, differentiating Christian populations from Muslims, Jews, and indigenous peoples. Her power continued through the independence period in Latin America, still uniting and dividing, but it was contested between those who supported continued Spanish control and the forces fighting for separation. The vision of Mary as protective, uniting, and powerful has maintained its psychological resonance

Processional pilgrimage from Villanueva, New Mexico, on the Feast Day of the Assumption of the Virgin Mary, August 15, 1995. While honoring the Virgin, the participants carry the flags of Mexico, New Mexico, and the United States. Photograph by Jacqueline Orsini Dunnington.

for those Latin Americans coming into the United States in the nineteenth and twentieth centuries, this time without the support of Spanish or any other military force. It also aided those in what is now the U.S. Southwest who saw their power and significance and access to land and resources diminished by the U.S. victory in the Mexican-American War. Advocations of the Virgin Mary have been associated with manifest expressions of nationalism—Spanish, Cuban, Mexican, Argentine, and now possibly even pan–Latin American, in locations from Los Angeles to Buenos Aires and beyond. In Texas and California and New Mexico, Mary in the form of Guadalupe may be beginning to stand for a dual Mexican/American identity, or a Latino identity, or even a Latino-U.S. identity as Hispanic populations assert their right to belong within U.S. borders. With Juan Diego's canonization, which took place in July 2002, Guadalupe's significance within all of the nations of the Americas seems certain to intensify, but other advocations will continue to be important as they differentiate one nation and/or group of people from another. A Latino population may claim multiple identities through Mary; the powerful images of Guadalupe underneath the highway in El Paso and of pilgrims on horseback in Villanueva, New Mexico, carrying Mexican, U.S., and New Mexican flags along with her banner show this manifold identification clearly.[1]

Though the way in which she is accessed may differ from one historical and regional setting to another, there are strong similarities that provide continuity. Her marvelous images may be associated with rock and thus earth, in the Andean highlands in the sixteenth century and in northern Mexico in the twentieth and twenty-first. Figures of her have appeared in living tree trunks in late medieval Spain and in contemporary California and New Mexico, the results of what were believed to be miracles or the loving touch of human artists.[2] Strength and solidity, life and liveliness are indicated here. Figures of her may be discovered in the water, off the coast of Brazil or the Canary Islands, or in Mexican rivers, again, a connection with life and fertility. She may save children who fall into wells from drowning in colonial Mexico or are imperiled in border territories in Reconquest Spain. She is called upon by those who brave the sea, from the Iberian mariners with Columbus in the fifteenth century to the Cuban rafters in our own time fleeing from that island to Florida. But the belief in the Virgin is flexible; the circumstances of her felt presence will change, depending on the changing needs and circumstances of those who seek her.

Virgin of Guadalupe carved in a tree trunk in Albuquerque's North Valley, New Mexico. Photograph by Baird Pogue.

A recent example is the appearance of an image of the Virgin of Guadalupe in the marble tiles in the Hidalgo station of the Mexico City subway. In early June 1997, a subway worker (or his daughter, depending on the account one chooses) who was mopping the floors spotted a water stain that bore a striking likeness to the image of the Virgin of Guadalupe. Word spread quickly, and lines of the devoted and the curious began to form to view the image, up to fifty visitors a minute on weekends, clogging the station and even imperiling the safety of travelers. Despite a rapid announcement by Mexico City's archbishop that the image was a result of water damage and not a miracle and his warning that such sightings might result in an "exploitation of popular devotion," thousands felt differently. Mexico at the time was suffering economic and political crises, the latter including assassinations, rebel uprisings in the south invoking the name of revolutionary hero Emiliano Zapata, and corruption scandals implicating government officials. By appearing in the center of Mexico City at one of the most heavily trafficked subway stops in a system not usually used by elites but more often by the poor, it seemed once again that the Virgin had made herself available in a convenient location to those who needed her.

The appearance of the image was publicized internationally, although most non-Mexican reporters seemed bemused by the events they were witnessing. Still, they reported what Mexicans were saying at the site: "It's the Virgin. Who else would it be? It is a miracle"; "We've had so many terrible things happen—corruption, assassinations, children in the streets—the country is in such a bad situation. She is the mother of all Mexico, and she has appeared to tell us she is here to help us"; "It's not just water, it's real. I touched her. I felt her. She didn't wipe away." All newspaper stories that I was able to find noted the remarkable resemblance to the original image, a remarkable resemblance to which I myself can attest. And the archbishop's disclaimer had little effect in dampening popular response. As one homemaker who had traveled an hour in from the suburbs of the city to have a look at the image commented, "I don't care what the Archbishop said. The Virgin appeared. Period." The incident illustrated yet again the unease of the hierarchical church in the face of this popular reverence. Moreover, the connection with Mexican nationalism was pointed out by observers: the metro station was named after Father Miguel Hidalgo y Costilla, the Mexican independence leader who had taken Guadalupe's banner as his standard.[3]

Bright orange partitions were erected quickly to move the public past the image, much as moving sidewalks had been installed to move the devout past the *tilma* in the basilica of Guadalupe, and the police presence was increased fivefold to help monitor the crowds. Despite the photocopied newspaper stories reporting the archbishop's stance on the issue that were posted around the site, crowds continued to come, many of them dropping to their knees to revere or to touch the image and leaving flowers, candles, and coins. The problems of crowd control soon led the municipal government to remove the tile from the station itself and to put it up, carefully protected with a heavy plastic shield, under a tarpaulin outside the station. Six years later, the faithful still pause on the way to work, stopping to talk to the image— sometimes weeping, sometimes very matter-of-factly, but without self-consciousness—as if she were there. On departing, most cross themselves and kiss their thumbs, then approach the image, putting a hand on the plastic covering in an intimate gesture of leave-taking.

The spot has become a little commercial area, with various kinds of goods including figures of Guadalupe for sale. The pavilion has become more permanent and substantial and now has a tin roof, and though a municipal government's disclaimer that what the viewer is seeing is a water stain remains on view, there is no question that through the image of Guadalupe, a bit of space in the center of Mexico City has been claimed for spiritual observance. Ordinary Mexicans can easily stop there and feel her presence, in an expression of community, nation, and personal reverence.

A question, of course, arises from the issue of Mary as a model of female sexuality and the use of the model for the purpose of "patriarchy" and male control. My own sense is that while such a model may induce heavy guilt feelings and complicated self-concepts for women, and certainly Latin American men try and have tried to use it to control the sexual behavior of "their" women, it is by no means always interpreted in this way. In my opinion, most women (and men) recognize that a contemporary human Virgin/Mother is indeed a superhuman impossibility, and focus rather on María's devotion to her Son (and, they believe, to themselves as her children) as a more reasonable ideal and model. There are striking examples of the faithful forgiving and understanding deviations from the model; Evita Perón is a stunning case of this phenomenon. The early use of Mary to promote the new kind of conjugality—monogamy—for indigenous elites during the colonial period impacted men as well as women; and Mary's example encouraged women to resist sexual violations, as in the stories of Mexico recounted by Motilinía. So while this model is important, it is very difficult to say that it operated to influence Latin American gender ideologies in only one way; the consequences were multiple for both men and women, and most of them were immeasurable. But certainly, Mary's image did not and does not simply victimize women; it provides a model of power as well. Ester Hernández's image of Guadalupe in karate garb emerging from the sun's rays and the young woman in the Chávez gym in Albuquerque show that the Virgin can inspire strength, physical and otherwise. As one Nicaraguan woman who had been active in the

Sandinista revolutionary movement observed, "We gave the Virgin Mary a whole new image. In spite of the pain she knew her son had a mission on earth and she stood by him. In the same way we knew our children had a mission and didn't oppose them. We always shared their struggle."[4]

This raises the issue of how ties with the mother are reflected in reverence for the Virgin. We have seen the ways in which the devotions of the mother within the family in Mexico, in Seville, and among Hispanic populations in the United States are reflected in reverence for Mary or one of the particular advocations of Mary. But these ties are also to others in the family and the community. These reverences are reinforced for children through community events in which they dress in elaborate costumes and take part in rituals, appearing as little Juan Diegos to celebrate Guadalupe's Day in Mexico; dressed as devils and dancing with other males for Mamacha Carmen, at the festival of the Virgin in Paucartambo; proceeding on the shoulders of one's father, going on his knees down the aisle at the basilica of the Virgin of Guadalupe in Mexico City; hastening through the streets with one's father to take part

Little Juan Diego at the basilica of Guadalupe in Mexico City on December 12, 1996. Photograph by Jacqueline Orsini Dunnington.

Adult and child devil dancers in Paucartambo, Peru, on July 15, 1998.
Photograph by María Elena Garcia.

Nazareno and child hurrying to a procession, Semana Santa, Seville, Spain, 1999.
Photograph by Linda B. Hall.

Little boy surrounded by adoring women waiting for a procession to emerge from a church, Semana Santa, Seville, Spain, 1999. Photograph by Linda B. Hall.

in a procession or being displayed and adored by the loving women of the family and community during Holy Week in Seville. It seems that the reverence for the Virgin reinforces important family memories, as for my friend's father, mentioned in the introduction, whose collection of paintings of Guadalupe may represent those family associations. The symbolism of the Virgin is also invoked to remember children, as with the white scarves of the Mothers of the Plaza de Mayo in Argentina.

The symbols and places of the Virgin are multiple. She is associated with light, from the candles carried by penitents in Seville's processions, to those carried by the first devotees in Mexico in the sixteenth century, to the electrically illuminated images of modern Brazilians and the nightlights available to Catholic children everywhere. She is identified by high places, from Montserrat in Spain (reflected at Monserrate, another sacred space, above Bogotá, Colombia) to the hills and mountains of indigenous pre-Columbian reverence at Tepeyac in Mexico and Sabaya in the Andean highlands. She provides a focus for healing, in the political realm—as the pope's appeal to the people of Argentina to unify peacefully around the Virgin of Luján underlines—to the physical and personal as with the mother who brought her child to King Alfonso X for healing and was sent instead to the Virgin, as well as the case of Alfonso himself. The belief in her power to heal and to save from danger and death ranges from Queen Isabel, visiting Guadalupe's monastery in Spain in the fifteenth century to immigrants crossing the Rio Grande into the United States in the twentieth and twenty-first centuries. And she is associated with movement and the instruments thereof: ships coming to the Spanish New World, mules in the colonial Andes, buses and trucks and taxis and other automobiles throughout the contemporary Hispanic world.

The figure of the Virgin Mary has been viewed in multiple ways, in different contexts, in the Hispanic world for many centuries. She has been used to differentiate populations devoted to her from others in contexts that range from overcoming or incorporating Moors and Jews in Spain's Reconquest to reinforcing solidarity in California barrios. Her advocations have been used to justify violence, as she traveled south in Spain with Fernando III in thirteenth century and with the Argentine military to the Falkland/Malvinas Islands in the twentieth century. She is deeply connected with identity: local, as we have seen in the reverence for the images of the Virgins of La Triana and La Macarena in Seville's Semana Santa and for the Virgin of Belén and others in Corpus Christi celebrations in Cuzco; national, with Guadalupe in

"Bus" for pilgrims east of the Guadalupe Basilica on the Virgin's feast day, December 12, 1996. Photograph by Jacqueline Orsini Dunnington.

Priest blessing car in Copacabana, Bolivia, 2000. Photograph by Susan Gandert.

Mexico and Luján in Argentina and Copacabana in Bolivia and Caridad in Cuba; and personal, as Rodríguez's interviews with Mexican-American women make clear. She is a personal source of strength and endurance, physical and psychological, for Mexican runners in Brooklyn—as she was for Bernal Díaz during the conquest of Mexico. She connects the out of place back to the homeland, for twentieth-century migrants from western Mexico to South Texas and for Pizarro in sixteenth-century Peru. She has been important in ties with believers' own mothers, as devotions to one advocation of the Virgin are passed down from mother to child in Seville, in Mexico, and among Mexican-Americans in the United States. She is invoked in repression and is used simultaneously for resistance, as in Argentina in the 1970s and 1980s by the military and the Mothers of the Plaza de Mayo. She may be beseeched for endurance or to justify submission or to call on inner resources of strength and power. As a contexts change, the ways in which the Virgin seems to operate change, too, and human interactions adjust as well. These, however, seem to me to be the overarching constants: strength, power, and connection.

Notes

CHAPTER ONE

1. William A. Christian Jr., *Apparitions in Late Medieval and Renaissance Spain* (Princeton: Princeton University Press, 1981), 4.

2. See the similar discussion in Christian, *Apparitions*, 7–8.

3. See especially David Freedberg, *The Power of Images: Studies in the History and Theory of Response* (Chicago: University of Chicago Press, 1989), 91–128, 136–146, and Hans Belting, *Likeness and Presence: A History of the Image before the Era of Art* (Chicago: University of Chicago Press, 1994), 30–36.

4. Richard P. McBrien, ed. *The Encyclopedia of Catholicism* (San Francisco: HarperSanFrancisco, 1995), 650.

5. See William H. Gentz, ed., *The Dictionary of Bible and Religion*, (Nashville: Abingdon, 1986), 477, 1063.

6. Peter Brown, "A Dark Age Crisis: Aspects of the Iconoclastic Controversy," *English Historical Review* 88, no. 346 (January 1973): 7, quoted in Marina Warner, *Alone of All Her Sex: The Myth and the Cult of the Virgin Mary* (New York: Vintage Books, 1983), 292.

7. Warner, *Alone*, 290–292.

8. Belting, *Likeness*, xxi.

9. Freedberg, *Power of Images*, 5.

10. Ibid., xxii.

11. Ibid., xxiii.

12. Ibid., xxiii.

13. *Lumen Gentium*, chapter 8, paragraph 60, quoted in Warner, *Alone*, 287–288.

14. Warner, *Alone*, xxii, 246–247. Suzanne L. Stratton, *The Immaculate Conception in Spanish Art* (Cambridge: Cambridge University Press, 1994), 39–66.

15. For a thorough discussion of this point see Warner, *Alone*, 285–290.

16. Leonardo Boff, *The Maternal Face of God: The Feminine and Its Religious Expressions*, translated by Robert R. Barr and John W. Diercksmeier (San Francisco: Harper & Row, 1987), 9; original passage in Portuguese, Leonardo Boff, *O rostro materno de Deus: Ensaio interdisciplinário sobre o feminino e suas formas religiosas* (Petrópolis, Brazil: Editora Vozes Ltda., 1979), 21–22.

17. Boff, *Maternal Face*, 5, and *O rostro materno*, 17–18.

18. See *Newsweek*, August 25, 1997, 48–56. The commission voted 23–0 against the promulgation of the doctrine, arguing that it was not in keeping with the Vatican Council II, that its wording was difficult to interpret, and that it might exacerbate "ecumenical difficulties." A large part of the difficulty lies with what exactly would happen theologically if such a step were taken, a point on which there is considerable disagreement. See also *Buffalo News*, March 3, 1998; *Columbus Dispatch*, November 28, 1997; *Plain Dealer*, November 22, 1997.

19. Rolena Adorno, "The Art of Survival in Early Colonial Peru," in *Violence, Resistance, and Survival in the Americas: Native Americans and the Legacy of Conquest*, edited by William B. Taylor and Franklin Pease (Washington, D.C.: Smithsonian Institution Press, 1994), 82–83.

20. Christian, *Apparitions*, 111.

21. An important discussion for Europe of the balance between the universal appeal of the Virgin and her attachment to more specific locations and roles may be found in Benedicta Ward, *Miracles and the Medieval Mind: Theory, Record, and Event 1000–1215* (Philadelphia: University of Pennsylvania Press, 1987), 143–148.

22. For more information on Gurumayi see Catherine Wessinger, "Woman Guru, Woman Roshi: The Legitimation of Female Religious Leadership in Hindu and Buddhist Groups in America," in Wessinger, ed., *Women's Leadership in Marginal Religions* (Urbana: University of Illinois Press, 1993), 124–146. Interestingly, Wessinger has found that many Catholics of Mexican descent in the United States are devotees of Gurumayi, whom they associate with the Virgin Mary.

23. Elisabeth Schussler Fiorenza, "Feminist Theology as a Critical Theology of Liberation," in *Churches in Struggle: Liberation Theology and Social Change in North America*, edited by William K. Tabb (New York: Monthly Review Press, 1986), 57–59.

24. Els Maeckelberghe, "'Mary': Maternal Friend or Virgin Mother?" in *Religion in the Eighties: Motherhood—Experience, Institution, Theology*, edited by Anne Carr and Elisabeth Schussler Fiorenza, *Concilium* 6, no. 206 (December 1989): 120.

CHAPTER TWO

1. Peggy K. Liss, *Isabel the Queen: Life and Times* (New York: Oxford University Press, 1992), 230.

2. I will use from time to time the term New World, speaking from a Spanish perspective. Obviously, the world was by no means new to the inhabitants. Unless I am speaking from a specifically Spanish perspective, I will discuss the interaction

of Columbus and the lands he discovered in the name of Spain as an encounter, a term which more reasonably describes the events in 1492 and the long period of interaction that follows.

3. John V. Fleming, "The 'Mystical Signature' of Christopher Columbus," in *Iconography at the Crossroads*, edited by Brendan Cassidy (Princeton: Index of Christian Art, Princeton University, 1993), 206–207.

4. This point is controversial, but I must agree with those who see it in this way. See arguments for Spain specifically in Christian, *Apparitions*, 21–22, in which he suggests that the "underground locations" in which, according to legend, Mary's statues were found, may support "the notion of Mary's role as successor to mother goddesses dealing with fertility"; and more generally in Stephen Benko, *The Virgin Goddess* (Leiden, Netherlands: E. J. Brill, 1993); Anne Baring and Jules Cashford, *The Myth of the Goddess: Evolution of an Image* (London: Penguin Books, 1991); and Lucia Chiavola Birnbaum, *Black Madonnas: Feminism, Religion, and Politics in Italy* (Boston: Northeastern University Press, 1993).

5. See the discussion in Peter Linehan, *History and the Historians of Medieval Spain* (Oxford: Clarendon Press, 1993), 5, 18.

6. Linehan, *History*, 262–264.

7. See Christian, *Apparitions*, 21–22; Amy Remensnyder, "The Colonization of Sacred Architecture: The Virgin Mary, Mosques, and Temples in Medieval Spain and Early Sixteenth-Century Mexico," in *Monks and Nuns, Saints and Outcasts: Religion in Medieval Society*, edited by Sharon Farmer and Barbara H. Rosenwein (Ithaca, New York: Cornell University Press, 2000), 194.

8. See the extensive discussion in William A Christian, "De los santos a María: Panorama de las devociones a santuarios españoles desde el principio de la Edad Media hasta nuestros dias," in *Temas de antropología española*, Carmelo Lisón, editor (Madrid: Akal Editor, 1976), 56–61.

9. Warner, *Alone*, 106–110.

10. See Leslie Brubacker, "Introduction: The Sacred Image," in Leslie Brubacker and Robert Ousterhout, *The Sacred Image East and West* (Urbana, Illinois: University of Illinois Press, 1995), 9.

11. Warner, *Alone*, 65–66. Warner notes that the celebrations of the virginity of Mary have been revived in the new liturgy as the Solemnity of the Mother of God.

12. Carmen García Rodríguez, *El culto de los santos en la España Romana y Visigoda* (Madrid: CSIC, 1966), 126.

13. Warner, *Alone*, 87.

14. For comment and translation see Christian, *Apparitions*, 21. For Law 43 see Alfonso X, *Setenario*, edited by Kenneth A. Vanderwood (Buenos Aires: Instituto de Filología, 1945), 73–76.

15. Quote from Linehan, *History*, 66. See also García Rodríguez, *El culto*, 129.

16. Linehan, *History*, 75.

17. Personal communication with Amy Remensnyder, April 21, 2000.

18. Linehan, *History*, 73, 273.

19. Christian, *Apparitions*, 52, attributes the stories to the monk Cixila in the ninth century, though the text may be later. For the thirteenth-century version see Alfonso X, *Las cantigas de loor de Alfonso X El Sabio*, bilingual edition translated by Luis Beltrán (Madrid: Ediciones Júcar, 1988), 193–196. Edition hereinafter cited as Beltrán, *Cantigas*.

20. Christian, *Apparitions*, 51–52.

21. García Rodríguez, *El culto*, 130–131.

22. Linehan, *History*, 95–96, 285.

23. See Lomax, "The Reconquest," 29–31, 62–63, 103–104; and Richard Fletcher, *St. James Catapult: The Life and Times of Diego Gelmirez of Santiago de Compostela* (Oxford Clarendon Press, 1984), 53–77, 296–300.

24. James Michener, *Iberia: Spanish Travels and Reflections* (New York: Random House, 1968), 715–716.

25. P. Arsenio Fernández Arenas and P. Pablo Huarte Arana, *Los caminos de Santiago* (Barcelona: Ediciones La Poligrafa, 1965), 20.

26. José Augusto Sánchez Pérez, *El culto mariano en España* (Madrid: Consejo Superior de Investigaciones Científicas, 1943), 321–324. The Spanish verse, provided in a personal communication from Aurora Morcillo, is:

La Virgen del Pilar dice,
que no quiere ser francesa,
que quiere ser capitana,
de la tropa aragonesa.

The Sánchez Pérez work, produced during the Franco period in Spain, contains no documentation and is illustrative of Marian legends at the time that he wrote his book. Thus, they are most clearly reflective of modern, rather than medieval, folklore.

27. Michener, *Iberia*, 715–716; Linehan, *History*, 170, 172.

28. Linehan, *History*, 102.

29. Sánchez Pérez, *El culto mariano*, 145.

30. Kenneth B. Wolf, *Christian Martyrs in Muslim Spain* (Cambridge: Cambridge University Press, 1988), 1–7. Jessica Coope, *The Martyrs of Córdoba: Community and Family in an Age of Mass Conversion* (Lincoln: University of Nebraska Press, 1995), 1–3, 6–10.

31. Wolf, *Christian Martyrs*, 1; Coope, *Martyrs of Córdoba*, ix.

32. Coope, *Martyrs of Córdoba*, ix–x, 12.

33. Eulogius, *Memoriale Sanctorum*, in Juan Gil, *Corpus Scriptorum Muzarabicorum*, vol. 2 (Madrid: Instituto Antonio Nebrija, 1973), 376, 409, 473, 485. I am indebted here to Donald Sullivan for assistance in translating the Latin text.

34. Liss, *Isabel*, 207.

35. An interesting sixteenth-century example of this tendency appears in a story of Ignacio de Loyola, the founder of the Jesuit order. It is said that he encountered a converted Moor or New Christian as he was departing on a pilgrimage and that their conversation turned on the issue of Mary's virginity. The New Christian agreed that it was possible that Mary had conceived Christ without sexual intercourse, but he doubted that she remained virgin after having given birth. Although Loyola

permitted the man to go on his way, he was later seized with fury and pursued him to fight for the Virgin's honor. The Moor had vanished, however, and Loyola set about establishing the Jesuit order. See Jean Lacouture, *Jesuits: A Multibiography* (Washington, D.C.: Counterpoint, 1995), 15–16. For Mary in the Koran see Jaroslav Pelikan, *Mary through the Centuries* (New Haven: Yale University Press, 1996), 67–79.

36. Paulino Iradiel, Salustiano Moreta, and Esteban Sarasa, *Historia medieval de la España cristiana* (Madrid: Ediciones Cátedra, 1989), 198.

37. Derek W. Lomax, *The Reconquest of Spain* (London: Longman, 1978), 98.

38. Quotation in Angus MacKay, "Religion, Culture, and Ideology of the Late Medieval Castilian/Granadan Frontier," in *Medieval Frontier Societies*, edited by Robert Bartlett and Angus MacKay (Oxford: Clarendon Press, 1989), 230.

39. Remensnyder, "Colonization," 194.

40. MacKay, "Religion," 230.

41. Remensnyder, "Colonization," 204. Original reads, "[N]unca Mafomete poder y averá; ca a conquereu ela e demais conquerrá Espanna e Marrocos e Ceta e Arcilla."

42. William A. Christian Jr., *Local Religion in Sixteenth-Century Spain* (Princeton: Princeton University Press, 1981), 74, 123.

43. José Goñi Gastambede, *Historia de la Bula de la Cruzada en España* (Vitoria, Spain: Pontificia Universitas Gregoriana, 1958), 32–33, 94–95.

44. *The Poem of My Cid*, translated by Peter Such and John Hodghinden (Warminster: Aris and Phillips, 1987), 45, 55, 57.

45. Ibid., 91.

46. Ibid., 57.

47. Richard Fletcher, *The Quest for El Cid* (New York: Oxford University Press, 1989), 182.

48. Lomax, *Reconquest of Spain*, 125–127, 146. See also Goñi Gastambede, *Historia de la Bula*, 126–127, and Sánchez Pérez, *El culto mariano*, 234–235.

49. Lomax, *Reconquest of Spain*, 118, 123, 133.

50. Sánchez Pérez, *El culto mariano*, 363. Carlos Ros, ed., *Historia de la Iglesia de Sevilla* (Barcelona: Editorial Castillejo, 1992), 160–164. Remensnyder, "Colonization," 202. It is unclear whether the images on view in the cathedral in Seville are actually the ones brought by Fernando.

51. Robert I. Burns, *Moors and Crusaders in Mediterranean Spain: Collected Studies* (London: Variorum Reprints, 1978), i, 15–17.

52. Lomax, *Reconquest of Spain*, 160–162. Sánchez Pérez, *El culto mariano*, 288–290.

53. Maricel E. Presilla, "The Image of Death and Political Ideology in the *Cantigas de Santa María*," in Israel J. Katz and John E. Keller, eds., *Studies on the Cantigas de Santa María: Art, Music, and Poetry* (Madison Wisconsin: Hispanic Seminary of Medieval Studies, 1987), 423.

54. Walter Mettmann, introduction to Alfonso X, *Cantigas de Santa María* (Madrid: Clásicos Castalia, 1986), vol. I, 11–12; collection cited hereinafter as Mettmann, *Cantigas* 1986, followed by volume and page number.

55. Presilla, "Image of Death," 424–425.

56. Ibid., 427.

57. Afonso X, *Cantigas de Santa María*, edited by Walter Mettmann (Coimbra, Portugal: Universidade de Coimbra, 1959), vol. 1, 1; edition cited hereinafter as Mettmann, *Cantigas* 1959, followed by volume and page number.

58. Joseph F. O'Callaghan, *The Learned King: The Reign of Alfonso X of Castile* (Philadelphia: University of Pennsylvania Press, 1993), 145–146.

59. Mettmann, *Cantigas* 1959, vol. 1, 7–8.

60. Presilla, "Image of Death," 429.

61. Linehan, *History*, 512–514.

62. Lomax, *Reconquest of Spain*, 144–147. Joseph F. O'Callaghan, "The *Cantigas* as an Historical Source: Two Examples," in Katz and Keller, *Studies on the Cantigas*, 388–389.

63. O'Callaghan, *Learned King*, 241.

64. Presilla, "Image of Death," 433–440.

65. Mettmann, *Cantigas* 1986, vol. 1, 63–66.

66. Mettmann, *Cantigas* 1986, vol. 2, 27–30. See also Alfonso X, *Cantigas*, edited by Jesús Montoya (Madrid: Ediciones Cátedra, 1988), 177–181.

67. Albert I. Bagby Jr., "The Figure of the Jew in the *Cantigas* of Alfonso X," in Katz and Keller, *Studies on the Cantigas*, 240–241. Angus MacKay with Vikki Hatton, "Anti-Semitism in the *Cantigas de Santa María*," in *Society, Economy, and Religion in Late Medieval Castile*, edited by Angus MacKay (London: Variorum Reprints, 1987), 190.

68. Benjamin Netanyahu, *The Origins of the Inquisition in 15th Century Spain* (New York: Random House, 1995), 168–175.

69. For the Moor as adversary see Cantigas 215 and 323, for example, as discussed in Jesús Montoya Martínez's introductory essay to his *Historia y anécdotas de Andalucía en las Cantigas de Santa María* (Granada, Spain: Universidad de Granada, 1988), 20. For the conversion of Moors see for example Cantigas 167, 192, and 205 in Mettmann, *Cantigas* 1959, vol. 2, 170–171, 229–233, and 265–267. Also discussed in Presilla, "Image of Death," 425.

70. O'Callaghan, *Learned King*, 165.

71. Ibid., 171–172.

72. Sánchez Pérez, *El culto mariano*, 259–260.

73. O'Callaghan, *Learned King*, 196. Montoya Martínez, introductory essay to *Historia y anécdotas*, 25–26.

74. For example see Cantigas 378, 381, and 389 in Montoya Martínez, *Historia y anécdotas*, 213–215, 219–220, 227–228.

75. Ibid., Cantigas 398 and 379, pp. 235–236, 217–218.

76. Ibid., Cantiga 364, pp. 191–192.

77. Christian, *Apparitions*, 88–92.

78. Linehan, *History*, 516–517.

79. Peter Linehan, *Past and Present in Medieval Spain* (Aldershot, England: Variorum, 1992), xii.

80. Christian, *Local Religion in Sixteenth-Century Spain* (Princeton: Princeton University Press, 1981), 36.

81. Liss, *Isabel*, 159.

82. Isabel, *Libro de Horas de Isabel la Católica*, edited by Matilde López Serrano (Madrid: Editorial Patrimonio Nacional, 1969), especially illustrations 3 and 16 and pages 27–31. For Juana's dark complexion see Nancy Rubin, *Isabella of Castile: The First Renaissance Queen* (New York: St. Martin's Press, 1992), 177.

83. Liss, *Isabel*, 160.

84. Ibid., 157.

85. MacKay, "Religion," 241.

CHAPTER THREE

1. Jacques Le Goff, for example, argues that "Ritual initial phrases, final clauses, dates, and lists of witnesses, to say nothing of the text itself, reflect not just concrete circumstances but ways of imagining power, society, time, and justice." Jacques Le Goff, *The Medieval Imagination*, translated by Arthur Goldhamer (Chicago: University of Chicago Press, 1988), 2. Ritual beginnings and endings to wills that invoke the Virgin, references to the Virgin and her Son in letters to the king, and a reiteration of faith and comfort in the Virgin all have a ritual sense on the one hand but do, as Le Goff asserts, indicate ways of "imagining," so important in spiritual matters. I do not believe that they indicate merely rote processes.

2. Alain Milhou, *Colón y su mentalidad mesianica en el ambiente franciscana español* (Valladolid: Casa Museo de Colón de la Universidad de Valladolid, 1983), 46. Valerie I. J. Flint, *The Imagined Landscape of Christopher Columbus* (Princeton: Princeton University Press, 1992), 187.

3. Flint, *Imagined Landscape*, 184.

4. Ibid., 175.

5. This issue is dealt with in the study by Mascarenhas Barreto, *The Portuguese Columbus: Secret Agent of King John II* (New York: St. Martin's Press, 1992), 99, 111, 188.

6. Fleming, "'Mystical Signature,'" 205, 207.

7. William D. Phillips Jr. and Carla Rahn Phillips, *The Worlds of Christopher Columbus* (Cambridge: Cambridge University Press, 1992), 145. See also Ferdinand Columbus, *The Life of the Admiral Christopher Columbus by His Son Ferdinand*, translated by Benjamin Keen (New Brunswick: Rutgers University Press, 1959), 27.

8. Ferdinand Columbus, *Life of the Admiral*, 58.

9. The story that follows in text of the vows, Columbus's doubts, and the difficulties on the Niña may be found in Christopher Columbus, *The Diario of Christopher Columbus's First Voyage to America*, translated by Oliver Dunn and James E. Kelley Jr. (Norman: University of Oklahoma Press, 1988), 362–385; and Samuel Eliot Morison, *Admiral of the Ocean Sea: A Life of Christopher Columbus* (Boston: Little, Brown & Co., 1946), 326–335.

10. Morison, *Admiral*, 392–394. Phillips and Phillips, *Worlds*, 193, indicate that although there is no direct evidence for this visit, it is almost certain that Columbus went to the monastery, given his later avowal that his naming of the island of

Guadalupe on the second voyage was a result of the promise he made to the monks there.

11. Morison, *Admiral*, 404, quoting Michele de Cuneo's narrative of the voyage.

12. Ibid., 404–410.

13. Ibid.

14. Ibid., map between 406 and 407.

15. Sánchez Pérez, *El culto mariano*, 269–270.

16. Ferdinand Columbus, *Life of the Admiral*, 116.

17. Ibid.

18. Matilda Webb, *The Churches and Catacombs of Early Christian Role: A Comprehensive Guide* (Brighton, England: Sussex Academic Press, 2001), 149–151. Richard Fletcher, *The Barbarian Conversion: From Paganism to Christianity* (Berkeley: University of California Press, 1999), 254.

19. Milhou, *Colón*, 438. See also Webb, *Churches*, 112–122.

20. Juan Martínez Alcalde, *Sevilla Mariana: Repertorio iconográfico* (Seville: Ediciones Guadalquivir, 1997), 35–36. This point is controversial, as the Dominican Republic has long claimed that Columbus's bones lie there. See also Hugh Thomas, *Conquest: Montezuma, Cortés, and the Fall of Old Mexico* (New York: Simon & Schuster, 1993), 126–127.

21. Roberta Vicchi, *The Major Basilicas of Rome* (Florence, Italy: SCALA, 1999), 124.

22. Fleming, "'Mystical Signature,'" 212.

23. Milhou, *Colón*, 54–55, 62–65.

24. See Fleming, "'Mystical Signature,'" 214.

25. Ferdinand Columbus, *Life of the Admiral*, 4.

26. See the discussions in Stratton, *Immaculate Conception*, 46–48, and in Warner, *Alone*, 236–254.

27. Fleming, "'Mystical Signature,'" 212.

28. For illuminating discussions of the issue of native American religions and idolatry in Spanish eyes see Fernando Cervantes, *The Devil in the New World: The Impact of Diabolism in New Spain* (New Haven: Yale University Press, 1994), 4–39, and Serge Gruzinski, *The Conquest of Mexico City: The Incorporation of Indian Societies into the Western World, 16th–18th Centuries*, translated by Eileen Corrigan (Cambridge, England: Polity Press, 1993), 146–183. Quotation is from Cervantes, *Devil*, 56.

29. Fleming, "'Mystical Signature,'" 212.

30. Milhou, *Colón*, 66.

31. Martínez Alcalde, *Sevilla Mariana*, 408–409.

32. Bernal Díaz del Castillo, *Verdadera y notable relación del descubrimiento y conquista de la Nueva España y Guatemala*, vol. 1 (Guatemala: Biblioteca Guatemalteca de Educación Pública, 1964), 9. Spanish reads, "Dios Nuestro Señor y a la Virgen Santa María su bendita madre." All citations of Díaz del Castillo are from this edition unless otherwise noted and cited as Díaz del Castillo, *Relación*, 1964, followed by volume and page number.

33. Thomas, *Conquest*, 121.

34. Ibid., 129.

35. Díaz del Castillo, *Relación*, 1964, vol. 1, 74. Spanish reads, "unos ídolos de muy disforme figuras."

36. Díaz del Castillo, *Relación*, 1964, vol. 1, 74–75. Spanish reads, "negro sermón." See also Thomas, *Conquest*, 159–160, and Francisco López de Gómara, *Historia de la conquista de México* (Mexico City: Editorial Pedro Robredo, 1943), 74–75.

37. Quoted in Fletcher, *Barbarian Conversion*, 254.

38. Díaz del Castillo, *Relación*, 1964, vol. 1, 77–81. Spanish reads, "ni mas ni menos era que indio"; "Dios y Santamaría e Sevilla"; "mal mascado y peor pronunciado"; "devoción y reverencia"; "que conocieran que por ello les vendría mucho bien."

39. Thomas, *Conquest*, 164.

40. Ibid., 160.

41. See reproduction in Bradley Smith, *Mexico City: A History in Art* (Garden City, New York: Doubleday, 1968), 163.

42. Díaz del Castillo, *Relación*, 1964, vol. 1, 143–146. Spanish reads, "buenas y muy sanctas doctrinas"; "como podíamos hacer ninguna cosa buena si no volvíamos por la honra de Díos y en quitar los sacrificios que hacían a los ídolos."

43. Ibid., 145. Spanish reads, "lloraban y tapaban los ojos" and "carne muerta."

44. Thomas, *Conquest*, 212–213.

45. Ibid., 237–255. Díaz del Castillo, *Relación*, 1964, vol. 1, 218–220. Spanish reads, "con su hijo precioso en los brazos" and "Marina y Aguilar, nuestras lenguas, estaban ya tan experto en ello, que se le daban a entender muy bien."

46. Thomas, *Conquest*, 237–255. Díaz del Castillo, *Relación*, 1964, vol. 1, 217–219.

47. Thomas, *Conquest*, 237–255. Díaz del Castillo, *Relación*, 1964, vol. 1, 213–214, 219. Spanish reads, "vuestro Díos y esa gran Señora."

48. Thomas, *Conquest*, 301.

49. Ibid., 301–302. Díaz del Castillo, *Relación*, 1964, vol. 2, 301.

50. Thomas, *Conquest*, 328. Spanish version of quotations from Tapia's report in Thomas are taken from Salvador de Madariaga, *Hernán Cortés* (Buenos Aires: Sudamericana, 1941), 394–395. The Spanish reads, "saltar sobrenatural" and "A algo nos hemos de poner por Dios."

51. Madariaga, *Hernán Cortés*, 396. Thomas, *Conquest*, 329. López de Gómara, *Historia*, 256–257, says the Spanish images originally were put up among the Aztec idols and were a source of *rencor mortal*—mortal rancor—on the part of Montezuma's priests, a rancor that would fester and lead to repeated attempts to remove the Christian images.

52. Hernán Cortés, *Cartas y relaciones de Hernán Cortés al Emperador Carlos V*, edited by Pascual de Gayangos (Paris: A. Chaix & Cia., 1866); passage is in "Segunda carta relación de Hernán Cortés al Emperador, October 30, 1520," 106–107. Spanish reads, "puse en ellas imágenes de nuestra Señora y de otros santos, lo que no poco el dicho Muteczuma y los naturales sintieron; los cuales primero me dijeron que no lo hiciese, porque si se sabía por los comunidades, se levantarían contra mí, porque tenian que aquellos ídolos les daban todos los bienes temporales, y que dejándoles

maltratar, se enojarian y no les darian nada, y les sacarían los frutos de la tierra, y moriria la gente de hambre. Yo les hice entender con las lenguas cuán engañados estaban en tener su esperanza en aquellos ídolos, que eran hechos por sus manos, de cosas no limpias, é que habían de saber que había un solo Dios."

53. Madariaga, *Hernán Cortés*, 396–398. Díaz del Castillo, *Relación*, 1964, vol. 2, 352–356.

54. Thomas, *Conquest*, 370. Madariaga, *Hernán Cortés*, 414. Díaz del Castillo, *Relación*, 1964, vol. 2, 374.

55. Thomas, *Conquest*, 379–380. Madariaga, *Hernán Cortés*, 425–428. Spanish reads, "Santa María, valéme, que muerto me han, e quebrado un ojo." Díaz del Castillo, *Relación*, 1964, vol. 2, 403.

56. Thomas, *Conquest*, 380.

57. Díaz del Castillo, *Relación*, 1964, vol. 2, 415–416.

58. Thomas, *Conquest*, 391. López de Gómara, *Historia*, 298. Spanish reads, "la mujer del altar."

59. Thomas, *Conquest*, 403.

60. Diego Durán, *The Aztecs: The History of the Indies of New Spain*, translated by Doris Heyden and Fernando Horcasitas and introduction by Ignacio Bernal (New York: Orion Press, 1964), 302.

61. Durán, *Aztecs*, 302.

62. Thomas, *Conquest*, 408–423.

63. Ibid., 424–425.

64. Ibid., 530.

65. Ibid., 567.

66. Ibid., 597.

67. Hernán Cortés, *Testamento de Hernán Cortés* (Mexico City: Imprenta del Asilo Patricio Sanz, 1925), 11. Spanish reads, "la gloriosísima y bienaventurada Virgen, su bendita madre, Señora y Abogada Nuestra."

68. Ibid., 12. Spanish reads, "mi villa de Coyoacan."

69. Ibid., 15–16.

70. Ibid., 16–19.

71. Mariano Cuevas, "Notas," in Cortés, *Testamento*, 42–43.

72. Bernal Díaz del Castillo, *La Conquista de Nueva España*, vol. 3 (Buenos Aires: Sociedad de Ediciones Louis-Michaud, 1853), 116–117, 198–199, 204–205.

73. Pedro Mártir de Anglería, *Décadas del Nuevo Mundo* (Mexico City: José Porrua e Hijos, 1964), vol. 1, 291, 314.

74. Pedrarias Dávila to the emperor, April 1525, in *Cartas del Perú*, vol. 3, edited by Raul Porras Barrenechea (Lima: Edición de la Sociedad de Bibliofilos Peruanos, 1959), 3.

75. Antón Cuadrada to royal functionary, August 1, 1527, in Porras Barrenechea, *Cartas del Perú*, 6–8. Spanish reads, "cabtiverio é carcel perpetua."

76. Prologue, Porras Barrenechea, *Cartas del Perú*, 10.

77. Francisco de Jerez, Pedro de Cieza de León, and Agustín de Zarate. *Crónicas de*

la conquista del Perú, edited by Julio Le Riverend (Mexico City: Editorial Nueva España), 557.

78. John Hemming, *The Conquest of the Incas* (New York: Harcourt Brace Jovanovich, 1970), 122, 193–194. Joseph de Acosta, *Historia natural y moral de las Indias,* vol. 2 (Madrid: R. Angles, Impresor, 1894), 349, also records the story, though briefly, and adds that Santiago and the Virgin appeared frequently in the air above the battles fought with indigenous peoples.

79. Phelipe Guaman Poma de Ayala, *El primer nueva Coronica i buen gobierno,* annotated by Arthur Posnansky (La Paz, Bolivia: Editorial del Instituto Tihuanacu de Antropología, Etnografía, y Prehistoria, 1944), folios 401–405. See also Rolena Adorno, *Guaman Poma: Writing and Resistance in Colonial Peru* (Austin: University of Texas Press, 1986), 20–21 and Plate 3.

80. Francisco Pizarro, *El testamento de Pizarro,* edited with prologue and notes by Raul Porras Barrenechea (Paris: Imprimeries les Presses Modernes, 1936) 21. Spanish reads, "En el nombre de dios padre hijo y espiritu sancto tres personas e vn solo dios verdadero que es la sanctisima trenidad e tomando primeramente por señora y abogada en esta obra que quiero y estoy determinado de hazer y efectuar a la sacratisima virgen maria madre de dios e nuestra señora vniversal e defensora de todo el genero vmano . . . vna yglesia e capellania en la cibdad de truxillo."

81. Pizarro, *El testamento,* 9–10. Spanish reads, "Devoción extremeña y andaluza, la de Nuestra Señora de la Concepción, se arraiga en el espíritu de Pizarro con el amor de las cosas del teruño y es garfio que le une a España y a los suyos." For the significance of the Virgin Mary in Spanish wills see Carlos M. N. Eire, *From Madrid to Purgatory: The Art and Craft of Dying in Sixteenth-Century Spain* (Cambridge: Cambridge University Press, 1995), 68–72.

82. Pizarro, *El testamento,* 21–22. Spanish reads, "yo he sido muy deboto y he tenydo y tengo especial debocion y creo y tengo firmemente que por la fee e debocion particular que yo he tenido e tengo y tendre syempre hasta que muera en esta sanctisima fiesta tendre siempre el fabor y ayuda necesaria de la santisima madre de dios para mi salbacion."

83. For Virgin's powers to deliver souls from purgatory see Warner, *Alone,* 325.

84. Pizarro, *El testamento,* 26–30.

85. Ibid., 10.

86. See Chapter I for a discussion of the correspondence between image and presence in the reverence for the Virgin.

87. Díaz del Castillo, *Relación,* 1964, vol. 3, 176. Spanish reads, "como yo quedaba solo y malherido, porque no me acabasen de matar, e sin sentido e poco acuerdo, me iba a meter entre unos matorrales altos, y volviendo en mí, con fuerte corazón dije: '¡Oh, válgame Nuestra Señora! Si es verdad que tengo que morir hoy en poder destos perros?' Y tomé tal esfuerzo, que salgo de las matas y rompo por los indios, que a buenas cuchilladas y estocadas me dieron lugar que salí de entre ellos; y aunque me tornaron á herir, y me fuí á las canoas, donde estaba ya mi compañero Francisco Martín, vizcaíno, con cuatro indios amigos."

88. Díaz del Castillo *Relación*, 1964, vol. 3, 96–97. Spanish reads, "acordándoseme de aquellas feísimas muertes . . . por esta causa desde entonces temí la muerte mas que nunca; y esto he dicho porque antes de entrar en las batallas se me ponía una grima y tristeza en el corazón, y ayunaba una vez o dos, y encomendándome á Díos y á su bendita madre y entrar en las batallas, todo era uno, y luego se me quitaba aquel temor; y también quiero decir qué cosa tan nueva os parecerá agora tener yo aquel temor no acostumbrado, habiéndome hallado en muchos batallas y reencuentros muy peligrosos de guerra ya había de estar curtido el corazón y esfuerzo y ánimo en mi persona, agora á la postre más arraigado que nunca."

89. See, for example, Díaz del Castillo *Relación*, 1964, vol. 2, 218.

90. *El Lienzo de Tlaxcala*, edited by Mario de la Torre with text by Josefina García Quintana and Carlos Martínez Marín (Mexico City: Cartón y Papel de México, 1983), 70.

CHAPTER FOUR

1. An outstanding work addressing this topic is Valerie I. J. Flint, *The Rise of Magic in Early Medieval Europe* (Princeton: Princeton University Press, 1991). See especially 3–4, 9.

2. Flint defines magic as "the exercise of a preternatural control over nature by human beings, with the assistance of forces more powerful than they." See Flint, *Rise of Magic*, 3.

3. For example, see Díaz del Castillo, *Relación*, 1964, vol. 1, 218–220.

4. Cervantes, *Devil*, 67–69, gives an example and discusses this issue.

5. See the fascinating argument for the development of a Nahua Christianity in Louise Burkhart, *The Slippery Earth: Nahua-Christian Moral Dialogue in Sixteenth-Century Mexico* (Tucson: University of Arizona Press, 1989), especially 189–190.

6. Quotes are in Fletcher, *Barbarian Conversion*, 254.

7. See discussion in William B. Taylor, "Santiago's Horse: Christianity and Colonial Indian Resistance in the Heartland of New Spain," in Taylor and Pease, *Violence, Resistance*, 154–155.

8. Jean-Michel Sallman with Serge Gruzinski, Antoinette Molinié Fiorivanti, and Carmen Salazar, *Visions Indiennes, Visions Baroques: Les Metissages de L'Inconscient* (Paris: Presses Universitaires de France, 1992), 120. French reads, "un imaginaire a opposer à l'imaginare indigène, sous la forme d'une représentation de l'au-dela qu'elle s'employa à rendre accessible aux Indiens des Andes et du Mexique."

9. Sallman et al., *Visions*, 120–121. Cervantes, *Devil*, 8–9. Quote in Sallman et al.; French reads, "invention du démon."

10. Cervantes, *Devil*, 14. Quotation from Toribio de Benavente (Motolinía), *Historia de los indios de la Nueva España*, transcribed by Edmundo O'Gorman (Mexico City: Editorial Porrúa, 1973), 20. Spanish reads, "carne de dios, o del demonio que ellos adoraban."

11. Sallman et al., *Visions*, 131–132. See, for example, the tale of Antonio Pérez,

dating from 1761, more than two centuries after the Conquest, in Serge Gruzinski, *Man-Gods in the Mexican Highlands: Indian Power and Colonial Society, 1520–1800* (Stanford: Stanford University Press, 1989), 105–121.

12. Mártir de Anglería, *Decadas*, vol. 1, 251–253. Spanish reads, "No le fue difícil al marinero convencer a aquella gente desnuda, y a ruegos del reyezuelo le regaló la imagen que traía."

13. A good discussion may be found in Bernard R. Ortiz de Montellano, *Aztec Medicine, Health, and Nutrition* (New Brunswick: Rutgers University Press, 1990), 37–40.

14. See representation in Erich Neumann, *The Great Mother: An Analysis of the Archetype* (Princeton: Princeton University Press, 1974), 154. A recreation of the image may be found in Gisele Díaz and Alan Rodgers, *The Codex Borgia: A Full-Color Restoration of the Ancient Mexican Manuscript*, with introduction and commentary by Bruce E. Byland (New York: Dover Publications, 1993), Plate 32, 46. A discussion appears on xiii–xiv and xxiii–xxiv. This figure is one of five noted as the "ritual sequence," in which the bodies of goddesses of death provide the central images. On bodily pain see Ortiz de Montellano, *Aztec Medicine*, 123, 127, 179.

15. Burkhart, *Slippery Earth*, 154.

16. Ortiz de Montellano, *Aztec Medicine*, 61, 132.

17. For a further discussion of these two goddesses see Salvador Mateos Higuera, *Enciclopedia gráfica del México antiguo*, vol. 3, *Los Dioses Creados* (Mexico City: Secretaría de Hacienda y Crédito Público, 1993), 121–152, 229-240; Silvia Trejo, *Dioses, mitos y ritos de México antiguo* (Mexico City: Secretaría de Relaciones Exteriores, 2000), 153–161; Philip P. Arnold, *Eating Landscape: Aztec and European Occupation of Tlalocan* (Niwot: University Press of Colorado, 1999), 90, 97–98, 146; and Linda B. Hall, "Visions of the Feminine: The Dual Goddesses of Ancient Mexico," *Southwest Review* 63, no. 2 (spring 1978): 133–143.

18. Burkhart, *Slippery Earth*, 116.

19. "Relación de Teotihuacan," in *Relaciones geográficas del siglo XVI: México* (Mexico City: Universidad Nacional Autónoma de México, 1986), 238. Spanish reads, "calenturas, fiebres, ciciones, tercianas, y cuartanas que curan con purgas, algunos suelen tener bubas . . . sangre corrompida."

20. Gruzinski, *Conquest*, 81.

21. Carmen Bernand and Serge Gruzinski, *Historia del Nuevo Mundo*, vol. 2, *Los mestizajes, 1550–1640* (Mexico City: Fondo de Cultura Económica, 1999), 155. Spanish reads, "las incertidumbres del mañana, más los cambios del modo de vida, de la alimentación, del hábitat, de las creencias, impuestas o aceptadas, difusas o espectaculares, tuvieron repercusiones sobre unos organismos a los que, por otra parte, diezmaban las enfermedades."

22. "Un canto triste de la conquista," in Miguel León-Portilla, *El reverso de la conquista: Relaciones aztecas, mayas e incas* (Mexico City: Editorial Joaquín Mortiz, 1964), 61-62. Spanish reads, "El llanto se extiende, las lágrimas gotean allí en Tlatelolco . . . hemos perdido la nación mexicana."

23. Text in Louise Burkhart, *Holy Wednesday: A Nahua Drama from Early Colonial Mexico* (Philadelphia: University of Pennsylvania Press, 1996) 233, translated from *Santoral en Mexicano* (n.d., MS 1476, Fondo Reservado, Biblioteca Nacional de México).

24. Warner, *Alone*, 180–182.

25. Toribio de Benavente, *Historia*, 131. Spanish reads, "Buscan mil modos para atraer a los indios al conocimiento de un sol Dios verdadero."

26. Justino Cortés Castellanos, *El catecismo en pictogramas de Fray Pedro de Gante* (Madrid: Fundación Universitaria Española, 1988), 57. See also Gruzinski, *Conquest*, 30–31.

27. Gruzinski, *Conquest*, 9.

28. Cortés Castellanos, *El catecismo*, 77.

29. Gruzinski, *Conquest*, 30.

30. Cortés Castellanos, *El catecismo*, annex 1, 438 and 440. Spanish reads, "Oh, Santa María, Dignate Alegrarte" and "Oh, Reina, Dignate Alegrarte." Nahua-to-Spanish translations are those of Cortés Castellanos; Spanish-to-English translations are mine. The Nahuatl-text catechisms that he uses are Alonso de Molina, *Doctrina christiana breve traduzida en lengua Mexicana* (Mexico City: n.p., 1546); Pedro de Gante, *Doctrina Christiana en lengua Mexicana*, (Mexico City: Juan Pablos, 1553), and Religiosos de la orden de Sancto Domingo, *Dotrina christiana en lengua Española y Mexicana* (Mexico City: Juan Pablos, 1548). The pictorial catechism that he uses is the *Catecismo en pictogramas de fray Pedro de Gante*, which is reproduced in full and in color in annex No. 2 in the Cortés Castellanos volume. The original is in the Biblioteca Nacional, Madrid, designated Vit. 26-9. References to the pictograms will be designated by number, followed by CPPG.

31. See a similar discussion on Nahuatl translations in Burkhart, *Holy Wednesday*, 47.

32. Cortés Castellanos, *El catecismo*, No. 17, 198, 453.

33. Ibid., No. 38, 208, 454.

34. Ibid., 438, 440. Spanish reads, "los que no hacemos más que llorar aquí en este de llantos lugar desierto."

35. Ibid., 217–218. A complete description of the Ave María pictograms appears on 213–221, and the pictograms themselves are Nos. 49 through 77, CPPG. Spanish reads, "Tú (que eres) la Madre venerada." The text for the second set appears on page 228 and reads, "verdaderamente virgen." The pictograms are on 454–455, CPPG.

36. Ibid., 244–245 and 456. The text reads in Spanish, "nosotros los que vivimos llorando sin cesar." A description of the pictograms for the *Salve* is on 241–250; the pictograms are No. 169 through No. 212, CPPG, 456.

37. Ibid., 243, reads, "desterrados, corridos" and "Eva." Pictograms on page 456.

38. Translations from the Nahuatl in Burkhart, *Slippery Earth*, 83–85.

39. Bartolomé de las Casas quoted in Gruzinski, *Conquest*, 30–31.

40. Gruzinski, *Conquest*, 31.

41. Burkhart, *Slippery Earth*, 182.

42. Sallman et al., *Visions*, 119. French reads, "la circulation des femmes."

43. Serge Gruzinski, "Individualization and Acculturation: Confession among

the Nahuas from the Sixteenth to the Eighteenth Century," in *Sexuality and Marriage in Colonial Latin America*, edited by Asunción Lavrín (Lincoln: University of Nebraska Press, 1989), 96–115, is a fascinating discussion of confession. Gruzinski notes the significance of the cult of Mary on page 107 in a fashion unlike my discussion in this chapter.

44. Alonso de Medina quoted in Gruzinski, "Individualization," 111.

45. Burkhart, *Slippery Earth*, 136–137.

46. Cortés Castellanos, *El catecismo*, 54.

47. In Toribio de Benavente, *Historia*, 131. Spanish reads, "y para apartarlos del error de los ídolos diéronles muchas maneras de doctrina. A el principio para les dar sabor enseñaronles el *per signum crucis*, el *pater noster, ave María, credo, salve*, todo cantado de un canto muy llano y gracioso."

48. Gruzinski, *Conquest*, 57.

49. See the discussion in Burkhart, *Holy Wednesday*, 81.

50. Burkhart, *Slippery Earth*, 79–80.

51. On the Nahua authorship see Burkhart, *Holy Wednesday*, 48–55.

52. Burkhart, *Holy Wednesday*, 11–12. See also Susan Verdi Webster, *Art and Ritual in Golden-Age Spain: Sevillian Confraternities and the Processional Sculpture of Holy Week* (Princeton, New Jersey: Princeton University Press, 1998), 93–99.

53. Burkhart, *Holy Wednesday*, 35.

54. Ibid., 43.

55. Ibid., 46.

56. Ibid., 90, on this point.

57. Ibid., 91.

58. Ibid., 97–98.

59. Ibid., 110–113. All translations are Burkhart's. The entire text of the two plays appears between pages 110 and 163.

60. Burkhart, *Holy Wednesday*, 118–119.

61. Ibid., 180. See also the discussion of the heart in Jill Leslie McKeever Furst, *The Natural History of the Soul in Ancient Mexico* (New Haven: Yale University Press, 1995), 14–19, 37–47.

62. Burkhart, *Holy Wednesday*, 158–159.

63. Ibid., 159–163.

64. Ibid., 249–252.

65. Toribio de Benavente, *Historia*, 24-28. Spanish reads, "templos del demonio"; "fue menester de darles también a entender quién era Santa María, porque hasta entonces solamente nombraban María, o Santa María, y diciendo este nombre pensaban que nombraban a Dios, y [a] todas las imágenes que veían llamaban Santa María"; "quíen era el demonio en quien ellos creían, y cómo los traía engañados; y las maldades que en sí tiene, y el cuidado que pone en trabajar que ninguna ánima se salve"; and "demandádole con lágrimas y suspiros y mucha importunación."

66. Sallman et al., *Visions*, 134.

67. Ibid., 141. Gruzinski, *Conquest*, 184; the French title of this work by Serge Gruzinski

is *La colonisation de l'imaginaire* (Paris: Editions Gallimard, 1988), a much better title than the English, meaning approximately, as I see it, the colonization of internal images and the imaginary, although this wording in no way implies that the imaginary is fantasy or simply imagination. It refers to the internalization of culture.

68. Sallman et al., *Visions*, 135, 138.

69. See discussion in Sallman et al., *Visions*, 137–138.

70. Gruzinski, *Conquest*, 219.

71. Sallman et al., *Visions*, 139.

72. Gruzinski, *Conquest*, 202.

73. See the interesting discussion of this case in Gruzinski, *Conquest*, 202–203.

74. See Jacinto de la Serna, "Manual de Ministros de Indias para el conocimiento de idolatria y la extirpación de ellas," in *Colección de documentos inéditos para la historia de España*, vol. 104 (Madrid: Imprenta de José Perales y Martínez, 1892), 59–67. Spanish reads, "de enfermedad que Dios le había dado."

75. Ibid., 67. Spanish reads, "todos estuvieron privados del juicio, que es el efecto de esta bebida."

76. Ibid., 66, 79. Spanish reads, "conocer no envuelvan con ellas alguna memoria de sus antiguos dioses."

77. Luis Weckmann, *La herencia medieval de México*, 2nd revised edition (Mexico City: El Colegio de Mexico, 1994), 231–232. Constantino Reyes-Valerio, *Arte indocristiano: Escultura del Siglo XVI en México* (Mexico City: Secretario de Educación Pública/ Instituto Nacional de Antropologia e Historia, 1978), 91.

CHAPTER FIVE

1. Elizabeth Wilder Weismann, *Art and Time in Mexico City: From the Conquest to the Revolution* (New York: Harper and Row, 1985), 33.

2. Toribio de Benavente, *Historia*, 24.

3. Quoted in Reyes-Valerio, *Arte Indocristiano*, 104. Spanish reads, "Los misterios e historias de nuestra redención es maravilla con cuanta perfección las hacen y señaladamente les he notado muchas veces en representar el *Descendimiento* de la cruz y recibir el cuerpo del Salvador, Nuestra Señora en su regazo, que llamamos la quinta angustia, tienen gracia especial."

4. Weismann, *Art and Time*, 151.

5. Reyes-Valerio, *Arte Indocristiano*, 124–126.

6. Burkhart has addressed the development of a Nahua version of Christianity in a number of places, including *Holy Wednesday*, 67, 80, as has William B. Taylor in, for example, *Magistrates of the Sacred: Priests and Parishioners in Eighteenth-Century Mexico* (Stanford: Stanford University Press, 1996), 59–62, and elsewhere. I believe that what was developed was not simply a syncretic sticking together of theological elements already existing in one or the other culture, but rather both a blending and a refiguring, the development of new concepts and elements, and the emergence of many variants of something that externally, at least, looked a great deal like Catholicism, but not exactly like the Spanish version.

7. Reyes-Valerio, *Arte Indochristiano*, 128. Spanish reads, "un nuevo medio de integración religioso-cultural del hombre a su nuevo medio."

8. Belting, *Likeness*, xxii.

9. Ibid., 1.

10. This discussion is heavily influenced by Belting, *Likeness*, 1–6.

11. Elizabeth Wilder Weismann, *Mexico in Sculpture, 1521–1821* (Cambridge, Massachusetts: Harvard University Press, 1950), 7 (quotes), 16–17.

12. The discussion of this image of the Virgin is based on Fred R. Kline, "The Lost Virgin of the New World: The Discovery of a Marian Sculpture of First Contact," unpublished paper, 1998, although I have added to Kline in my interpretation. The figure is dated by Constantino Reyes-Valerio in his unpublished "Opinion," April 15, 1996. Reyes-Valerio indicates his belief that it was probably made before the middle of the sixteenth century, and it is "one of the early rare examples of religious art made in the New World and one of the finest Mexican Colonial 'Indian Madonna' single-figure sculptures known to exist."

13. Burr Cartwright Brundage, *The Jade Steps: A Ritual Life of the Aztecs* (Salt Lake City: University of Utah Press, 1985), 105.

14. Inga Clendinnen, *The Aztecs: An Interpretation* (Cambridge: Cambridge University Press, 1991), 299. Quote is from Clendinnen. See also Cervantes, *Devil*, 41, 54, and Furst, *Natural History*, 90–93.

15. Luis Barjau, *Tezcatlipoca: Elementos de una teología nahua* (Mexico City: Universidad Nacional Autónoma de México, 1991), 93–94. Spanish reads, "un medio sagrado de conocimiento del universo y del hombre mismo."

16. Burkhart, *Slippery Earth*, 40–41.

17. Solange Alberro, *Inquisición y sociedad en México, 1571–1700* (Mexico City: Fondo de Cultura Económica, 1988), 463, 475. Serge Gruzinski, *La guerra de las imágenes de Cristóbal Colón a 'Blade Runner' (1492–2019)* (Mexico City: Fondo de Cultura Económica, 1994), 163.

18. Elsa Cecilia Frost, "Un estilo de vida," in *Artes de Mexico*, vol. 4, *Guía Franz Mayer* (n.d.), 37–40.

19. Beatriz Sánchez Navarro de Pintado, "El arte blanco," *Tepotzotlan: La vida y la obra en Nueva España*, Miguel Fernández Félix, coordinator (Mexico City: Editorial Joaquín Mortiz, 1988), 111–112.

20. Belting, *Likeness*, 4.

21. Corpus Christi in Cuzco and Guadalupe's Day in Mexico City are among the many ceremonies that I have personally witnessed. See Chapter IX.

22. Freedberg, *Power of Images*, 28, 90–91.

23. Toribio de Benavente, *Historia*, 54. Spanish reads, "Adornan sus iglesias muy pulidamente con los paramentos que pueden haber, y lo que les falta de tapicería suplen con muchos ramos, flores, espadañas y juncia que echan por el suelo, yerbabuena, que en esta tierra se ha multiplicado cosa increíble, y por donde tiene de pasar la procesión hacen muchos arcos triunfales, hechos de rosas, con muchas labores y lazos de las mismas flores; y hacen muchas piñas de flores, cosa muy de ver, y por esto hacen en esta tierra todos mucho por tener jardines con rosas, y no

las teniendo ha acontecido enviar por ellas diez o doce leguas a los pueblos de tierra caliente, que casi siempre las hay, y son de muy suave olor."

24. Ibid., 54. Spanish reads, "parecen de noche un cielo estrellado."

25. Ibid., 55.

26. Ibid. Spanish reads, "precioso Hijo"; "siempre hasta ahora va creciendo en ellos la devoción de este día"; "porque tienen gran devoción con Nuestra Señora, y por ser benditas en su santo día las guardan mucho."

27. Ibid., 57. One anonymous reader of this manuscript suggests a possible connection with the pre-Columbian tribute in textiles.

28. Ibid., 57.

29. There are literally hundreds of examples of this phenomenon. Some may be found in *Relaciones geográficas del Arzobispado de México, 1743*, edited by Francisco de Solano (Madrid: Consejo Superior de Investigaciones Científicas, 1988), vols. 1 and 2.

30. Gruzinski, *Conquest*, Plate 15.

31. Florencia quoted in Gruzinski, *La guerra*, 139. Spanish reads, "¿Esta correspondencia en los cuatro como polos de la ciudad destas cuatro prodigiosas imágenes puede ser acaso? ¿Que las del Oriente y Poniente ambas sean de talla y de un mismo tamaño? . . . A cargo del Señor y de la Señora están los cuatro ángulos desta tierra"; "la Estrella del Norte de México." A large portion of Florencia's text corresponding to the Guadalupe story is available in Francisco de Florencia, "La estrella del norte de México," in *Testimonios históricos guadalupanas*, compiled by Ernesto de la Torre Villar and Ramiro Navarro de Anda (Mexico City: Fondo de Cultura Económica, 1982), 359–399. Specific quote about the North Star is on 394.

32. Gruzinski, *La guerra*, 114. See also Gruzinski, *Conquest*, 190–191.

33. Freedberg, *Power of Images*, 84–85.

34. A similar discussion appears in Gruzinski, *La guerra*, 143.

35. Weckmann, *La herencia medieval*, 281.

36. Ibid., 169.

37. Ibid., 279–280.

38. Ibid., 280.

39. Ibid., 279.

40. Ibid., 276–278.

41. See, for example, the discussion of Remedios of Querétaro, in Weckmann, *La herencia medieval*, 280.

42. Ibid., 281. The quote is from José Antonio de Villaseñor y Sánchez, *Theatro americano*, vol. 2 (Mexico City: Imprenta de la Viuda de don J. Bernardo de Hogal, 1746–1748), xxx. Spanish reads, "la cesación del diluvio de la idolatría."

43. Rafael Alarcón, *La última Virgen Negra del Temple: El enigma templario de Candelaria* (Mexico City: Ediciones Roca, 1991), 53–59.

44. Elizabeth Kiddy, "Brotherhoods of Our Lady of the Rosary of the Blacks: Community and Devotion in Minas Gerais, Brazil" (Ph.D. diss., University of New Mexico, 1998), 369–371.

45. Weckmann, *La herencia medieval*, 277.

46. Ibid., 278.

47. Ibid., 280.

48. Ibid., 231–232.

49. Ibid., 275.

50. Ibid., 278; Spanish reads, "mojado y lleno de lodo."

51. Ibid., 278.

52. Ibid., 277.

53. Toribio de Benavente, *Historia*, 183. Spanish reads, "el demonio despertó a otro"; "Dios la había dado la mano."

54. Ibid., 183; Spanish reads, "¿Piensas que porque no tengo marido que me guarde, has de ofender conmigo a Dios? Ya que otra cosa no mirases, sino que ambos somos cofrades de la hermandad de Nuestra Señora, y que en esto la ofenderíamos mucho, y con razón que tú me dejases, y ya que tú por esto no me quieras dejar, sábete que yo estoy determinada de antes morir que cometer tal maldad."

55. Florencia, "La estrella," 394–395. Spanish reads, "Si nos guarda y defienden [*sic*] en México el Señor por medio de su Madre por cuatro partes: si puso Dios por centinelas, que por nosotros velan, cuatro milagrosas imágenes de María en los cuatro ángulos della, ¿quién podrá invadir y ofender a esta ciudad?"

56. Weckmann, *La herencia medieval*, 274–275. An important new work on the cults of Remedios and Guadalupe is Francisco Miranda Godínez, *Dos cultos fundantes: Los Remedios y Guadalupe (1521–1649)* (Zamora, Michoacán: El Colegio de Michoacán, 2001).

57. The story is reconstructed from Weckmann, *La herencia medieval*, 274–275, and Linda Curcio-Nagy, "Native Icon to City Protectress to Royal Patroness: Ritual, Political Symbolism and the Virgin of Remedies," *Americas* 52, no. 3 (January 1996), 369–370.

58. Curcio-Nagy, "Native Icon," 372.

59. Ibid., 374–375.

60. Ibid., 378–379.

61. This account is taken from Luis Lasso de la Vega, "El gran acontecimento con que se le apareció la Señora Reina del Cielo Santa María, nuestra querida Madre de Guadalupe, aquí cerca de la Ciudad de México, en el lugar nombrado Tepeyácac," Spanish translation of Nahuatl document, in Torre Villar, *Testimonios*, 289–310. The portion of the document which recounts the apparition story is known as the *Nican Mopohua* for its beginning words, "Here is recounted." This version has become the standard account of the apparition. See Stafford Poole, *Our Lady of Guadalupe: The Origins and Sources of the Mexican National Symbol, 1531–1797* (Tucson: University of Arizona Press, 1995), 110–111.

62. Lasso de la Vega, "El gran acontecimento"; Spanish reads, "el más pequeño de mis hijos"; "Señora y niña mía, tengo que llegar a tu casa de México Tlatelolco, a seguir las cosas divinas que nos dan y enseñan nuestros sacerdotes, delegados de Nuestro Señor"; "yo soy la siempre Virgen Santa María, Madre del verdadero Dios . . . Señor del cielo y de la tierra."

63. Ibid.; Spanish reads, "soy hoja, soy gente menuda."

64. Ibid.; Spanish reads, "bien está, hijito mío, volverás aqui mañana para que lleves al obispo la señal que te ha pedido; con eso creerá."

65. Ibid.; Spanish reads, "mi embajador, muy digno de confianza."

66. Ibid.; Spanish reads, "un poco moreno."

67. Ibid.; Spanish reads, "Mucho le maravillaba que se hubiese aparecido por milagro divino; porque ninguna persona de este mundo pintó su preciosa imagen."

68. See Lasso de la Vega, "El gran aconticimento, 282–284; Poole, *Our Lady*, 110–126; Xavier Noguez, *Documentos guadalupanos: Un estudio sobre las fuentes de información tempranas en torno a las mariofanías en el Tepeyac* (Mexico City: Fondo de Cultura Económica, 1993), 19–29.

69. Louise Burkhart, "The Cult of the Virgin of Guadalupe in Mexico," in Gary H. Gossen and Miguel León-Portilla, editors, *South and Meso-American Native Spirituality* (New York: Crossroad, 1993), 201–203, 210, 216.

70. James Lockhart, *The Nahuas after the Conquest* (Stanford: Stanford University Press, 1992), 14.

71. Brundage, *Jade Steps*, 59–60.

72. Ibid., 59, 83.

73. Ibid., 75–77.

74. Ibid., 79.

75. Solange Alberro, *El águila y la cruz: Orígenes religiosos de la conciencia criolla. México, siglos XVI–XVII* (Mexico City: Fondo de Cultura Económica, 1999), 128.

76. Burkhart, "Cult of the Virgin," 207–208.

77. See the highly interesting argument in Johanna Broda, "The Sacred Landscape of Aztec Calendar Festivals: Men, Nature, and Society," in David Carrasco, editor, *To Change Place: Aztec Ceremonial Landscapes* (Niwot: University Press of Colorado, 1991), 89–92.

78. Richard F. Townsend, "The Mount Tlaloc Project," in Carrasco, *To Change Place*, 30.

79. Broda, "Sacred Landscape," 90.

80. Alberro, *El águila*, 124–129.

81. Jacques Galinier, *La mitad del mundo. Cuerpo y cosmos en los rituales otomíes* (Mexico City: Universidad Nacional Autónoma de México, 1990), 577. Quoted in Alberro, *El águila*, 129. Spanish reads, "La relación entre el maguey y la fertilidad cósmica persiste actualmente a través de diversos símbolos de la religión cristiana. De este modo, la Virgen de los Remedios se ha convertido en la santa protectora de los magueyes. En la iconografía popular, esta virgen es representada sobre un maguey, a imagen de *mayahuel*, la divinidad azteca de esta misma planta."

82. Alberro, *El águila*, 130–132.

83. The following discussion is based on Hugo G. Nutini and Betty Bell, *Ritual Kinship: The Structure and Historical Development of the Compadrazgo System in Rural Tlaxcala*, vol. 1 (Princeton, New Jersey: Princeton University Press, 1980), 294–304.

84. Nutini saw this document and transcribed it in the summer of 1963, when it

was in the collection of Rafael Lozano Lavalle of Tlaxcala. He believes it to have been from the collection of the Archivo del Ayuntamiento of Tlaxcala; it was probably taken from there sometime before 1948 when the room in which it would have been located was being repaired. The report focuses on the apparition and subsequent developments. Professor Wigberto Jiménez Moreno, in a personal communication with Nutini, indicated his belief that the document might be a forgery, possibly from the end of the sixteenth century. Nutini and Bell, however, believe that it is authentic. Nutini and Bell, *Ritual Kinship*, 295, 448–449. On later documentation see Rodrigo Martínez Baracs, *La secuencia tlaxcalteca: Orígenes del culto a Nuestra Señora de Ocotlán* (Mexico City: Colección Biblioteca del INAH, 2000), 17–43. Cervantes, *Devil*, 54–56, notes that it would be difficult to date the document befote 1647, when the first publication of the Guadalupe story appeared.

85. Quote is from Nutini and Bell, *Ritual Kinship*, 295.

86. Nutini and Bell, *Ritual Kinship*, 291.

87. Ibid., 297–301.

88. Cervantes, *Devil*, 55.

CHAPTER SIX

1. Carol Damian, *The Virgin of the Andes: Art and Ritual in Colonial Cuzco* (Miami Beach, Florida: Grassfield Press, 1995), 22. Damian's work, coming from an art history perspective, is an excellent source.

2. Garcilaso de la Vega, *Royal Commentaries of the Incas*, translated by Harold Livermore (Austin: University of Texas Press, 1966), part 2, book 2, chapter 25, 805.

3. Carolyn Dean, *Inka Bodies and the Body of Christ: Corpus Christi in Colonial Cuzco, Peru* (Durham, North Carolina: Duke University Press, 1999), 112, 147–154.

4. Barbara Duncan, "Statue Paintings of the Virgin," in *Gloria in Excelsis: The Virgin and Angels in Viceregal Painting of Peru and Bolivia*, edited by John Stringer, Barbara Duncan, and Teresa Gisbert (New York: Center for Inter-American Relations, 1986), 32–33.

5. Guaman Poma de Ayala, *Primer nueva Coronica*, 120–143, 173–174. Duncan, "Statue Paintings," 34.

6. Guaman Poma de Ayala, *Primer nueva Coronica*, 138–139.

7. Damian, *Virgin*, 50.

8. Ibid., 50–53. Teresa Gisbert, *Iconografía y mitos indígenas en el arte* (La Paz, Bolivia: Linea Editorial Fundación BHN, 1994), Plate 2.

9. Damian, *Virgin*, 55.

10. Gisbert, *Iconografía*, Plate 3a. Spanish reads, "La forma mas usual de representar a la Virgen como la Pachamama es pintádola sobre una piedra en forma triangular en su advocación de la Candelaria; así se enfatiza el concepto María-Cerro y María-Piedra."

11. Gisela Cánepa Koch, *Máscara, transformación e identidad en los Andes: La fiesta de la Virgen del Carmen Paucartambo-Cuzco* (Lima: Pontificia Universidad Católica del Perú, Fondo Editorial, 1998), 165–167.

12. Gisbert, *Iconografía*, 24–25.

13. Ibid., 23–24.

14. Ibid., 24–25.

15. On this point see Duncan, "Statue Paintings," 38–39.

16. Damian, *Virgin*, 71–73.

17. Duncan, "Statue Paintings," 55.

18. Gisbert, *Iconografía*, 28. Adorno, *Guaman Poma*, 18–21.

19. Dean, *Inka Bodies*, 27.

20. Gisbert, *Iconografía*, 28; Spanish reads, "Fue visto salir el Patrón de las Españas . . . y atónita la idolatría veneró Rayo el Hijo del Trueno."

21. Felipe Guaman Poma de Ayala, *Nueva crónica y buen gobierno*, edited by John V. Murra, Rolena Adorno, and Jorge L. Urioste (Mexico City: Siglo XXI, 1987), 412.

22. Pablo Joseph de Arriaga, *The Extirpation of Idolatry in Peru*, translated and edited by L. Clark Keating (Lexington: University of Kentucky Press, 1968), 53–54.

23. Gisbert, *Iconografía*, 29, Plate 20, 196–197. See also Verónica Salles-Reese, *From Viracocha to the Virgin of Copacabana: Representations of the Sacred at Lake Titicaca* (Austin: University of Texas Press, 1997), 189 n. 81.

24. Duncan, "Statue Paintings," 47.

25. Dean, *Inka Bodies*, 100–101, 142. Damian, *Virgin*, 57, 80–89.

26. Dean, *Inka Bodies*, 174.

27. Ibid., Plate 52; 88.

28. Ibid., 57–58.

29. Ibid., 79.

30. Ibid., 79–80.

31. Ibid., Plate 43, 79–80.

32. See ibid., 63–70, for a discussion of this point. For use of the term "Double Mistaken Identity" see Lockhart, *Nahuas*, 445; he defines it as "a process . . . whereby each side takes it that a given form or concept is essentially one already known to it, operating in much the same manner as in its own tradition, and hardly takes cognizance of the other side's interpretation."

33. Arriaga, *Extirpation*, 70. See also Nicholas Griffiths, *The Cross and the Serpent: Religious Repression and Resurgence in Colonial Peru* (Norman: University of Oklahoma Press, 1995), 39, 213–214.

34. Arriaga, *Extirpation*, 81–84.

35. Ibid., 85–89.

36. Dean, *Inka Bodies*, 33–37.

37. Garcilaso de la Vega, *Royal Commentaries*, 1415–1416. Also quoted in Dean, *Inka Bodies*, 180–181.

38. Garcilaso de la Vega, *Royal Commentaries*, 1417–1418. See the extensive discussion of this incident in Dean, *Inka Bodies*, 58–59, 180–181. Dean, 181, translates *auca* as "savage or traitor."

39. Dean, *Inka Bodies*, 187–189.

40. Ibid., 79–80.

41. Ibid., 63–78.

42. Burr C. Brundage, *Lords of Cuzco: A History and Description of the Inca People in Their Final Days* (Norman: University of Oklahoma Press, 1967), 296.

43. Dean, *Inka Bodies*, 27-28, 216.

44. Damian, *Virgin*, 67 and figures 36 and 53. Figure 36 is identified as La Linda but is actually Santa Ana. See also Luis A. Huayhuaca Villasante, *La festividad del Corpus Christi en el Cusco* (Cuzco: Talleres Gráficas de Villanueva, 1988), 38, and Jorge Flores Ochoa, *El Cuzco: Resistencia y continuidad* (Cuzco: Centro de Estudios Andinos Cusco, 1990), 103.

45. For a list of native parishes see Dean, *Inka Bodies*, 80.

46. Luis Eduardo Wuffarden, "Notas de los cuadros," in *La procesión del Corpus en el Cuzco* (Seville: Unión Latina, 1996), 85–86, and Plate 14. See also Dean, *Inka Bodies*, 90–92.

47. Dean, *Inka Bodies*, 140–145.

48. See Wuffarden, "Notas," Plate 14, and Dean, *Inka Bodies*, 133.

49. See the important discussion of birds and plumage in Dean, *Inka Bodies*, 170–175.

50. Wuffarden, "Notas," 77–78 and Plate 7.

51. Ibid., Plates 7 and 24.

52. See Damian, *Virgin*, Plates 40, 41, and 43.

53. Wuffarden, "Notas," Plate 24.

54. Alfonsina Barrionuevo, *Cuzco mágico* (Lima: Editorial Universo, n.d.), 85–87.

55. Ibid., 85–86. Huayhuaca Villasante, *La festividad*, 140–141.

56. On these points, see Dean, *Inka Bodies*, 182–187.

57. Salles-Reese, *From Viracocha*, 10.

58. Ibid., 8, 13.

59. Ibid., 47, 53–54.

60. Sabine MacCormack, "From the Sun of the Incas to the Virgin of Copacabana," *Representations* 8 (fall 1984), 43.

61. Salles-Reese, *From Viracocha*, 93.

62. Ibid., 47.

63. Alonso Ramos Gavilán, *Historia del Santuario de Nuestra Señora de Copacabana*, transcription, editor's notes, and indexes by Ignacio Prado Pastor (Lima: Talleres Gráficos de P. L. Villanueva, 1988), 218–228. Spanish reads, "Pues los de Copacabana, antes que la Virgen descubriesse milagros en su pueblo, se estavan en su Gentilidad, porque como avía sido cabeca de Idolatría durava todavía en ella."

64. Ramos Gavilán, *Historia*, 238–425. MacCormack, "From the Sun," 50–53.

65. MacCormack, "From the Sun," 46.

66. Ibid., 48–49.

67. Ibid., 55.

CHAPTER SEVEN

1. Benedict Anderson, *Imagined Communities: Reflections on the Origin and Spread of Nationalism* (London: Verso, 1991), 13.

2. Ramos Gavilán, *Historia*. Antonio de la Calancha, *Corónica moralizada del Orden de San Augustín en el Perú*, 6 vols., transcription, critical study, bibliographical notes, and indexes by Ignacio Prado Pastor (Lima: Universidad Nacional Mayor de San Marcos, 1974).

3. Ruben Vargas Ugarte, *Historia del culto de María en Iberoamerica y de sus imagines y santuarios mas celebrados* (Buenos Aires: Editorial Huarpes, 1947), 679.

4. Quotation from Alan Kolata, *The Tiwanaku: Portrait of an Andean Civilization* (Cambridge, Massachusetts: Blackwell, 1993), 5.

5. Julio María Elías, *Copacauana-Copacabana* (La Paz, Bolivia: Editorial Offset, 1978) 79–83.

6. Ramos Gavilán, *Historia*, 415–419. Spanish reads, "joyas, y perlas de mucha valor"; "personas de lustre," "Indios, e Indias forasteros."

7. Elías, *Copacauana*, 113.

8. Ibid., 112–114.

9. Jan Szeminski, "Why Kill the Spaniard? New Perspectives on Andean Insurrectionary Ideology in the 18th Century," in *Resistance, Rebellion, and Consciousness in the Andean Peasant World, 18th to 20th Centuries*, edited by Steve J. Stern (Madison: University of Wisconsin Press, 1987), 166–192, provides an excellent discussion of these issues.

10. Leon G. Campbell, "Ideology in Factionalism during the Great Rebellion, 1780–1782," in Stern, *Resistance*, 110–127. Quotation appears on 126. On the Independence movement see Marie-Danielle Demélas, *L'invention politique: Bolivie, Equateur, Pérou au XIXe siecle* (Paris: Editions Recherche sur les Civilisations, 1992), 224.

11. Gisbert, *Iconografía*, 210.

12. Ibid., 208.

13. Campbell, "Ideology," 118, 123–124. Gisbert, *Iconografía*, 214–216, figures 247 and 247a.

14. The account below is taken from Matías de la Borda to Sebastían de Segurola, May 30, 1781, in *Colección documental de la independencia del Perú*, edited by Carlos Daniel Valcarcel, vol. 2 (Lima: Comisión Nacional del Sesquicentenario de la Independencia del Perú, 1971), 801–818. Spanish reads, "quienes ya parece estuvieron conbocados de antemano."

15. Ibid.; Spanish reads, "toda persona que sea o parezca ser española, o que a lo menos esté vestida a imitación de tales Españoles"; and "funestísimo lago de sangre."

16. Ibid.; Spanish reads, "eran todos los Españoles unos Excomulgados, tambien unos demonios."

17. Ibid.; Spanish reads, "llevase la Imagen milagrosa de Ntra. Sra. de Copacabana a otra parte."

18. Ibid.; Spanish reads, "con bastante irreverencia"; "sin el menor respeto ni veneración."

19. Ibid.; Spanish reads, "aquellos Yndios que no habían perdido en el todo la Devoción a aquella Divina Ymagen."

20. Ibid.; Spanish reads, "al instante fueron Almas que Dios dispuso."

21. Nicholas A. Robins, *El mesianismo y la semiótica indígena en el Alto Peru: La gran rebelión de 1780–1781*, translated by Silvia San Martín and Sergio del Río (La Paz, Bolivia: Hisbol, 1998), 132–133.

22. See, for example, José Santos Vargas, *Diario de un comandante de la independencia americana, 1814–1825* (Mexico City: Siglo XXI Editores, 1982), 24.

23. Bartolomé Mitre, *Historia de Belgrano y de la independencia argentina*, vol. 2, 5th edition (Buenos Aires: n.p., 1902), 97–98. Spanish reads, "ejército patriota"; "la conciencia de los pueblos." On Our Lady of Mercies in the independence struggle and issues of religion and nationalism see also Demélas, *L'invention*, 223, 231.

24. Javier Marion, "Inkarra Myths and Class Conflict: An Interpretive Study of Juana Azurduy de Padilla's Life as Seen through Late Colonial Currents" (master's thesis, University of New Mexico, 1997), 64–72.

25. Marion, "Inkarra Myths," 67. Santos Vargas, *Diario*, 31.

26. This account is taken from Tristan Platt, "Simón Bolívar, the Sun of Justice and the Amerindian Virgin: Andean Conceptions of the *Patria* in Nineteenth-Century Potosí," *Journal of Latin American Studies* 25 (1995): 171–177.

27. See, for example, Ramos Gavilán, *Historia*, 217–222, 288, 295, 299, 302, 372, 391.

28. Elías, *Copacauana*, 121–122.

29. Ibid., 128, 132.

30. Ibid., 134–138.

31. Ibid., 139–141.

32. Quoted in ibid., 142. Spanish reads, "tan querida como venerada."

33. Ibid., 147.

34. Ibid., 150. Spanish reads, "Confiérese a la Santíssima Virgen de Copacabana, declarada PATRONA PRINCIPAL ANTE DIOS, DE TODA LA FUERZA NAVAL DE BOLIVIA, el Alto Grado de ALMIRANTE DE LA FUERZA NAVAL BOLIVIANA, con todas las prerrogativas correspondientes a su alta jerarquía, como un acto de fé cristiana de las Fuerzas Armadas de la Nación." Emphasis in the original.

35. Salles-Reese, *From Viracocha*, 18.

36. Félix Coluccio, *Fiestas y celebraciones de la República Argentina*, 3rd ed. (Buenos Aires: Editorial Plus Ultra, 1992), 347.

37. Juan Uribe Echevarría, *Fiesta de la Virgen de la Candelaria de Copiapó* (Valparaiso: Ediciones Universitarias de Valparaiso, 1978), 111.

38. Coluccio, *Fiestas*, 35, 347.

39. Isabel Laumonier, *Festividad de Nuestra Señora de Copacabana* (Buenos Aires: Centro de Estudios Migratorios Latinoamericanos, 1990), 5–15.

40. Ibid., 14–17. Spanish reads, "prestar el santo."

41. Ibid., 22–28. Spanish reads, "para que descanse de la caminata"; "es fiestera"; "también se cansa, pues."

42. Ibid., 28–31.

43. Ibid., 26–27.

44. Poole, *Our Lady*, 58–64.

45. Miguel Sánchez, "Imagen de la Virgen María Madre de Dios de Guadalupe," in Torre Villar, *Testimonios*, 230. Spanish reads, "Apareciéndose María en México entre las flores, es señalarla por su tierra, no sólo como posesión, sino como su patria"; "renace milagrosa en la ciudad donde ellos nacen; y la patria aunque es madre común, es amantísima madre." See also the discussion in D. A. Brading, *Mexican Phoenix: Our Lady of Guadalupe: Image and Tradition Across Five Centuries* (Cambridge: Cambridge University Press, 2001), 68–69.

46. Sánchez, "Imagen," 246–247. Spanish reads, "Milagro fue muy público y que engendró en todos los indios afectuosa devoción a la milagrosa imagen de Guadalupe"; "La Virgen María Señora Nuestra en los principios de la conversión de aqueste Nuevo Mundo esmeró sus favores con los indios, para aficionarlos, enseñarlos y atraerlos a la fe católica y al amparo de su intercesión, pues vemos que las dos imágenes milagrosas que hoy gozamos a la vista de México, entregó y descubrió a dos indios; aquesta en el santuario de Guadalupe; la otra en el de los Remedios."

47. Curcio-Nagy, "Native Icon," 377.

48. Ibid., 387.

49. Poole, *Our Lady*, 136–137, 142.

50. Brading, *Mexican Phoenix*, 99, 111. The house of Mary was said to have been carried in its entirety from Nazareth, with several stops in between, to Loreto on the Adriatic coast of Italy. The small stone structure is now incorporated into a basilica that continues to attract pilgrims. The story, however, is now considered to be unhistorical. See McBrien, *Encyclopedia of Catholicism*, 795.

51. Poole, *Our Lady* 175–176.

52. Ibid., 172, 181.

53. Ibid., 180.

54. Brading, *Mexican Phoenix*, 163–164.

55. Poole, *Our Lady*, 176–177.

56. Ibid., 233–234. Brading, *Mexican Phoenix*, 132–133.

57. William B. Taylor, "The Virgin of Guadalupe in New Spain: An Inquiry into the Social History of Marian Devotion," *American Ethnologist* 14 (1987): 20–21. Quotations as rendered in Taylor.

58. Taylor, "Virgin of Guadalupe," 22–23.

59. Eric Van Young, *El crisis del orden colonial: Estructura agraria y rebeliones populares de la Nueva España, 1750–1821* (Mexico City: Alianza Editorial, 1992), 399–400. For more on Mariano also see Van Young's *The Other Rebellion: Popular Violence, Ideology, and the Mexican Struggle for Independence, 1810–1821* (Stanford, California: Stanford University Press, 2001), in which he notes that Mariano is now believed to have been aprocryphal, perhaps the invention of an indigenous leader, but that authorities took the conspiracy seriously nonetheless.

60. Quotation as translated in Brading, *Mexican Phoenix*, 228–229.

61. Brading, *Mexican Phoenix*, 229. Taylor, "Virgin of Guadalupe," 24.

62. Censura de Señor Marques de Castañiza, Rector de San Ildefonso, in Josef

Mariano Beristain de Souza, "Declamación que en la solemne función de desagravios a María Santísima de Guadalupe," (Mexico City: Imprenta Arizpe, 1811.) Spanish reads, "el nombre dulcíssimo de María de Guadalupe para promover insubordinación, el hurto, el homicidio y quanto ha traido consigo la revolución, es un horrendo sacrilegio que quiere hacer a la madre de Dios protectora de los excesos y horrores que prohibe y condena la ley santo de su hijo, que vino la Señora a establecer en estos reynos."

63. Revisión del Sr. Doctor y Maestro Don Josef Angel Gazano, in Beristain de Souza, "Declamación." Spanish reads, "la invocación del augusto nombre de Ma. Sma. de Guadalupe, para proteger un proyecto que envuelve en si un acervo de los mayores males destructivos todos de la religion, del estado, de las vidas, de las haciendas y de la paz pública y privada de todos los habitantes de este Nuevo mundo."

64. Beristain de Souza, "Declaraciones." Spanish reads, "¿Estamos todos conformes en que ha sido blasfemia, insulto y desacato apellidar el santo y dulce nombre de María para santificar los desórdenes que han afligido y afligen todavia a nuestros Pueblos?" "Solo el Parayso terrenal pudiera compararse en esto con nuestra tierra." For Pilar see Brading, *Mexican Phoenix*, 231, 234.

65. F. Diego Miguel Bringas, "Sermon en honor de Ma. Sma. De Guadalupe," (n.p.: Imprenta de Doña María Fernández de Jauregui, 1812). Spanish reads, "la injusticia manifesta de su causa ni es, ni será jamas, un empeño digno de la protección de María"; "por medio de María."

66. Taylor, "Virgin of Guadalupe," 23.

67. Curcio-Nagy, "Native Icon," 389–390. Brading, *Mexican Phoenix*, 230.

68. Brading, *Mexican Phoenix*, 237–241, 288.

69. Ibid., 312.

70. Ibid., 313–314.

71. Ibid., 317.

72. Ibid., 317–318.

73. Poole, *Our Lady*, 12.

74. Quotation from Poole, *Our Lady*, 225.

75. I am deeply indebted in this discussion to Eloisa Martín and her photocopied works, "Aparecida, Guadalupe y Luján como símbolos religiosos y nacionales: Un análisis comparativo," 1998, and "La Virgen de Luján: El milagro de una identidad nacional católica," 1997.

76. Juan Antonio Presas, *Anales de Nuestra Señora de Luján: Trabajo histórico-documental 1630–1982* (Buenos Aires: Talleres Gráficos Abel, 1983), 15–16.

77. Presas, *Anales*, preliminary notes.

78. Ibid., 316–317.

79. Loris Zanatta, *Del estado liberal a la nación Católica. Iglesia y Ejército en los orígenes del peronismo, 1930–1943* (Buenos Aires: Universidad Nacional de Quilmes, 1996), 25, 32–33. Spanish reads, "por tradición y ello no implicaba un determinado comportamiento social"; "aconfesional"; "invocación común de la tradición"; "antipatriótico."

80. Quoted in Eloisa Martín, "La Virgen," 11. Spanish reads, "Jurar el Patronato de la Virgen de Luján es, desde el punto de vista nacional, empeñar el honor ante Dios y la Patria por mantener la incolumnidad de la tradición que ella encarna y que es religiosa y patriótica . . . sin cuyos principios cardinales perece la identidad histórica de la Patria, que debe ser indivisible y única. ¿Y cuáles son esos principios cardinales que a toda costa y no obstante cualquier evolución debemos mantener? Dios, Patria, Familia y Propiedad." Emphasis in Martín. See also Eloisa Martín, "Aparecida," which has informed my thinking throughout this chapter.

81. The definition is from Fortunato Mallimaci as used in Martín, "La Virgen," 2.

82. Martín, "La Virgen," 12–13. Anthony Gill, *Rendering unto Caesar: The Catholic Church and the State in Latin America* (Chicago: University of Chicago Press, 1998), 157.

83. Martín, "La Virgen," 14. Michael A. Burdick, *For God and the Fatherland: Religion and Politics in Argentina* (Albany: State University of New York Press, 1995), 55.

84. Presas, *Anales*, 269–271.

85. For a discussion of Perón's activities in this regard see Roberto Bosca, *La iglesia nacional peronista: Factor religioso y poder político* (Buenos Aires: Editorial Sudamericana, 1997).

86. Presas, *Anales*, 277.

87. Ibid., 280, 282.

88. Martín, "La Virgen," 18–19.

89. Presas, *Anales*, 283.

90. Ibid., 286, 289.

91. Ibid., 300. Spanish reads, "No hacemos más que venir a cumplir con una promesa hecha en los momentos difíciles. La Virgen de Luján nos ayudó y es justo que vengamos a agradecérselo."

92. Ibid., 307–309.

93. See the illustrations on pages 17, 31, and 68 and poems "The Disappeared Are Dead" and "Springtime of a Son," pages 23 and 29, in *Selection of Poems of the Mothers of the Plaza de Mayo* (Oxford: Busqueda, 1983).

94. Presas, *Anales*, 309–310.

CHAPTER EIGHT

1. Otelo Borroni and Roberto Vacca, *La vida de Eva Perón: Testimonios para su historia*, vol. 1 (Buenos Aires: Editorial Galerna, 1970), 13–15.

2. Nicolas Fraser and Marysa Navarro, *Eva Perón* (New York: W. W. Norton, 1985), 2–5.

3. Alicia Dujovne Ortiz, *Eva Perón*, translated by Shawn Fields (New York: St. Martin's Press, 1996), 87.

4. Fraser and Navarro, *Eva Perón*, 11.

5. Ibid., 12–27.

6. Ibid., 29–33.

7. Ibid., 30–31.

8. Joseph A. Page, *Perón: A Biography* (New York: Random House, 1983), 84–85. On Evita as a blond, see Ortiz, *Eva Perón*, 78–79.

9. Fraser and Navarro, *Eva Perón*, 58–60.

10. Ibid., 60–61, 69.

11. Marysa Navarro, "Evita's Charismatic Leadership," in *Latin American Populism in Comparative Perspective*, edited by Michael L. Conniff (Albuquerque: University of New Mexico Press, 1981), 47–49. Quotes from Weber appear in Navarro's text; the term "shared" charisma is hers.

12. Eva Perón, *La razón de mi vida* (Buenos Aires: Ediciones Peuser, 1951), 84. Spanish reads, "el pueblo y sobre todo los trabajadores, encontrasen siempre libre el camino de su Lider."

13. Navarro, "Evita's Charismatic Leadership," 60. Spanish reads, "El puente de amor entre Perón y el pueblo."

14. Fraser and Navarro, *Eva Perón*, 88–89.

15. See, for example, the description of an article from *Time* in Borroni and Vacca, *La vida*, 183.

16. First quote in Navarro, "Evita's Charismatic Leadership," 61. Second quote in Eva Perón, *Discursos completos, 1946–1948*, vol. 1 (Buenos Aires: Editorial Megafón, 1985), 44. Spanish reads, "Yo que soy la mas modesta de los colaboradores del general Perón."

17. David I. Kertzer, *Ritual, Politics, and Power* (New Haven: Yale University Press, 1988), 9–10.

18. Fraser and Navarro, *Eva Perón*, 122–126.

19. María Julia Carozzi, "La religiosidad popular en las políticas del patrimonio cultural," *Estudios sobre religión: Newsletter de la Asociación de Cientistas Sociales de la Religión en el Mercosur* 13 (July 2002): 6.

20. Fraser and Navarro, *Eva Perón*, 90–91.

21. Ibid., 93.

22. Ortiz, *Eva Perón*, 178.

23. Borroni and Vacca, *La vida*, 168.

24. Personal visit by the author to the basilica of the Virgen de la Macarena, March 1998. For an interesting discussion of the significance of La Macarena in Francoist Spain see Hilario Arenas González, "Historia XIV: El simbolismo de un reinado: 1936–1964," in *Esperanza Macarena* (Seville: Ediciones Qualdalquivir, 1989), 115–141.

25. Bosca, *La iglesia*, 180.

26. Ortiz, *Eva Perón*, 179.

27. Lila M. Caimari, *Perón y la iglesia católica: Religión, estado y sociedad en la Argentina (1943–1955)* (Buenos Aires: Ariel Historia, 1995), 219. Spanish reads, "Legado de una reina que atendío lo universal, la fe católica y la expansión de su reino cristiano. Legado de Isabel, la mujer que estuvo más cerca de Dios en el tiempo sagrado de España, cuando estar cerca de Dios era combatir y rezar."

28. Borroni and Vacca, *La vida*, 173.

29. Tomás de Elia and Juan Pablo Queiroz, *Evita: El retrato de su vida* (Buenos Aires: Brambila, 1997), 83.

30. Ortiz, *Eva Perón*, 196–197.

31. Fraser and Navarro, *Eva Perón*, 137–139. Mariano Plotkin, *Mañana es San Perón* (Buenos Aires: Ariel Historia Argentina, 1993), 239.

32. Fraser and Navarro, *Eva Perón*, 135.

33. Ibid., 143–146. Spanish, 144, reads, "Perón-Eva Perón, la fórmula de la patria." Ortiz, *Eva Perón*, 264–267.

34. Eva Perón, *La razón de mi vida* (Buenos Aires: Editorial Relevo, 1973), 68–69. Spanish reads, "mujer del Líder de un pueblo que ha depositado en él toda su fe, toda su esperanza y todo su amor"; "Evita, puente tendido entre las esperanzas del pueblo y las manos realizadoras de Perón."

35. Eva Perón, *La razón*, 72. Spanish reads, "Cuando un pibe me nombra 'Evita' me siento madre de todos los pibes y de todos los débiles y humildes de mi tierra."

36. Anderson, *Imagined Communities*, 143, links the idea of "political love" with the "vocabulary of kinship." However, Anderson uses these concepts to describe something that he sees as "natural" and "unchosen." In this case, the working class of Argentina was actively choosing Evita, at her explicit invitation.

37. Fraser and Navarro, *Eva Perón*, 148–149.

38. Ibid., 148–150.

39. Ibid., 150–152.

40. Lawrence K. Altman, "From the Life of Evita, a New Chapter on Medical Secrecy," *The New York Times*, June 6, 2000.

41. Ortiz, *Eva Perón*, 270.

42. Ibid., 270–271. De Elia and Queiroz, *Evita*, 155.

43. Fraser and Navarro, *Eva Perón*, 155.

44. De Elia and Queiroz, *Evita*, 161. Spanish reads, "iremos a hacernos justicia por nuestras propias manos."

45. Fraser and Navarro, *Eva Perón*, 155–156.

46. Ibid., 156.

47. Ortiz, *Eva Perón*, 277. Fraser and Navarro, *Eva Perón*, 162–163.

48. Fraser and Navarro, *Eva Perón*, 163.

49. Bosca, *La iglesia*, 186–187.

50. Pedro Ara, *El caso Eva Perón* (Madrid: CVS Ediciones, n.d.), 62–63. Spanish reads, "Sobre su lecho dormía para siempre el espectro de una rara, tranquila belleza, liberada, al fin, del cruel tormento de una materia hasta el límite corroída y de la tortura mental sostenida por la ciencia que, esperando el milagro, prolonga el suplicio."

51. Ara, *El caso*, 66–67.

52. Fraser and Navarro, *Eva Perón*, 164.

53. Ara, *El caso*, 68–69.

54. Fraser and Navarro, *Eva Perón*, 165.

55. Ortiz, *Eva Perón*, 278–279.

56. Austen Ivereigh, *Catholicism and Politics in Argentina 1810–1960* (New York: St. Martin's Press, 1995), 153–155.

57. Eva Perón, *Mi mensaje* (Buenos Aires: Ediciones del Mundo, 1987), 55. Spanish reads, "hombres fríos"; "inconcebible indiferencia frente a la realidad sufriente de los pueblos"; "generosidad y amor."

58. Ibid., 55–56. Spanish reads, "La religión volverá a tener prestigio entre los pueblos si sus predicadores la enseñan así . . . como fuerza de rebeldía y de igualdad . . . no como instrumento de opresión."

59. Ibid., 61. Spanish reads, "apagar aquella sed" "traiciones"; "Dios le exigirá algún día la cuenta precisa y meticulosa de sus traiciones . . . con mucho más severidad que a quienes con menos teología pero con más amor nos decidimos a darlo todo por el pueblo . . . con toda el alma, con todo el corazón."

60. For a discussion of the Peronist ideology in this regard as it developed after her death see Bosca, *La iglesia*, 207–211.

61. Eva Perón, *La razón* (1951), cover, frontispiece, 6–10. Spanish reads, "la figura, el alma y la vida"; "una humilde mujer"; "Y el era y es el cóndor gigante que vuela alto y cerca de Dios."

62. Eva Perón, *Mi mensaje*, 18. Spanish reads, "Yo ya sabía que el como los condores volaba alto y solo . . . ¡y sin embargo yo tenía que volar con el!"

63. *El mundo peronista*, June 15, 1954. Spanish reads "Evita, tu nombre no se olvida ya"; "La obra del amor y el sublime sacrificio de la Inmortal Evita tiene eterna presencia en el corazón de su Pueblo"; "un Amor de fuego"; "fuera del Tiempo y Espacio, eterna."

64. Fraser and Navarro, *Eva Perón*, between 182 and 183. The image is reproduced as well on a cover of *El pregonero*, the official publication of the Sindicato de Vendedores de Diarios y Revistas de Capital Federal y Gran Buenos Aires, December 1998, with the caption "May happiness reign in all homes." Spanish reads, "Que la felicidad reine en todos los hogares."

65. *Cancionero de Juan Perón y Eva Perón*, edited by Dario Alessandro (Buenos Aires: Grupo Editor de Buenos Aires, 1966), 286–288, 293–294. Spanish reads, "Dios-Patria-Perón"; "Eva Perón no ha muerto"; "En la esfera sublime vibra el canto. Es música de luz su eterna aurora. En su esencial pureza se decora y esplende en el Empireo sacrosanto"; "Redentora de pueblos"; "Bajo tu advocación sueña la Patria, Redentora de pueblos, luz del pobre, para decir tu nombre, o iluminada, un tiempo de campanas y flores"; "Alúmbranos, Señora, en las espigas; un campo de esperanzas es tu imagen. Bajo la Cruz del Sur nace tu gloria: ¡Santa Eva Perón, bandera y Mártir!"

66. Plotkin, *Mañana*, 157–158.

67. Fraser and Navarro, *Eva Perón*, 134.

68. Plotkin, *Mañana*, 197–198.

69. Ibid., 171, 175.

70. Graciela Albornoz de Videla, *Evita: Libro de Lectura para Primer Grado Inferior*, (Buenos Aires: Editorial Luis Lasserre S.R.L., 1953), 10. Spanish reads, "Mamita me enseñó a rezar. En mis oraciones, nunca olvido a Eva Perón, nuestra Madre Espiritual."

71. Albornoz de Videla, *Evita*, 3. Spanish reads, "Perón ama a los ninos. Mi mamá. Mi papá. Perón. Evita."

72. Albornoz de Videla, *Evita*, 26–28. Spanish reads, "Fué un hijo modelo, obediente y sumiso"; "Nuestra Patria es un nidito, nuestra Patria es un hogar . . . los chiquillos, hermanitos, y es Evita la mamá."

73. Albornoz de Videla, *Evita*, vocabulary list.

74. Ara, *El caso*, 91–112.

75. Fraser and Navarro, *Eva Perón*, 169–170.

76. Ivereigh, *Catholicism*, 175–177.

77. Ortiz, *Eva Perón*, 289–290. Fraser and Navarro, *Eva Perón*, 173.

78. Fraser and Navarro, *Eva Perón*, 172–174.

79. Quoted in Ortiz, *Eva Perón*, 282.

80. Ibid., 283. Fraser and Navarro, *Eva Perón*, 176.

81. Ara, *El caso*, 241–242. Spanish reads, "Esta medallista . . . debe ser de la Inmaculada. !Pobrecita! Que Dios la haya perdonado."

82. Fraser and Navarro, *Eva Perón*, 175–177. Ortiz, *Eva*, 283–285.

83. Ortiz, *Eva Perón*, 285.

84. Ibid., 273–274, 299.

85. *The New York Times*, May 5, 1996.

86. Ortíz, *Eva Perón*, 299.

87. Ibid., 299–300. Ara, *El caso*, 266–267.

88. Page, *Perón*, 425.

89. Ortiz, *Eva Perón*, 302–303. Fraser and Navarro, *Eva Perón*, 190–191.

90. Fraser and Navarro, *Eva Perón*, 181–182. J. M. Taylor, *Eva Perón: The Myths of a Woman* (Chicago: University of Chicago Press, 1979), 4.

91. Carozzi, "La religiosidad," 8. Spanish reads, "Cuando pienso en eso de subir al púlpito y encarar a la gente, yo tengo en mi cabeza todo lo que hizo Evita. Ella fue . . . increíble. Porque ella trajo mucho para las mujeres. Ella fue la primera en jugar al futbol, en hacer política . . . No se dejaba pasar por arriba. Y yo hago como ella. Cuando algún pastor me dice que yo soy mujer y que no debería ser pastora, les digo que eso era antes. Pero ahora no. *Que yo soy como Evita.*" Emphasis in Carozzi.

92. Nicholas Perry and Loreto Echeverría, *Under the Heel of Mary* (London: Routledge, 1988), 281–282.

93. Perry and Echavarría, *Under the Heel*, 286.

94. Marguerite Guzmán Bouvard, *Revolutionizing Motherhood: The Mothers of the Plaza de Mayo* (Wilmington, Delaware: Scholarly Resources, 1994), 70–74.

95. Bouvard, *Revolutionizing Motherhood*, 74–77.

96. *Selection of Poems*, 17, 31, 68.

97. Ibid., 74.

CHAPTER NINE

1. On this point I agree with Isidoro Moreno Navarro, *La Semana Santa de Sevilla: Conformación, mistificación, y significaciones* (Seville: Biblioteca de Temas Sevillanos, 1982),

232–233, and not with Timothy Mitchell, *Passional Culture: Emotion, Religion, and Society in Southern Spain* (Philadelphia: University of Pennsylvania Press, 1990), 7. Mitchell believes that the Sevillanos, in this ritual, have set themselves "against the very dogma of the Resurrection."

2. Quotation in English and Spanish is from Susan Webster, *Art and Ritual*, 95. Spanish reads, "llevado por Capitan delante de nuestros ojos a Jesu Christo, y las espaldas amparadas con su diuina Madre, seamos libres del demonio, en esta dicha Prosession [*sic*]."

3. Carol Ann Fiedler, "Corpus Christi in Cuzco: Festival and Ethnic Identity in the Peruvian Andes" (Ph.D. diss., Tulane University, 1985), 271–276.

4. Arenas González, "Historia XIV," 118.

5. Belting, *Likeness*, xxi. Also see Chapter I of this volume.

6. See Chapter VI of this volume.

7. Author's interview with Jorge Flores Ochoa, June 1998.

8. Ibid.

9. Fiedler, "Corpus Christi," 173.

10. Martínez Alcalde, *Sevilla Mariana*, 200–206.

11. Ibid., 206. Spanish reads, "garbo castizo, su consonancia con el tipismo de su barrio"; "empaque femenil y moreno"; "no es reliquía trágica sino señal cierta de Esperanza, donde se anuncia la Corredención obtenida mediante su propio Dolor"; "De ahí la alegría que la rodea durante su desfile processional"; "'*Capitana de los mares que no tienen puertas,*' áncora de salvación y faro en radiante singladura." Emphasis in the original.

12. For the antiquity of the brotherhoods see Webster, *Art and Ritual*, 207–209. The exact name of La Macarena's sodality is Real, Ilustre, y Fervorosa Hermandad y Cofradía de Nazarenos de Nuestra Señora del Santo Rosario, Nuestro Padre Jesús de la Sentencia y María Santísima de la Esperanza Macarena; La Triana's is Pontificia, Real e Ilustre Hermandad Sacramental y Archicofradía de Nazarenos del Santísimo y de la Pura y Limpia Concepción de la Virgen María, del Santísimo Cristo de las Tres Caidas, Nuestra Señora de la Esperanza y San Juan Evangelista.

13. Martínez Alcalde, *Sevilla Mariana*, 200–206. Quotation on 201 reads, "la tierra y el cielo, lo humano y lo divino, el llanto y la sonrisa, la pena y la gracia."

14. Antonio Burgos, *Folklore de los cofradias de Sevilla* (Seville: Universidad de Sevilla, 1972), 46–50.

15. Mitchell, *Passional Culture*, 43.

16. Webster, *Art and Ritual*, 192.

17. Quoted in Mitchell, *Passional Culture*, 123.

18. *Diario de Sevilla*, March 3, 1999, special insert, 15.

19. Victor Turner and Edith Turner, *Image and Pilgrimage in Christian Culture* (New York: Columbia University Press, 1978), 103.

20. Turner and Turner, *Image*, 250–251.

21. Ibid., 8, 124. Turner and Turner acknowledge possible nationalistic consequences resulting from these sorts of pilgrimages but address the issue only briefly in a discussion of Saint Patrick and Ireland.

22. Ana Rita Valero, "Peregrinación al Tepeyac. Una observación analítica de las romerías guadalupanas," in Beatriz Barba de Piña Chan, editor, *Caminos terrestres al cielo: Contribución al estudio del fenómeno romero* (Mexico City: Instituto Nacional de Antropología e Historia, 1998), 65–68. Spanish reads, "un viaje que se dirige a un lugar sagrado con la intención de tener un encuentro con lo divino."

23. *The New York Times*, June 6, 2001.

24. Mitchell, *Passional Culture*, 113.

25. Webster, *Art and Ritual*, 91–95.

26. *Diario de Sevilla*, special insert, April 1, 1999.

27. Webster, *Art and Ritual*, 113–121. Quotation is on 117.

28. Moreno Navarro, *La Semana Santa*, 99–100. Spanish reads, "individualizándose extraordinariamente la figura central de los mismos."

29. Mitchell, *Passional Culture*, 113. Emphasis in the original.

30. Ibid., 114–116.

31. Ibid., 170.

32. Huayhuaca Villasante, *La festividad*, 136–146. See also Kathryn Burns, *Colonial Habits: Convents and the Spiritual Economy of Cuzco, Peru* (Durham: Duke University Press, 1999), 72–77, for the move from Arequipa to Cuzco.

33. See discussion in Gutierre Aceves, "Imagenes de la inocencio eternal," in *Artes de México: El Arte Ritual de la Muerte Niña* 15 (spring 1992), 27.

34. Author's discussion with Jorge Flores Ochoa, June 1998. See Huayhuaca Villasante, *La festividad*, 148–149, for usual arrangement of the images in the cathedral and discussion in "La fiesta de los cuzqueños: La procesión del Corpus Christi," in *El Cuzco*, 138–144.

35. Fiedler, "Corpus Christi," 117, 277. See also Flores Ochoa, "La fiesta," 144. Flores Ochoa links eleven of the fifteen images that actually processed during Corpus Christi in 1988 to Andean symbols on an early colonial drawing of the Coricancha produced by the Andean Juan Santa Cruz Pachacuti dating from the late sixteenth or early seventeenth century.

36. Flores Ochoa, "La fiesta," 131–132.

37. See the discussion of Tepeyac and quotations in Poole, 78. For highland Mexican pilgrimages in the pre-Columbian period see Beatriz Barba de Piña Chan, "Peregrinaciones prehispanicos del Altiplano mesoamericano," in Barba de Piña Chan, 17–47.

38. Victor Turner, *Dramas, Fields, and Metaphors: Symbolic Action in Human Society* (Ithaca, New York: Cornell University Press, 1996), 225–226.

39. Poole, *Our Lady*, 118.

40. For example, see *Metro* (Mexico City), December 12, 1999.

41. *Machetearte* 50 (December 7, 1999).

42. See *The New York Times*, June 21, 1996; *Proceso*, January 10, 2000; *Reforma*, December 9 and 12, 1999; *Albuquerque Journal*, December 5, 1999; *Mexico City News*, December 12, 1999; *Uno mas uno*, December 1, 1999. Quote in *Reforma*, December 9, 1999. Spanish reads, "Creo que una persona que vive como vive no tiene derecho a hacer esas

acusations. Que se convierta, que pida perdón. Dios lo perdonará, y si se quiere, en mi confesionario, yo también lo perdonaré."

43. *Reforma,* December 9, 1999. Spanish reads, "inmediatemente, mi corazón se convirtió en un pájaro de fuego que voló hacia ella, empecé a llorar como nunca lo había hecho y ella me dijo: 'Calmate, respira profundo que yo estoy contigo'"; "todos somos de la Virgen de Guadalupe y Juan Diego."

44. *Uno más uno,* December 10, 1999.

45. *Albuquerque Journal,* June 24, 2000.

46. *Proceso,* December 3, 2000.

47. *La Jornada,* December 11, 2000. Spanish reads, "Que la Virgen de Guadalupe, Patrona de los Trabajadores de México, los bendiga"; "el único santo que será el santo contrato colectivo."

48. *The New York Times,* June 25, 2001.

49. Carlos Monsivais, *Mexican Postcards,* edited and translated by John Kraniasuskas (London: Verso, 1997), 37–38.

CHAPTER TEN

1. *The New York Times,* June 9, 2002. The report notes that the data collection was somewhat different in the two censuses so that the numbers may not be exactly comparable.

2. Personal observations by the author. See also Turner and Turner, *Image,* 76, and Turner, *Dramas,* 187.

3. Quoted in Thomas A. Tweed, *Our Lady of Exile: Diasporic Religion at the Cuban Catholic Shrine in Miami* (New York: Oxford University Press, 1997), 43. Tweed's book is an outstanding study of this figure in interaction with the Cuban American population.

4. *Miami Herald,* September 6, 1998.

5. Tweed, *Our Lady,* 15–16.

6. *Miami Herald,* July 14, 1999.

7. Tweed, *Our Lady,* 104.

8. Ibid.

9. Nelson P. Valdés, "The Meaning of Elián González—Miracles, Dolphins, and Orishas," unpublished paper. The entire discussion of the Elián González situation is much influenced by conversations with Nelson Valdés, and I am indebted to him for sharing his ideas with me.

10. Jorge Durand and Douglas S. Massey, *Miracles on the Border: Retablos of Mexican Migrants to the United States* (Tucson: University of Arizona Press, 1995), 59–66, 70–71.

11. Conversation by the author with secretary of Saint Lawrence Church, San Antonio, Texas, October 28, 1999.

12. Durand and Massey, *Miracles,* 63.

13. Thomas J. Steele, *Santos and Saints: The Religious Folk Art of Hispanic New Mexico* (Santa Fe, New Mexico: Ancient City Press, 1974), 98–109.

14. Jeanette Rodríguez, *Our Lady of Guadalupe: Faith and Empowerment among Mexican-American Women* (Austin: University of Texas Press, 1994), 98.

15. Ibid., 122.

16. Ibid., 122–134.

17. *The New York Times*, July 21, 1996.

18. Callejo was aided in the project by Steve Salazar and Fabian Araiza. Students Daniel Hernández, Gregorio García, Mike Vargas, Janet Becerra, David Ramírez, Gilbert Chen, Christián Hernández, Arlene Caudillo, Beatriz Moreno, Yvonne Ortega, Liz Landeros, and Irene Juárez participated in the section of the mural project in which this image of the Virgin appears.

19. *Santa Fe New Mexican*, April 17, 1998.

20. Ibid., April 18, 1998.

21. Ibid., April 23, 1998.

22. Documents pertinent to the controversy may be found on http:// www.almalopez.net. Archbishop Sheehan's March 26, 2001, statement is reproduced, along with a chronology of the events, a statement by Alma López, and statements by a number of the other participants. The description of events on March 31, 2001, is taken from the report in the *Albuquerque Journal*, April 1, 2001.

23. Quotes from Villegas, Nunn, López, and Cisneros appear in *Albuquerque Journal*, April 1, 2001.

24. Patricia Gonzales, "Guadalupe Represents the Feminine Energy of God," *Albuquerque Journal*, May 23, 2001.

CHAPTER ELEVEN

1. For the Villanueva and other New Mexico pilgrimages see Jacqueline Orsini Dunnington, *Guadalupe: Our Lady of New Mexico* (Santa Fe: Museum of New Mexico Press, 1999), 101–150.

2. See New Orleans *Times-Picayune*, December 21, 1997, for the likeness of the Virgin of Guadalupe as it appeared in the sap of a pine tree in Olivet Memorial Park cemetery of Colma, California, and of the crowds that began to gather there. The cemetery is nonsectarian.

3. See, for example, newspaper reports in *The Washington Post*, June 9, 1997; *Times-Picayune*, June 12, 1997; *Ottawa Citizen*, June 14, 1997. Quotations appear in the stories.

4. Quoted in Norma Galb, "Communism, Religion, and War," *Voices from Nicaragua: A U.S.-Based Journal of Culture in Reconstruction* 1 (2–3): 9.

Glossary

abuela—grandmother

adelantado—a Spanish explorer/warrior with governance responsibilities

Alto Peru—the area of the southern Andean highlands now approximately
   contiguous with modern Bolivia

ayllu—Andean kinship group

basilica (minor)—a church of particular importance, historical, devotional,
   or artistic, that has been so honored by the pope

C.G.T.—Confederación General del Trabajo, central labor organization
   in Argentina

camarín—(also recamarín) dressing room, often a sort of chapel, for an image
   of the Virgin

chasuble—vestment worn by priests at Mass

cofrade—member of religious brotherhood

cofradía—religious brotherhood

Coya—Inka queen

estanciero—estate owner

hermandad—religious brotherhood

huaca—Andean sacred object or place (shrine)

Huitzilopochtli—principal Aztec God, Blue-Hummingbird-on-the-Left, associated with the sun

illapa—Andean term for lightning and also for Saint James, Santiago

imagenes de vestir—statues that have carved faces and hands but only a framework for a body, which is covered with clothing; a dressed image

integral Catholicism—term characterizing an intense relationship between
   Catholicism and the nation/state

ixiptla—representative, substitute; human who stood in for one of the Gods
 in Aztec ceremonials; also, literally, envelope, bark, or skin
maguey—a type of agave plant from which fiber for cloth is made
mallqui—mummy of Andean leader
mamacha—Andean term used for the Virgin in connection with the name
 of an advocation
mamaconas—Inka chosen women, often called the Virgins of the Sun
maskaypacha—characteristic fringe worn on the forehead by Inka head of state
mezquita—mosque
nahualli—shaman with ability to take other forms, especially those of animals
Noche Triste—night of June 30–July 1, 1520, when Spanish forces under Cortés
 were forced to battle their way out of Tenochtitlan, the Aztec capital
ñusta—Andean princess
ocote—resinous pine tree whose wood is used for torches
ololiuhqui—hallucinogen used in Mesoamerica; identified with various plants
Pachamama—Andean earth deity, gendered female
peyote—hallucinogen taken from cactus
Plaza de Mayo—central plaza in Buenos Aires
raza—race, often used to denote Hispanics
recamarín—see camarín
repartidor—Spanish individual charged with the distribution of native peoples
 to the conquerors
saeta—a song presented as an offering to one of the images in the Semana
 Santa procession in Seville
saetero—singer, often professional, who specializes in the singing of saetas
Semana Santa—Holy Week
suntur pakar—Andean headdress denoting nobility
Tenochtitlan—Aztec capital
Tezcatlipoca—the Smoking Mirror, the mysterious Aztec god associated with
 the night wind, a trickster who introduced the random and the unexpected
 into the cosmos
titixtli—native wraparound skirt
tlacatecolotl—owl man, used by the Spanish to connote devil
Viracocha—Andean culture hero, creating God
tlacuilo—native scribe in New Spain
wak'as—Andean sacred objects and shrines
zemi—small, numinous object revered by the indigenous peoples of the
 Caribbean

Bibliography of Works Cited

Aceves, Gutierre. "Imágenes de la inocencio eternal." In *Artes de México: El Arte Ritual de la Muerte Niña* 15 (spring 1992).

Acosta, Joseph de. *Historia natural y moral de las Indias.* Madrid: R. Angles, Impresor, 1894.

Adorno, Rolena. "The Art of Survival in Early Peru." In *Violence, Resistance, and Survival in the Americas: Native Americans and the Legacy of the Conquest.* Edited by William B. Taylor and Franklin Pease. Washington: Smithsonian Institution Press, 1994.

————. *Guaman Poma: Writing and Resistance in Colonial Peru.* Austin: University of Texas Press, 1986.

Alfonso X. *Cantigas de Santa María.* Edited by Walter Mettmann. Coimbra, Portugal: Universidade de Coimbra, 1959.

Alarcón, Rafael. *La última Virgen Negra del Templo: El enigma templario de Candelaria.* Mexico City: Ediciones Roca, 1991.

Alberro, Solange. *El águila y la cruz: Orígenes religiosos de la conciencia criolla. México, siglos XVI-XVII.* Mexico City: Fondo de Cultura Económica, 1999.

————. *Inquisición y sociedad en México, 1571–1700.* Mexico City: Fondo de Cultura Económica, 1988.

Albornoz de Videla, Graciela. *Evita: Libro de Lectura para Primer Grado Inferior.* Buenos Aires: Editorial Luis Lasserre S.R.L., 1953.

Alessandro, Dario, ed. *Cancionero de Juan Perón y Eva Perón.* Buenos Aires: Grupo Editor de Buenos Aires, 1966.

Alfonso X. *Cantigas.* Ca. 1257–1283 Edited by Jesús Montoya. Madrid: Ediciones Cátedra, 1988.

————. *Cantigas de Santa María.* Edited by Walter Mettmann. 2 vols. Madrid: Clásicos Castalia, 1986.

————. *Las Cantigas de loor de Alfonso X El Sabio.* Bilingual edition translated by Luis Beltrán. Madrid: Ediciones Júcar, 1988.

————. *Setenario.* Edited by Kenneth Vanderwood. Buenos Aires: Instituto de Filología, 1945.

Altman, Lawrence K. "From the Life of Evita, a New Chapter on Medical Secrecy." *New York Times,* June 6, 2000.

Amigo Vallejo, Carlos, presenter. *Esperanza Macarena en el XXV aniversario de su canonización canónica.* Seville: Ediciones Guadalquivir, 1989.

Anderson, Benedict. *Imagined Communities: Reflections on the Origin and Spread of Nationalism.* London: Verso, 1991.

Anglería, Pedro Martir de. *Décadas del Nuevo Mundo.* Mexico City: José Porrua e Hijos, 1964.

Ara, Pedro. *El caso Eva Perón.* Madrid: CVS Ediciones, n.d.

Arenas González, Hilario. "Historia XIV: El simbolismo de un reinado: 1936–1964." In *Esperanza Macarena.* Presented by Carlos Amigo Vallejo. Seville: Ediciones Quadalquivir, 1989.

Arnold, Philip P. *Eating Landscape: Aztec and European Occupation of Tlalocan.* Niwot: University Press of Colorado, 1999.

Arriaga, Pablo Joseph de. *The Extirpation of Idolatry in Peru,* translated and edited by L. Clark Keating. Lexington: University of Kentucky Press, 1968.

Bagby, Albert I. Jr. "The Figure of the Jew in the *Cantigas of Alfonso X.*" In *Studies on the Cantigas de Santa María: Art, Music, and Poetry.* Edited by Israel J. Katz and John E. Keller. Madison, Wisconsin: Hispanic Seminary of Medieval Studies, 1987.

Barba de Piña Chan, Beatriz. "Peregrinaciones prehispanicos del Altiplano mesoamericano." In *Caminos terrestres al cielo: Contribución al estudio del fenómeno romero.* Edited by Barba de Piña Chan. Mexico City: Instituto Nacional de Antropología e Historia, 1998.

————, ed. *Caminos terrestres al cielo: Contribución al estudio del fenómeno romero.* Mexico City: Instituto Nacional de Antropología e Historia, 1998.

Baring, Anne, and Jules Cashford. *The Myth of the Goddess: Evolution of an Image.* London: Penguin Books, 1991.

Barjau, Luis. *Tezcatlipoca: Elementos de una teología nahua.* Mexico City: Universidad Nacional Autónoma de México, 1991.

Barreto, Mascarenhas. *The Portuguese Columbus: Secret Agent of King John II.* New York: St. Martin's Press, 1992.

Barrionuevo, Alfonsina. *Cuzco mágico.* Lima: Editorial Universo, n.d.

Bartlett, Robert, and Angus MacKay, eds. *Medieval Frontier Societies.* Oxford: Clarendon Press, 1989.

Belting, Hans. *Likeness and Presence: The History of the Image before the Era of Art.* Chicago: University of Chicago Press, 1994.

Benavente, Toribio de (Motolinía). *Historia de los indios de la Nueva España.* Transcribed with critical study, appendices, notes, and index by Edmundo O'Gorman. Mexico City: Porrúa, 1973.

Benko, Stephen. *The Virgin Goddess.* Leiden, Netherlands: E. J. Brill, 1993.

Beristain de Souza, Josef Mariano. "Declamación que en la solemne función de desagravios a María Santísima de Guadalupe." Mexico City: Imprenta Arizpe, 1811.

Bernand, Carmen, and Serge Gruzinski. *Historia del Nuevo Mundo.* Vol. 2: *Los mestizajes, 1550–1640.* Mexico City: Fondo de Cultura Económica, 1999.

Birnbaum, Lucía Chiavola. *Black Madonnas: Feminism, Religion, and Politics in Italy.* Boston: Northeastern University Press, 1993.

Boff, Leonardo. *The Maternal Face of God: The Feminine and Its Religious Expressions.* San Francisco: Harper & Row, 1987.

———. *O rostro materno de Deus: Ensaio interdisciplinario sobre o femenino e suas formas religiosas.* Petrópolis, Brazil: Editora Vozes, 1979.

Bosca, Roberto. *La iglesia nacional peronista: Factor religioso y poder político.* Buenos Aires: Editorial Sudamericana, 1997.

Borroni, Otelo, and Roberto Vacca. *La vida de Eva Perón: Testimonios para su historia.* Vol. 1. Buenos Aires: Editorial Galerna, 1970.

Brading, David A. *Mexican Phoenix: Our Lady of Guadalupe: Image and Tradition Across Five Centuries.* Cambridge: Cambridge University Press, 2001.

Bringas, F. Diego Miguel. "Sermon en honor de Ma. Sma. De Guadalupe." N.p.: Imprenta de Doña María Fernández de Jauregui, 1812.

Broda, Johanna. "The Sacred Landscape of Aztec Calendar Festivals: Men, Nature, and Society." In *To Change Place: Aztec Ceremonial Landscapes.* Edited by David Carrasco. Niwot: University Press of Colorado, 1991.

Brown, Peter. "A Dark Age Crisis: Aspects of the Iconoclastic Controversy." *English Historical Review* 88, no. 346 (January 1973).

Brundage, Burr C. *The Jade Steps: The Ritual Life of the Aztecs.* Salt Lake City: University of Utah Press, 1985.

———. *Lords of Cuzco: A History and Description of the Inca People in Their Final Days.* Norman: University of Oklahoma Press, 1967.

Burdick, Michael A. *For God and the Fatherland: Religion and Politics in Argentina.* Albany: State University of New York Press, 1995.

Burgos, Antonio. *Folklore de las cofradías de Sevilla.* Seville: Universidad de Sevilla, 1972.

Burkhart, Louise M. "The Cult of the Virgin of Guadalupe in Mexico." In Gary H. Gossen and Miguel León-Portilla, editors. *South and Meso-American Native Spirituality.* New York: Crossroad, 1993.

———. *Holy Wednesday: A Nahua Drama from Early Colonial Mexico.* Philadelphia: University of Pennsylvania Press, 1996.

———. *The Slippery Earth: Nahua-Christian Moral Dialogue in Sixteenth-Century Mexico.* Tucson: University of Arizona Press, 1989.

Burns, Kathryn. *Colonial Habits: Convents and the Spiritual Economy of Cuzco, Peru.* Durham: Duke University Press, 1999.

Burns, Robert I. *Moors and Crusaders in Mediterranean Spain: Collected Studies.* London: Variorum Reprints, 1978.

Caimari, Lila M. *Perón y la iglesia católica: Religión, estado y sociedad en la Argentina (1943–1955).* Buenos Aires: Ariel Historia, 1995.

Campbell, Leon G. "Ideology in Factionalism during the Great Rebellion, 1780–1782." In *Resistance, Rebellion, and Consciousness in the Andean Peasant World, 18th to 20th Centuries*. Edited by Steve J. Stern. Madison: University of Wisconsin Press, 1987.

Cánepa Koch, Gisela. *Máscara, transformación e identidad en los Andes: La fiesta de la Virgen del Carmen Paucartambo-Cuzco*. Lima: Pontificia Universidad Católica del Perú, Fondo Editorial, 1998.

Carozzi, María Julia. "La religiosidad popular en las políticas del patrimonio cultural." *Estudios sobre religión*. Newsletter de la Asociación de Cientistas Sociales de la Religión en el Mercosur.

Carr, Anne, and Elisabeth Schussler Fiorenza, eds. *Religion in the Eighties: Motherhood—Experience, Institution, Theology. Concilium* 6, no. 206 (December 1989).

Carrasco, David, ed. *To Change Place: Aztec Ceremonial Landscapes*. Niwot, Colorado: University Press of Colorado, 1991.

Cassidy, Brendan, ed. *Iconography at the Crossroads*. Princeton: Index of Christian Art, Princeton University, 1993.

Cervantes, Fernando. *The Devil in the New World: The Impact of Diabolism in New Spain*. New Haven: Yale University Press, 1994.

Christian, William A. Jr. *Apparitions in Late Medieval and Renaissance Spain*. Princeton: Princeton University Press, 1981.

———. "De los santos a María: Panorama de las devociones a santuarios españoles desde el principio de nuestros días." In *Temas de antropología española*, edited by Carmelo Lisón. Madrid: Alcal Editor, 1976.

———. *Local Religion in Sixteenth-Century Spain*. Princeton: Princeton University Press, 1981.

Clendinnen, Inga. *The Aztecs: An Interpretation*. Cambridge: Cambridge University Press, 1991.

Coluccio, Félix. *Fiestas y celebraciones de la República Argentina*. 3rd ed. Buenos Aires: Editorial Plus Ultra, 1992.

Columbus, Christopher. *The Diario of Christopher Columbus's First Voyage to America*. Translated by Oliver Dunn and John E. Kelley Jr. Norman: University of Oklahoma Press, 1988.

Columbus, Ferdinand. *The Life of the Admiral Christopher Columbus by His Son Ferdinand*. Translated by Benjamin Keen. New Brunswick: Rutgers University Press, 1959.

Coope, Jessica. *The Martyrs of Córdoba: Community and Family in an Age of Mass Conversion*. Lincoln: University of Nebraska Press, 1995.

Cortés, Hernán. *Cartas y relaciones de Hernán Cortés al Emperador Carlos V. 1519–1525*. Edited by Pascual de Gayangos. Paris: A. Chaix & Cia., 1866.

———. *Testamento de Hernán Cortés*. Mexico City: Imprenta del Asilo Patricio Sanz, 1925.

Cortés Castellanos, Justino. *El catechismo en pictogramas de Fray Pedro de Gante*. Madrid: Fundación Universitaria Española, 1988.

Curcio-Nagy, Linda. "Native Icon to City Protectress to Royal Patroness: Ritual,

Political Symbolism and the Virgin of Remedies." *Americas* 52, no. 3 (January 1996).

Damian, Carol. *The Virgin of the Andes: Art and Ritual in Colonial Cuzco*. Miami Beach, Florida: Grassfield Press, 1995.

de Elia, Tomás, and Juan Pablo Queiroz. *Evita: El retrato de su vida*. Buenos Aires: Brambila, 1997.

de Jerez, Francisco, Pedro de Cieza de León, and Agustín de Zarate. *Crónicas de la conquista del Perú*. Edited by Julio Le Riverend. Mexico, Editorial Nueva Espána.

de la Calancha, Antonio. *Corónica moralizada del Orden de San Antonio en el Perú*. Transcription, critical study, bibiographical notes, and indices by Ignacio Prado Pastor. Lima: Universidad Nacional Mayor de San Marcos, 1974.

de la Serna, Jacinto. "Manual de Ministros de Indias para el conocimiento de idolatria y la estirpación de ellas." In *Colección de documentos inéditos para la historia de España*. Vol. 104. Madrid: Imprenta de José Perales y Martínez, 1892.

de la Torre, Mario, ed., with text by Josefina García Quintana and Carlos Martínez Marín. *El Lienzo de Tlaxcala*. Mexico City: Cartón y Papel de México, 1983.

de la Vega, Garcilaso. *Royal Commentaries of the Incas*. Translated by Harold Livermore. Austin: University of Texas Press, 1966.

Dean, Carolyn. *Inka Bodies and the Body of Christ: Corpus Christi in Colonial Cuzco, Peru*. Durham: Duke University Press, 1999.

Demélas, Marie-Danielle. *L'invention politique: Bolivie, Equateur, Pérou au XIXe siecle*. Paris: Editions Recherche sur les Civilisations, 1992.

Díaz, Gisele, and Alan Rodgers, *The Codex Borgia: A Full-Color Restoration of the Ancient Mexican Manuscript*, with an introduction and commentary by Bruce E. Byland New York: Dover Publications, 1993.

Díaz del Castillo, Bernal. *La Conquista de Nueva España*. Buenos Aires: Sociedad de Ediciones Louis-Michaud, 1853.

———. *Verdadera y notable relación del descubrimiento y conquista de la Nueva España y Guatemala*. 4 vols. Guatemala City: Biblioteca Guatemalteca de Educación Pública, 1964.

Duncan, Barbara. "Statue Paintings of the Virgin." In *Gloria in Excelsis: The Virgin and Angels in Viceregal Painting of Peru and Bolivia*. Edited by John Stringer, Barbara Duncan, and Teresa Gisbert. New York: Center for Inter-American Relations, 1986.

Dunnington, Jacqueline Orsini. *Guadalupe: Our Lady of New Mexico*. Santa Fe: Museum of New Mexico Press, 1999.

Durán, Diego. *The Aztecs: The History of the Indies of New Spain*. Translated by Doris Heyden and Fernando Horcasitas and introduction by Ignacio Bernal. New York: Orion Press, 1964.

Durand, Jorge, and Douglas S. Massey. *Miracles on the Border: Retablos of Mexican Migrants to the United States*. Tucson: University of Arizona Press, 1995.

Eire, Carlos M. N. *From Madrid to Purgatory: The Art and the Craft of Dying in Sixteenth-Century Spain*. Cambridge: Cambridge University Press, 1995.

Elías, Julio María. *Copacauana-Copacabana*. La Paz, Bolivia: Editorial Offset, 1978.

Eulogius. *Memoriale Sanctorum*. In Juan Gil, *Corpus Scriptorum Muzarabicorum*. Vol. 2. Madrid: Instituto Antonio Nebrija, 1973.

Fernández Arenas, P. Arsenio, and P. Pablo Huarte Arana. *Los caminos de Santiago*. Barcelona: Ediciones La Polígrafa, 1965.

Fiedler, Carol Ann. "Corpus Christi in Cuzco: Festival and Ethnic Identity in the Peruvian Andes." Ph.D. dissertation, Tulane University, 1985.

Fiorenza, Elisabeth Schussler. "Feminist Theology as a Critical Theology of Liberation." In *Churches in Struggle: Liberation Theology's and Social Change in North America*. Edited by William Tabb. New York: Monthly Review Press, 1986..

Fleming, John V. "The 'Mystical Signature' of Christopher Columbus." In *Iconography at the Crossroads*. Edited by Brendan Cassidy. Princeton: Index of Christian Art, Princeton University, 1993.

Fletcher, Richard. *The Barbarian Conversion: From Paganism to Christianity*. Berkeley: University of California Press, 1999.

———. *The Quest for El Cid*. New York: Oxford University Press, 1989.

———. *St. James's Catapult: The Life and Times of Diego Gelmírez of Santiago de Compostela*. Oxford: Clarendon Press, 1984.

Flint, Valerie I. J. *The Imagined Landscape of Christopher Columbus*. Princeton: Princeton University Press, 1992.

———. *The Rise of Magic in Early Medieval Europe*. Princeton: Princeton University Press, 1991.

Florencia, Francisco de. "La estrella del norte de México." In *Testimonios históricos guadalupanas*. Compiled by Ernesto de la Torre Villar and Ramiro Navarro de Anda. Mexico City: Fondo de Cultura Económica, 1982.

Flores Ochoa, Jorge, ed. *El Cuzco: Resistencia y continuidad*. Cuzco, Peru: Centro de Estudios Andinos Cusco, 1990.

———. "La fiesta de los cuzqueños: la procession del Corpus Christi." In Flores Ochoa, *El Cuzco*.

Fraser, Nicholas, and Marysa Navarro. *Eva Perón*. New York: W. W. Norton, 1985.

Freedberg, David. *The Power of Images: Studies in the History and Theory of Response*. Chicago: University of Chicago Press, 1989.

Frost, Elsa Cecilia. "Un estilo de vida." *Artes de México*. Vol. 4 of *Guía Franz Meyer*. n.d.

Furst, Jill Leslie McKeever. *The Natural History of the Soul in Ancient Mexico*. New Haven: Yale University Press, 1995.

Galb, Norma. *Voices from Nicaragua: A U.S.-Based Journal of Culture in Reconstruction* 1 (2–3), n.d.

Galinier, Jacques. *La mitad del mundo. Cuerpo y cosmos en los rituales otomíes*. Mexico City: Universidad Nacional Autónoma de México, 1990.

García Rodríguez, Carmen. *El culto de los santos en la España Romana y Visigoda*. Madrid: CSIC, 1966.

Gentz, William H., ed. *The Dictionary of Bible and Religion*. Nashville: Abingdon Press, 1986.

Gil, Juan. *Corpus Scriptorum Muzarabicorum*. Vol. 2. Madrid: Instituto Antonio Nebrija, 1973.

Gill, Anthony. *Rendering unto Caesar: The Catholic Church and the State in Latin America.* Chicago: University of Chicago Press, 1998.

Gisbert, Teresa. *Iconografía y mitos indígenas en el arte*. La Paz, Bolivia: Linea Editorial Fundación BHN, 1994.

Goñi Gastambede, José. *Historia de la Bula de la Cruzada en España*. Vitoria, Spain: Pontificia Universitas Gregoriana, 1958.

Gossen, Gary H., and Miguel León-Portilla, editors. *South and Meso-American Native Spirituality*. New York: Crossroad, 1993.

Griffiths, Nicholas. *The Cross and the Serpent: Religious Repression and Resurgence in Colonial Peru.* Norman: University of Oklahoma Press, 1995.

Gruzinski, Serge. *The Conquest of Mexico City: The Incorporation of Indian Societies into the Western World, 16th–18th Centuries.* Translated by Eileen Corrigan. Cambridge, England: Polity Press, 1993.

————. "Individualization and Acculturation: Confession among the Nahuas from the Sixteenth to the Eighteenth Century." In *Sexuality and Marriage in Colonial Latin America*. Edited by Asunción Lavrín. Lincoln: University of Nebraska Press, 1989.

————. *La guerra de las imágenes de Cristóbal Colón a "Blade Runner (1492–2019)."* Mexico City: Fondo de Cultura Económica, 1994.

————. *Man-Gods and the Mexican Highlands: Indian Power and Colonial Society, 1520–1800.* Stanford: Stanford University Press, 1989.

Guzmán Bouvard, Marguerite. *Revolutionizing Motherhood: The Mothers of the Plaza de Mayo.* Wilmington, Delaware: Scholarly Resources, 1994.

Hall, Linda B. "Visions of the Feminine: The Dual Goddesses of Ancient Mexico." *Southwest Review* 63, no. 2 (spring 1978).

Hemming, John. *The Conquest of the Incas*. New York: Harcourt Brace Jovanovich, 1970.

Huayhuaca Villasante, Luis A. *La festividad del Corpus Christi en el Cusco*. Cuzco, Peru: Talleres Gráficas de Villanueva, 1988.

Iradiel, Paulino, Salustiano Moreta, and Esteban Sarasa. *Historia Medieval de la España Cristiana.* Madrid: Ediciones Cátedra, 1989.

Isabel. *Libro de Horas de Isabel la Católica*. Edited by Matilde López Serrano. Madrid: Editorial Patrimonio Nacional, 1969.

Ivereigh, Austen. *Catholicism and Politics in Argentina 1810–1960*. New York: St. Martin's Press, 1995.

Katz, Israel J., and John E. Keller, eds. *Studies on the Cantigas de Santa Maria: Art, Music, and Poetry.* Madison, Wisconsin: Hispanic Seminary of Medieval Studies, 1987.

Kertzer, David. *Ritual, Politics, and Power*. New Haven: Yale University Press, 1988.

Kiddy, Elizabeth. "Brotherhoods of Our Lady of the Rosary of the Blacks: Community and Devotion in Minas Gerais, Brazil." Ph.D. dissertation, University of New Mexico, 1998.

Kline, Fred R. "The Lost Virgin of the New World: The Discovery of a Marian Sculpture of First Contact." 1998. Photocopy.

Kolata, Alan. *The Tiwanaku: Portrait of an Andean Civilization*. Cambridge, Massachusetts: Blackwell, 1993.

Lacouture, Jean. *The Jesuits: A Multibiography*. Washington, D.C.: Counterpoint, 1995.

La procesión del Corpus en el Cuzco. Seville: Unión Latina, 1996.

Lasso de la Vega, Luis. "El gran acontecimiento . . ." In *Testimonios históricos guadalupanas*. Compiled by Ernesto de la Torre Villar and Ramiro Navarro de Anda. Mexico City: Fondo de Cultura Económica, 1982.

Laumonier, Isabel. *Festividad de Nuestra Señora de Copacabana*. Buenos Aires: Centro de Estudios Migratorios Latinoamericanos, 1990.

Lavrin, Asunción, ed. *Sexuality and Marriage in Colonial Latin America*. Lincoln: University of Nebraska Press, 1989.

Le Goff, Jacques. *The Medieval Imagination*. Translated by Arthur Goldhamer. Chicago: University of Chicago Press, 1988.

León-Portilla, Miguel. *El reverso de la conquista: Relaciones aztecas, mayas e incas*. Mexico City: Editorial Joaquín Mortiz, 1964.

Linehan, Peter. *History and the Historians of Medieval Spain*. Oxford: Clarendon Press, 1993.

———. *Past and Present in Medieval Spain*. Aldershot, England: 1992.

Liss, Peggy K. *Isabel the Queen: Life and Times*. New York: Oxford University Press, 1992.

Lockhart, James. *The Nahuas after the Conquest*. Stanford: Stanford University Press, 1992.

Lomax, Derek W. *The Reconquest of Spain*. New York: Longman, 1978.

López de Gómara, Francisco. *Historia de la conquista de México*. Mexico City: Editorial Pedro Robredo, 1943.

MacCormack, Sabine. "From the Sun of the Incas to the Virgin of Copacabana." *Representations* 8 (Fall 1984).

MacKay, Angus. "Religion, Culture, and Ideology of the Late Medieval Castilian/Granadan Frontier." In *Medieval Frontier Societies*. Edited by Robert Bartlett and Angus MacKay. Oxford: Clarendon Press, 1989.

———, ed. *Society, Economy, and Religion in Late Medieval Castile*. London: Variorum Reprints, 1987.

MacKay, Angus, with Vikki Hatton. "Anti-Semitism in the *Cantigas de Santa María*." In MacKay, ed., *Society, Economy*.

Madariaga, Salvador de. *Hernán Cortés*. Buenos Aires: Sudamericana, 1941.

Maeckelberghe, Els. "'Mary': Maternal Friend or Virgen Mother?" *Religion in the Eighties: Motherhood—Experience, Institution, Theology*, edited by Anne Carr and Elisabeth Schussler Fiorenza. *Concilium* 6, no. 206 (December 1989).

Marion, Javier. "Inkarra Myths and Class Conflict: An Interpretive Study of Juana Azurduy de Padilla's Life as Seen through Late Colonial Currents." Master's thesis, University of New Mexico, 1997.

Martín, Eloisa. "Aparecida, Guadalupe y Luján como símbolos religiosos y nacionales: Un análisis comparativo." 1998. Photocopy.

————. "La Virgen de Luján: El milagro de una identidad nacional católica." 1997. Photocopy.

Martínez Alcalde, Juan. *Sevilla Mariana: Repertorio iconográfica.* Seville: Ediciones Guadalquivir, 1997.

Martínez Baracs, Rodrigo. *La secuencia tlascalteca: Orígenes del culto a Nuestra Señora de Ocotlán.* Mexico City: Colección Biblioteca del INAH, 2000.

Mateos Higuera, Salvador. *Enciclopedia gráfica del México antiguo.* Vol. 3: *Los dioses creados.* Mexico City: Secretaria de Hacienda y Crédito Público, 1993.

McBrien, Richard P., ed. *Encyclopedia of Catholicism.* New York: HarperCollins, 1995.

Michener, James. *Iberia: Spanish Travels and Reflections.* New York: Random House, 1968.

Milhou, Alain. *Colón y su mentalidad mesiánica en el ambiente franciscana español.* Valladolid, Spain: Casa Museo de Colón de la Universidad de Valladolid, 1983.

Miranda Godínez, Francisco. *Dos cultos fundantes: Los Remedios y Guadalupe (1531–1649).* Zamora, Mexico: El Colegio de Michoacán, 2001.

Mitchell, Timothy. *Passional Culture: Emotion, Religion, and Society in Southern Spain.* Philadelphia: University of Pennsylvania Press, 1990.

Mitre, Bartolomé. *Historia de Belgrano y de la independencia argentina.* Vol. 2. Buenos Aires, 1902.

Monsivais, Carlos. *Mexican Postcards.* Edited and translated by John Kraniasuskas. London: Verso, 1999.

Montoya Martínez, Jesús. *Historia y anécdotas de Andalucía en las Cantigas de Santa María.* Granada, Spain: Universidad de Granada, 1988.

Moreno Navarro, Isidoro. *La Semana Santa de Sevilla: Conformación, mixtificación, y significaciones.* Seville: Biblioteca de Temas Sevillanos, 1982.

Morison, Samuel Eliot. *Admiral of the Ocean Sea: A Life of Christopher Columbus.* Boston: Little, Brown & Company, 1946.

Navarro, Marysa. "Evita's Charismatic Leadership." In *Latin American Populism in Comparative Perspective.* Edited by Michael L. Conniff. Albuquerque: University of New Mexico Press, 1981.

Netanyahu, Benjamin. *The Origins of the Inquisition in 15th Century Spain.* New York: Random House, 1995.

Neumann, Erich. *The Great Mother: An Analysis of the Archetype.* Princeton: Princeton University Press, 1974.

Noguez, Xavier. *Documentos guadalupanos: Un estudio sobre las fuentes de información tempranas en torno a las marifanías en el Tepeyac.* Mexico City: Fondo de Cultura Económica, 1993.

Nutini, Hugo G., and Betty Bell. *Ritual Kinship: The Structure and Historical Development of the Compadrazgo System in Rural Tlaxcala.* Vol. 1. Princeton: Princeton University Press, 1980.

O'Callaghan, Joseph F. "The *Cantigas* as an Historical Source: Two Examples." In *Studies on the Cantigas de Santa Maria: Art, Music, and Poetry.* Edited by Israel J. Katz and John E. Keller. Madison, Wisconsin: Hispanic Seminary of Medieval Studies, 1987.

————. *The Learned King: The Reign of Alfonso X of Castile.* Philadelphia: University of Pennsylvania Press, 1993.

Ortiz, Alicia Dujovne. *Eva Perón.* Translated by Shawn Fields. New York: St. Martin's Press, 1996.

Ortiz de Montellano, Bernard R. *Aztec Medicine, Health, and Nutrition.* New Brunswick, New Jersey: Rutgers University Press, 1990.

Page, Joseph A. *Perón: A Biography.* New York: Random House, 1983.

Pelikan, Jaroslav. *Mary through the Centuries.* New Haven: Yale University Press, 1996.

Perón, Eva. *Discursos completos 1946–1948.* Buenos Aires: Editorial Megafón, 1985.

————. *La razón de mi vida.* Buenos Aires: Ediciones Preuser, 1951.

————. *La razón de mi vida.* Buenos Aires: Editorial Relevo, 1973.

————. *Mi mensaje.* Buenos Aires: Ediciones del Mundo, 1987.

Perry, Nicholas, and Loreto Echeverría. *Under the Heel of Mary.* London: Routledge, 1988.

Phillips, William D. Jr., and Carla Rahn Phillips. *The Worlds of Christopher Columbus.* Cambridge: Cambridge University Press, 1992.

Pizarro, Francisco. *El testamento de Pizarro.* Edited with prologue and notes by Raul Porras Barrenechea. Paris: Imprimeries les Presses Moderne, 1936.

Platt, Tristan. "Simón Bolívar, the Sun of Justice and the Amerindian Virgin: Andean Conceptions of the Patria in the Nineteenth-Century Potosí." *Journal of Latin American Studies* 25 (1995): 171–177.

Plotkin, Mariano. *Mañana es San Perón.* Buenos Aires: Ariel Historia Argentina, 1993.

Poem of My Cid, The. Translated by Peter Such and John Hodghinden. Warminster: Aris and Phillips, 1987.

Poma de Ayala, Guaman. *El primer Coronica i buen gobierno.* Annotated by Arthur Posnansky. La Paz, Bolivia: Editorial del Instituto Tihuanacu de Tropología, Etnografía, y Prehistoria, 1944.

————. *Nueva crónica y buen gobierno.* Edited by John V. Murra, Rolena Adorno, and Jorge L. Urioste. Mexico City: Siglo XXI, 1987.

Poole, Stafford. *Our Lady of Guadalupe: The Origins and Sources of the Mexican National Symbol, 1531–1797.* Tucson: University of Arizona Press, 1995.

Porras Barrenechea, Raul. *Cartas del Peru.* Lima: Edición de la Sociedad de Bibliofilos Peruanos, 1959.

Presas, Juan Antonio. *Anales de Nuestra Señora de Luján: Trabajo histórico-documental 1630–1982.* Buenos Aires: Talleres Gráficos Abel, 1983.

Presilla, Maricel E. "The Image of Death and Political Ideology in the *Cantigas de Santa María.*" In *Studies on the Cantigas de Santa Maria: Art, Music, and Poetry.* Edited by Israel J. Katz and John E. Keller. Madison, Wisconsin: Hispanic Seminary of Medieval Studies, 1987.

Ramos Gavilán, Alonso. *Historia del Santuario de Nuestra Señora de Copacabana.* Transcription, editor's notes, and indices by Ignacio Prado Pastor. Lima: Talleres Gráficos de P.L. Villanueva, 1988.

Relaciones geográficas del Arzobispado de México, 1743. Edited by Francisco de Solano. 2 vols. Madrid: Consejo Superior de Investigaciones Científicas, 1988.

Relaciones geográficas del siglo XVI: México. Mexico City: Universidad Nacional de México, 1986.

Remensnyder, Amy. "The Colonization of Sacred Architecture: The Virgin Mary, Mosques, and Temples in Medieval Spain and Sixteenth-Century Mexico." In *Monks and Nuns, Saints, and Outcasts*. Edited by Sharon Farmer and Barbara H. Rosenwein. Ithaca: Cornell University Press, 2000.

Reyes-Valerio, Constantino. *Arte indocristiano: Escultura del Siglo XVI en México*. Mexico City: SEP/INAH, 1978.

Robins, Nicholas A. *El mesianismo y la semiótica indígena en el Alto Peru: La gran rebelión de 1780–1781*. La Paz, Bolivia: Hisbol, 1998.

Rodríguez, Jeanette. *Our Lady of Guadalupe: Faith and Empowerment among Mexican-American Women*. Austin: University of Texas Press, 1994.

Ros, Carlos, ed. *Historia de la Iglesia de Sevilla*. Barcelona: Editorial Castillejo, 1992.

Rubin, Nancy. *Isabella of Castile: The First Renaissance Queen*. New York: St. Martin's Press, 1992.

Salles-Reese, Verónica. *From Viracocha to the Virgin of Copacabana: Representations of the Sacred at Lake Titicaca*. Austin: University of Texas Press, 1997.

Sallman, Jean-Michel, with Serge Gruzinski, Antoinette Molinié Fiorivanti, and Carmen Salazar. *Visions Indiennes, Visions Baroques: Les Metissages de L'Inconscient*. Paris: Presses Universitaires de France, 1992.

Sánchez, Miguel. "Imagen de la Virgen María Madre de Dios de Guadalupe." In *Testimonios históricos guadalupanas*. Compiled by Ernesto de la Torre Villar and Ramiro Navarro de Anda. Mexico City: Fondo de Cultura Económica, 1982.

Sánchez Navarro de Pintado, Beatriz. "El arte blanco." In *Tepozotlan: La vida y la obra en Nueva España*. Coordinated by Miguel Fernández Félix. Mexico City: Editorial Joaquín Mortiz, 1998.

Sánchez Pérez, José Augusto. *El culto mariano en España*. Madrid: Consejo Superior de Investigaciones Científicas, 1943.

Santos Vargas, José. *Diario de un comandante de la independencia americana, 1814–1825*. Mexico City: Siglo XXI Editores, 1982.

Selection of Poems of the Mothers of the Plaza de Mayo. Oxford: Busqueda, 1983.

Smith, Bradley. *Mexico City: A History in Art*. Garden City, New York: Doubleday, 1968.

Steele, Thomas J. *Santos and Saints: The Religious Folk Art of Hispanic New Mexico*. Santa Fe, New Mexico: Ancient City Press, 1974.

Stern, Steve J., ed. *Resistance, Rebellion, and Consciousness in the Andean Peasant World, 18th to 20th Centuries*. Madison: University of Wisconsin Press, 1987.

Stratton, Suzanne L. *The Immaculate Conception in Spanish Art*. Cambridge: Cambridge University Press, 1994.

Stringer, John, Barbara Duncan, and Teresa Gisbert, eds. *Gloria in Excelsis: The Virgen and Angels in Viceregal Painting of Peru and Bolivia*. New York: Center for Inter-American Relations, 1986.

Szeminski, Jan. "Why Kill the Spaniard? New Perspectives on Andean Insurrectionary Ideology in the 18th Century." In *Resistance, Rebellion, and Consciousness in the Andean Peasant World, 18th to 20th Centuries.* Edited by Steve J. Stern. Madison: University of Wisconsin Press, 1987.

Tabb, William, ed. *Churches in Struggle: Liberation Theology and Social Change in North America.* New York: Monthly Review Press, 1986.

Taylor, J. M. *Eva Perón: The Myths of a Woman.* Chicago: University of Chicago Press, 1979.

Taylor, William B. *Magistrates of the Sacred: Priests and Parishioners in Eighteenth-Century Mexico.* Stanford: Stanford University Press, 1996.

————. "Santiago's Horse: Christianity and Colonial Indian Resistance in the Heartland of New Spain." In Taylor and Pease, *Violence, Resistance.*

————. "The Virgin of Guadalupe in New Spain: An Inquiry into the Social History of Marian Devotion." *American Ethnologist* 14 (February 1987).

Taylor, William B., and Franklin Pease, eds. *Violence, Resistance, and Survival in the Americas: Native Americans and the Legacy of the Conquest.* Washington, D.C.: Smithsonian Institution Press, 1994.

Thomas, Hugh. *Conquest: Montezuma, Cortés, and the Fall of Old Mexico.* New York: Simon & Schuster, 1993.

Torre Villar, Ernesto de la, and Ramiro Navarro de Anda, compilation, prologue, bibliographic notes, and indices. *Testimonios históricos guadalupanas.* Mexico City: Fondo de Cultura Económica, 1982.

Townsend, Richard F. "The Mount Tlaloc Project." In *To Change Place: Aztec Ceremonial Landscapes.* Edited by David Carrasco. Niwot: University Press of Colorado, 1991.

Trejo, Silvia. *Dioses, mitos y ritos del México antiguo.* Mexico City: Secretaria de Relaciones Exteriores, 2000.

Turner, Victor. *Dramas, Fields, and Metaphors: Symbolic Action in Human Society.* Ithaca, New York: Cornell University Press, 1996.

Turner, Victor, and Edith Turner. *Image and Pilgrimage in Christian Culture.* New York: Columbia University Press, 1978.

Tweed, Thomas A. *Our Lady of Exile: Diasporic Religion at a Cuban Catholic Shrine in Miami.* New York: Oxford University Press, 1997.

Uribe Echevarría, Juan. *Fiesta de la Virgen de la Candelaria de Copiapó.* Valparaiso: Ediciones Universitarias de Valparaiso, 1978.

Valcarcel, Carlos Daniel, ed. *Colección documental de la independencia del Perú.* Vol. 2. Lima: Comisión Nacional del Sesquicentenario de la Independencia del Perú, 1971.

Valdés, Nelson P. "The Meaning of Elían González—Miracles, Dolphins, and Orishas." Photocopy.

Valero, Ana Rita. "Peregrinación al Tepeyac. Una observación analítica de las romerías guadalupanas." In *Caminos terrestres al cielo: Contribución al estudio del fenómeno romero.* Edited by Beatriz Barba de Piña Chan. Mexico City: Instituto Nacional de Antropología e Historia, 1998.

Van Young, Eric. *El crisis del orden colonial: Estructura agraria y rebeliones populares de la Nueva España, 1750–1821.* Mexico City: Alianza Editorial, 1992.

————. *The Other Rebellion: Popular Violence, Ideology, and the Mexican Struggle for Independence, 1810–1821*. Stanford, California: Stanford University Press, 2001.

Vargas Ugarte, Ruben. *Historia del culto de María en Iberoamerica y de sus imagines y santuarios mas celebrados*. Buenos Aires: Editorial Huarpes, 1947.

Vicchi, Roberta. *The Major Basilicas of Rome*. Florence: SCALA, 1999.

Villaseñor y Sánchez, José Antonio de. *Theatro americano*. Mexico City: Imprenta de la viuda de d. Bernardo de Hogal, 1746–1748.

Ward, Benedicta. *Miracles of the Medieval Mind: Theory, Record and Event 1000–1215*. Philadelphia: University of Pennsylvania Press, 1987.

Warner, Marina. *Alone of All Her Sex: The Myth and the Cult of the Virgin Mary*. New York: Vintage Books, 1983.

Webb, Matilda. *The Churches and Catacombs of Early Christian Rome*. Brighton, England: Sussex Academic Press, 2001.

Webster, Susan Verdi. *Art and Ritual in Golden-Age Spain: Sevillian Confraternities and the Processional Sculpture of Holy Week*. Princeton: Princeton University Press, 1998.

Weckmann, Luis. *La herencia medieval de México*. 2nd revised edition. Mexico City: El Colegio de México, 1996.

Weismann, Elizabeth Wilder. *Art and Time in Mexico City: From the Conquest to the Revolution*. New York: Harper & Row, 1985.

————. *Mexico in Sculpture, 1521–1821*. Cambridge, Massachusetts: Harvard University Press, 1950.

Wessinger, Catherine. "Woman Guru, Woman Roshi: The Legitimation of Female Religious Leadership in Hindu and Buddhist Groups in America." In Wessinger, ed., *Woman's Leadership*.

————, ed. *Woman's Leadership in Marginal Religions*. Chicago: University of Illinois Press, 1993.

Wolf, Kenneth B. *Christian Martyrs in Muslim Spain*. Cambridge: Cambridge University Press, 1988.

Wuffarden, Luis Eduardo. "Notas de los cuadros." In *La procesión del Corpus en el Cuzco*. Seville: Unión Latina, 1996.

Zanatta, Loris. *Del estado liberal a la nación Católica. Iglesia y ejército en los orígenes del peronismo, 1930–1943*. Buenos Aires: Universidad Nacional de Quilmes, 1996.

Index

Note: Italic page numbers refer to illustrations.

✢ ✢ ✢

indigenous artists, 108–110, 138, 146; and indigenous populations, 6, 58–67, 83, 89, 105, 107, 155, 187; and indigenous rebellions, 173–174; and light, 258–259, 298; and miracles, 19, 105, 107, 121–136, 142, 278; and Monte Serrado, 52; and mountains, 140–141, 142, 146, 298; and Pelayo, 25; and Peru, 138, 139, 140–142, 144, 145, 146, 148, 149–151, 156–167; power of, 2, 4, 5, 6–7, 110, 140, 295, 300; and presence of Virgin, 4, 5, 7, 77, 78–79, 107, 110, 116, 117, 243, 248, 274; public manifestations of, 3; and Reconquest of Spain, 4, 17, 32, 33, 38, 110; and rocks, 141–142, 293; treatment as a person, 5, 110, 116, 117, 185, 243, 248, 249–250; and tree trunks, 121, 293, 293; and water, 121, 123–124, 293; and Woman of the Apocalypse, 8, 43, 56–57

Immaculate Conception (artist unknown), 8
Immaculate Conception, The (Bartolomé Esteban Murillo), *41*
Immigrants and immigration: Cuban immigrants, 276–278, 292, 293; and Marian reverence, 273, 278–279, 299; and September 11 attacks, 273–274; and Virgin of Luján, 200, 206, 207
Indigenous goddesses: identification of Eve with, 82, 93–94; identification of Virgin with, 57, 121, 131–132, 133, 134–136, 138, 140–141, 149, 151, 266–267; representations of, 85–88, *86*
Indigenous populations: Christians as distinct from, 291; and conversion to Catholicism, 6, 18; cultures of, 13, 81, 95, 114, 126, 295; and disease, 18, 70, 72, 83, 88–89, 115, 189; and images of Mary, 6, 58–67, 83, 89, 105, 107, 155, 187; and Marian reverence, 10, 12; and power of Virgin, 12, 89, 110, 120, 122, 127; rebellions of eighteenth century, 173–177; resistance to conversion, 65–66, 83, 91, 109, 110, 114, 151, 167
Indigenous religious practices: and

Catholic Church, 81–84, 109, 121, 133, 135–136, 137, 144, 151, 162, 167, 274, 316n.6; Christ's suffering compared to, 98; and Church festivals, 96, 151; and conquest of Spanish New World, 59–65, 79; Mary associated with, 81, 89, 153; and owls, 112, 114; sacred feminine in, 81, 82, 85, 111, 133, 138; Spanish reaction to, 81, 84; and Virgin of Guadalupe, 130–131
Indigenous sacred places: altars, 57, 59, 64; Christian incorporation of, 60, 83; Cortés placing crosses in, 60, 110; Cortés placing images of Mary in, 59, 60, 62, 64, 65, 67, 68, 85; and images of Mary, 4, 79, 81, 122, 126–127, 131, 132, 134–136, 137, 140–141, 163, 167, 170, 186, 197–198, 266–267; and independence movements, 178–179; and indigenous rebellions, 173–174; pyramids, 57, 63–67; temples, 59, 62, 64, 67–68, 72–73, 136
Inka empire: and birds, 148–149, 159; and Capacocha festival, 244–245; and Copacabana region, 166; and ethnic rivalries, 163; and Inti Raymi ceremony, 154, 156, 244; and Spanish conquest, 73–74, 137–139, 146, 155, 162; and Virgins of the Sun, 265–266
Inka mummies, *153*, 156, 264
Innocent III (pope), 31
Inquisition, 114, 121
Investiture of Saint Ildefonsus (Juan de Borgoña), *23*
Isabel (queen of Castile and Aragon): and Columbus, 45, 48, 52–53, 55; and Marian devotion, 17, 40–43, 298; and Reconquest of Spain, 33, 40–41, 43, 44, 57; succession of, 18; and Virgin of Guadalupe, 40, 41, 51
Italy, 51, 243
Iturbide, Agustín, 194–195
Izquierdo Zebrero, Ausías, 97, 98, 99

James, Saint, 10, 23, 24–25, 35, 68, 145. *See also* Santiago
Jaume I (king of Aragon), 32, 33, 46